# SouL

Memphis' Original Sound

FRONT COVER: BEN CAULEY

BACK COVER: SHURE 556 UNIDYNE MIC (c. 1947) FROM SUN STUDIOS

*Director of production*
Marco Jellinek

*Graphic design and layout*
Paola Gallerani

*Editorial assistant*
Serena Solla

*Editing*
Yarwood Editorial Services

*Color separation*
Eurofotolit, Cernusco sul Naviglio, Milan

*Printed by*
Petruzzi Stampa, Città di Castello (Perugia)



isbn: 978-88-97737-47-6
isbn: 978-88-97737-43-3 LIMITED EDITION


Officina Libraria
via Carlo Romussi, 4
20125 Milan, Italy
www.officinalibraria.com

Printed in Italy

THOM GILBERT

# SOUL
## Memphis' Original Sound

with a foreword by
**DAN AYKROYD**

OFFICINA
LIBRARIA

# Table of Contents

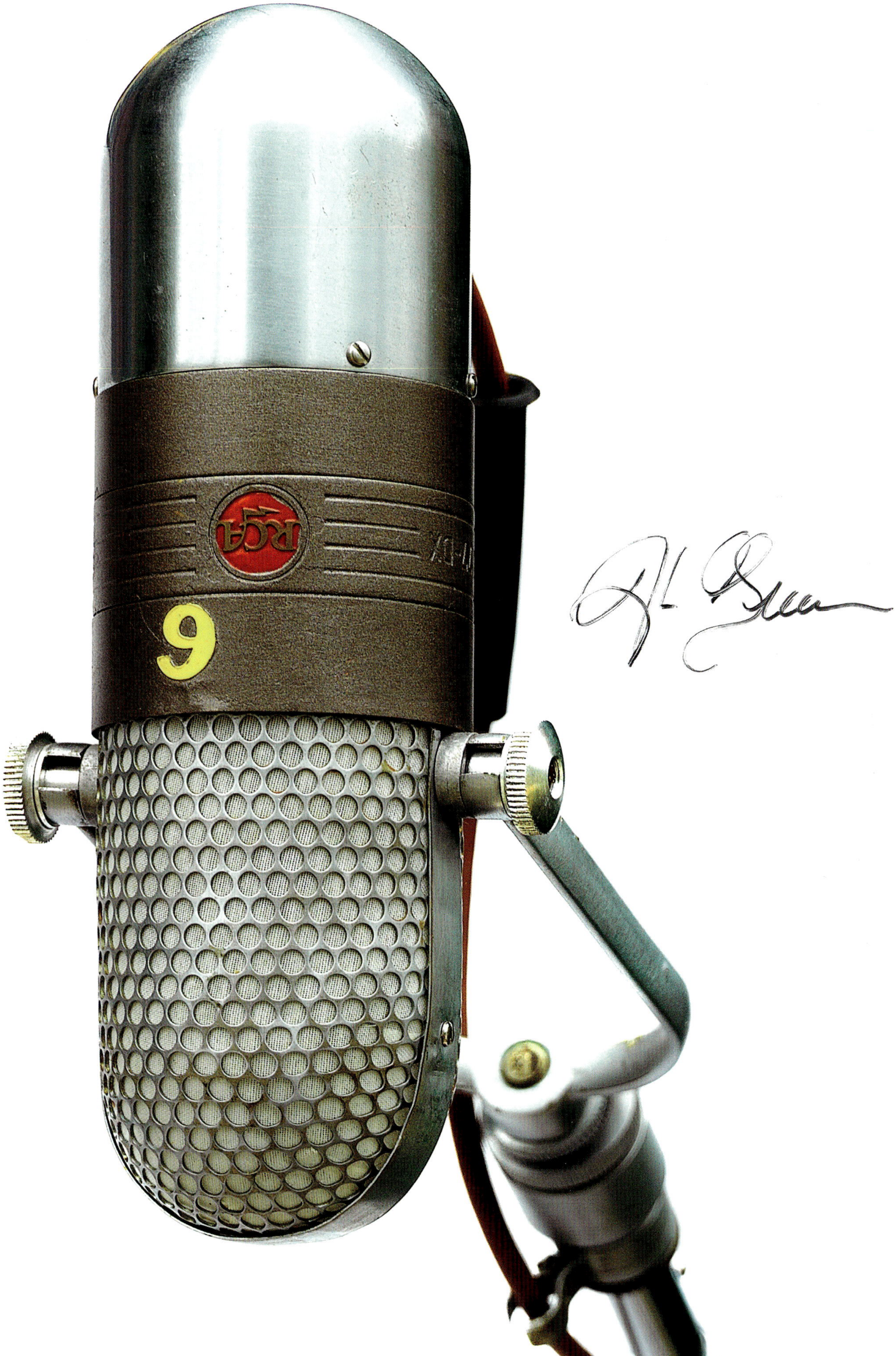

AL GREEN'S RECORDING MIC AT ROYAL STUDIOS, MEMPHIS

# "In Performance at the White House: *Memphis Soul*" *

* Extracted from Office of the White House Press Secretary, "Remarks by the President at 'In Performance at the White House: Memphis Soul,'" *White House Press Release* (April 9, 2013). Available at: http://www.whitehouse.gov/the-press-office/2013/04/09/remarks-president-performance-white-house-memphis-soul.
On Tuesday, April 9, 2013, as part of their "In Performance at the White House" series, the President and First Lady invited music legends and contemporary major artists to the White House for a celebration of Memphis Soul music. The program included performances by Alabama Shakes, William Bell, Steve Cropper, Al Green, Ben Harper, Queen Latifah, Cyndi Lauper, Joshua Ledet, Sam Moore, Charlie Musselwhite, Mavis Staples, and Justin Timberlake, with Booker T. Jones as music director and band leader.

THE PRESIDENT: Al [Green] once said, about the Memphis Soul sound that he helped create, "We don't even know ourselves how that music has endured for so long and how that came out of us." ...

[L]et's face it, who does not love this music? These songs get us on the dance floor. ... They get stuck in our heads. We go back over them again and again. And they've played an important part in our history.

In the sixties and seventies, Memphis knew its share of division and discord and injustice. But in that turbulent time, the sound of Hi, and Duke, and Sun, and Stax Records tried to bridge those divides—to create a little harmony with harmony. The great Memphis musician Don Nix went to an all-white school, and he described what it was like. He said, "If you could imagine, nobody's ever heard R&B music before. White kids had never heard it. And you can imagine what that did to us."

So he and others kept playing music that everybody could get into. They created a whole new sound, and, as they did, they broke down barriers. On McLemore Avenue, in the heart of a segregated city, Stax Records was integrated from the studio musicians all the way to upper management. Booker T. Jones and Steve Cropper ... helped form one of the city's first integrated bands. They weren't allowed to go to school together. They weren't always allowed to travel or eat together. But no one could stop them from playing music together.

And that was the spirit of their music—the sound of Soulsville, USA, a music that, at its core, is about the pain of being alone, the power of human connection, and the importance of treating each other right. After all, this is the music that asked us to try a little tenderness. It's the music that put Mr. Big Stuff in his place. And it's the music that challenged us to accept new ways of thinking with four timeless words: "Can you dig it?"

So it's really no surprise that Memphis Soul swept the nation, and it has stood the test of time. ...

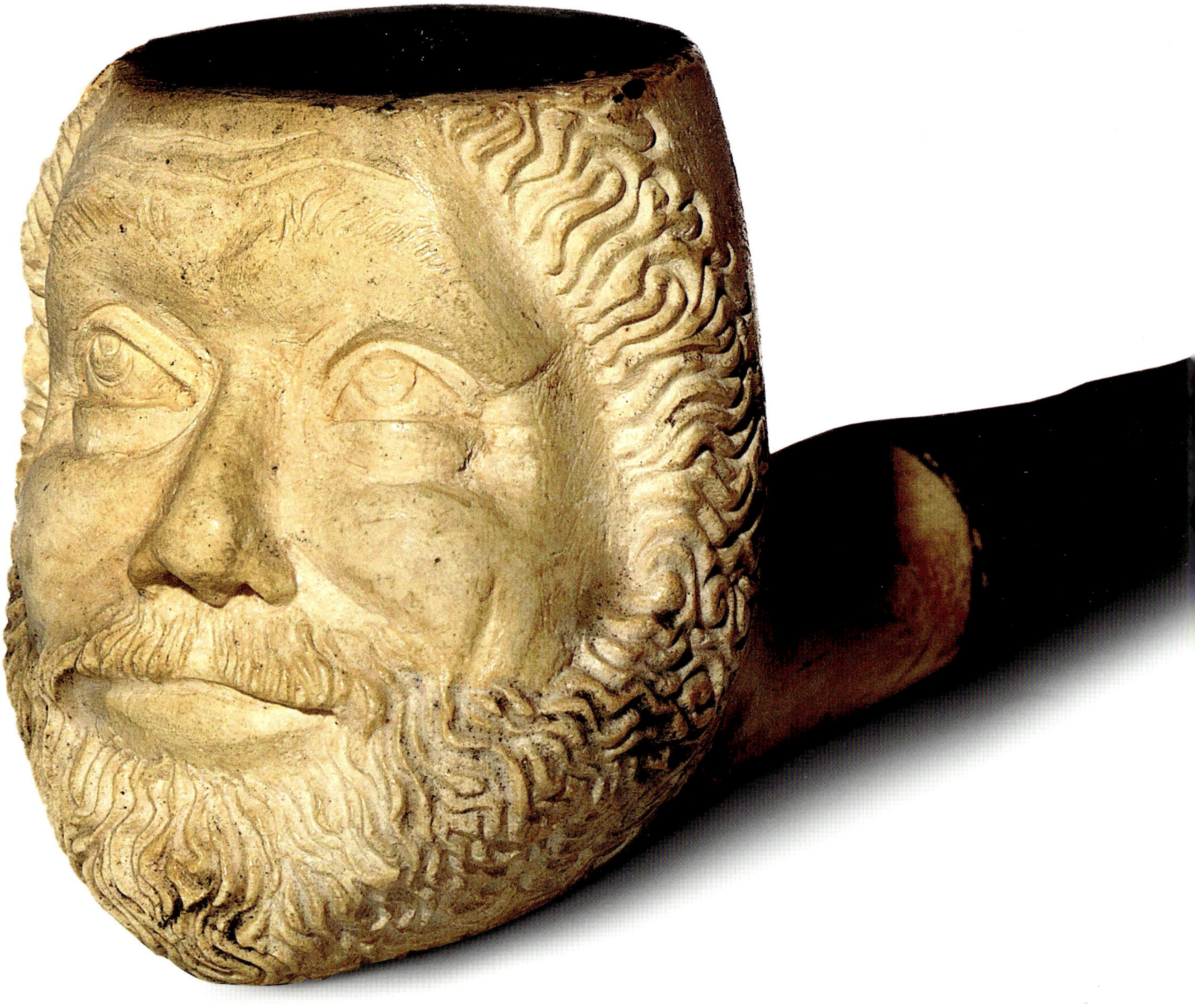

DONALD "DUCK" DUNN CUSTOM-MADE "LOOK-ALIKE" PIPE & MEMORIAL CURRENCY

# A Foreword

When Tom “Bones” Malone, Paul Shaffer, John Belushi, and I assembled The Blues Brothers Band, we recruited three Memphis guitar players – Donald “Duck” Dunn, Steve Cropper, and Matt Murphy.

Matt migrated to the Chicago urban blues scene in the ’50s and ’60s. “Duck” and Steve provided the musical backbone for many of the Stax artists featured in this historical assembly of beautiful portraits.

Cropper and Dunn also brought their talent to the Blues Brothers, at once legitimizing our entire existence and furnishing us with the knowledge of their catalog, which had us cover “Soul Man,” the Sam & Dave hit that became a no. 1 record for us. To me, seeing Sam & Dave live at Expo 67 in Montreal was an epiphany that broadened my understanding of the African American songbook beyond blues. This book of photographs is essential to any serious scholar of American music and culture. It is a vibrant companion to the living careers of Sam Moore, Eddie Floyd, and Steve Cropper, plus the many other still-working, still-playing Stax artists who keep this great body of music alive today.

*Dan Aykroyd a.k.a. “Elwood Blues”*

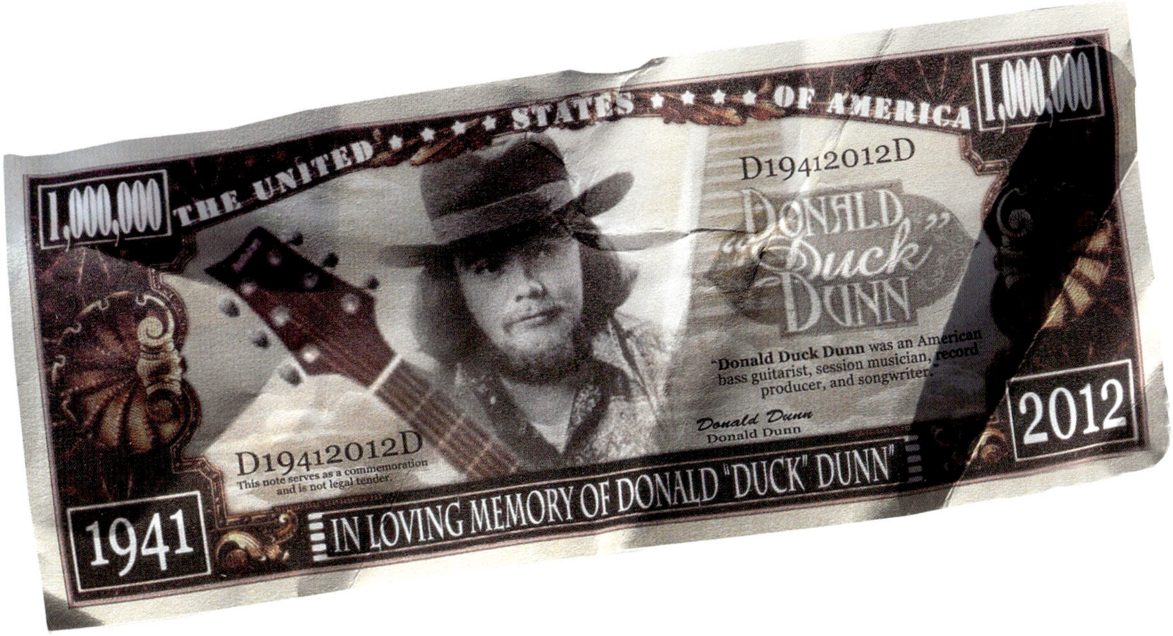

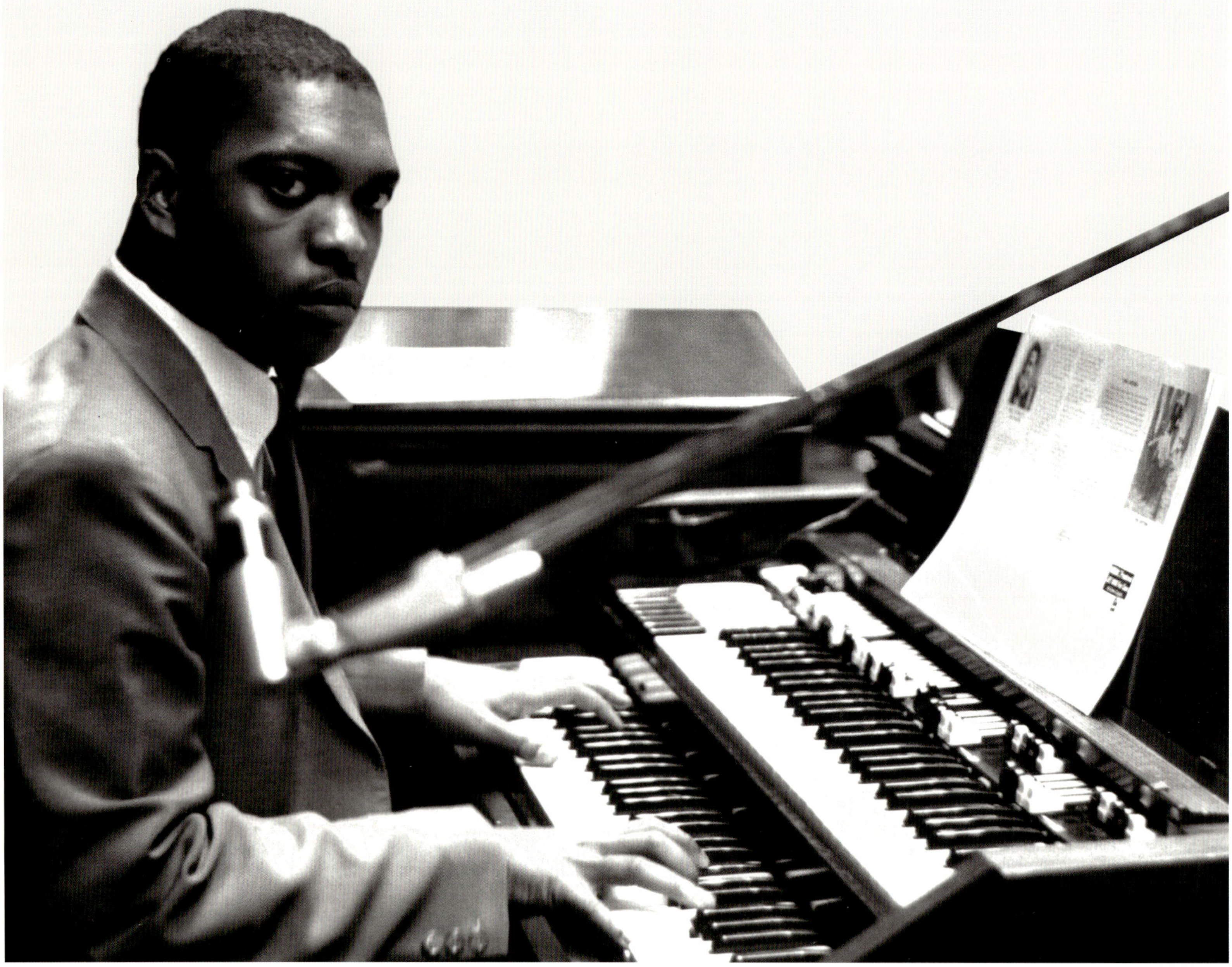

Hang 'Em High

BOOKER T. JONES

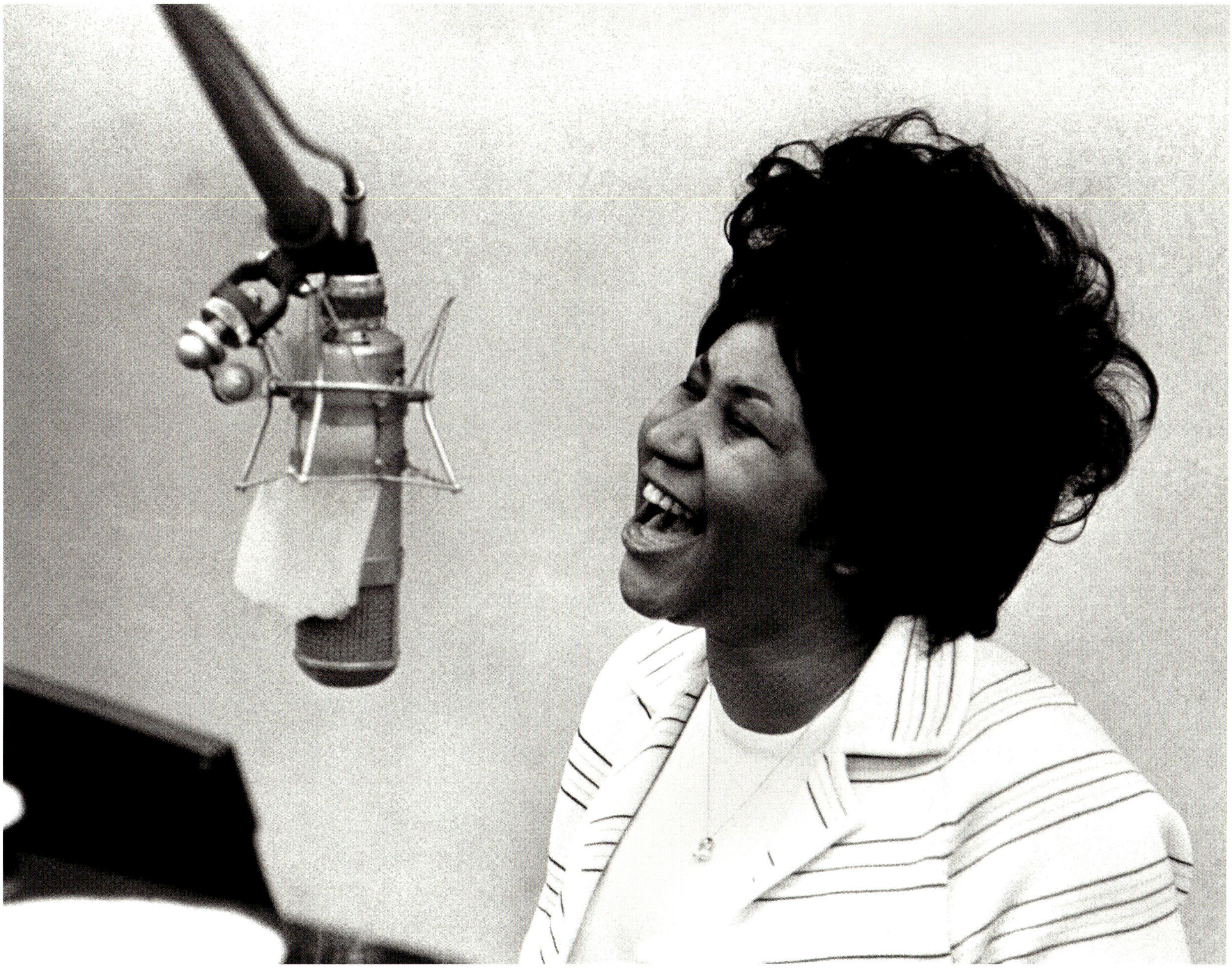

Peace + love
best
"Aretha"

ARETHA LOUISE FRANKLIN

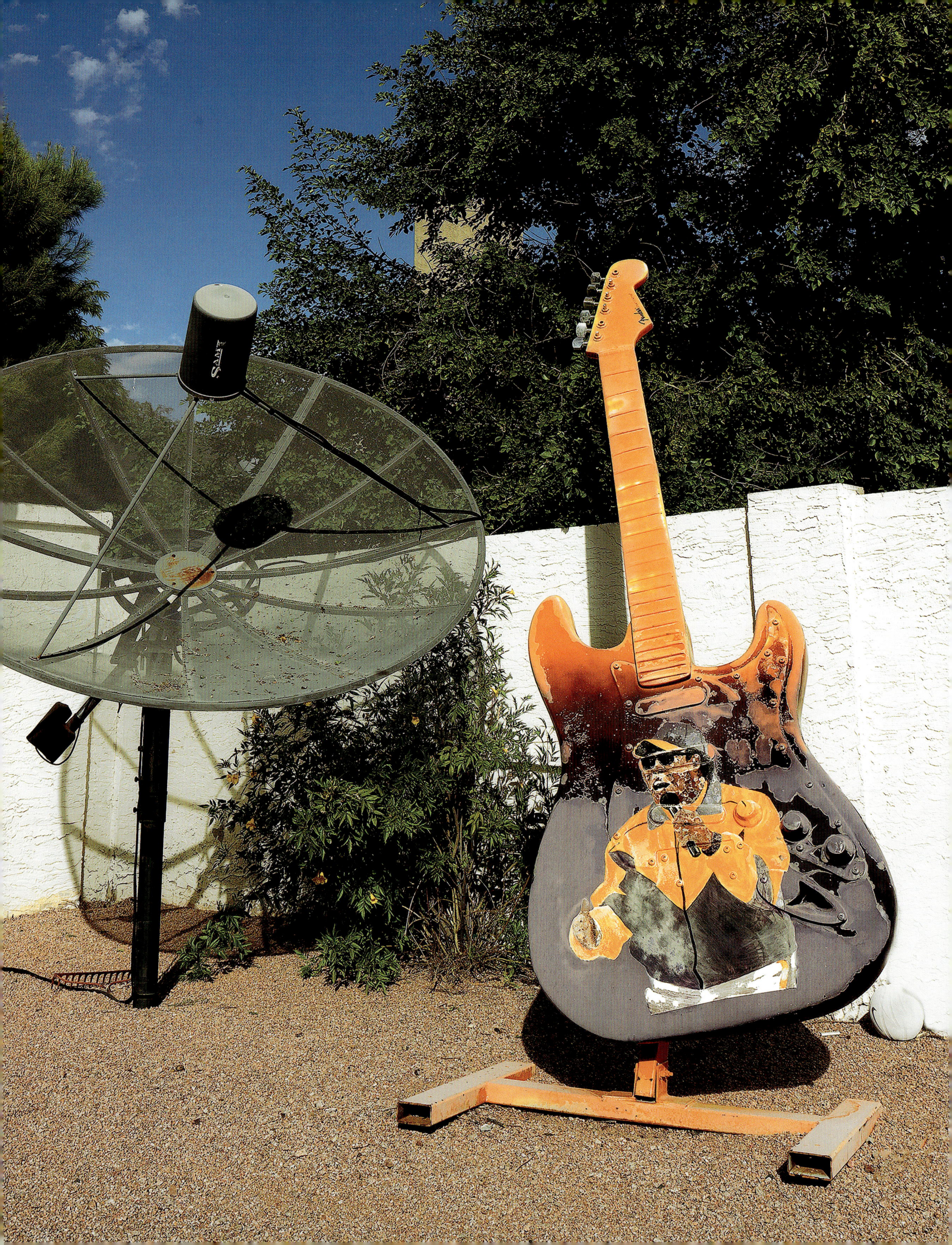

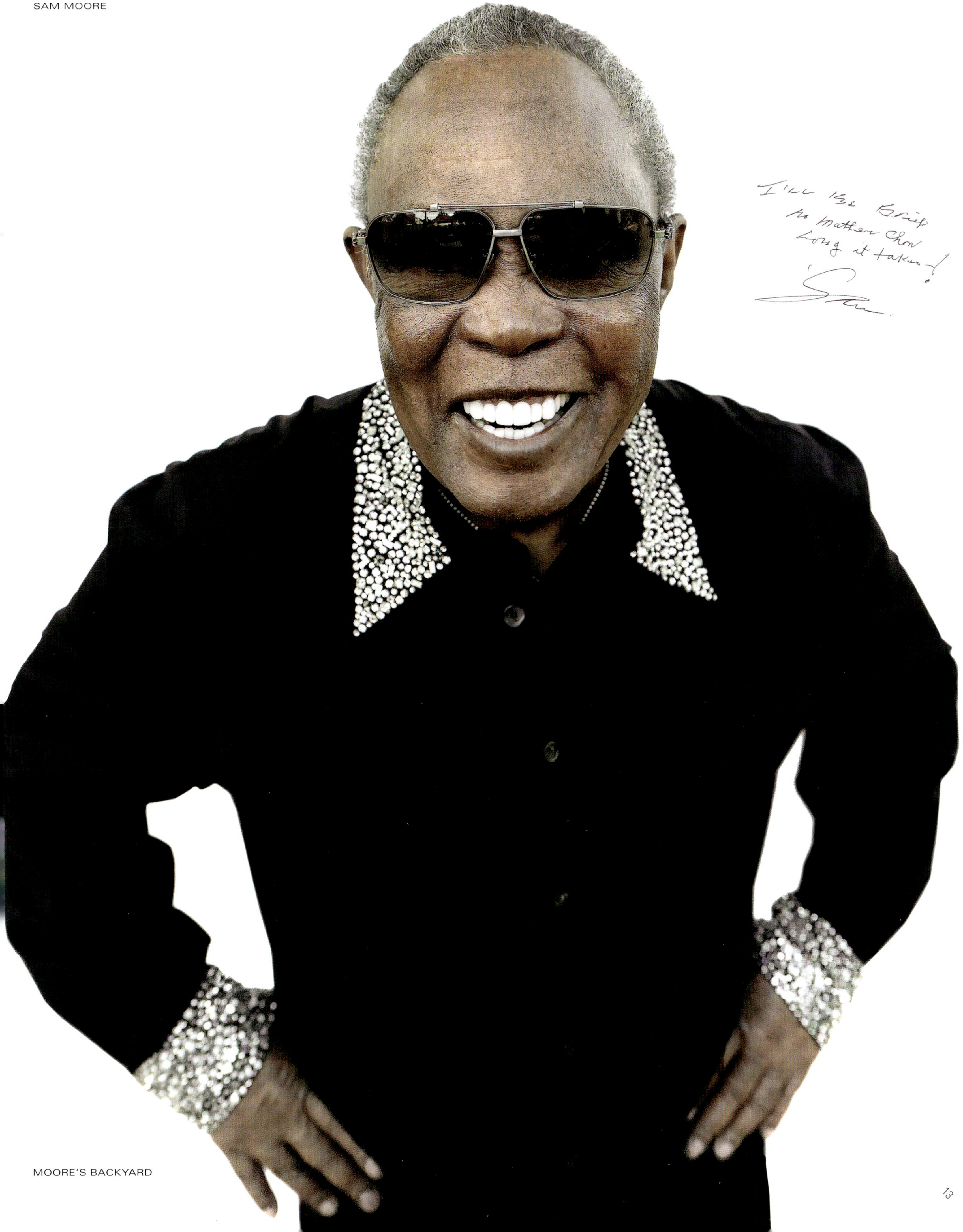


MOORE'S BACKYARD

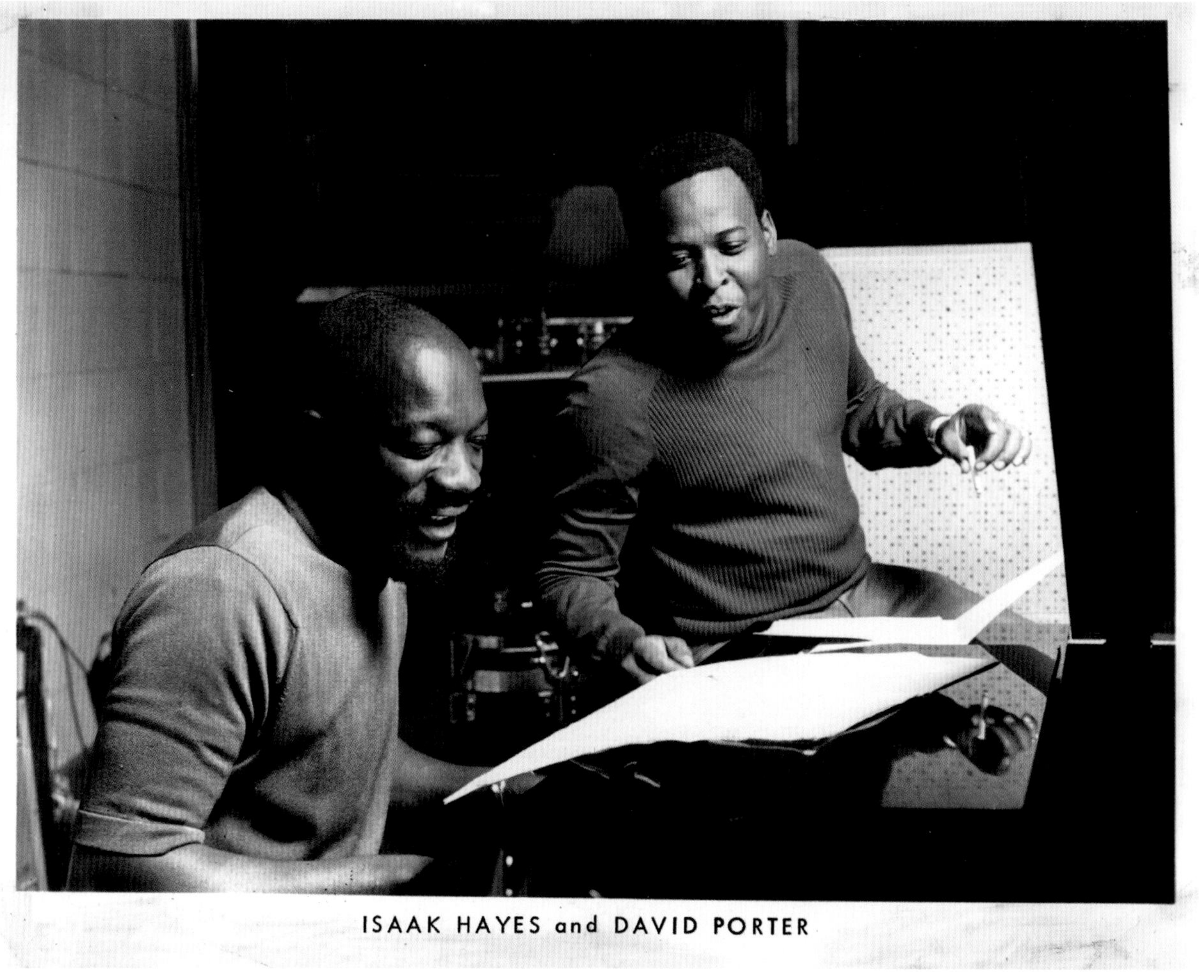


ISAAC HAYES & DAVID PORTER

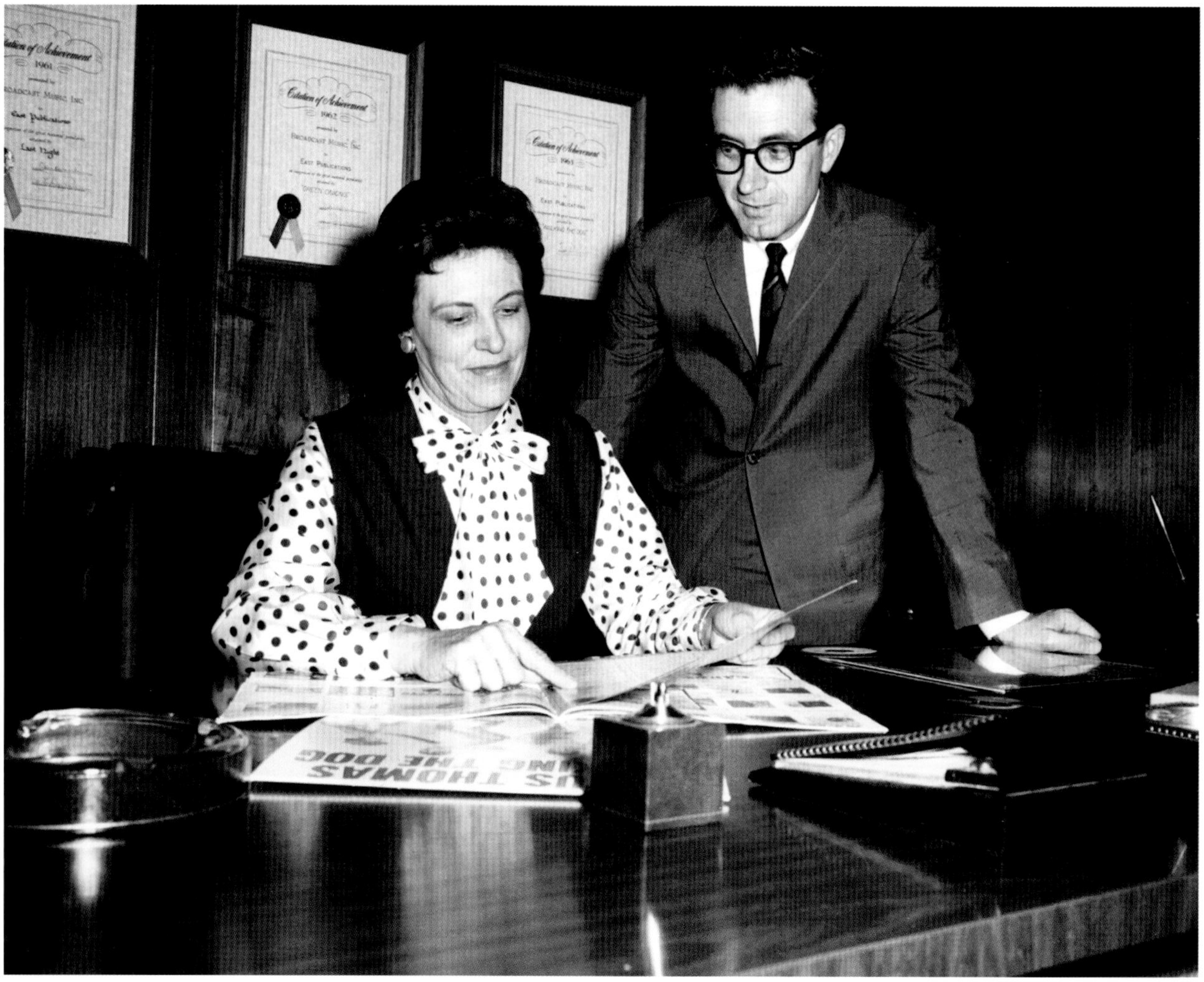

ESTELLE AXTON & JIM STEWART

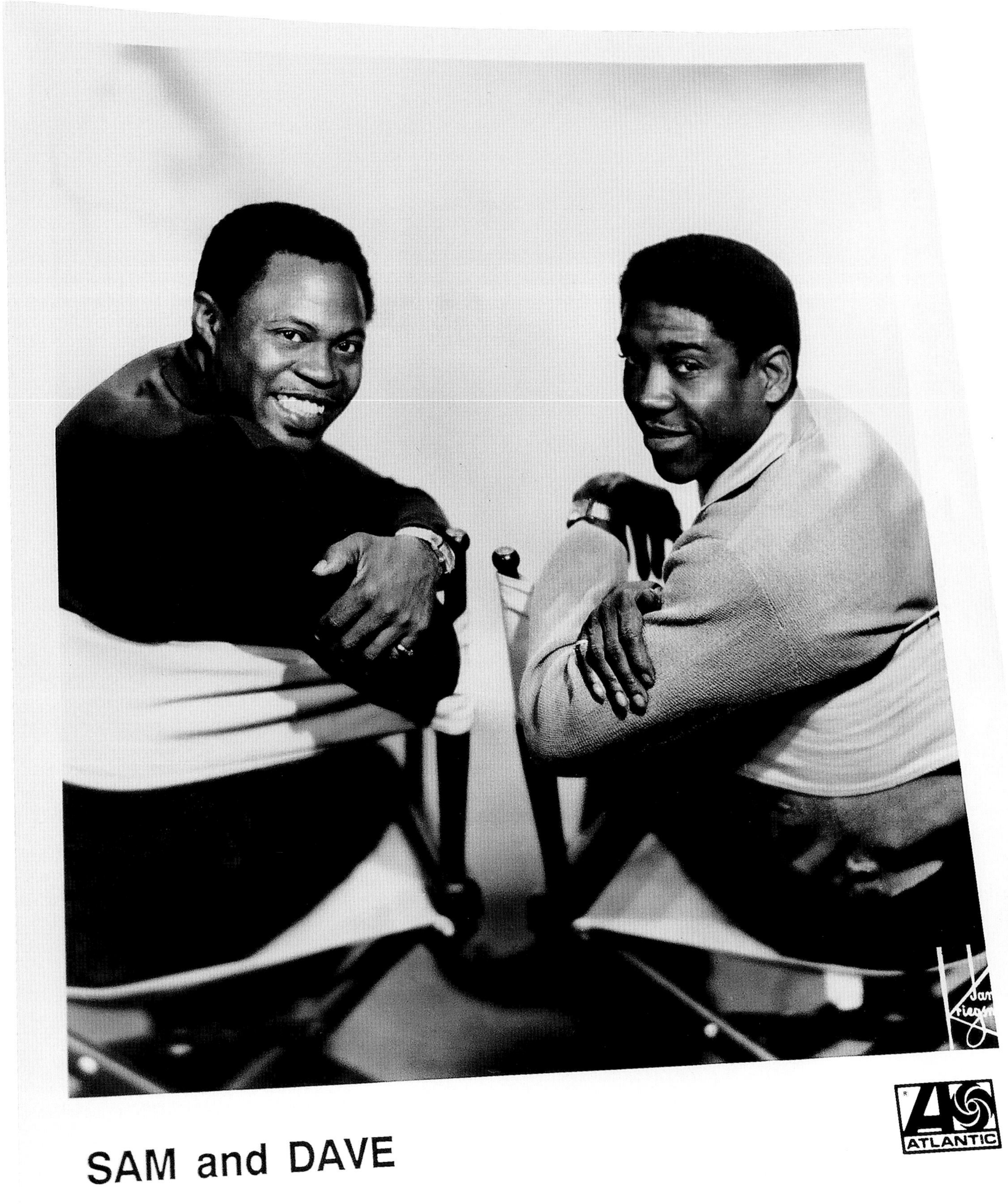


SAMUEL MOORE & DAVE PRATER

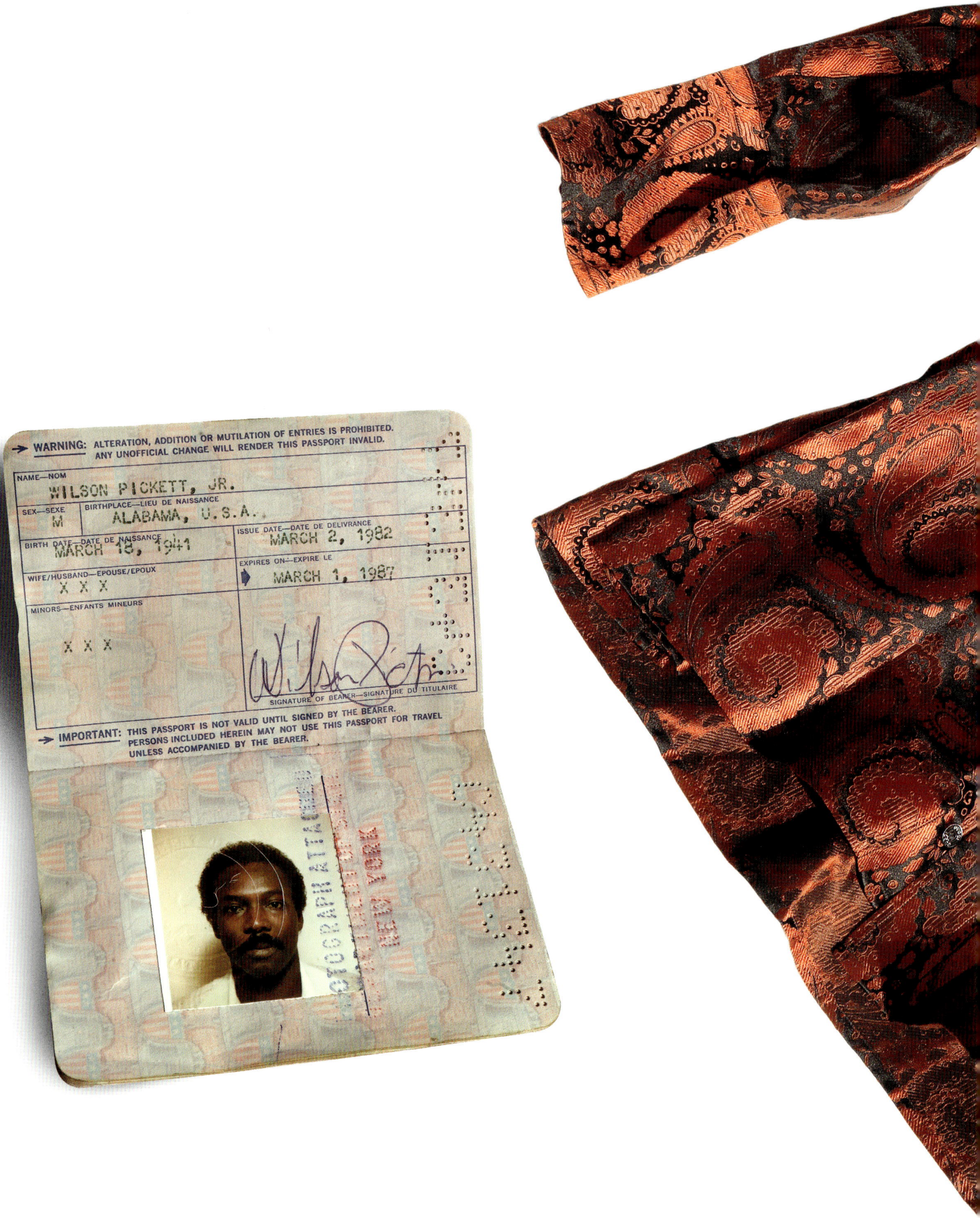


WILSON PICKETT - PASSPORT AND GUCCI STAGE SHIRT

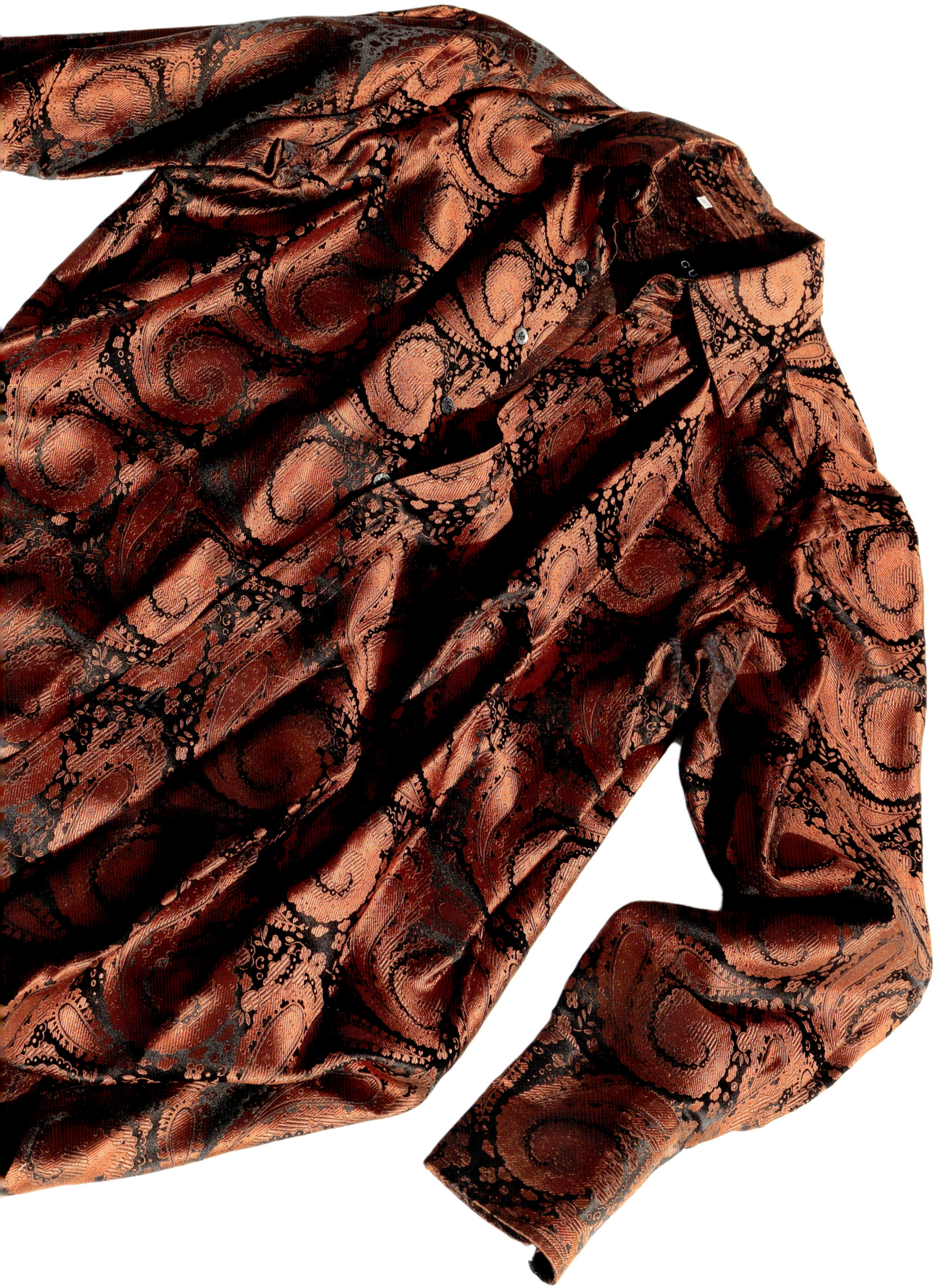

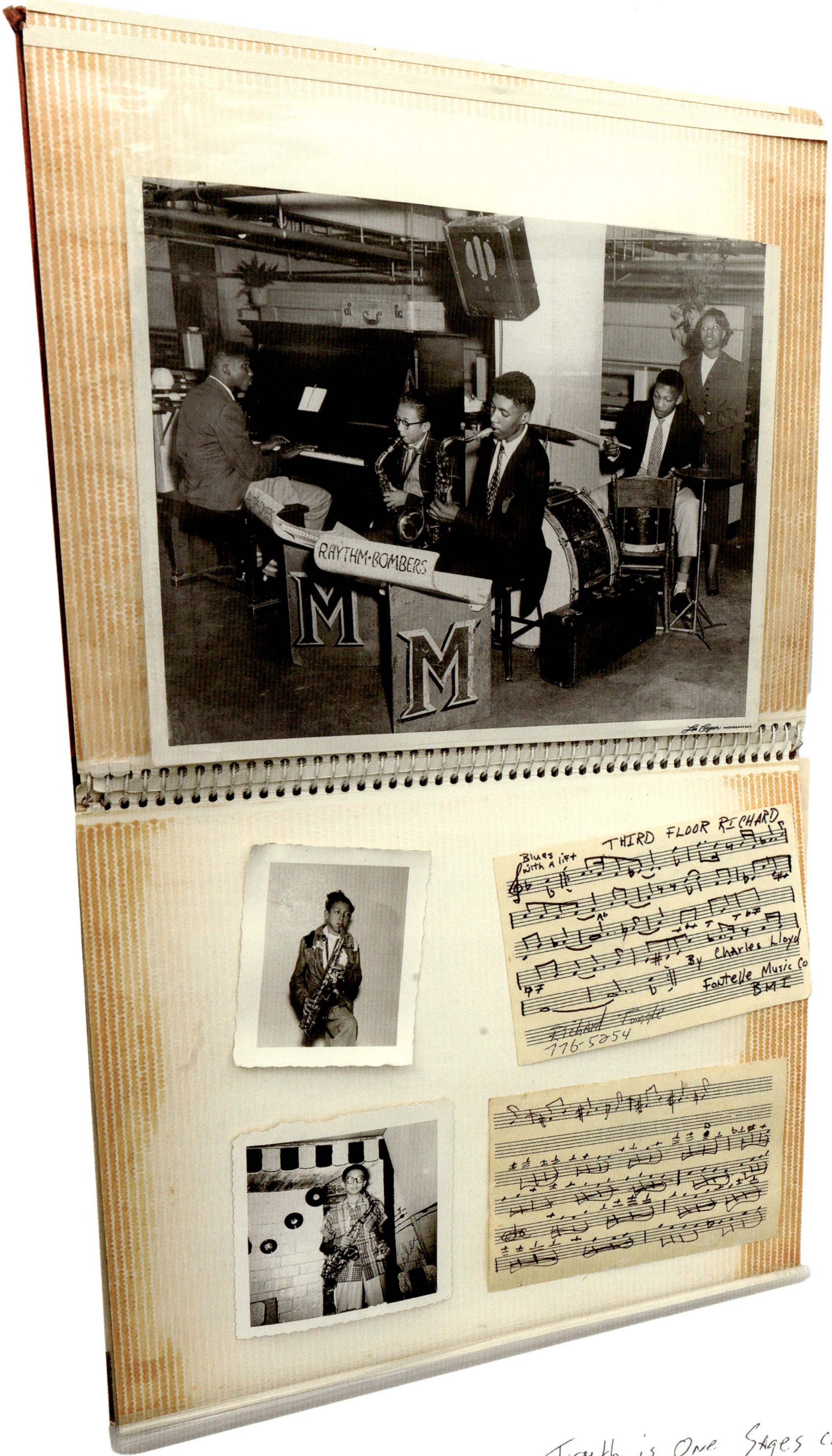


Truth is One Sages call it by various Names

TOP IMAGE: MAYBERN, LLOYD, DAVIDS & DUB

CHARLES LLOYD

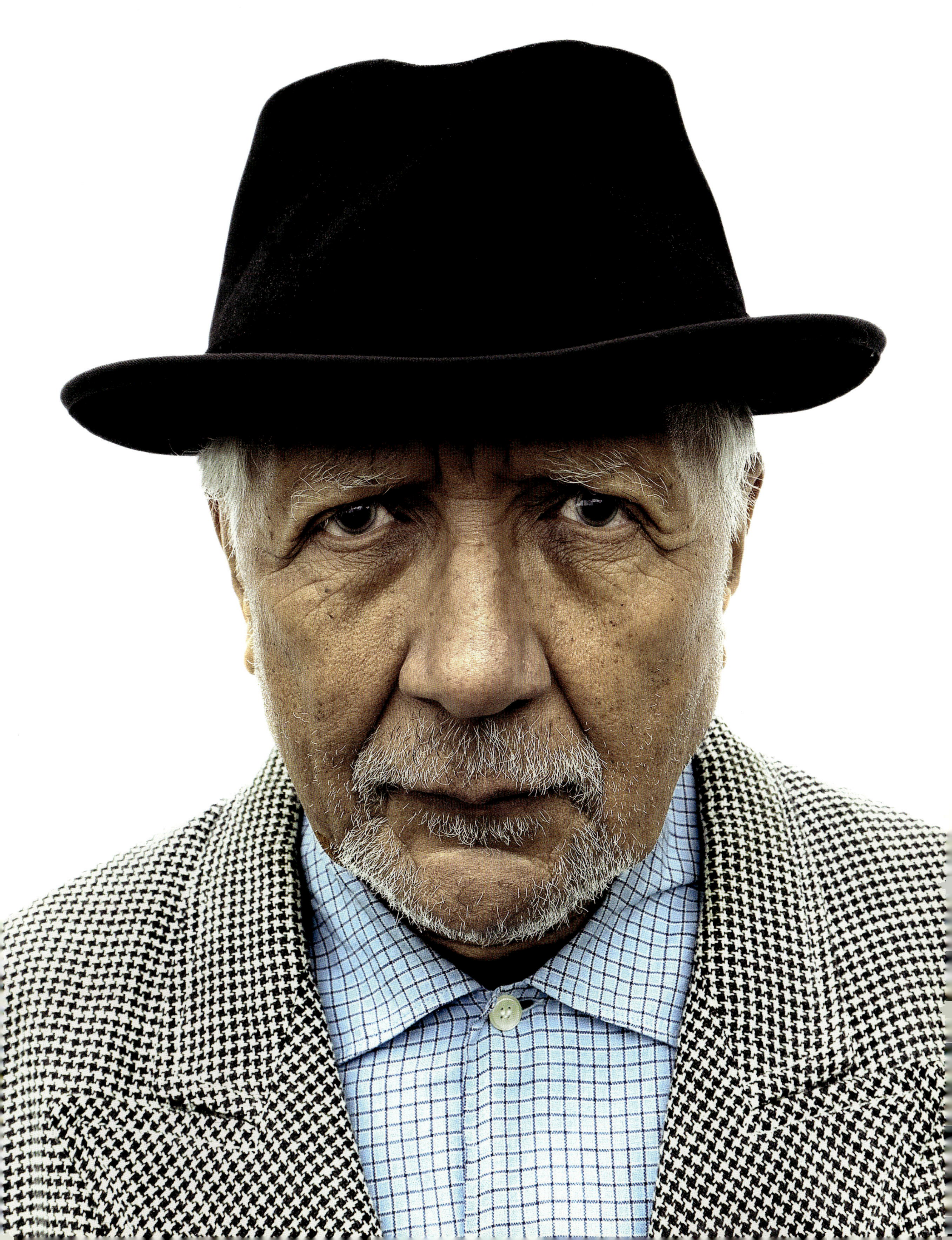

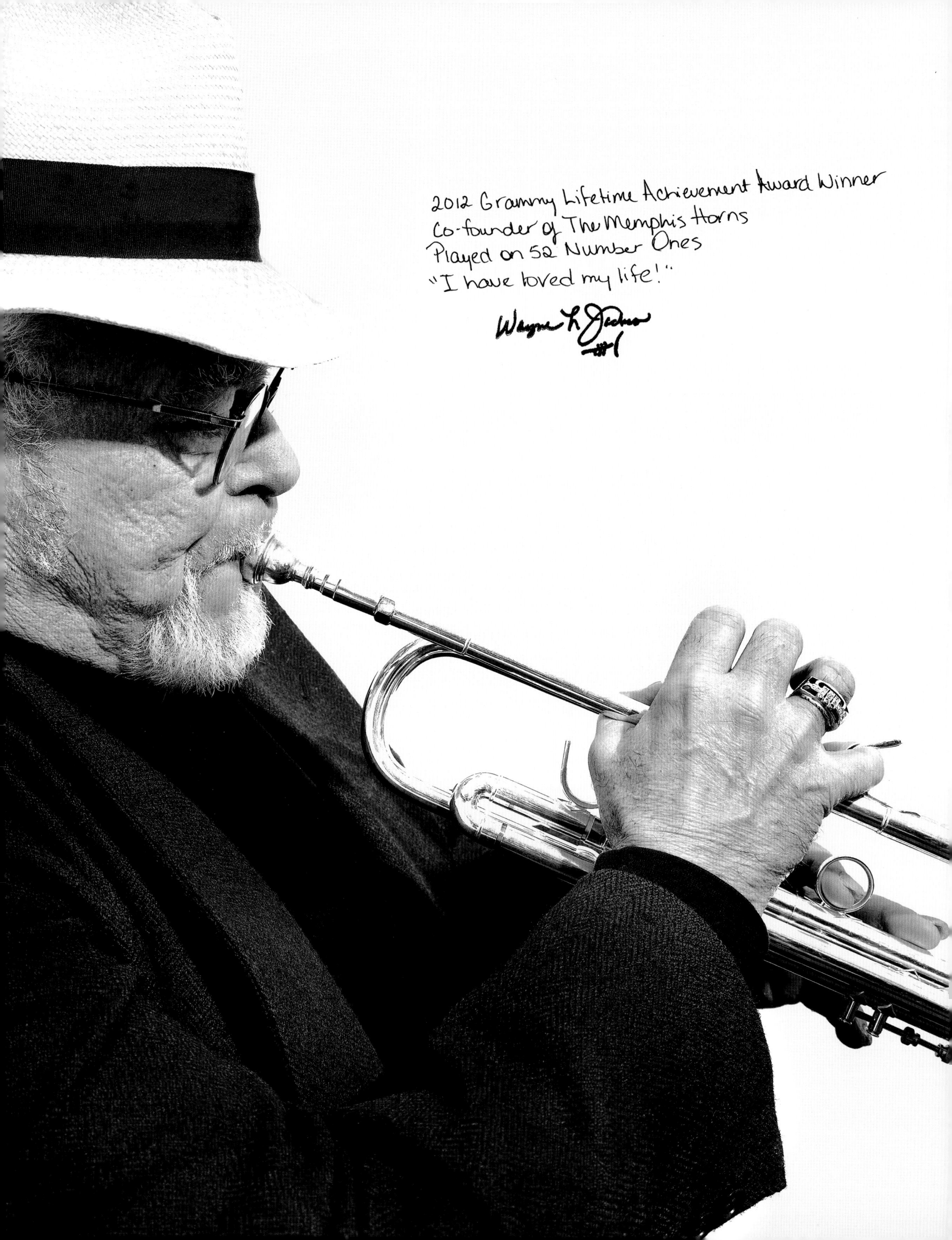
2012 Grammy Lifetime Achievement Award Winner
Co-founder of The Memphis Horns
Played on 52 Number Ones
"I have loved my life!"
Wayne L. Jackson
#1

# Wayne Jackson talks about meeting, hearing and playing for the first time with:

## Elvis

I was a boy in the backseat of Dad's car when Elvis first came on the radio. He shocked us all with his power. I followed him through the years until I wound up in the studio with him in 1969. The day he walked into American Studio was the day I understood his personal power. Elvis lit up whatever room he was in. I played on "Suspicious Minds," "Kentucky Rain," and "In the Ghetto." Sitting there listening to him sing "In the Ghetto," man, you could have hung clothes on the electricity he generated. The fact that I got to spend time with him and be a musician with him is something I'll never forget.

## Isaac Hayes

I was in the studio at Stax the day Isaac showed up. He was dressed like the rest of us, nice but nothing special. He even went on some gigs with me and the boys to Jonesboro. Isaac was always full of laughter. He was not much of a piano player, he was a singer. We all loved him and enjoyed his company. This was before he and David Porter began to write songs together. I don't know how they got started, but they were a natural fit. Isaac knew he was headed for the top one day as a singer, and we were glad to be there for the ride.

## Aretha Franklin

Andrew and I made the trip to New York for Atlantic Records many times, but the time I remember most was the day that Aretha came to the studio, sat down at the piano, and began to sing. Our worlds would never be the same. Aretha was a great musician. She plays piano like a man, with a lot of force and authority. She knows what she wants. And of course, her singing speaks for itself. I'm glad I got to know her and make records with her.

She is a genius. One of the highlights of my recording career was working with her. And I haven't even mentioned being on stage with her, which was a personal triumph of my life. She was a true powerhouse!

## Wilson Pickett

Wilson was a real work of art. Nobody could scream like Wilson. Being with him in the studio was like being with a bomb. You just never knew when it was going to go off, but we knew it would. And the hair on the back of our necks would stand up in anticipation. He set the whole studio on its ear when he started singing. I loved Wilson. I talked to him on the phone not long before he died. There will never be another guy like Wilson. He is irreplaceable. His insanity was a thing to behold.

## Otis Redding

When I first got a load of Otis Redding in the studio at Stax, it was almost too heavy to carry. There was a star standing back behind that big telefunken microphone. There was never any doubt about it. Otis would have the entire studio wound up tight, and he would come over to where the horns were standing and sing our parts to us. He was a genius! His enthusiasm carried over to everyone. You would know when Otis came through the front door. It was almost like the pictures on the wall would dance, and we knew we would be in for a hell of a day. Thank you, Otis.
And being on the stage with him during the 1967 Stax/Volt Tour and Monterey Pop Festival was like being tied to a firecracker!

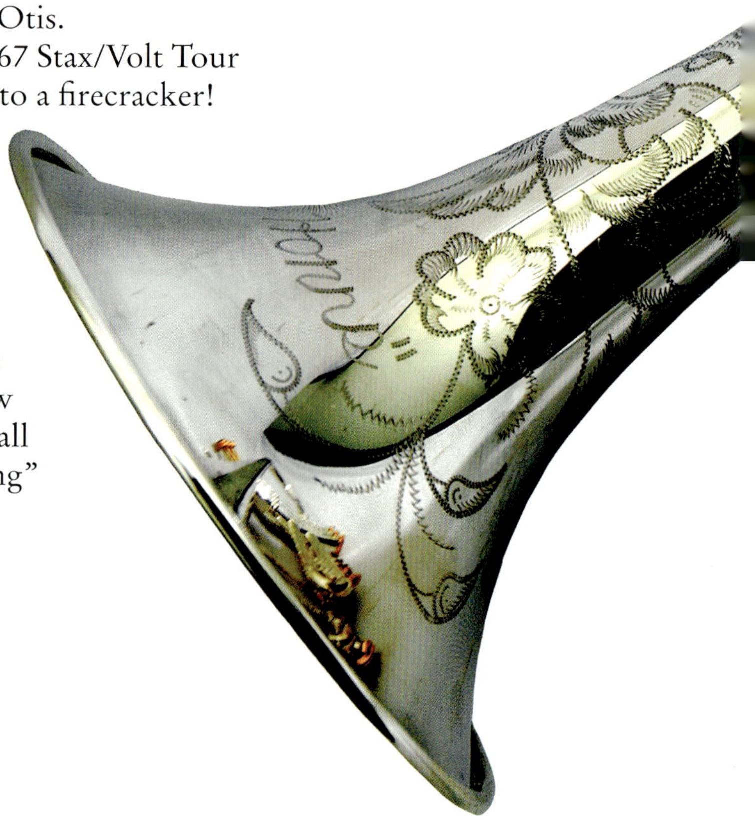

## Sam & Dave

Sam & Dave came to Stax bringing their own box of dynamite, and, believe me, when you lit one up with them, you had to get ready to blow the roof off the building! It was that way with all their recordings. I think "Hold On, I'm Coming" is one of the all-time classic R&B hits.
We all knew it the day we worked on it.

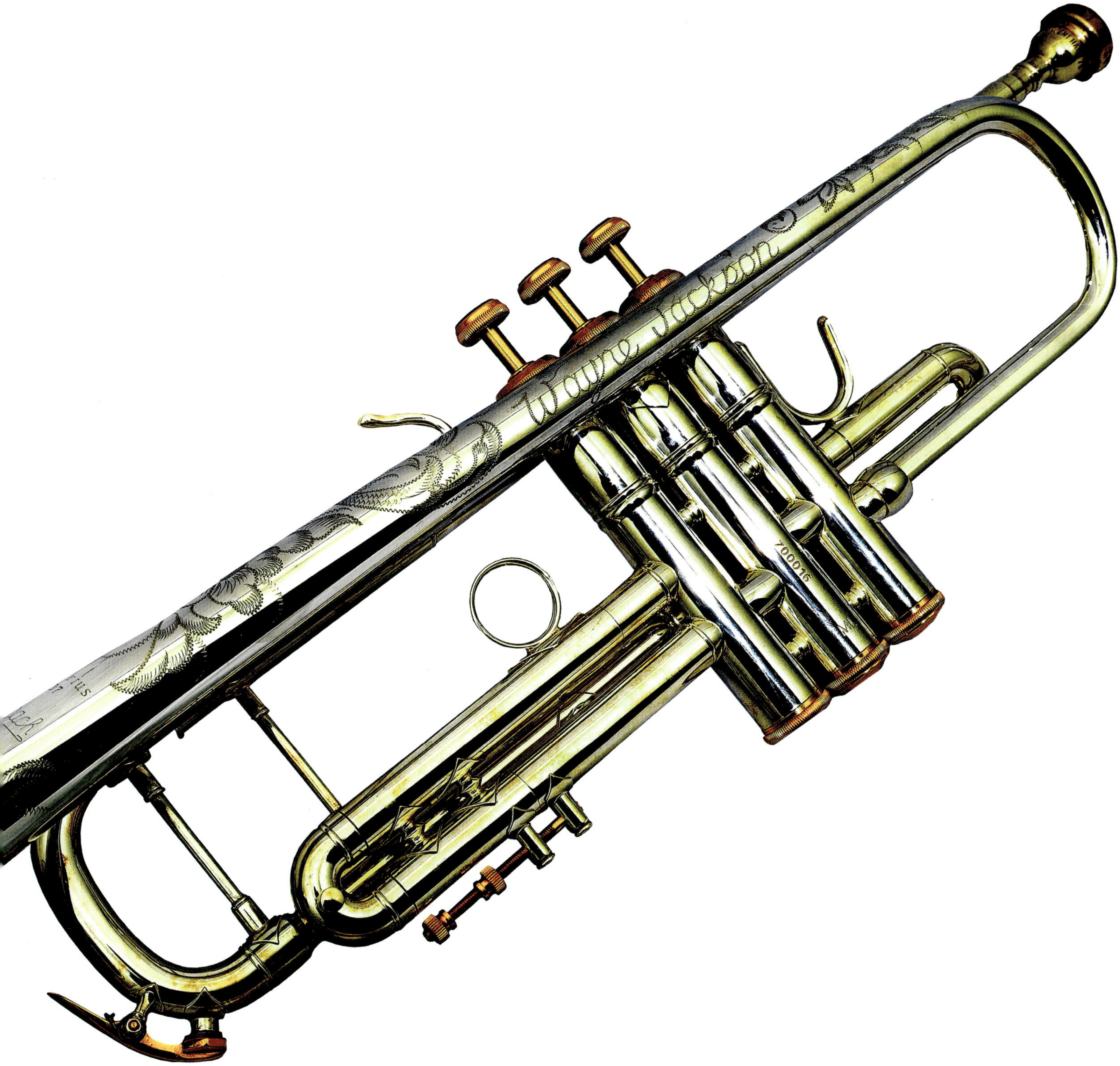


WAYNE JACKSON'S CONN-SELMER "MEMPHIS HORNS" STRADIVARIUS TRUMPET

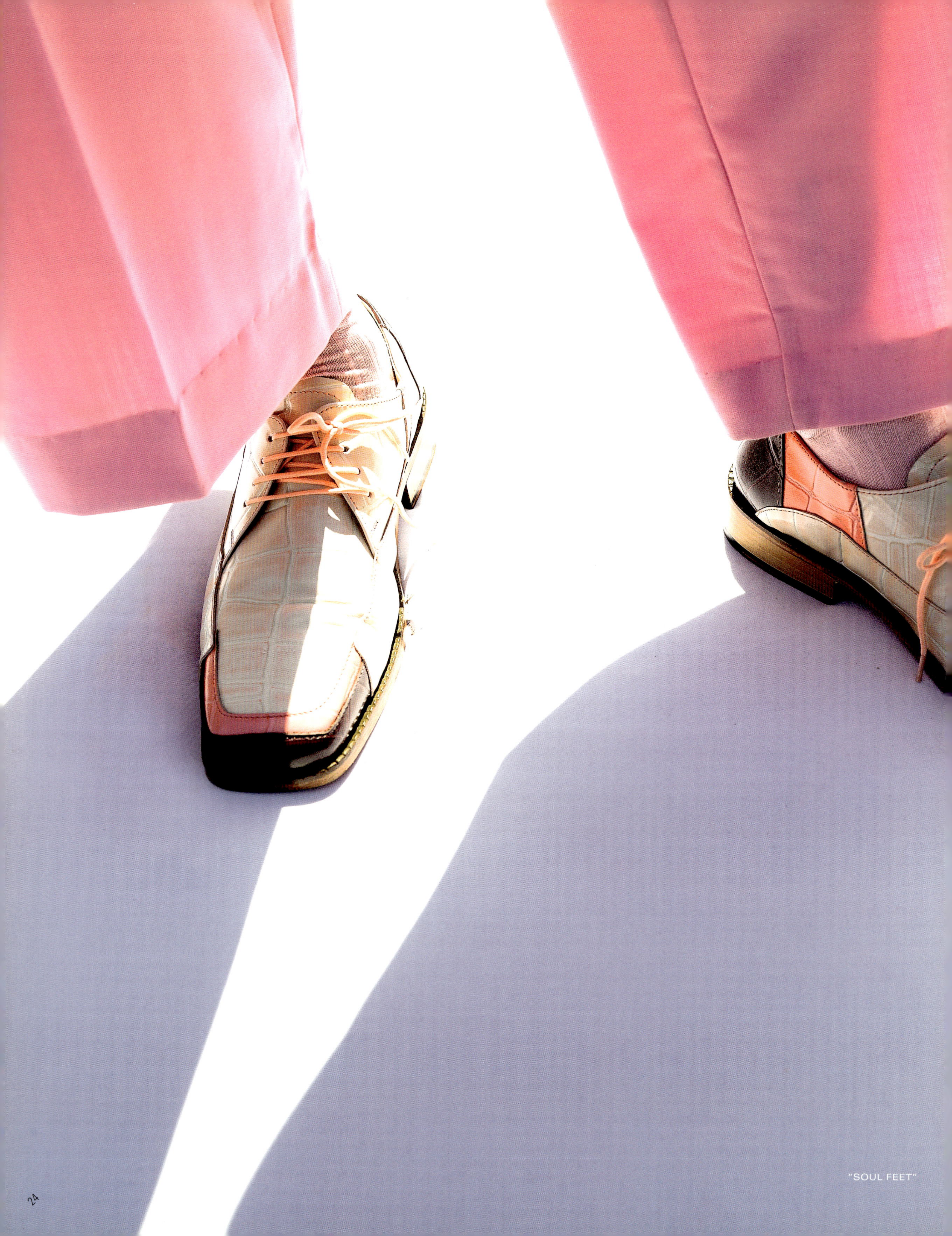

"SOUL FEET"

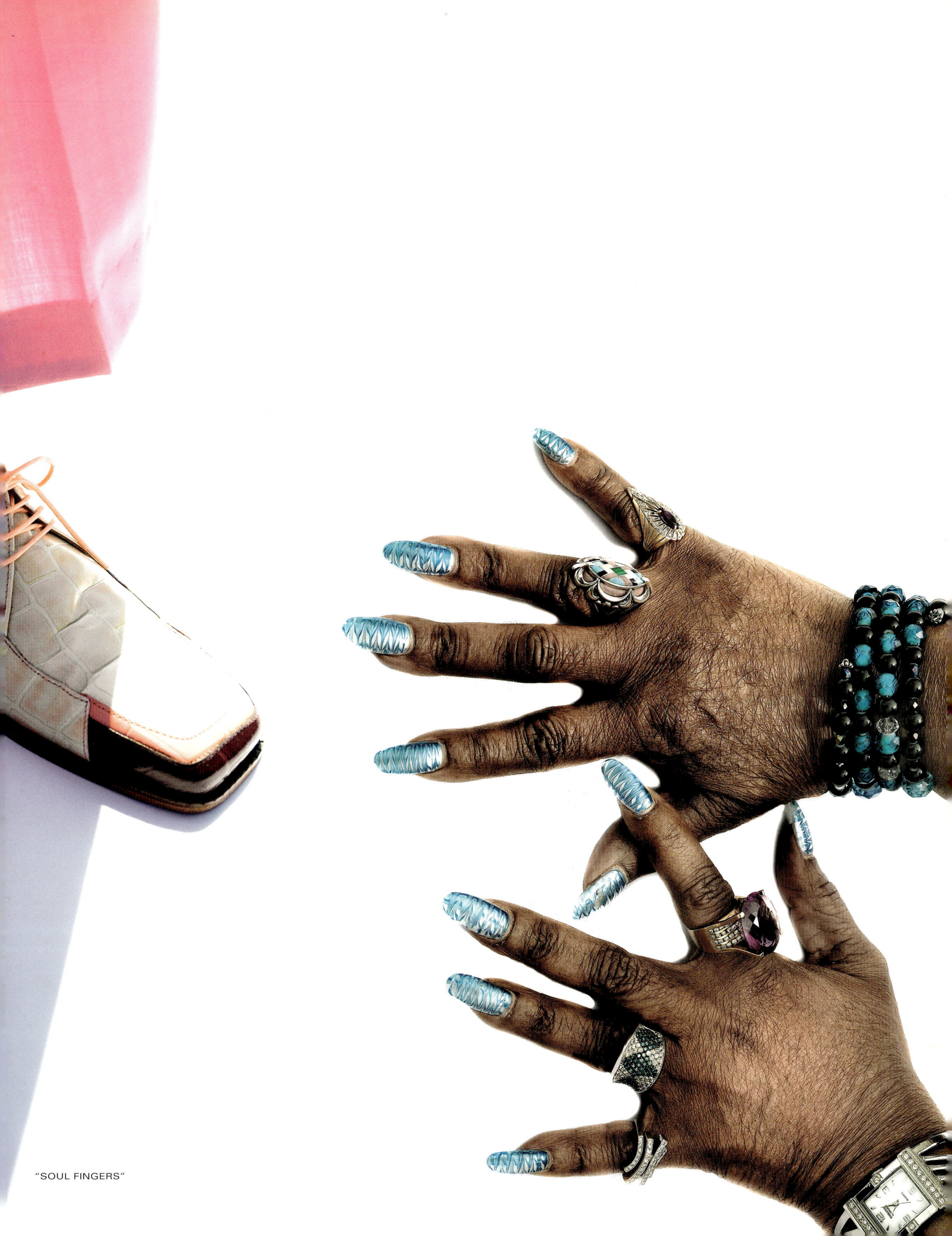

"SOUL FINGERS"

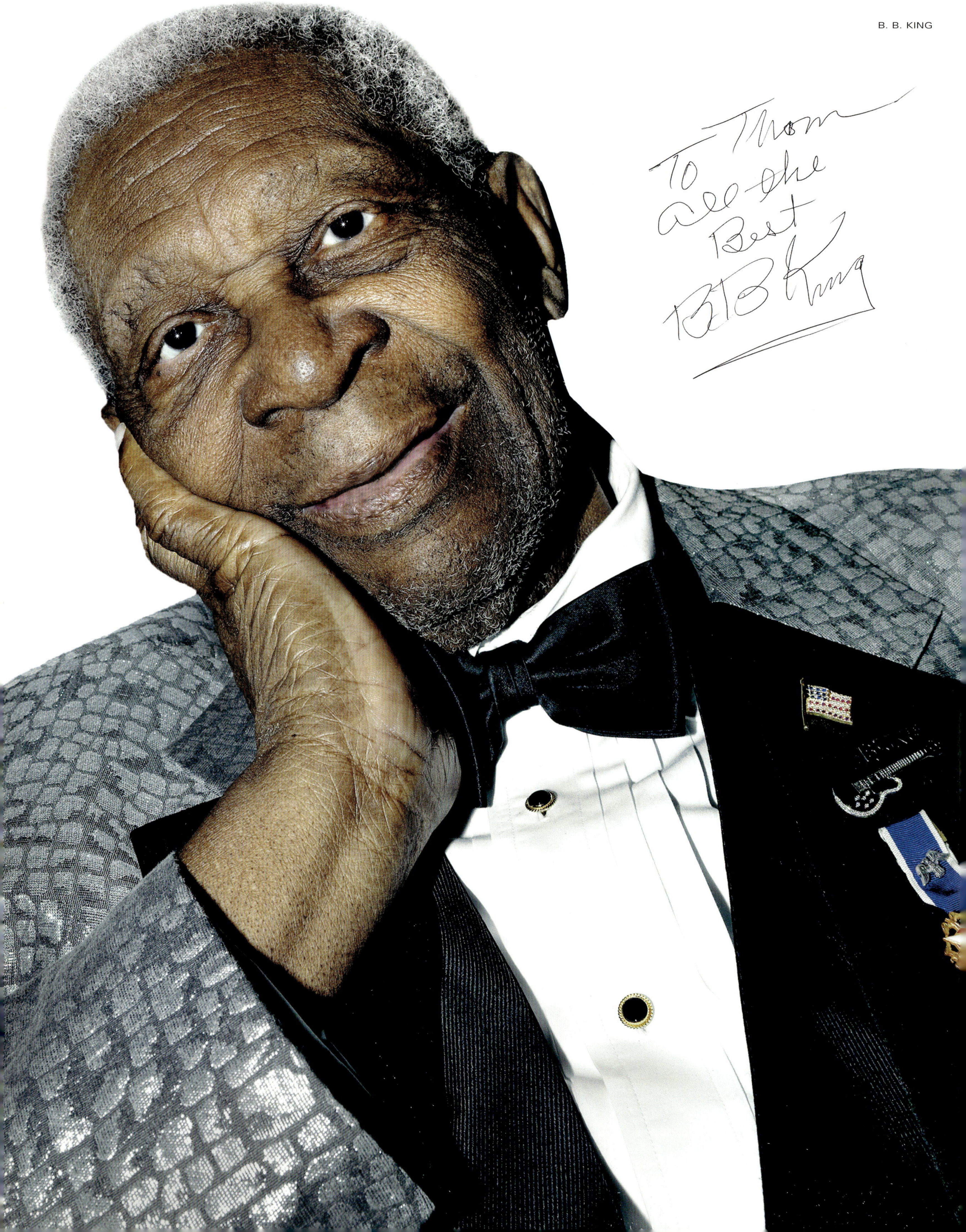
To Thom
all the
Best
B B King

AND HIS GUITAR "LUCILLE"

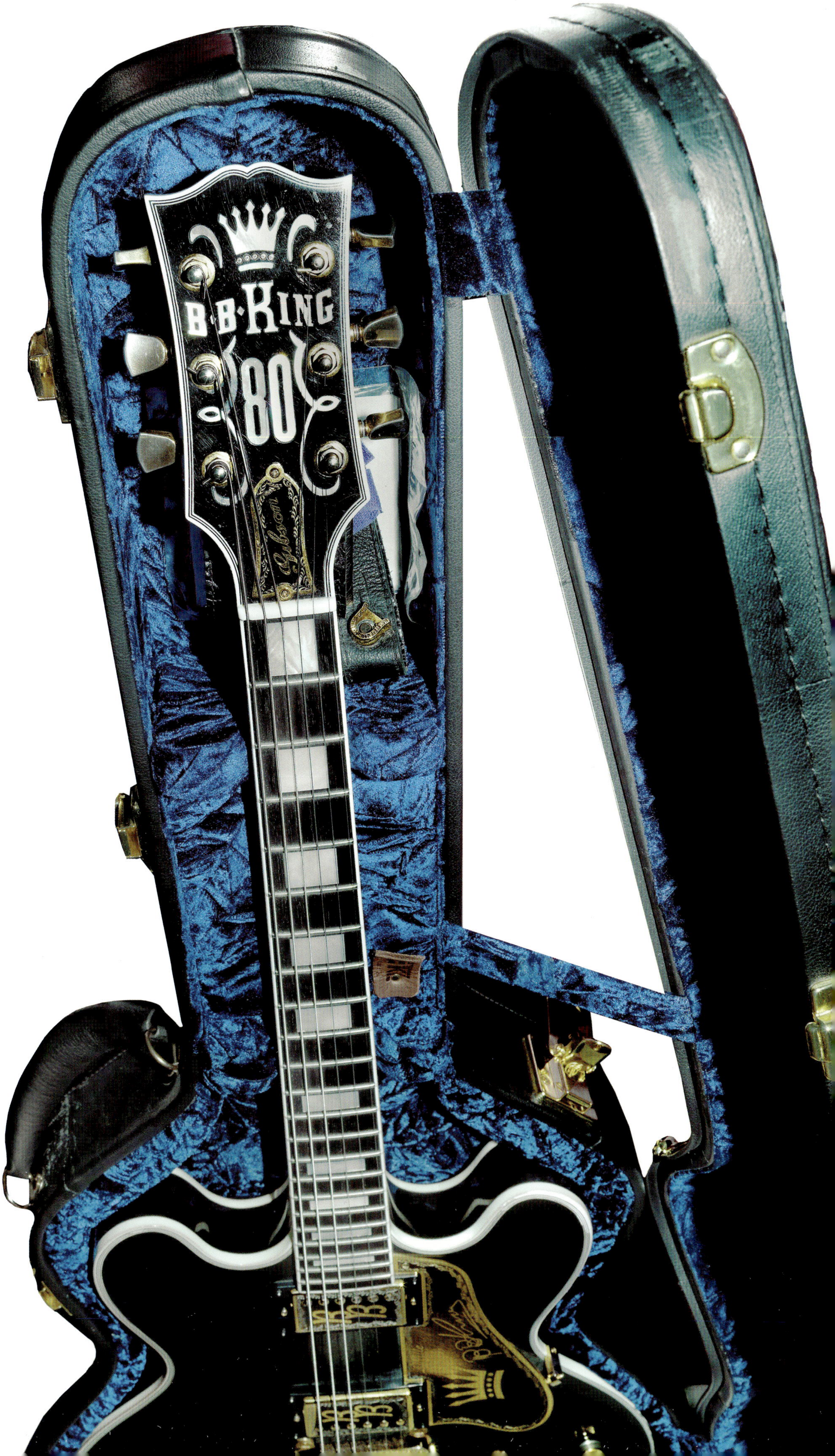

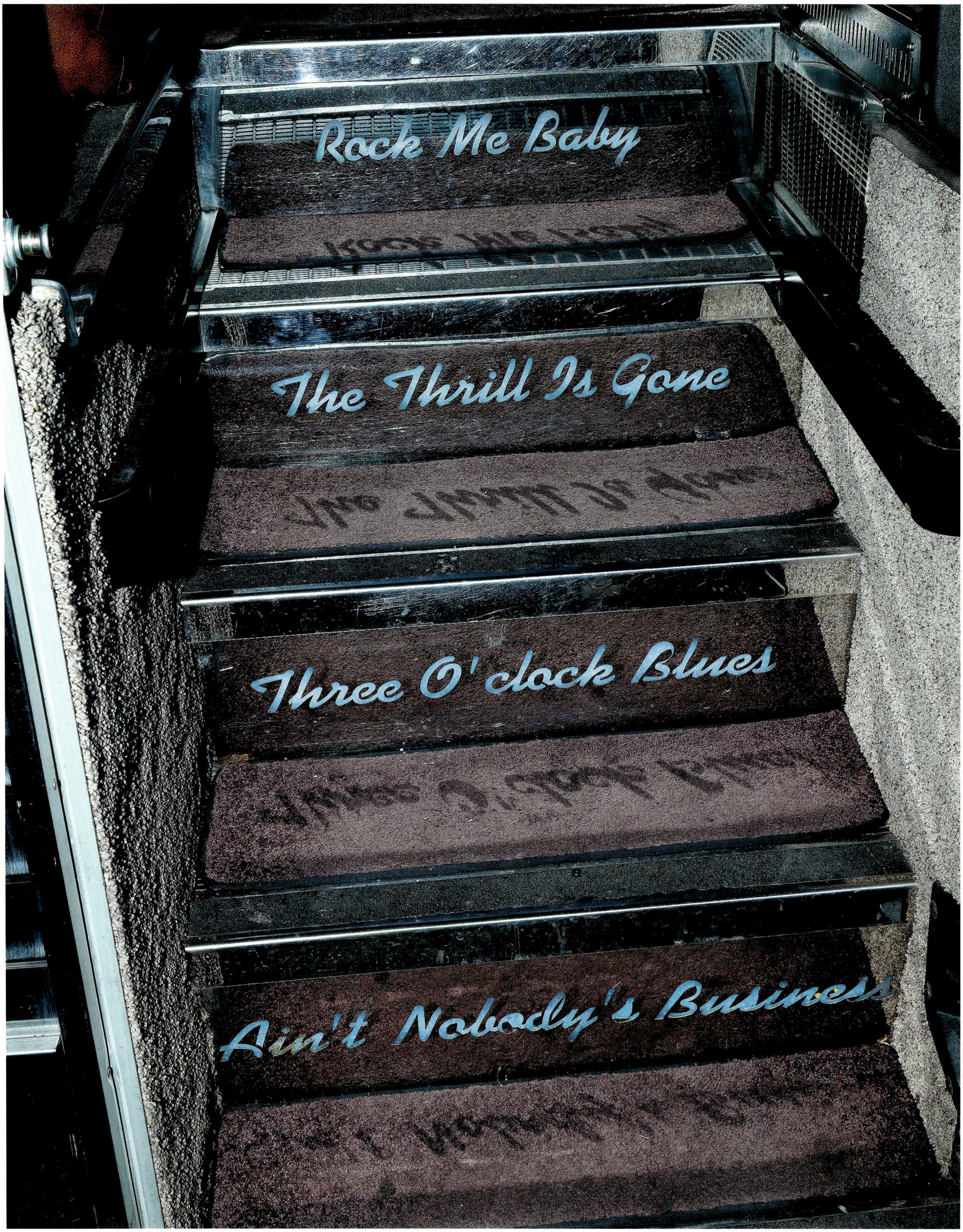


STEPS OF B. B. KING'S TOUR BUS

NORMAN MATTHEWS, B. B. KING'S ASSISTANT THEN TOUR MANAGER SINCE 1946

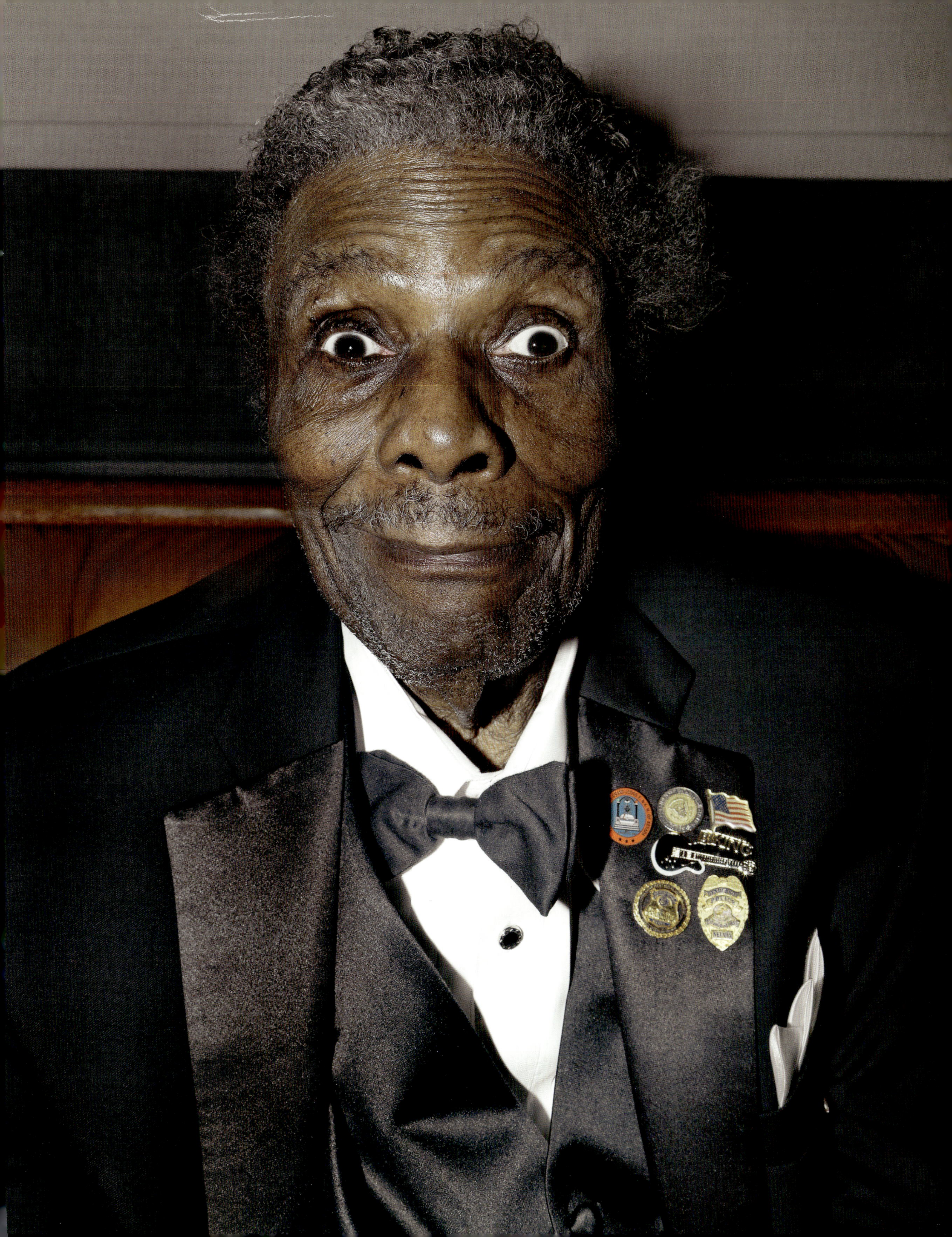

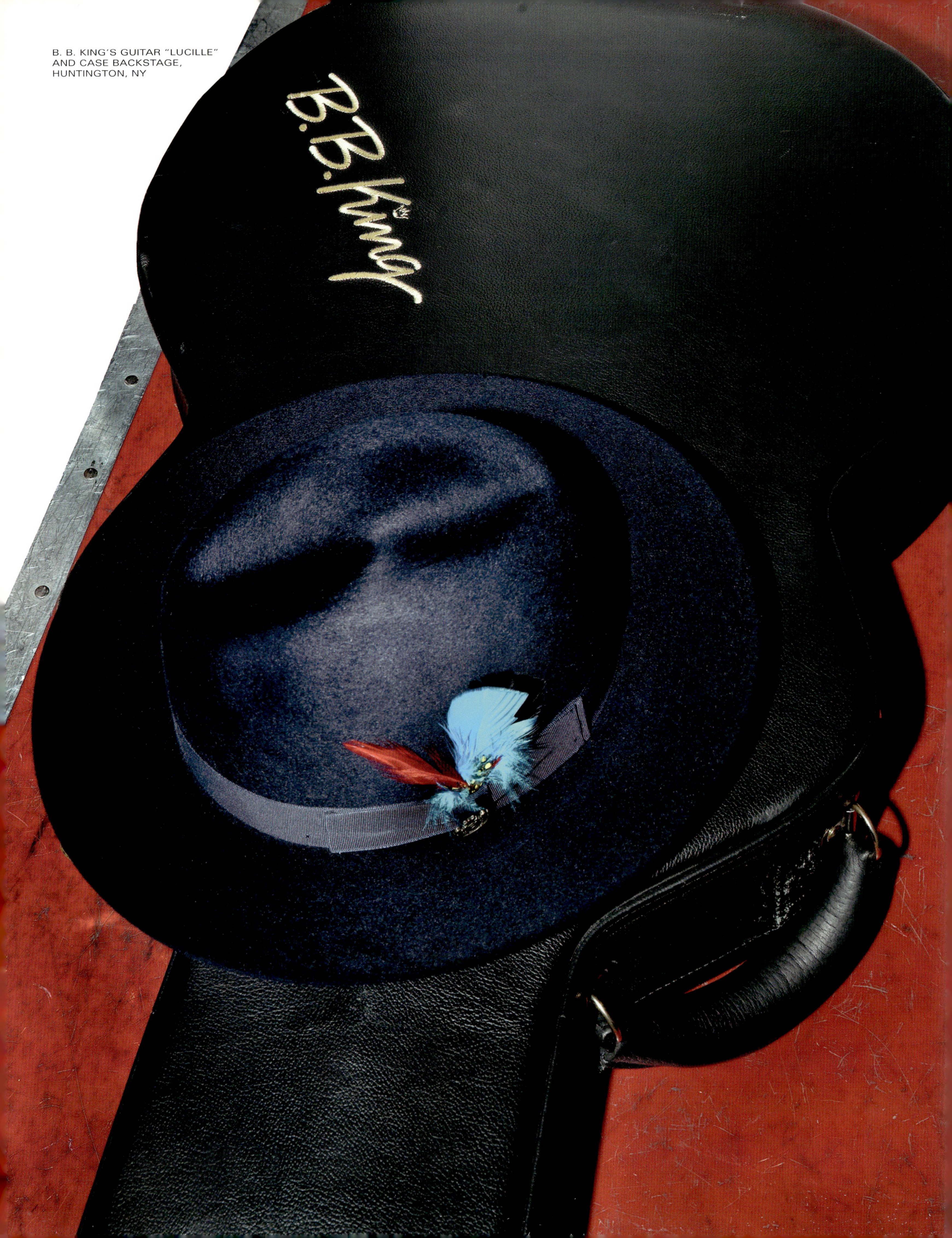


B. B. KING'S GUITAR "LUCILLE"
AND CASE BACKSTAGE,
HUNTINGTON, NY

IKE TURNER AND ANN PEEBLES'S
STAGE CLOTHING c. 1960s

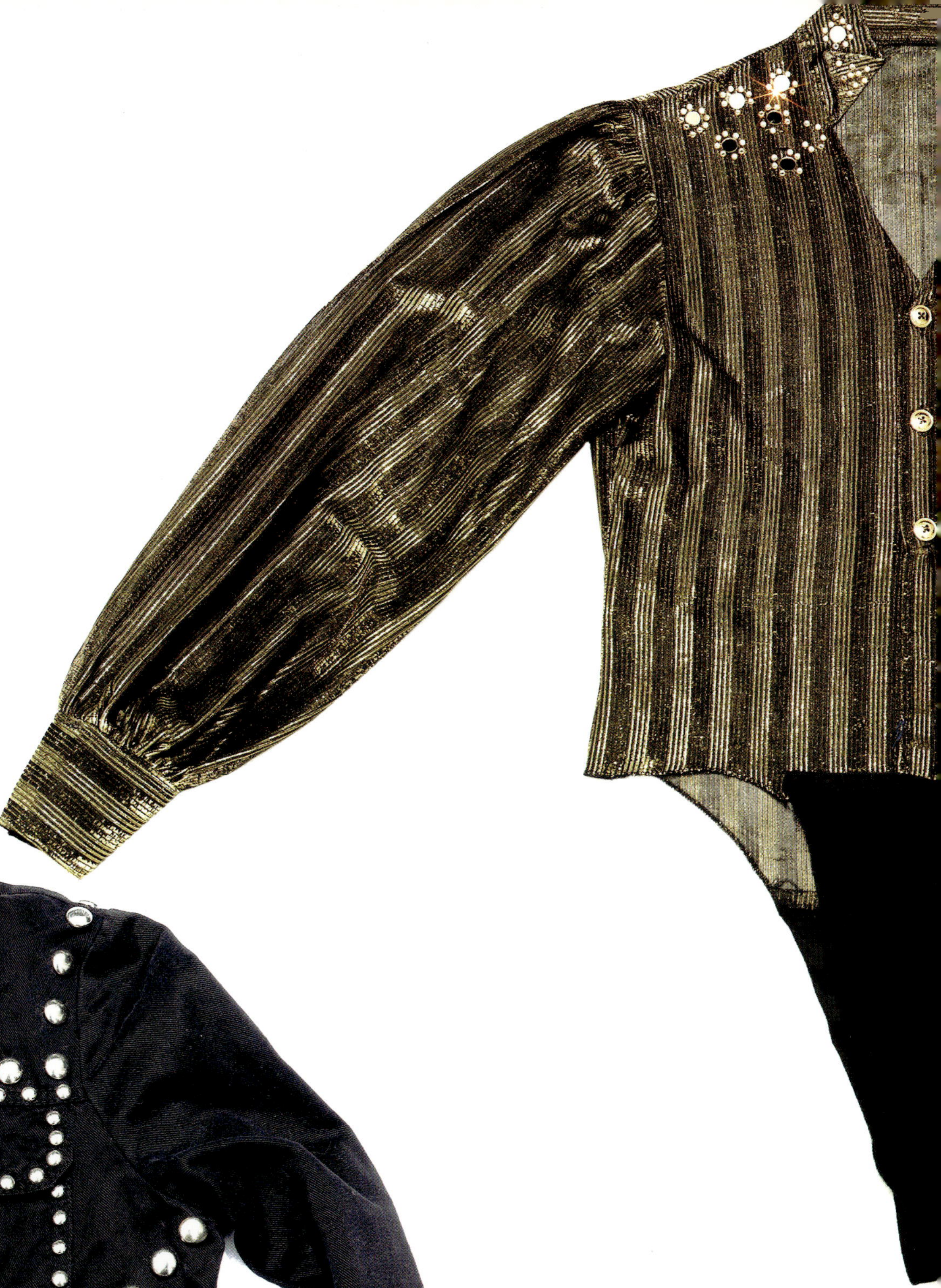

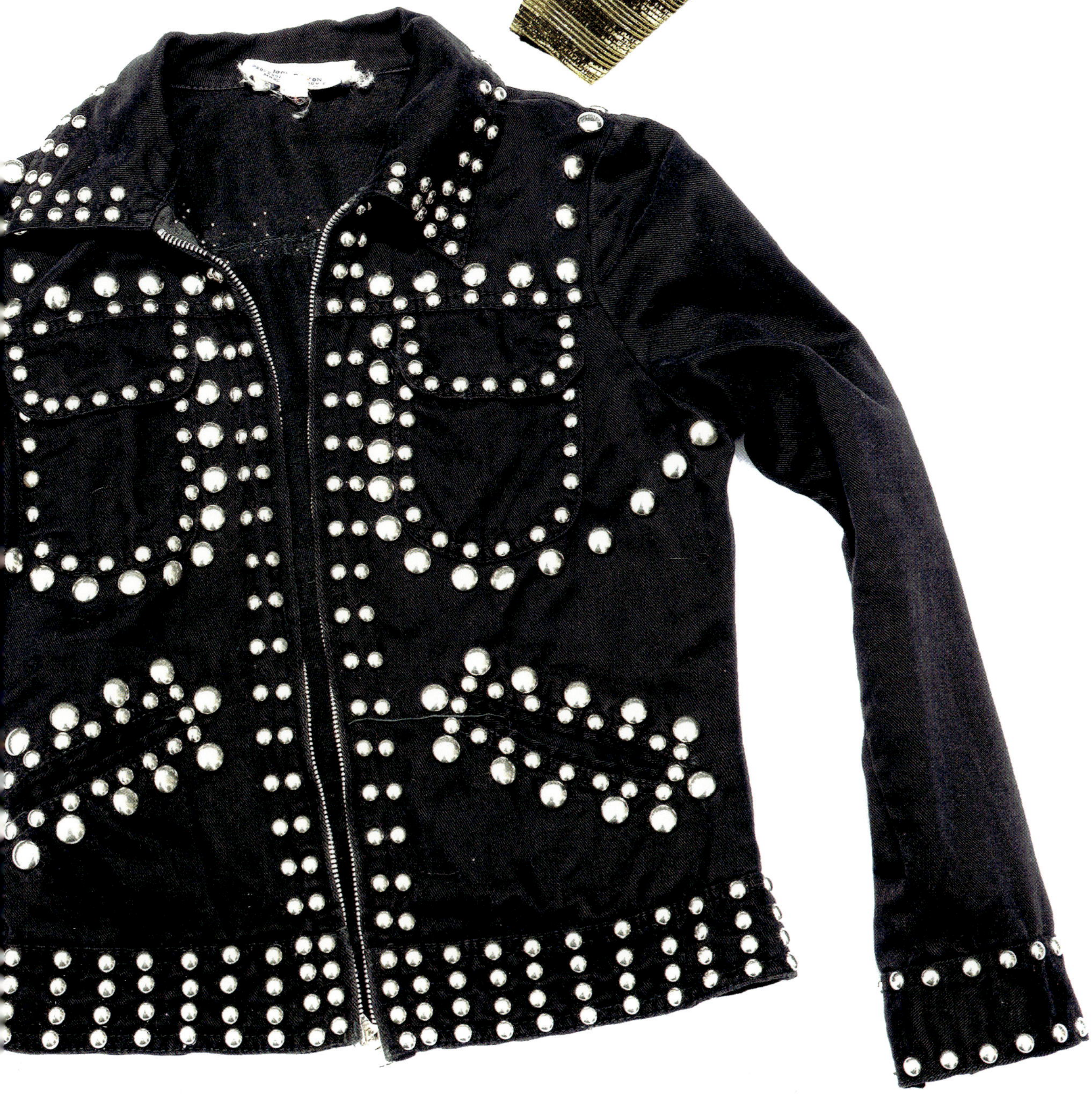

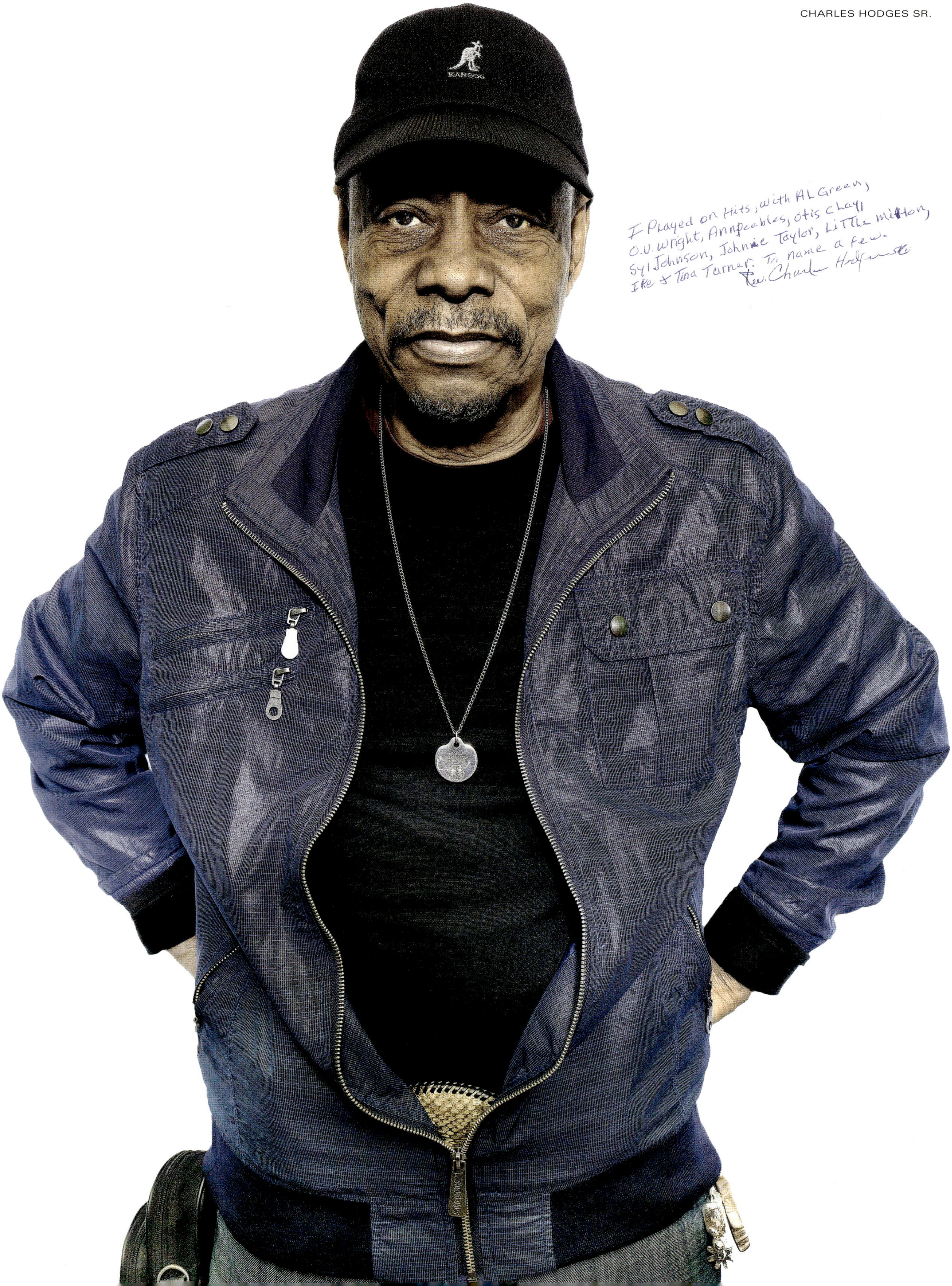


I Played on Hits, with AL Green,
O.V. wright, Annpeebles, otis clay,
Syl Johnson, Johnnie Taylor, LiTTle milton,
Ike & Tina Turner. To name a few.
Rev. Charles Hodges Sr.

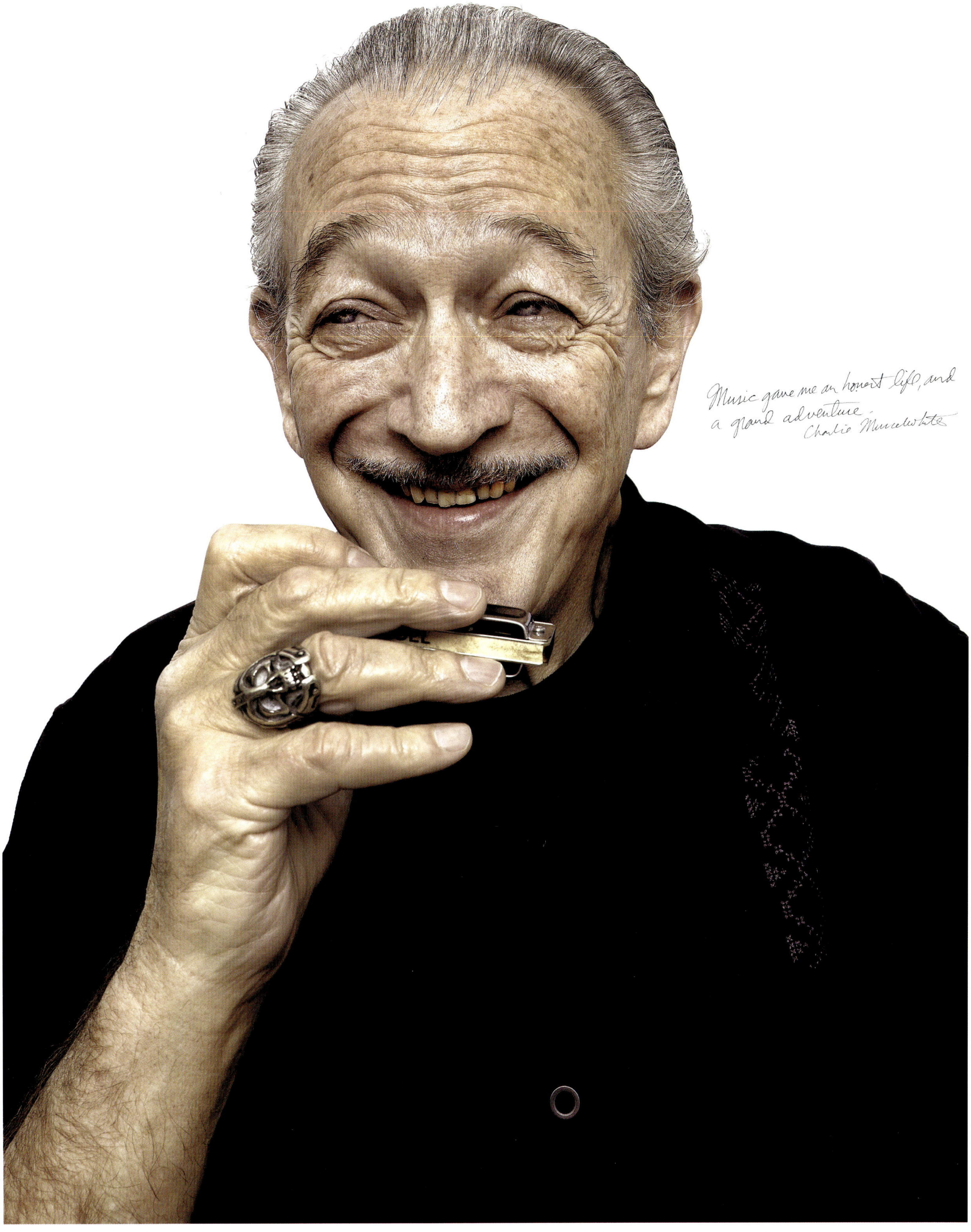
Music gave me an honest life, and
a grand adventure.
Charlie Musselwhite

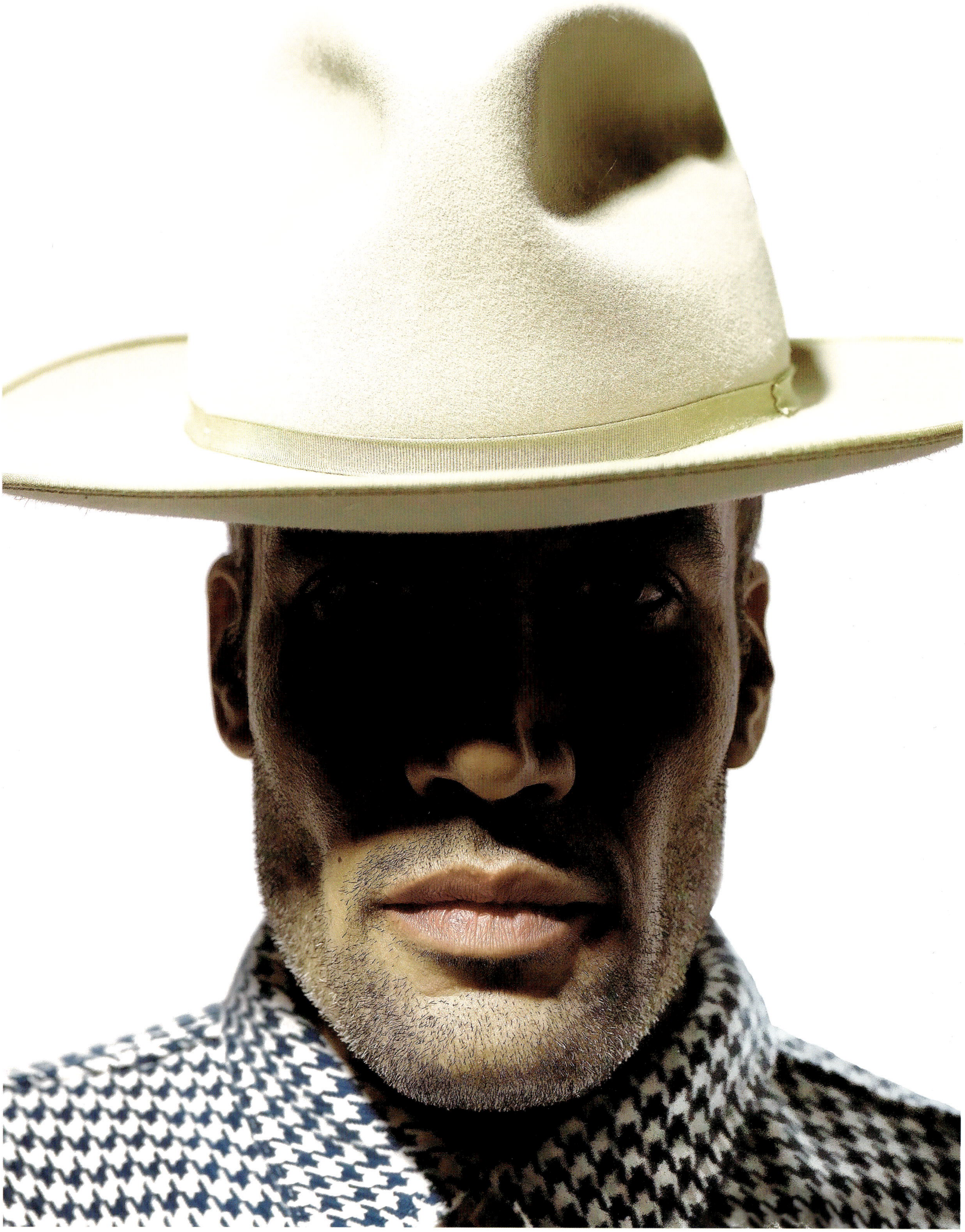

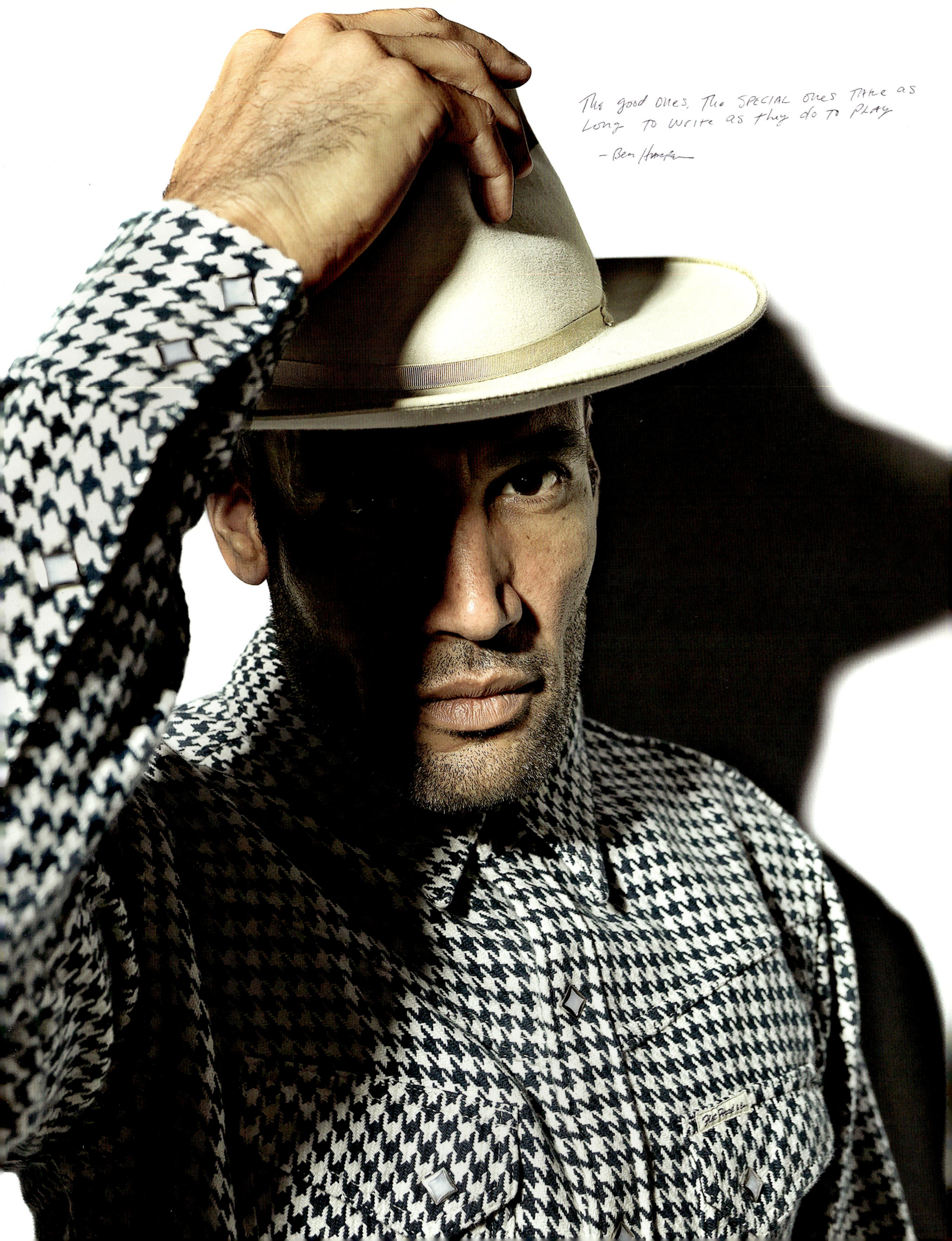

The good ones, the SPECIAL ones take as long to write as they do to play

– Ben Harper

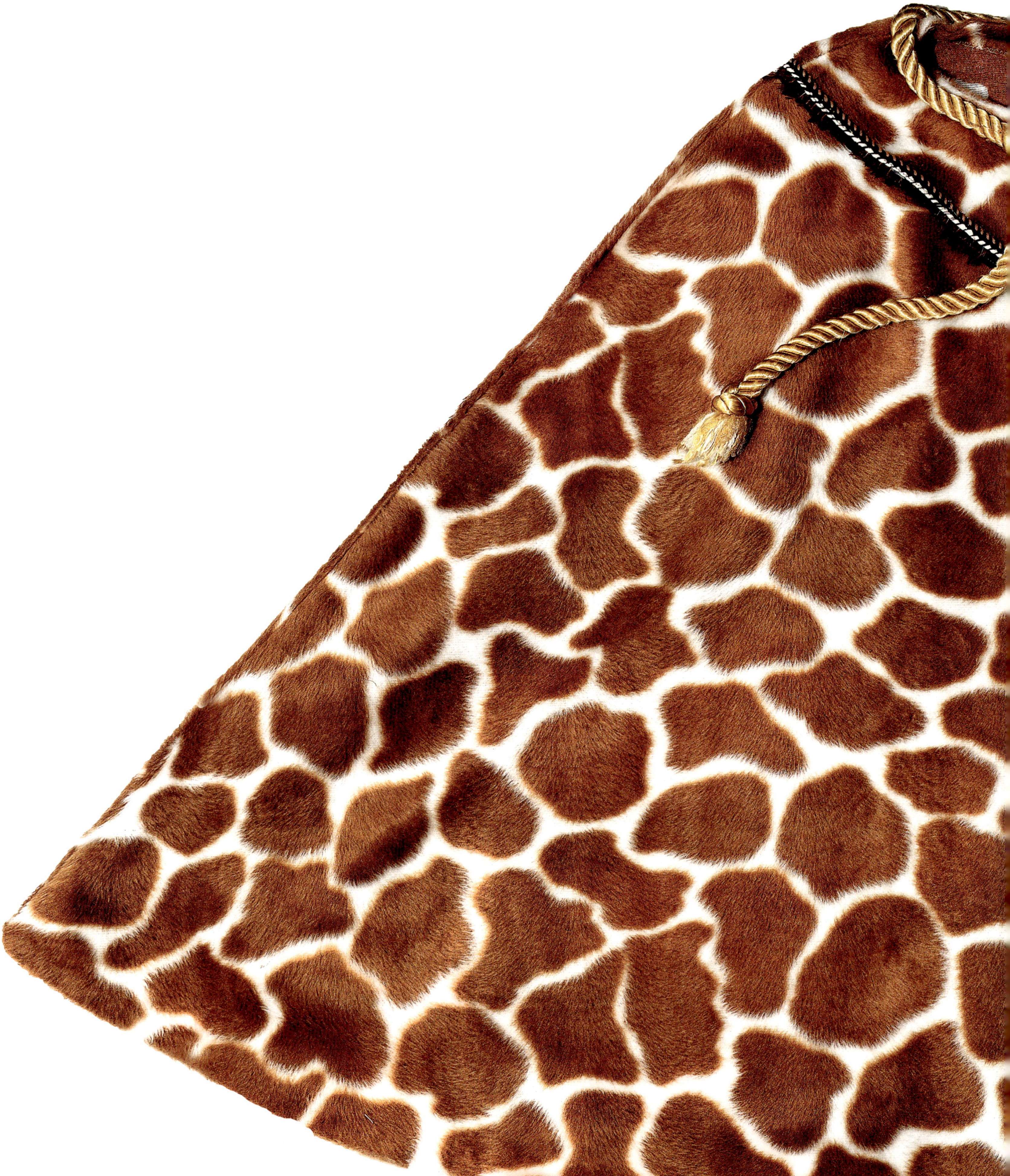

RUFUS THOMAS'S 1970s' FUR STAGE CAPE

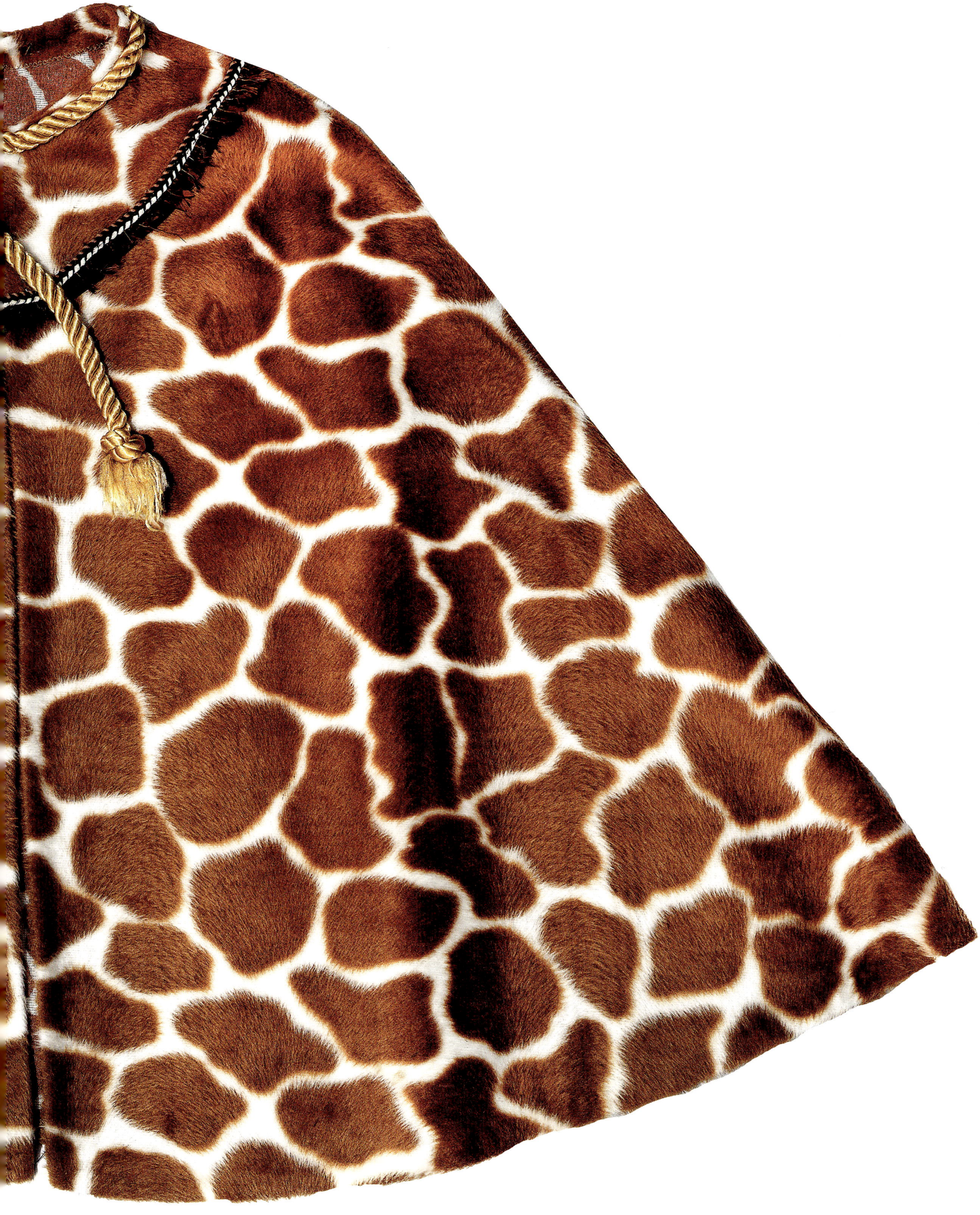

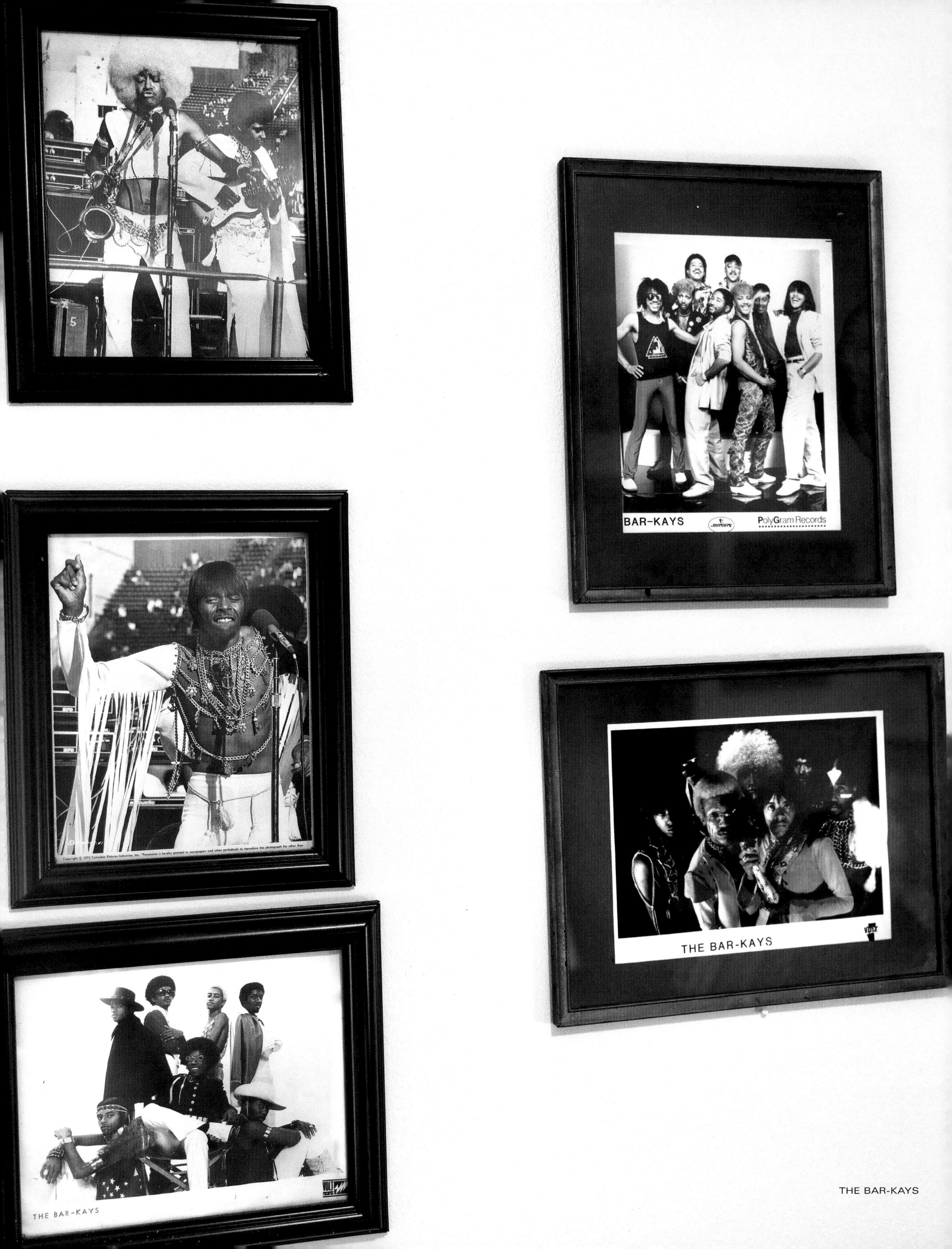
5
BAR-KAYS
mercury
PolyGram Records
THE BAR-KAYS
VOLT
THE BAR-KAYS
VOLT

THE BAR-KAYS

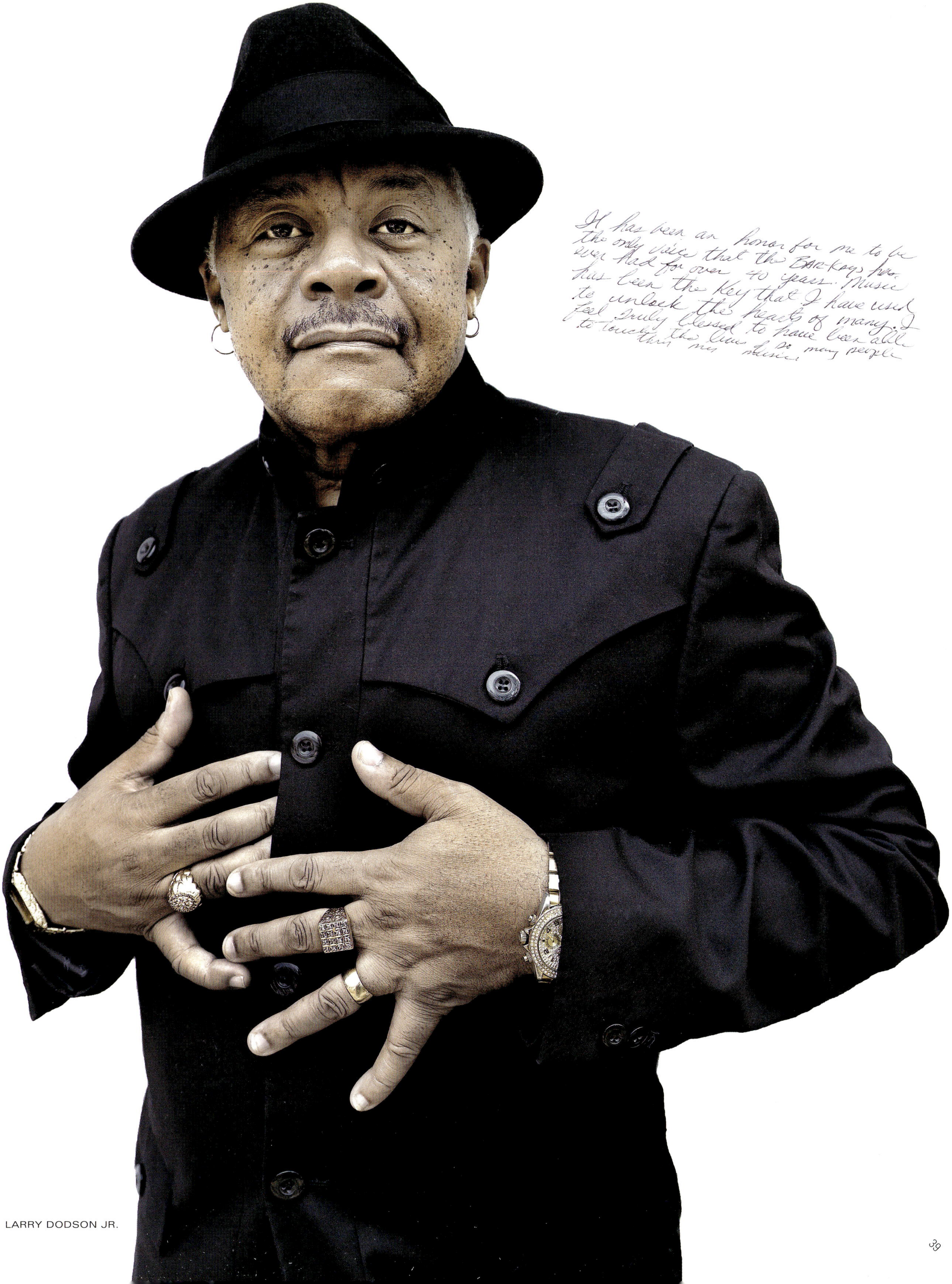


LARRY DODSON JR.

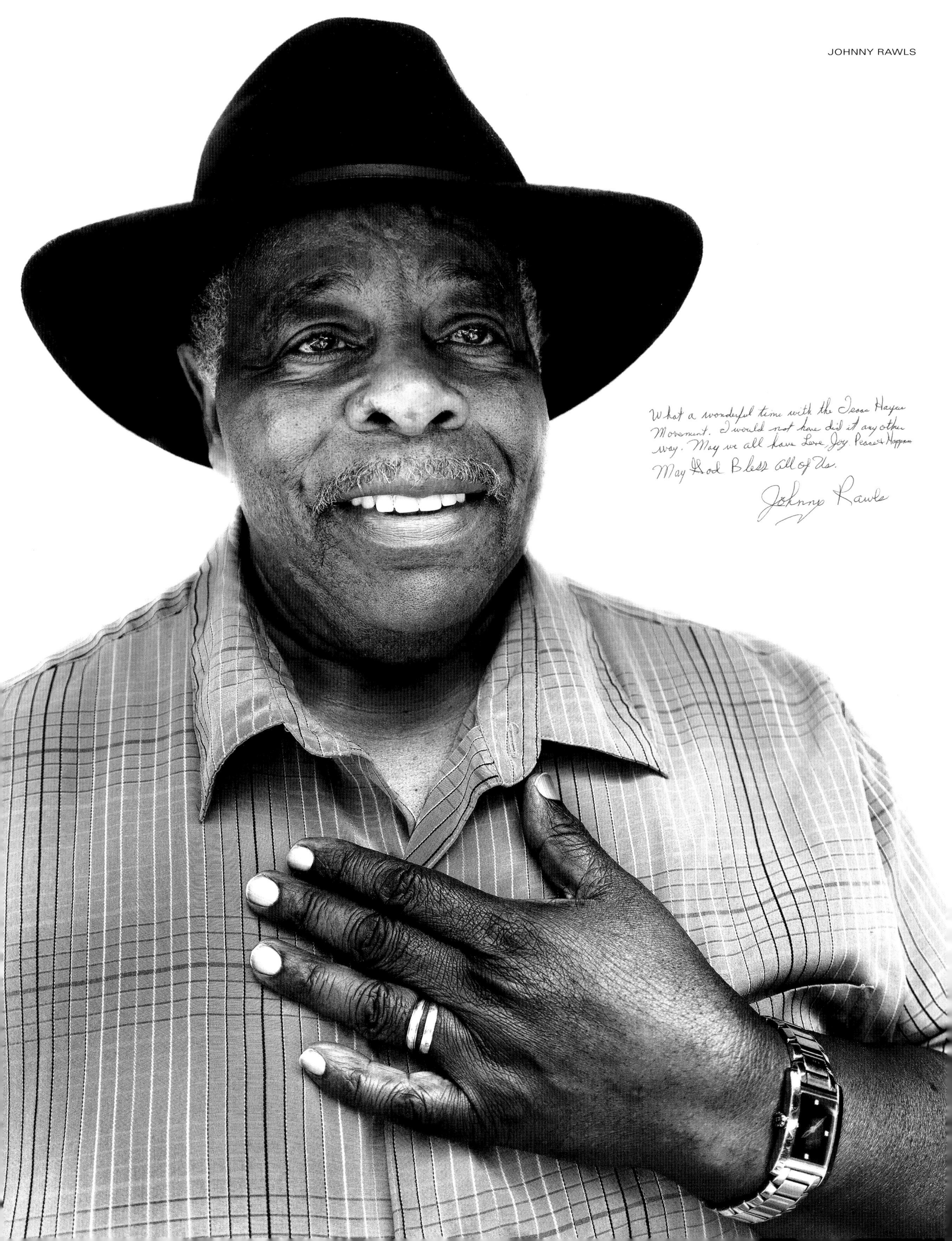
What a wonderful time with the Isaac Hayes
Movement. I would not have did it any other
way. May we all have Love, Joy. Peace & Happ
May God Bless all of Us.
Johnny Rawls

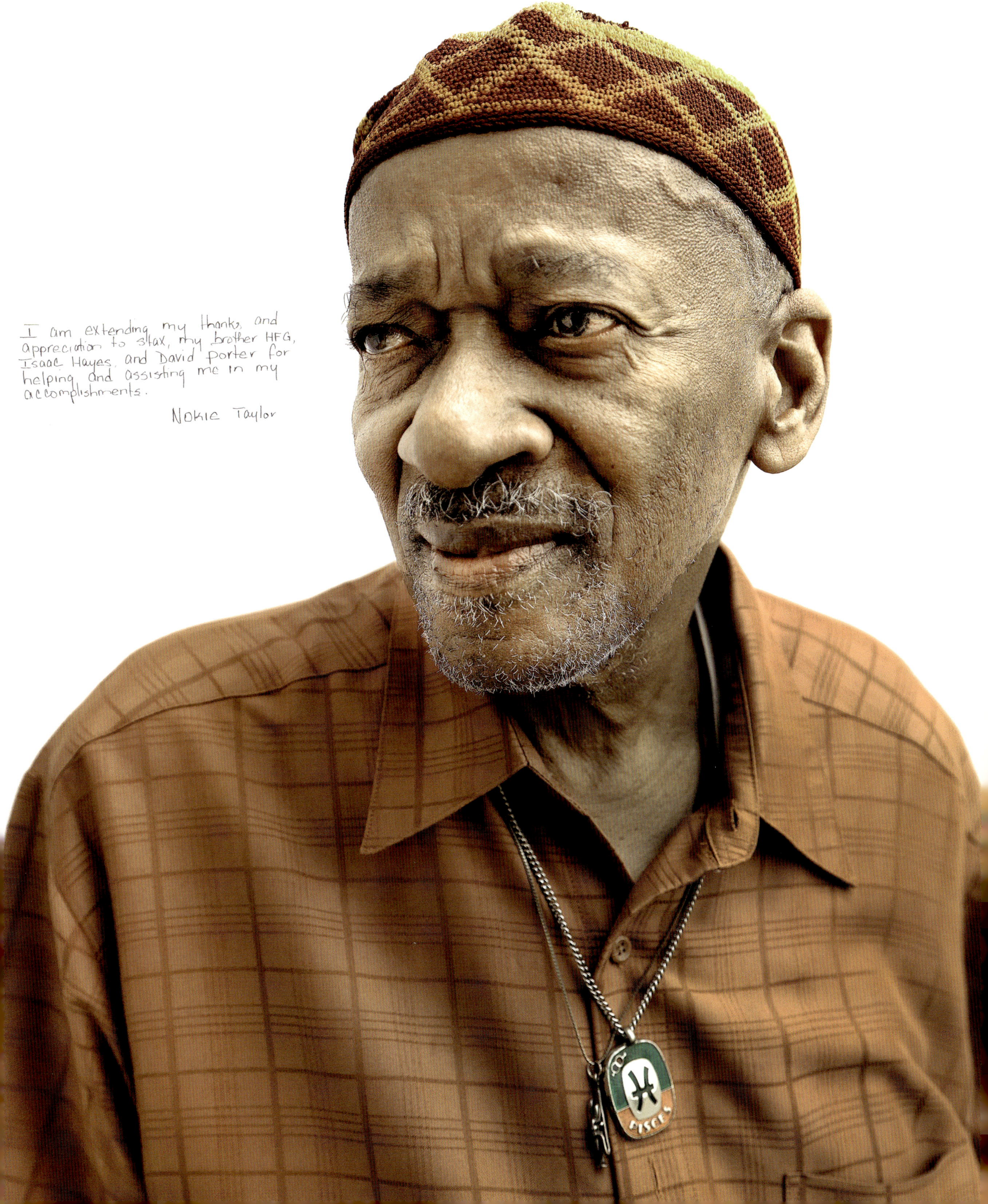

I am extending my thanks and appreciation to stax, my brother HFG, Isaac Hayes, and David porter for helping and assisting me in my accomplishments.

Nokie Taylor

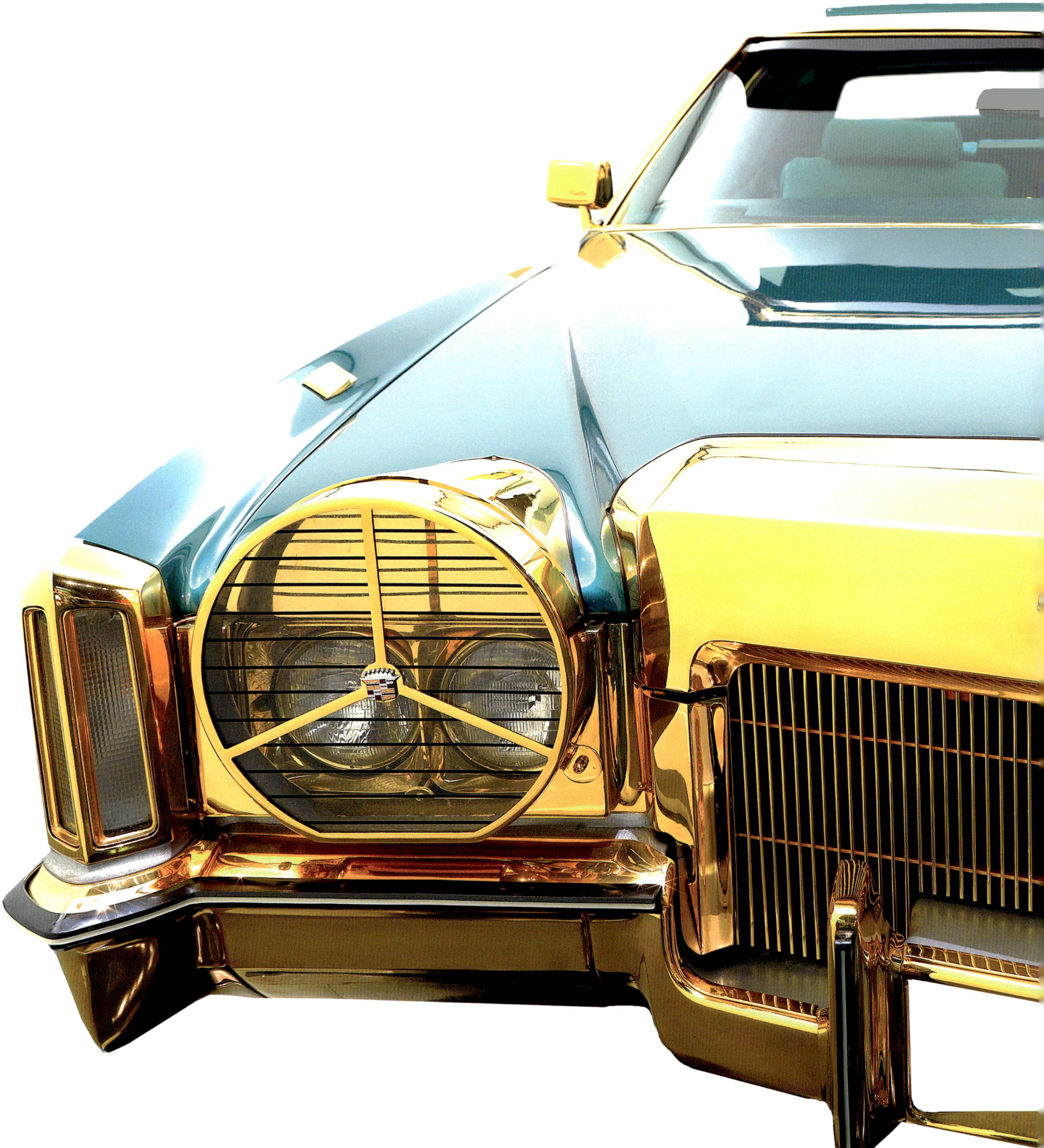

ISAAC HAYES'S 1972 CADILLAC ELDORADO IN PEACOCK BLUE WITH GOLD-PLATED TRIM

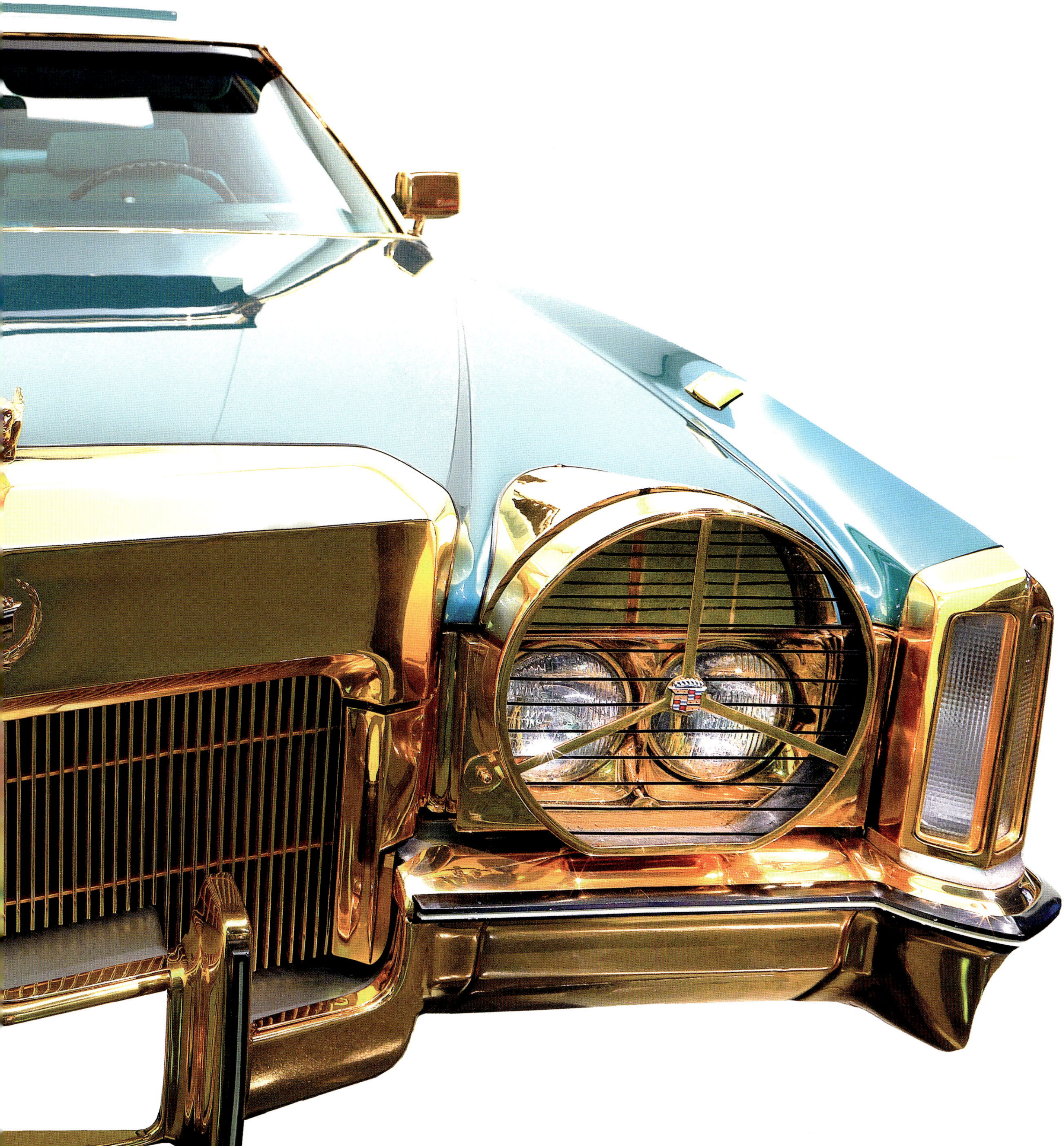

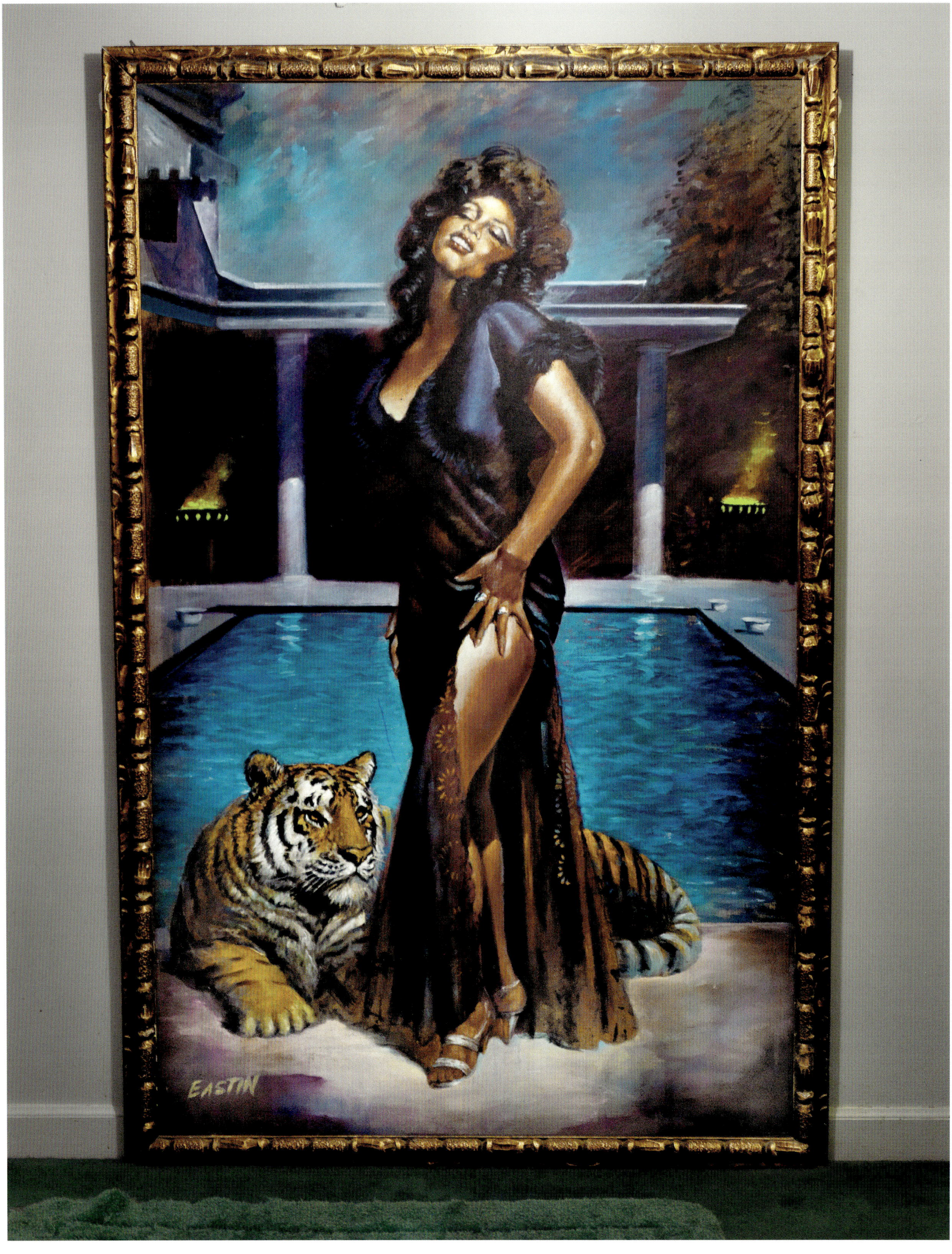
EASTIN

People ask me about the songs I write
and record. I have to tell them that
I write what I feel is real.
I believe in telling it like it is

Denise LaSalle

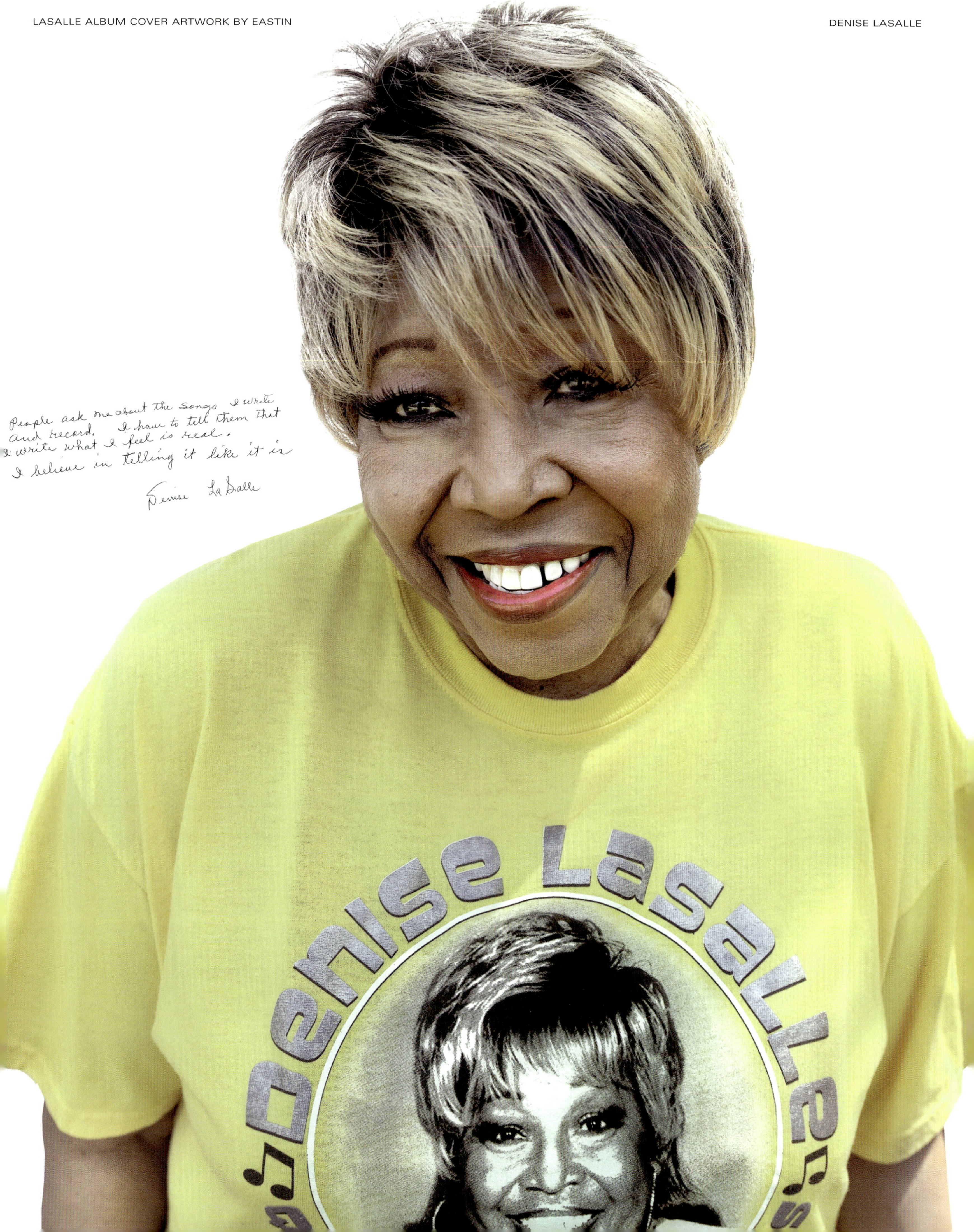

Today in my life live a highlight, are
healing and inspiration that will live forever.
The Creator of the Universe continues to
bless me!!! Al Bell 04/22/13

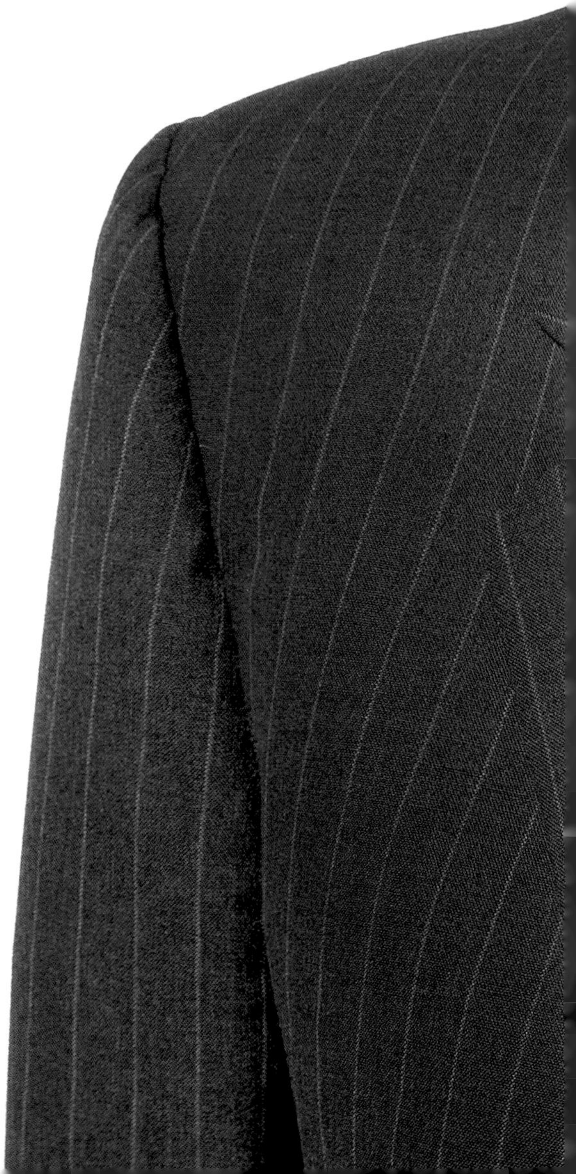

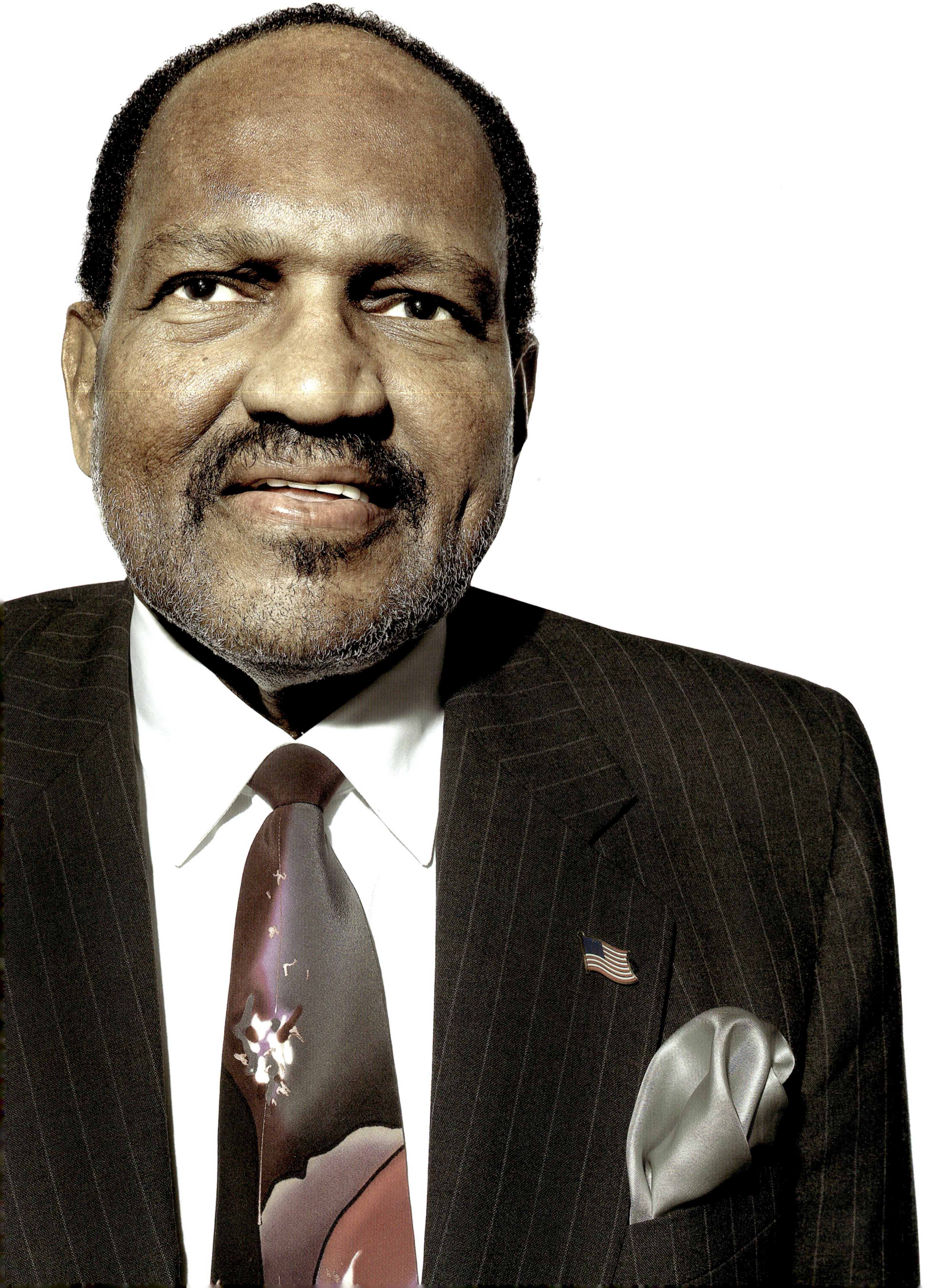

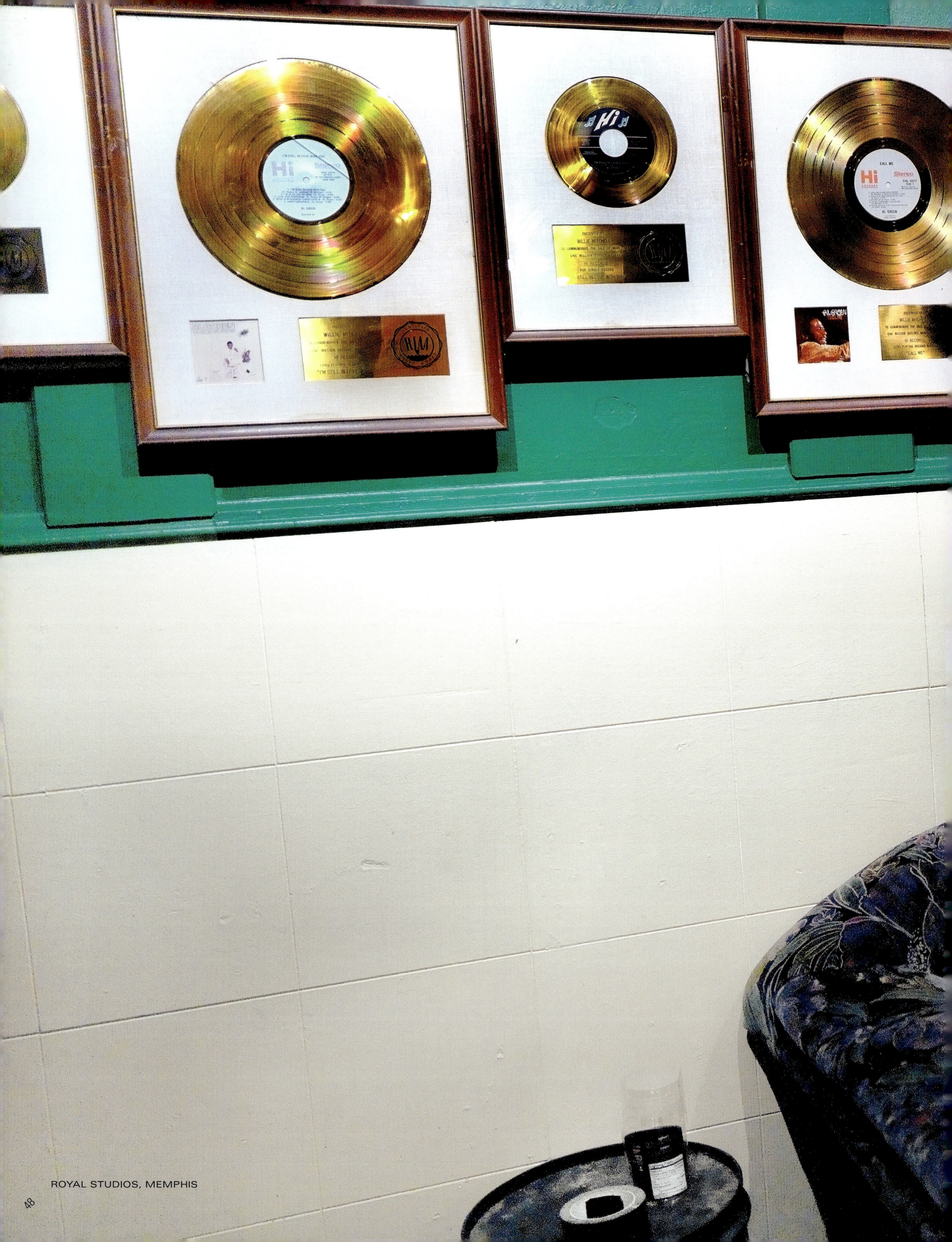


ROYAL STUDIOS, MEMPHIS

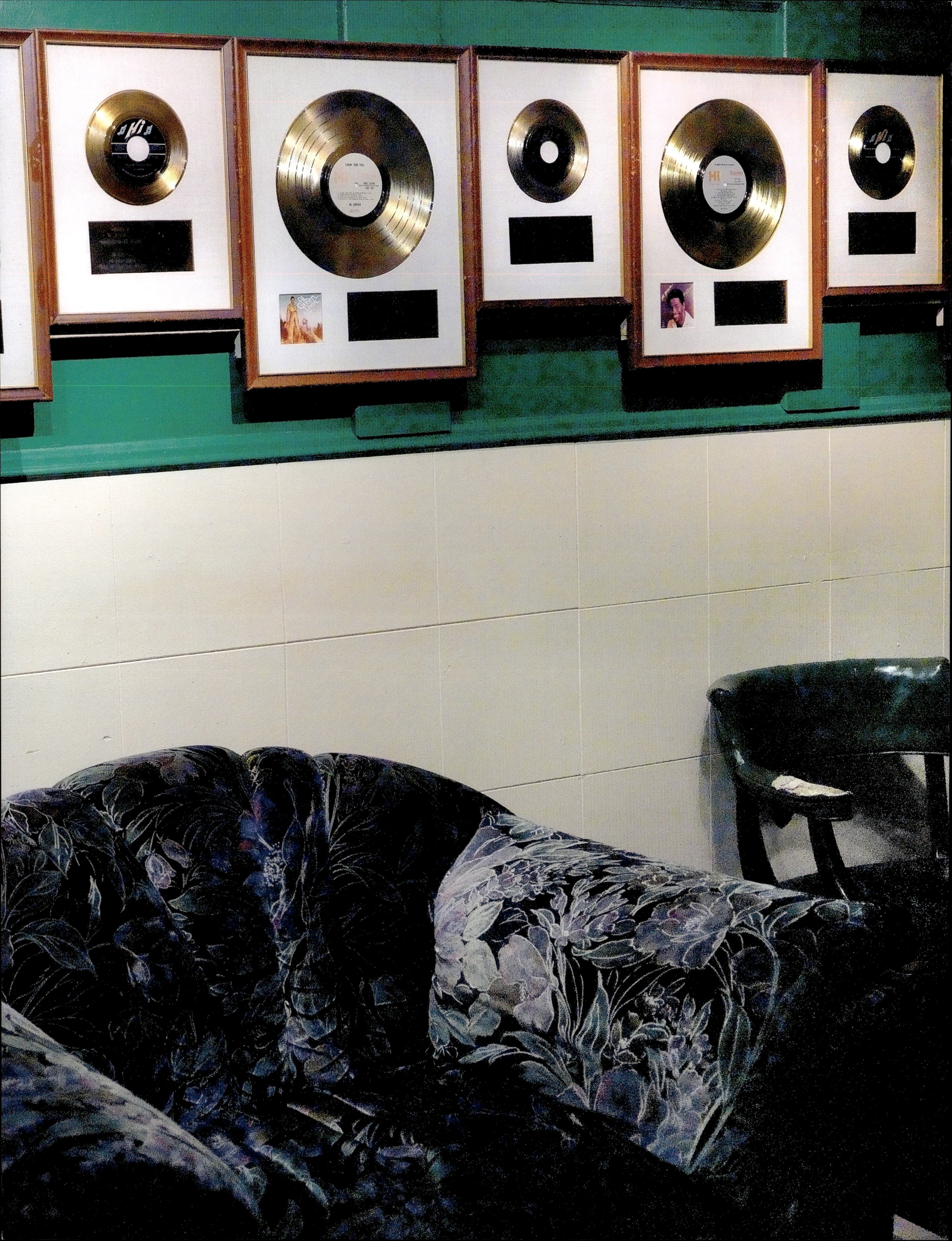

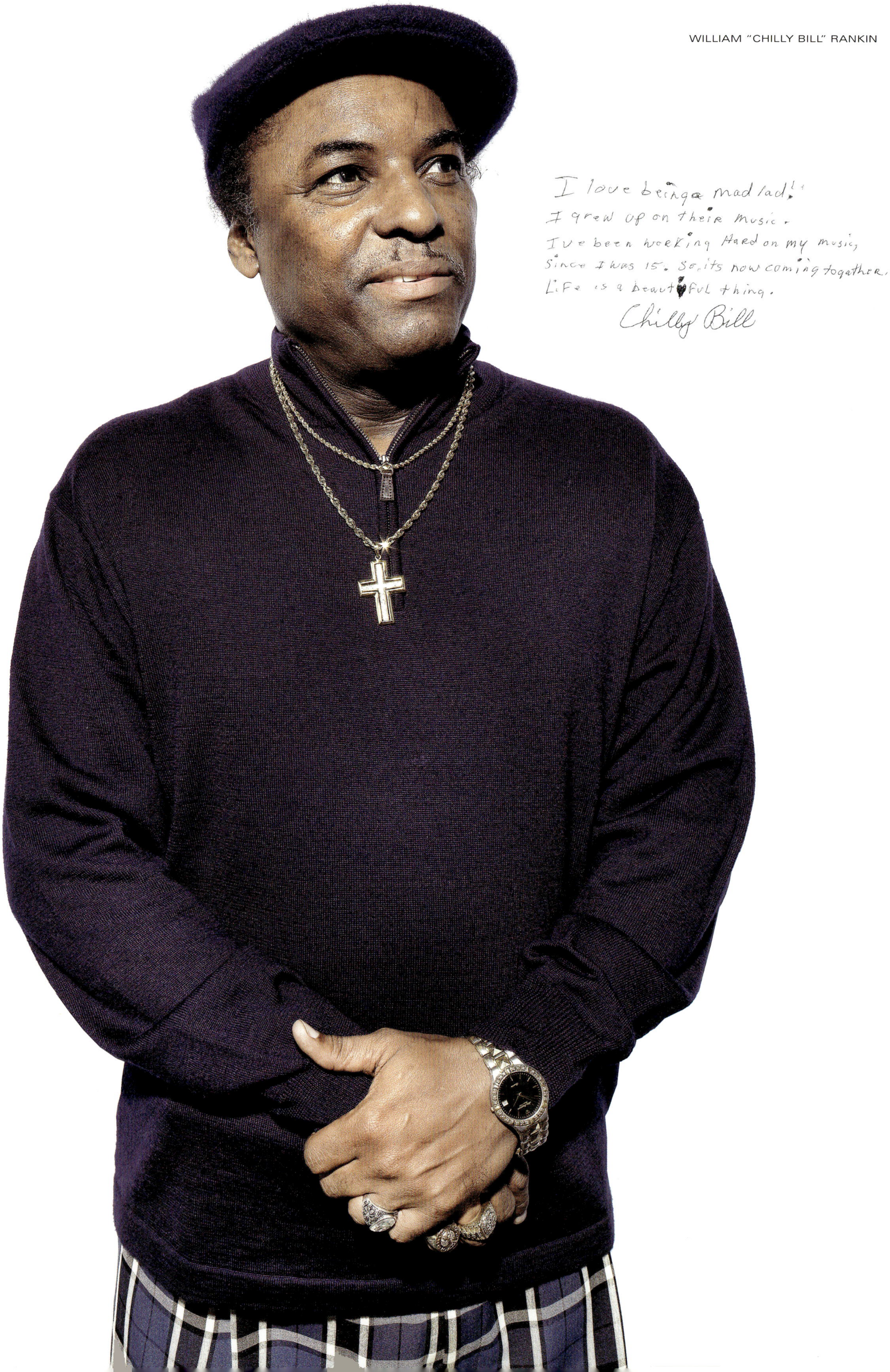
I love being a mad lad!!
I grew up on their music.
Ive been working Hard on my music,
since I was 15. So its now coming together.
Life is a beautiful thing.
Chilly Bill

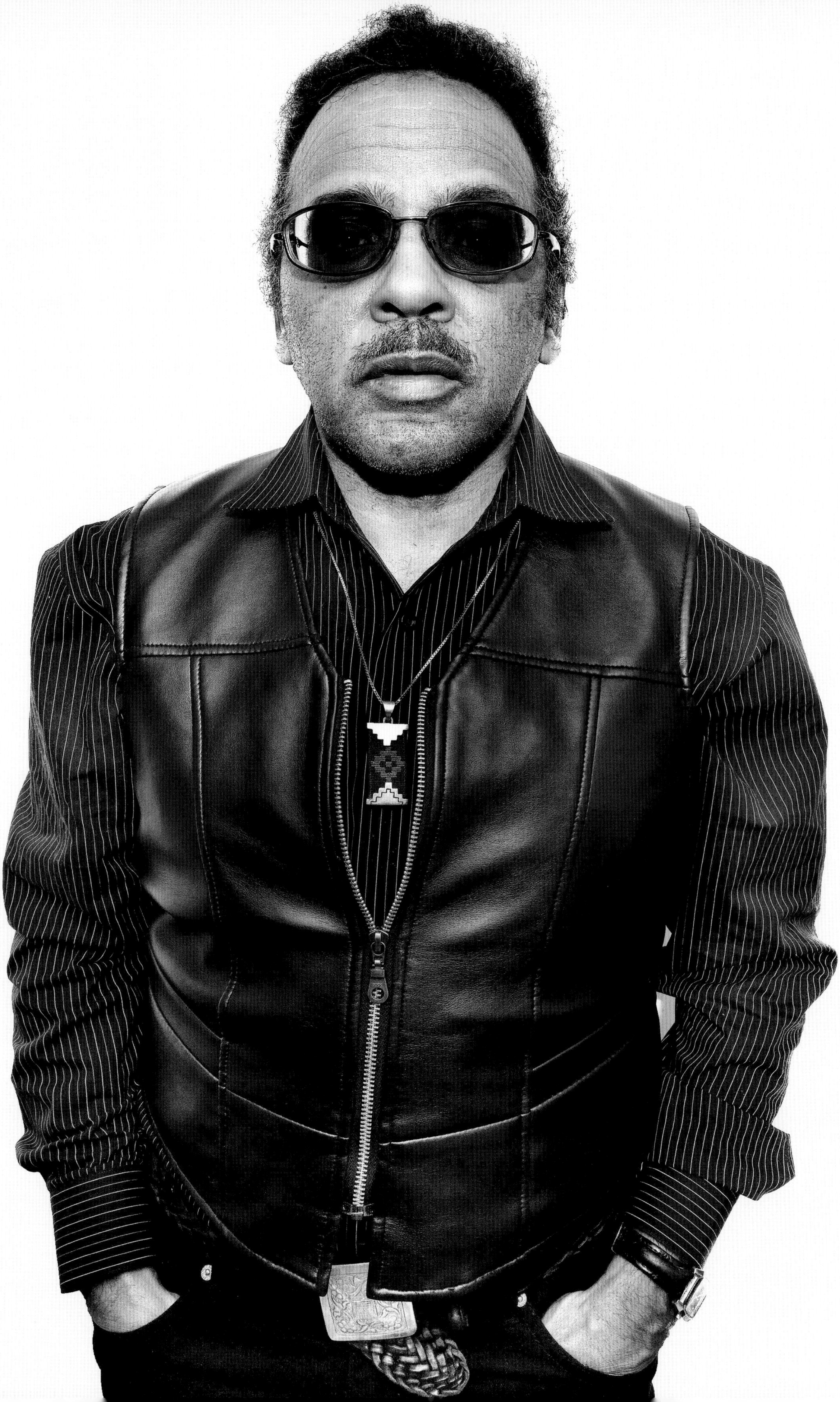

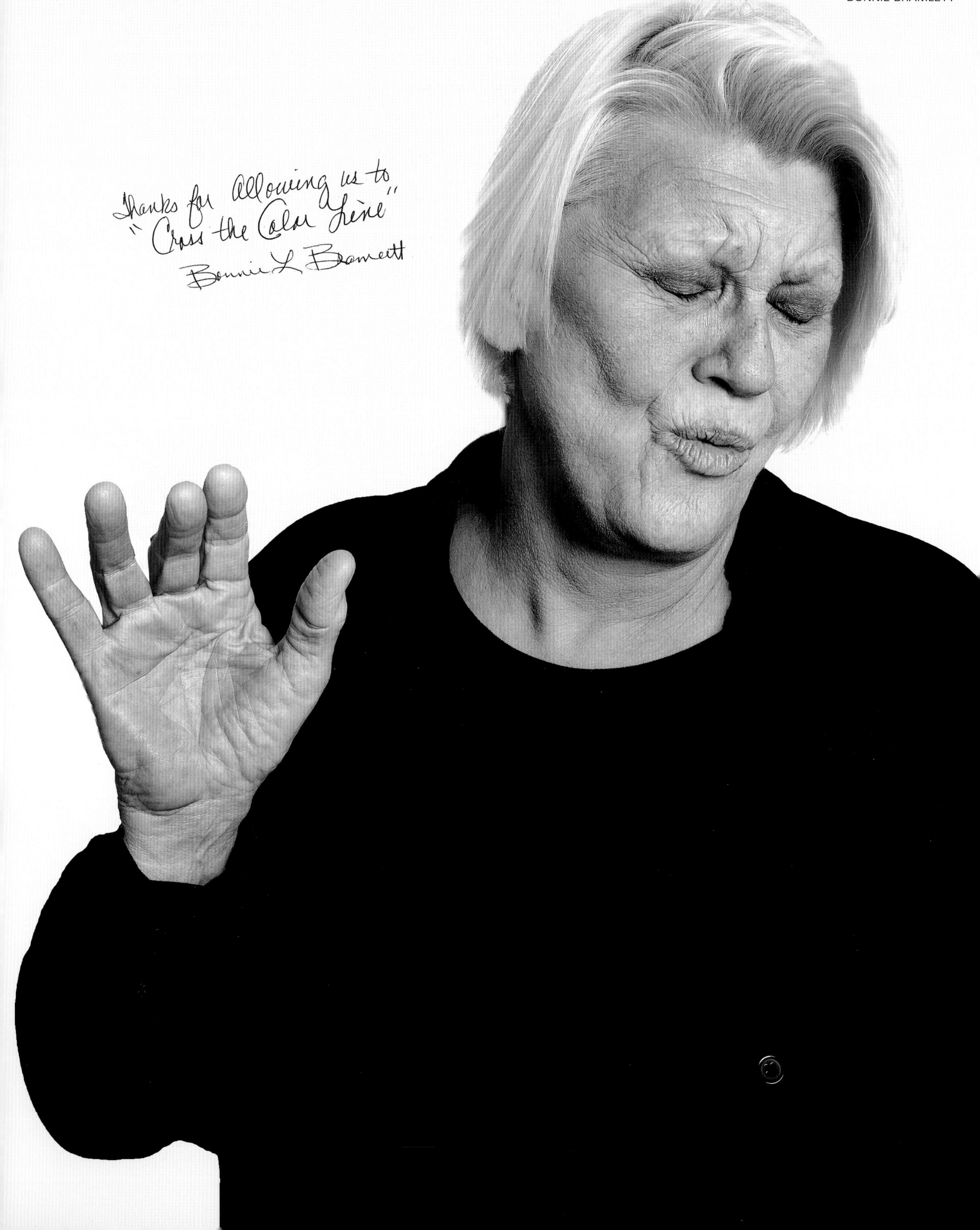
Thanks for allowing us to
"Cross the Color Line"
Bonnie L Bramlett

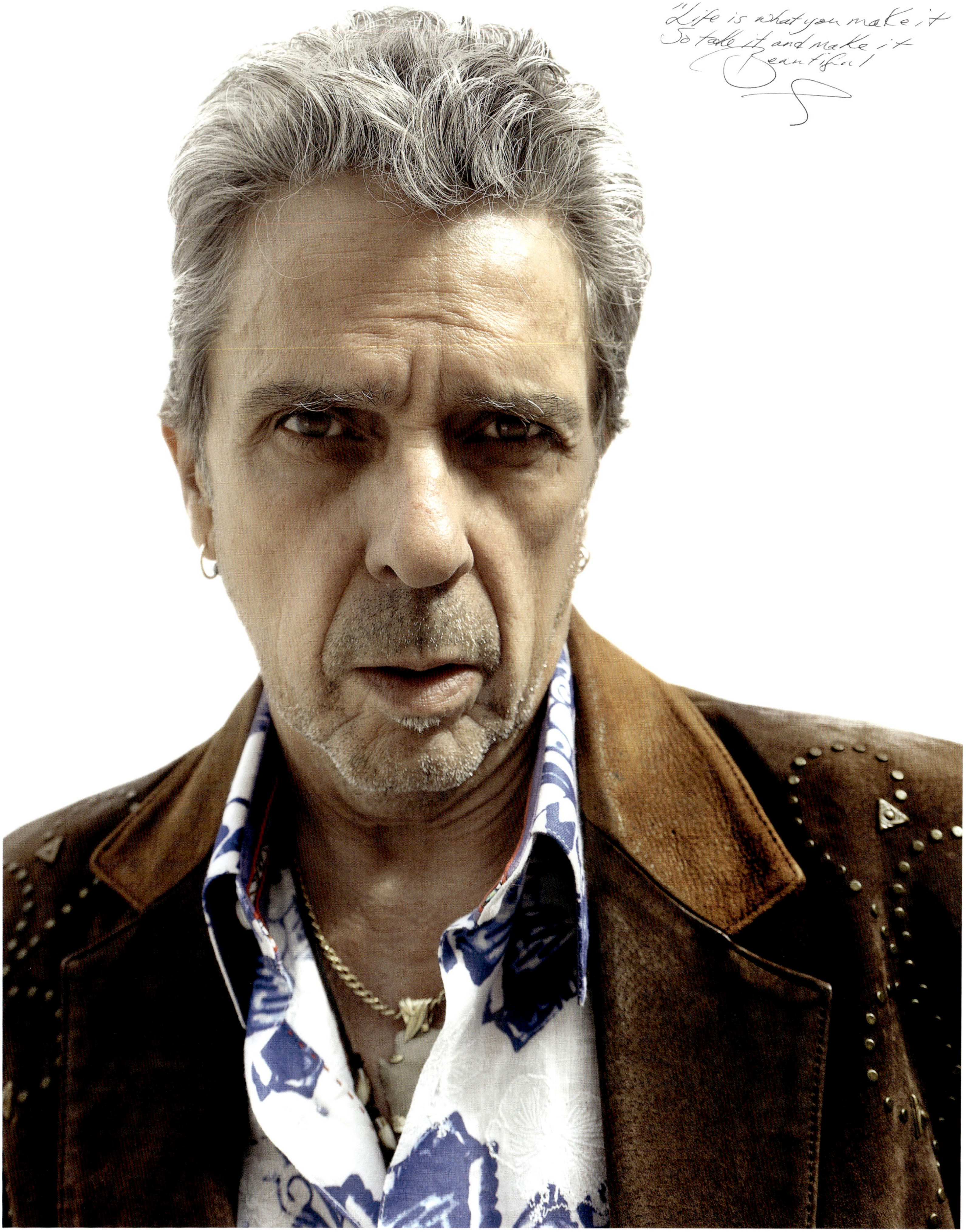
"Life is what you make it
So take it and make it
Beautiful

Life is a journey of many
experiences. Take the time to
enjoy each and every one of
them, for too soon it's over.
Have a happy Life.
William Bell

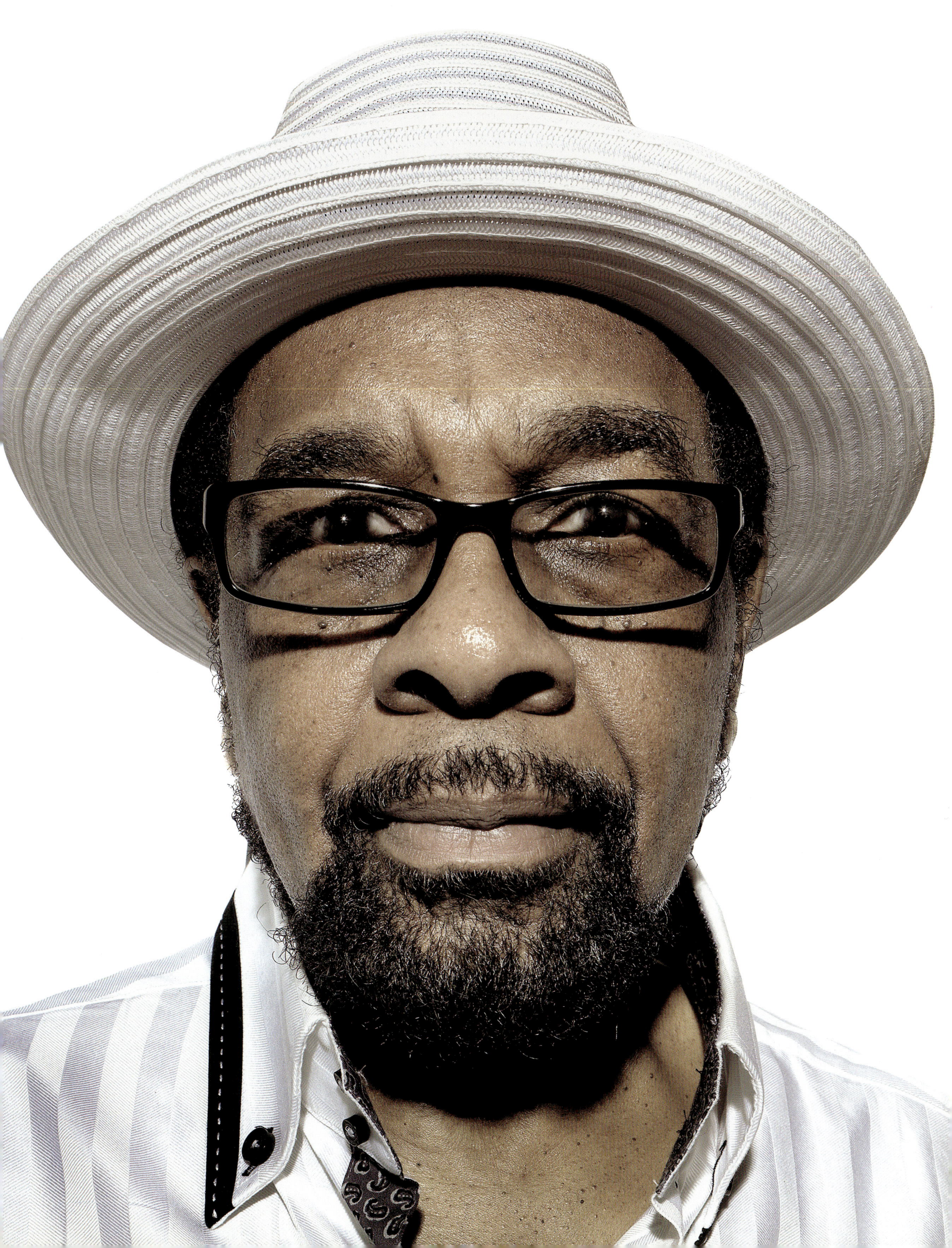

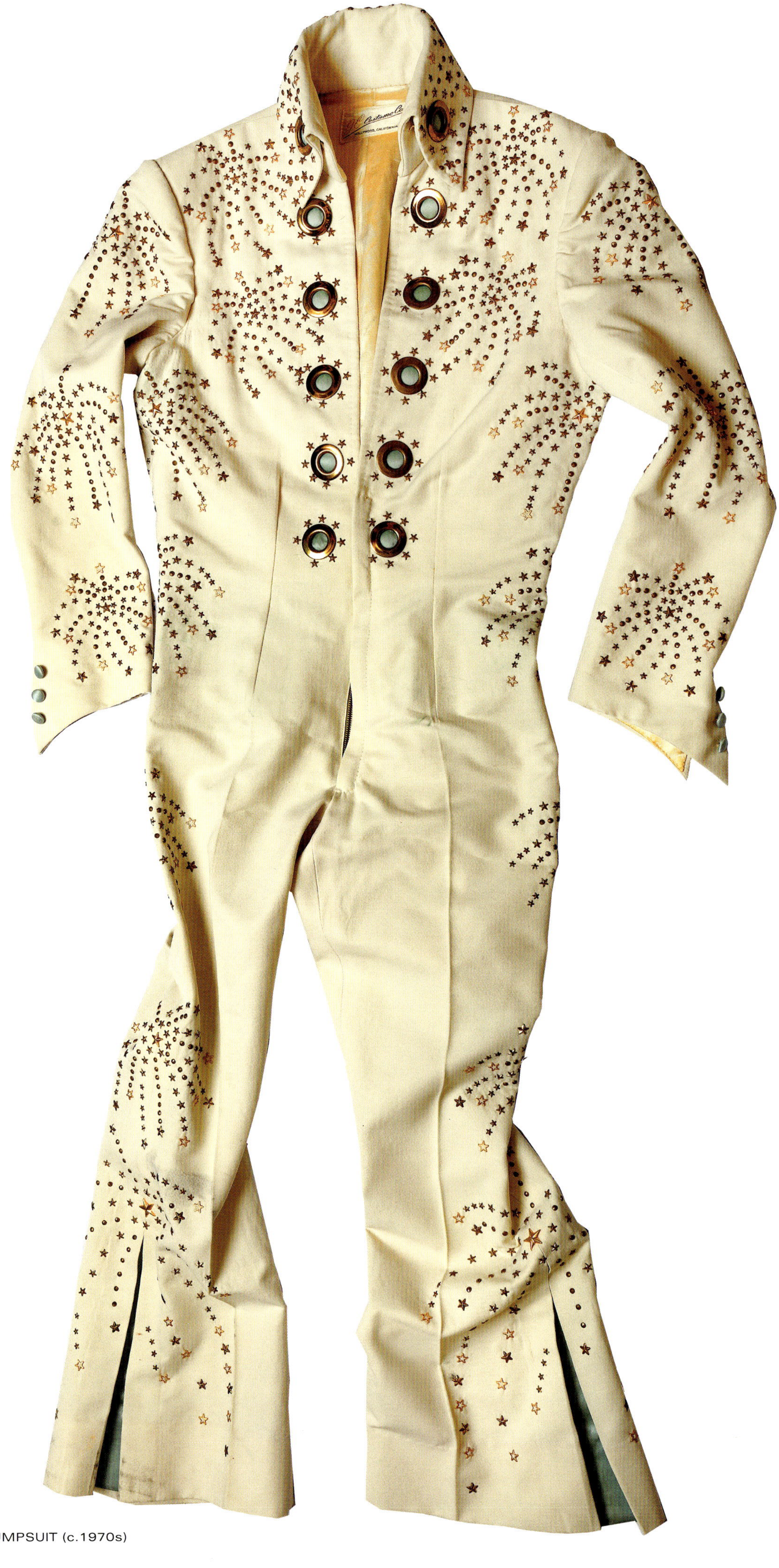

ELVIS PRESLEY'S STAGE JUMPSUIT (c.1970s)

CLAYTON IVEY

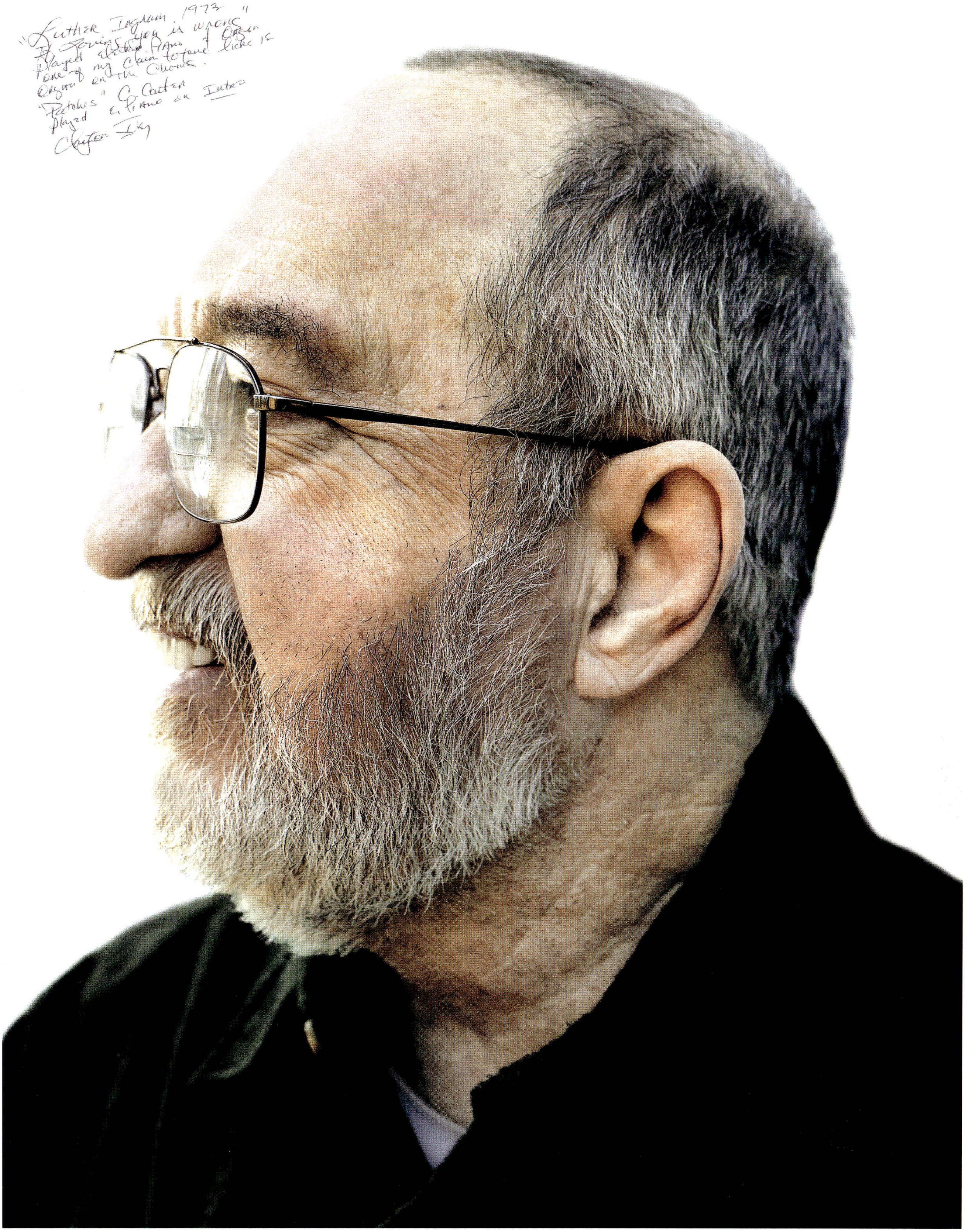
"Luther Ingram 1973
"If Loving You is wrong"
Played Electric Piano & Organ
one of my claim to fame licks is
Organ on the chorus.
"Patches" C. Carter
Played E. Piano on Intro
Clayton Ivey

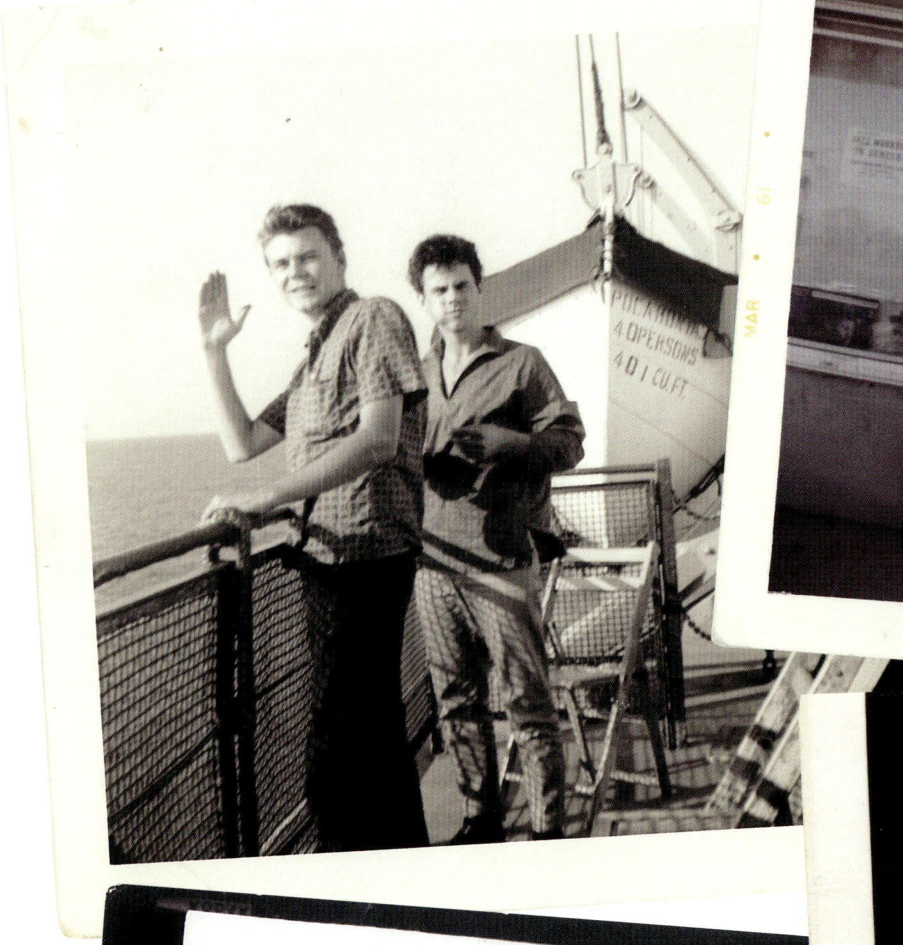

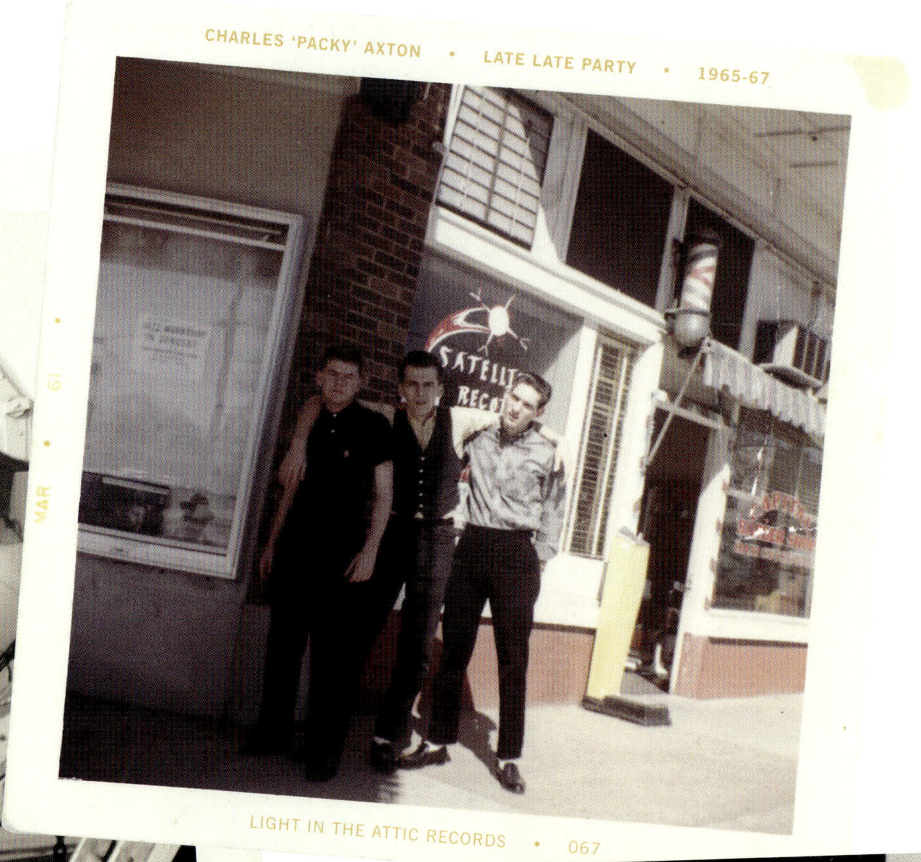


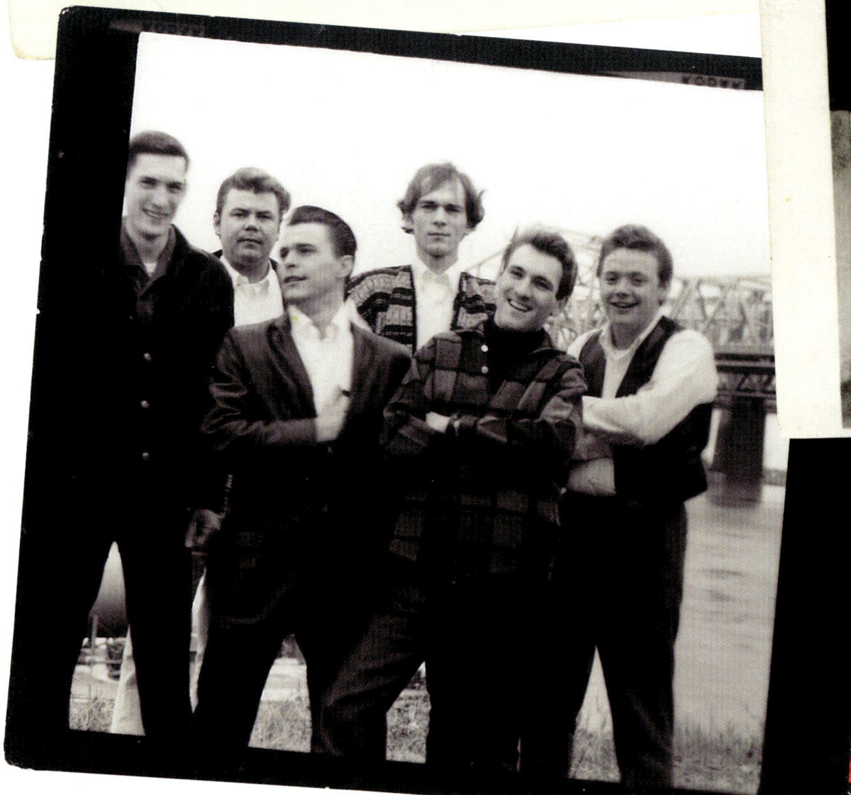

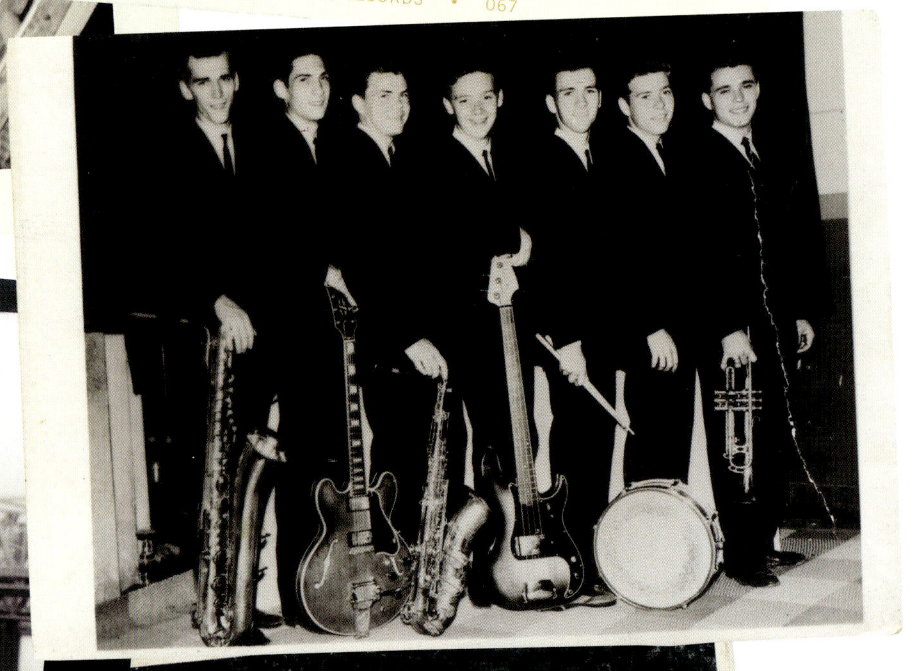

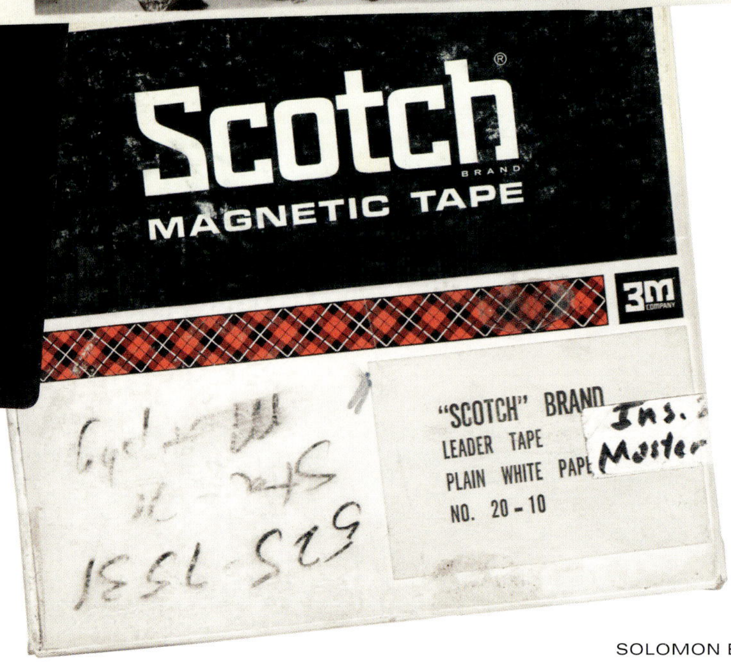


CHARLES "PACKY" AXTON
"PACKY" AXTON WITH STEVE CROPPER, DON NIX, DONALD "DUCK" DUNN,TERRY JOHNSON, RONNIE STOOTS AND WAYNE JACKSON

SOLOMON BURKE

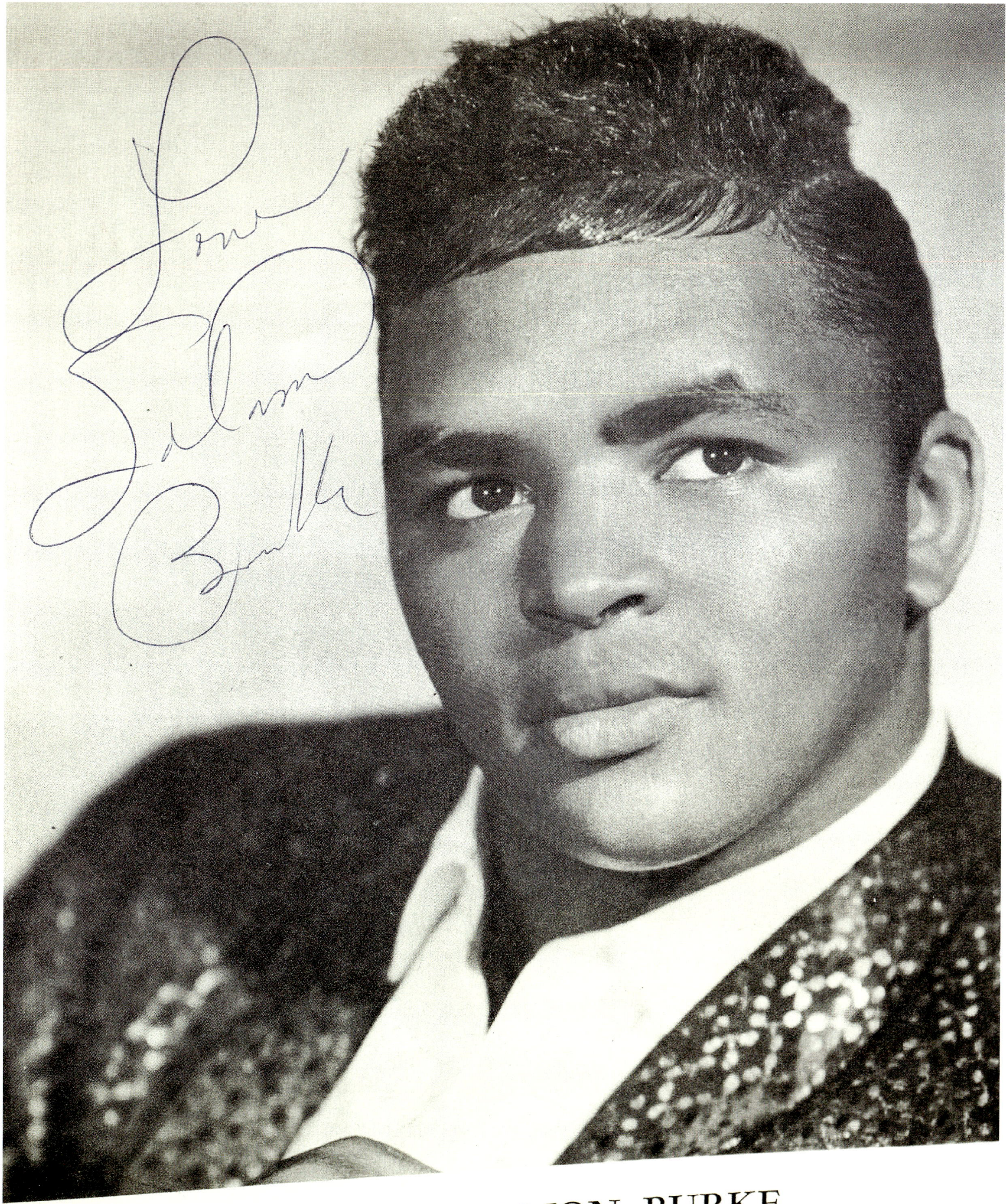


# SOLOMON BURKE

Solomon Burke, the exciting new Atlantic record-
...tar, comes from Philadelphia. Like many other
...incipal vocal training

Heaven", written by Solomon for his grandmo
before her death. He cut three other dis
authored by former champ Joe Louis,
...seen on the Steve Allen Sho

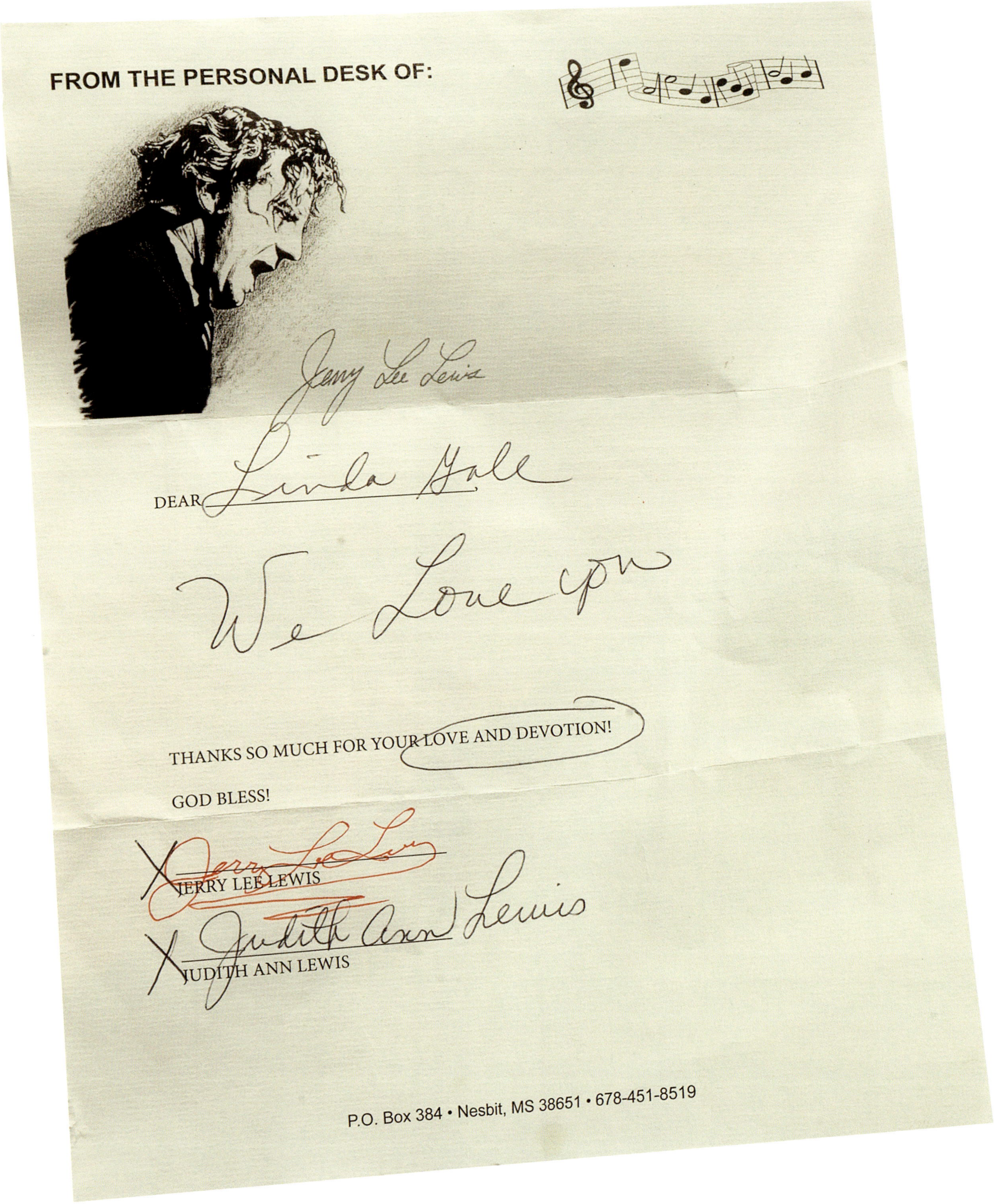

FROM THE PERSONAL DESK OF:

Jerry Lee Lewis

DEAR Linda Gail

We Love you

THANKS SO MUCH FOR YOUR LOVE AND DEVOTION!

GOD BLESS!

X Jerry Lee Lewis
JERRY LEE LEWIS

X Judith Ann Lewis
JUDITH ANN LEWIS

P.O. Box 384 • Nesbit, MS 38651 • 678-451-8519

JERRY LEE LEWIS' PERSONAL STATIONERY AND DIAMOND RING

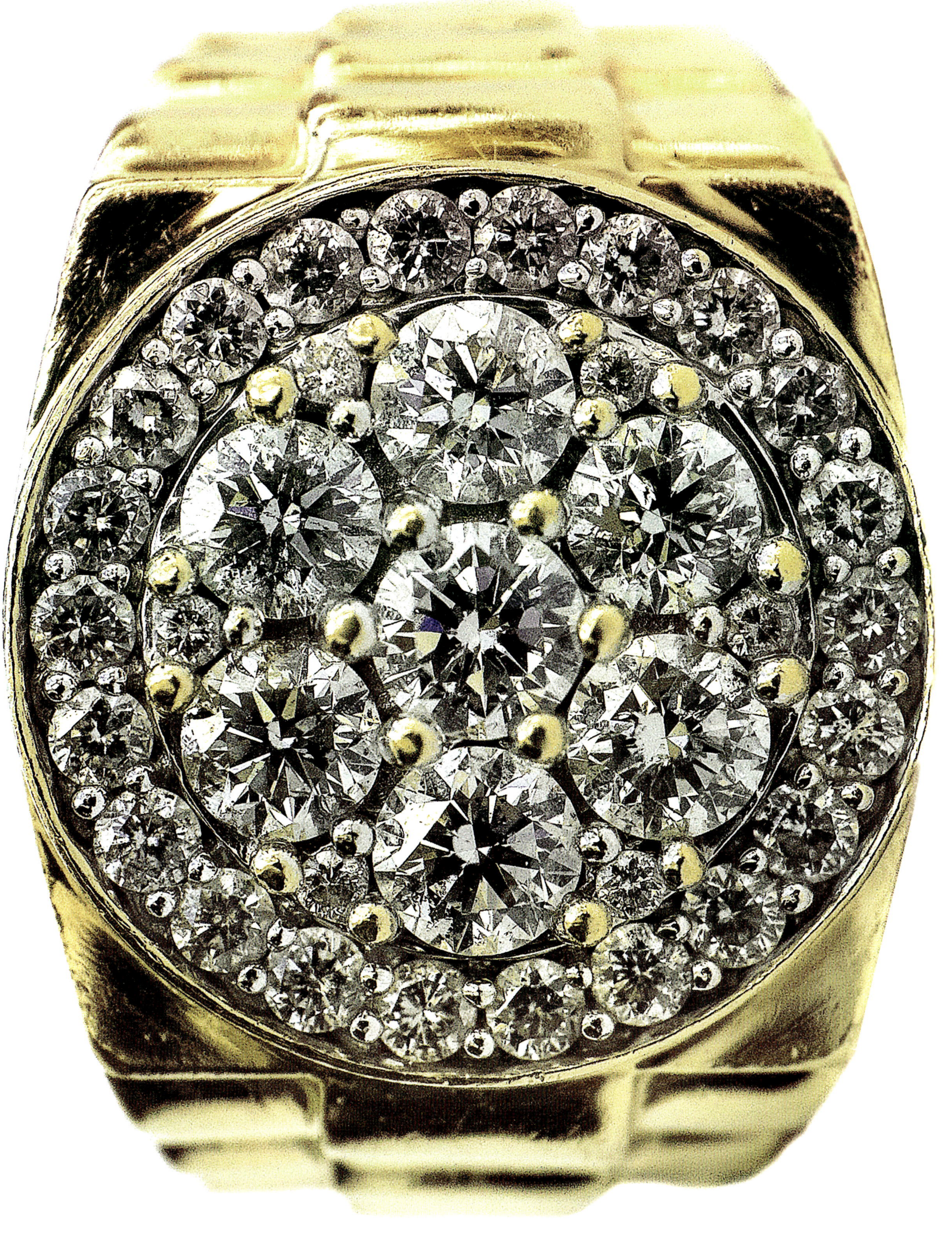

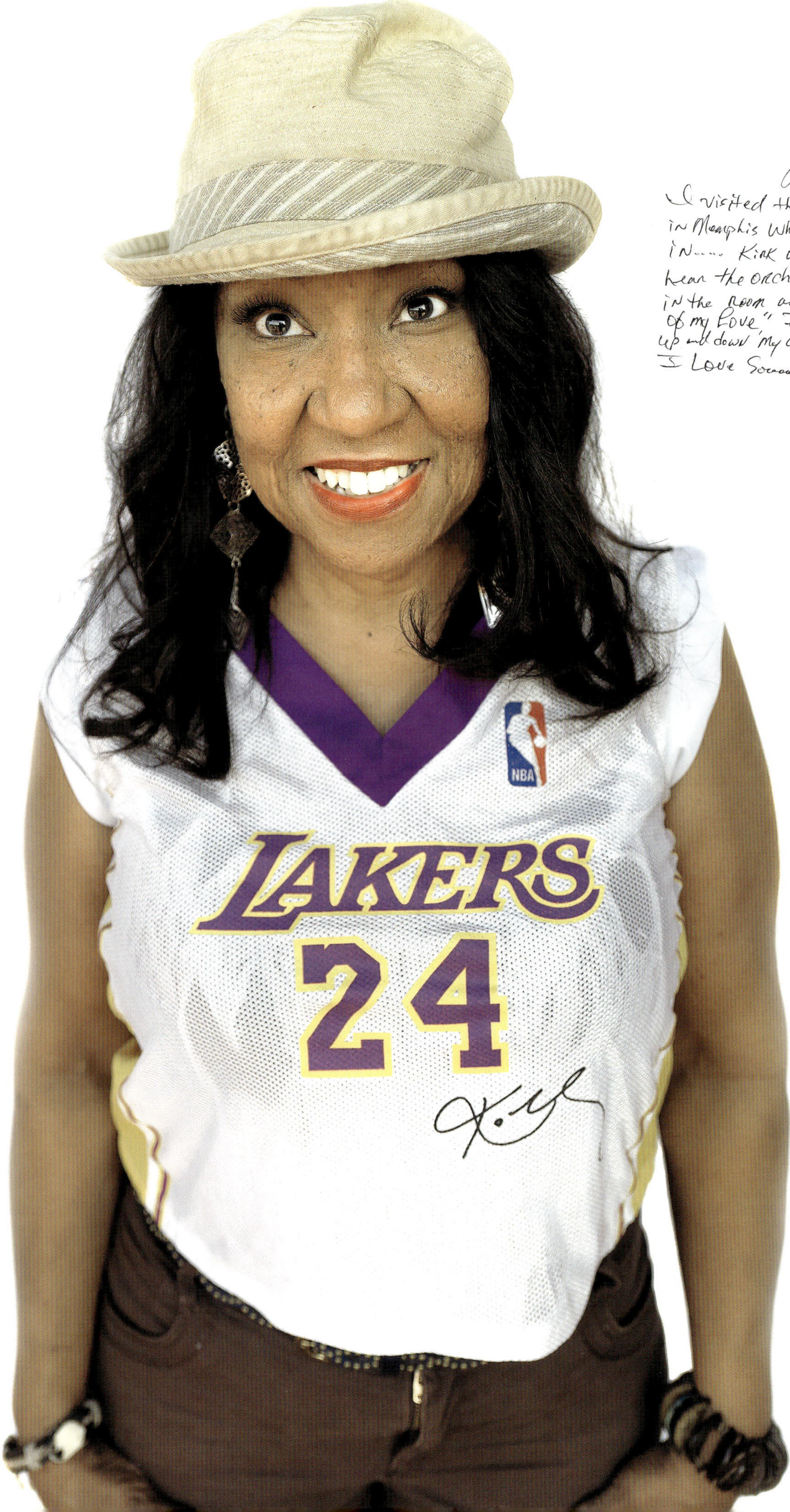


A Wonderful momory I have when I visited the Stax Muesemm, after doing a peformance in Memphis while viewing Ike's Car that I was actually in...... Kirk Whalen came out and invited us over to hear the orchestra next door in the School. We walked in the room and they started playing beautifully "Best of my Love" I couldn't stop crying with chill bumps up and down my arms. God Bless STAX: David Porter I Love Sooooo Much!

Wanda Hutchinson

"Blessed That Be The Ties That Bind" us and ALL mankind
I always felt that our singing was a blessing from God. A gift and I'm always glad to share it with people all over the world.
Pamela Hutchinson

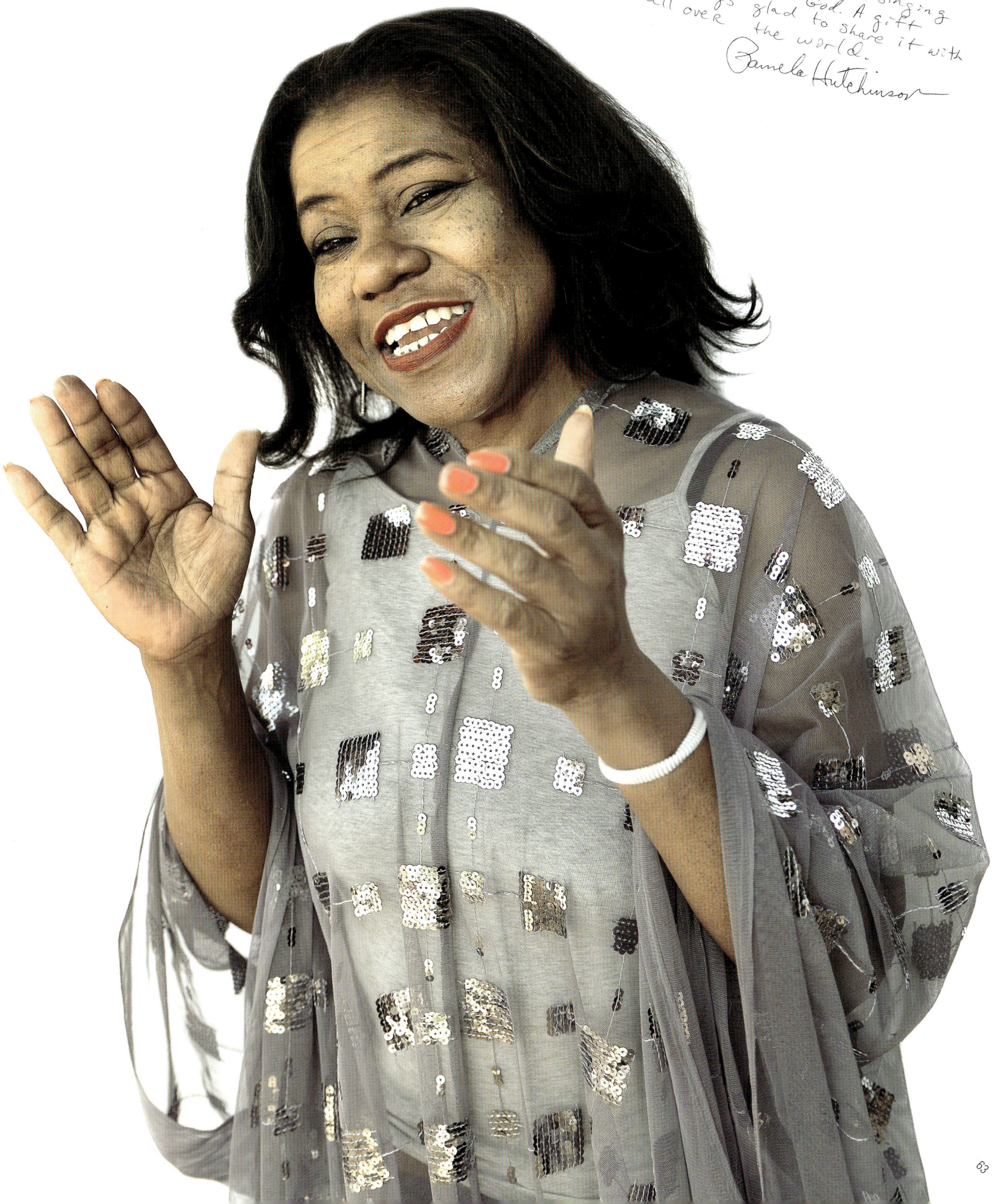

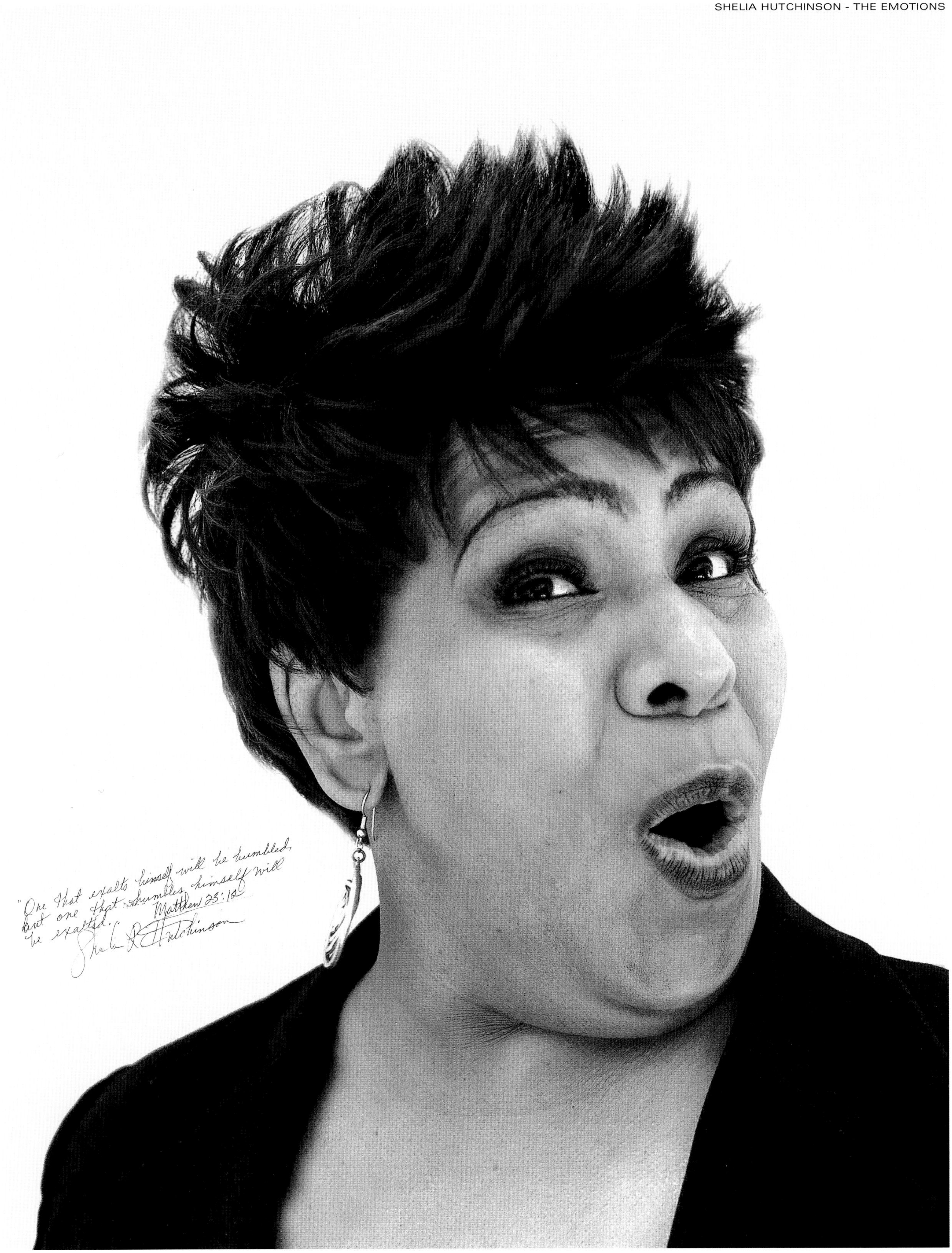
"One that exalts himself will be humbled,
but one that humbles himself will
be exalted."
Matthew 23:12
Shelia R Hutchinson

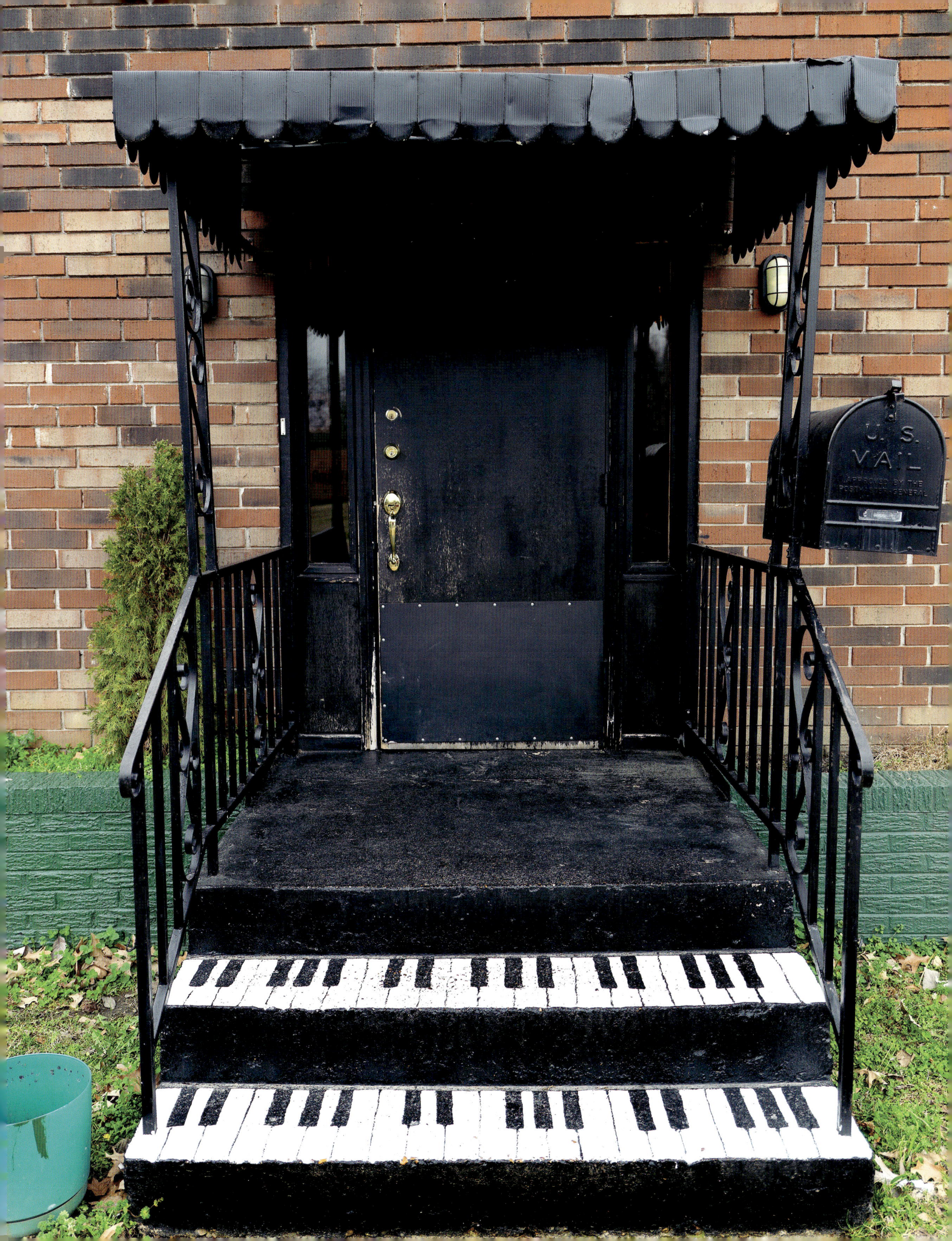
U. S.
MAIL
APPROVED BY THE

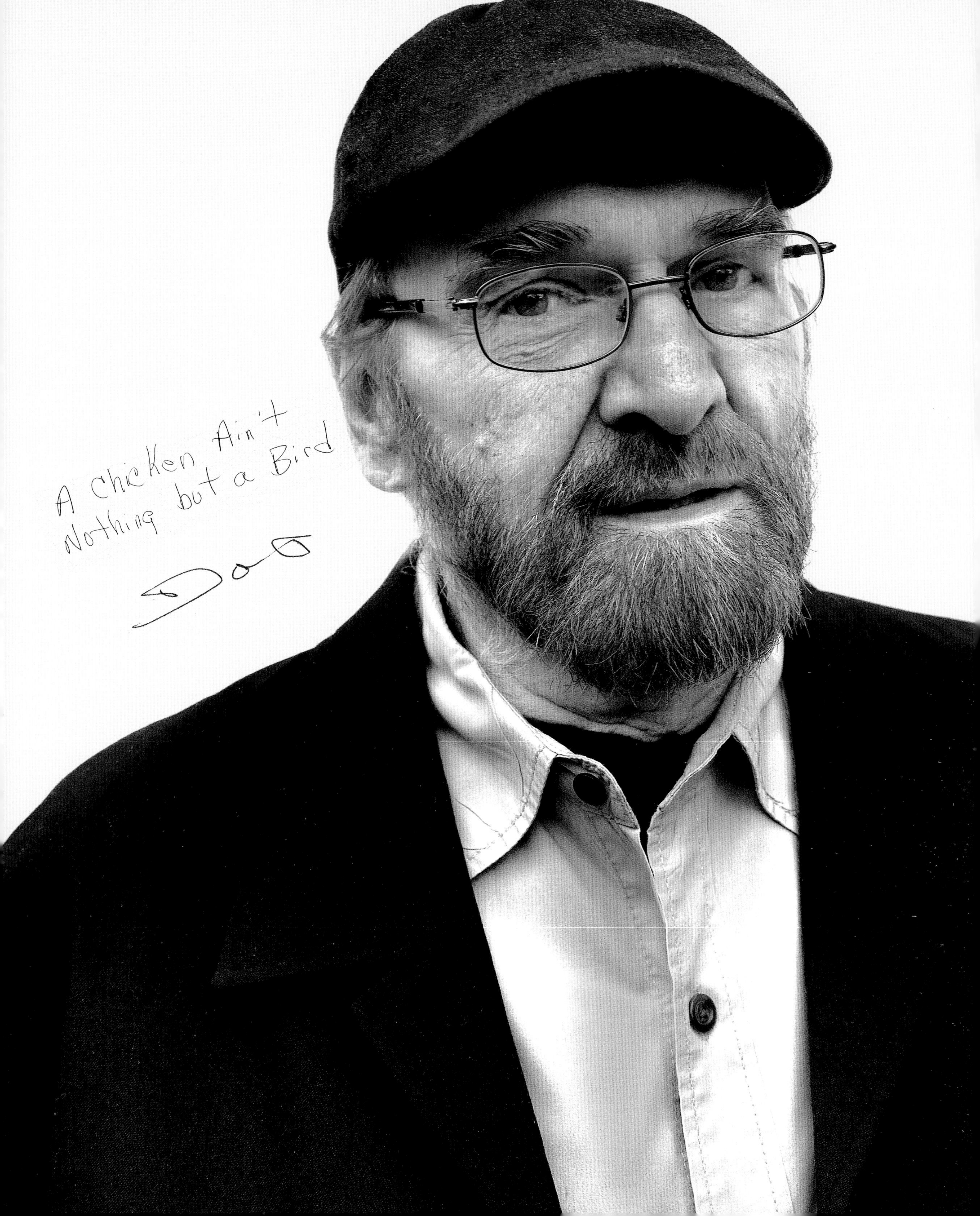
A Chicken Ain't Nothing but a Bird

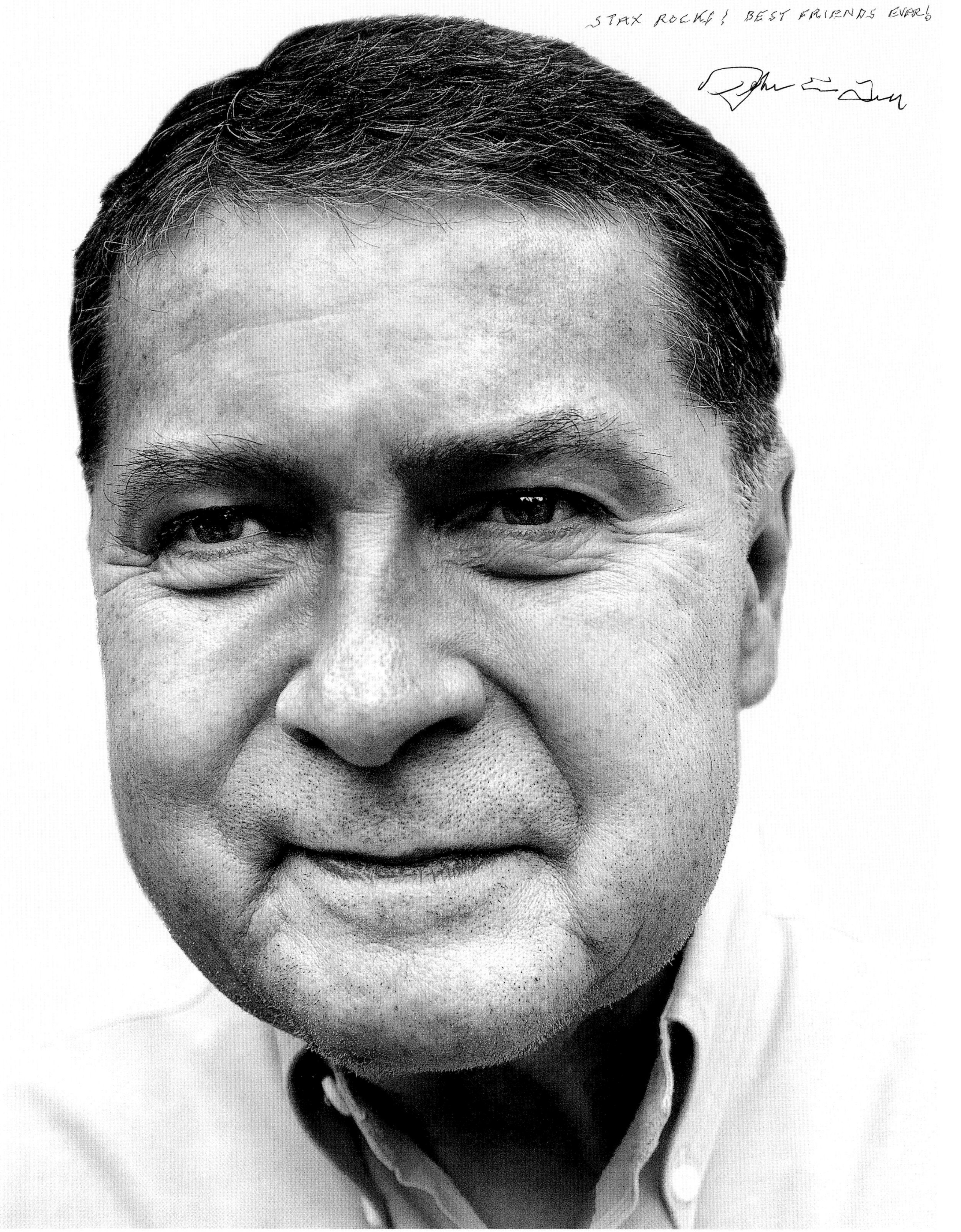
STAX ROCKS! BEST FRIENDS EVER!

Howard L. Grimes

Syl Johnson
Al Green
Willie Mitchell
Otis Clay
O.V. Right
Ann Peebles

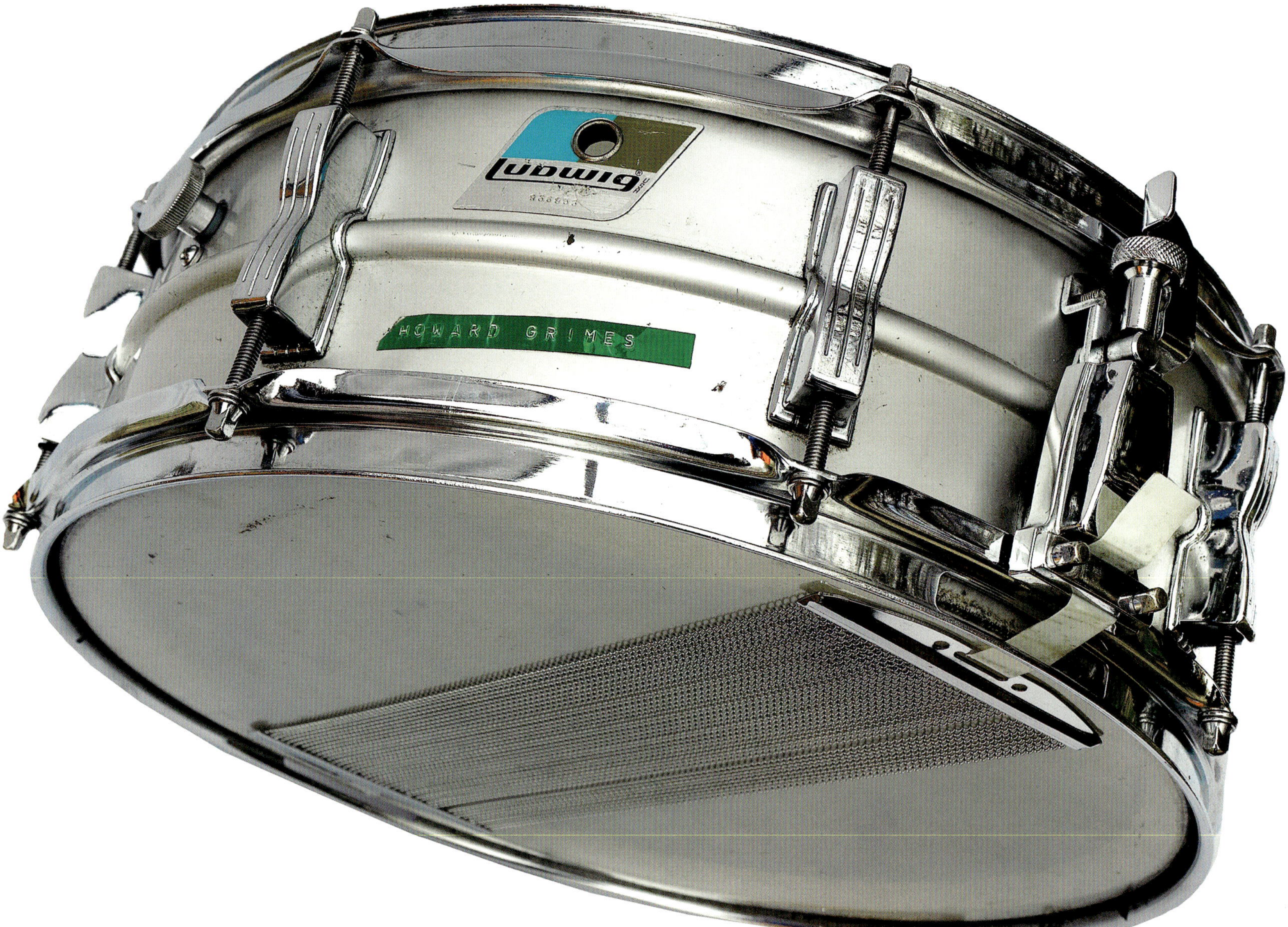


HOWARD GRIMES'S 1970s' LUDWIG SNARE DRUM USED AT ROYAL STUDIOS RECORDINGS

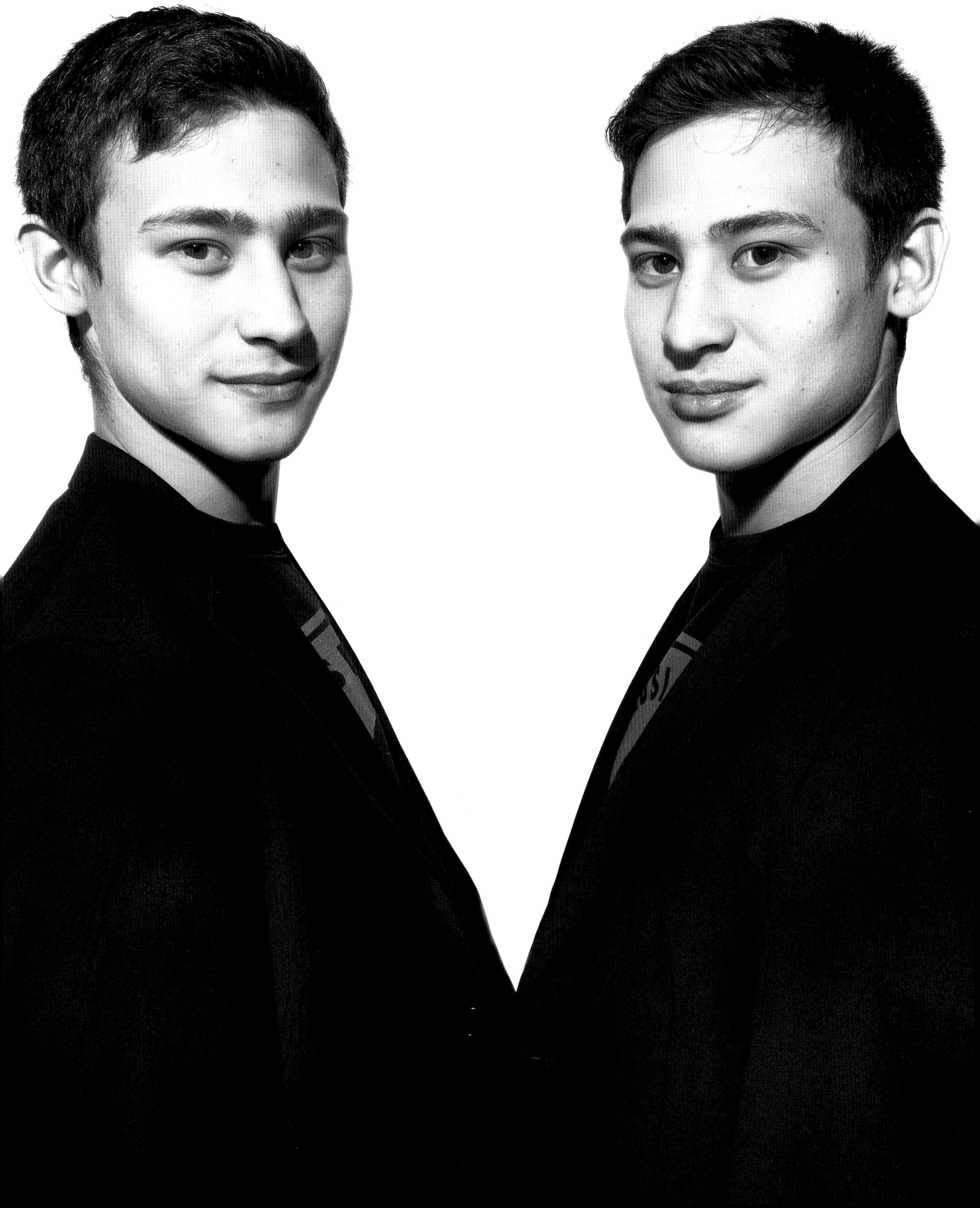

Ann Peebles

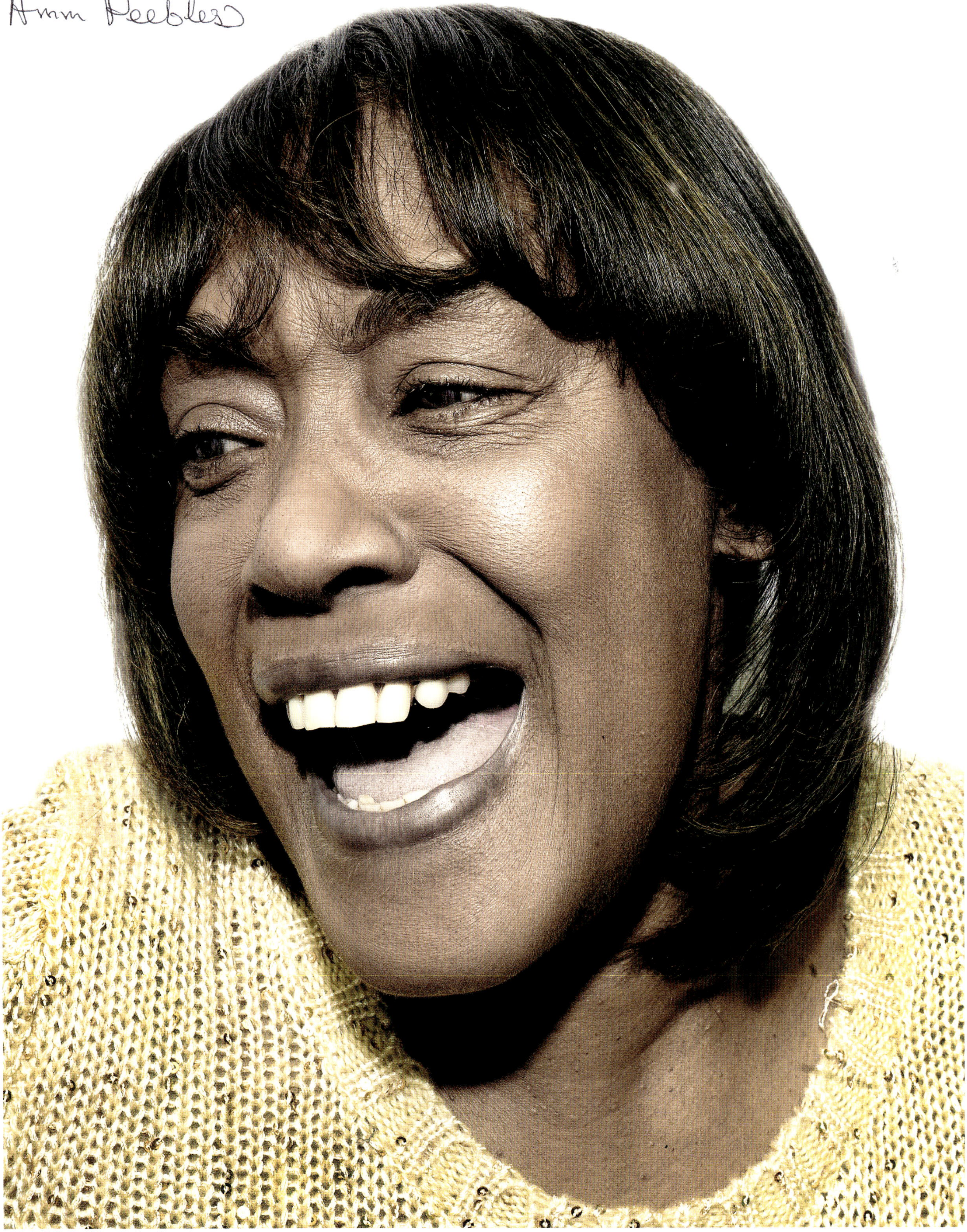

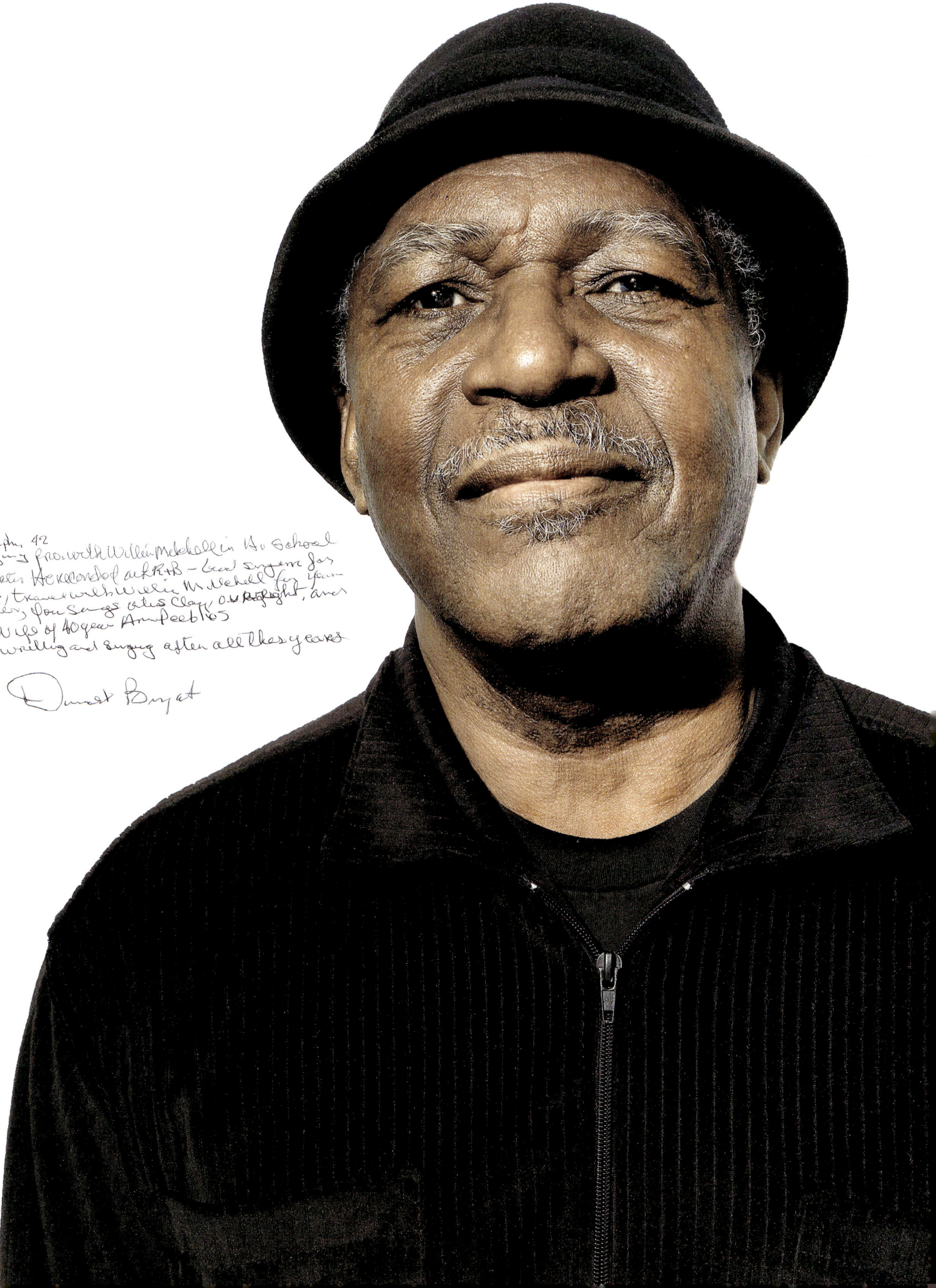

born Memphis 42
start singing pro. with Willie Mitchell in Hi School
fines after He recorded of all R+B - lead singer for
4 Kings, travel with Willie Mitchell for years
then writer, for songs Otis Clay, O.V. Wright, and
My Wife of 40 year Ann Peebles
still writing and singing after all these years

Donald Bryant

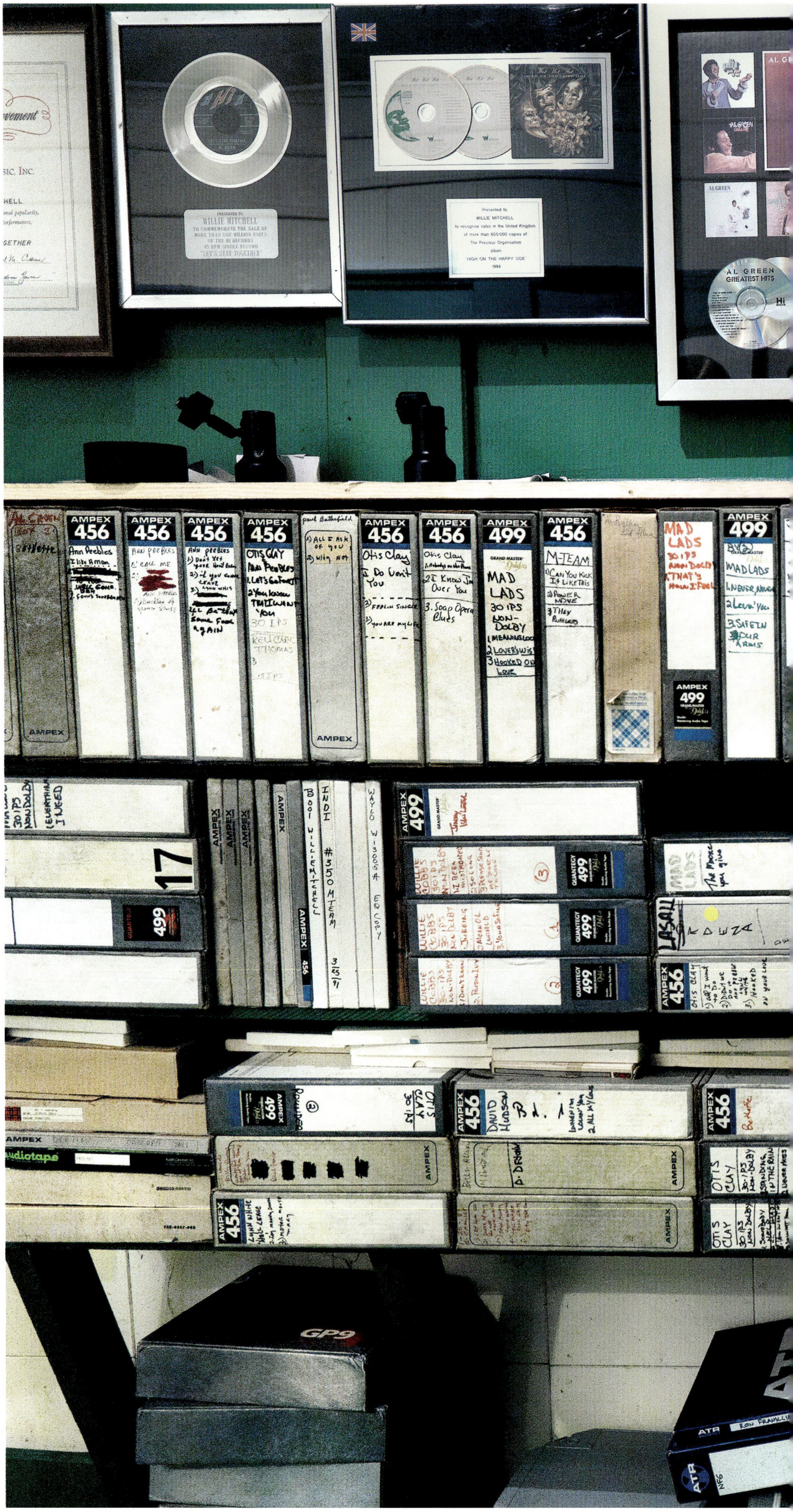

WILLIE MITCHELL
LET'S STAY TOGETHER
HIGH ON THE HAPPY SIDE
AL GREEN GREATEST HITS
AMPEX 456
AMPEX 499
Ann Peebles
Otis Clay
MAD LADS
M-TEAM
AMPEX
QUANTEGY 499
audiotape
GP9
ATR

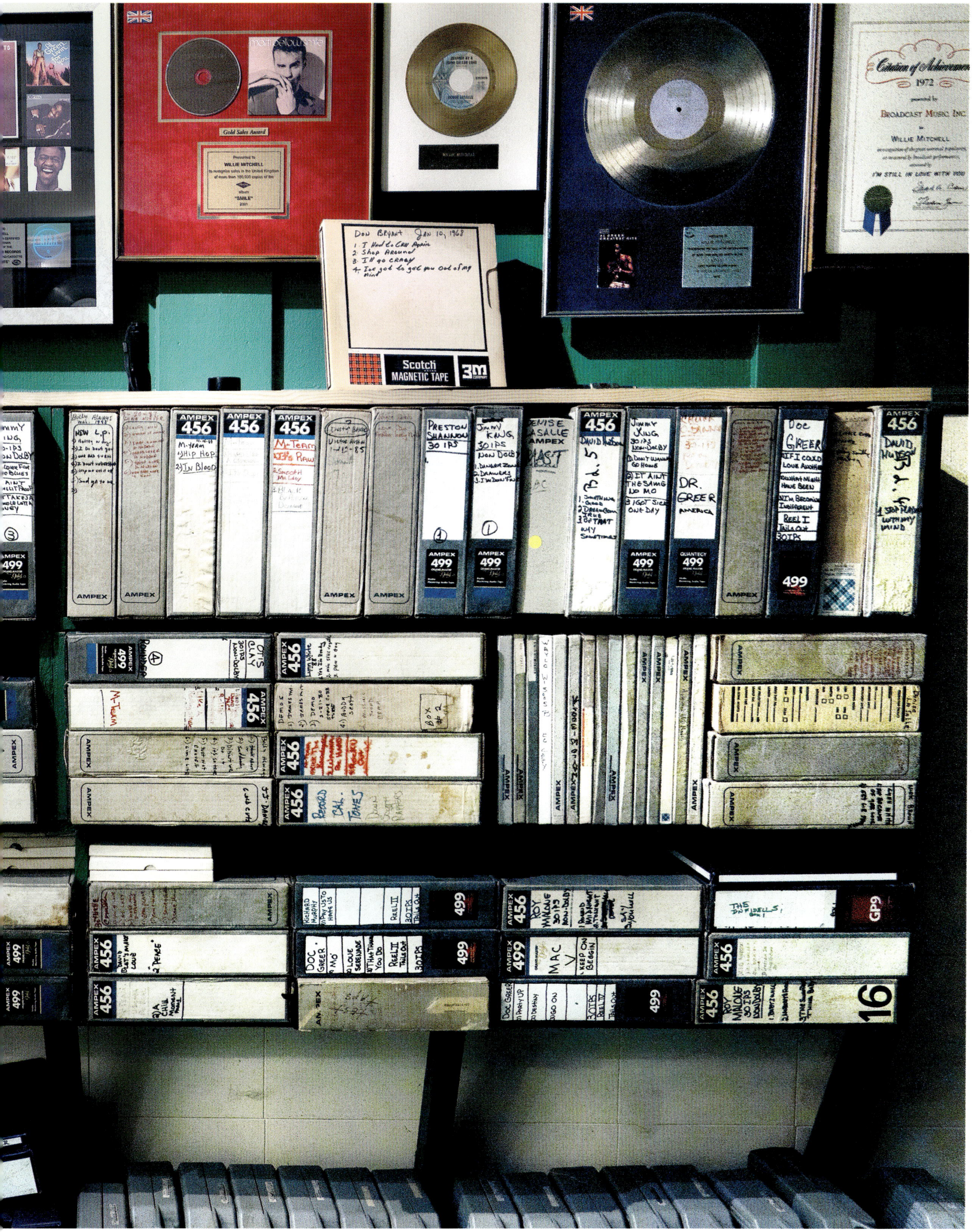

Gold Sales Award
Don Bryant Jan 10, 1968
1. I Had to Cry Again
2. Shop Around
3. I'll go crazy
Scotch MAGNETIC TAPE
3M
Citation of Achievement
1972
Broadcast Music, Inc.
Willie Mitchell
I'm Still in Love with You
AMPEX
456
499
PRESTON SHANNON 30 IPS
JIMMY KING 30 IPS
DENISE LASALLE
DR. GREER AMERICA
DOC GREER
OTIS CLAY
M-Team
RECORD BAL. TAPES
DAVID HUDSON
ROY MALONE
THE DYNELLS
16

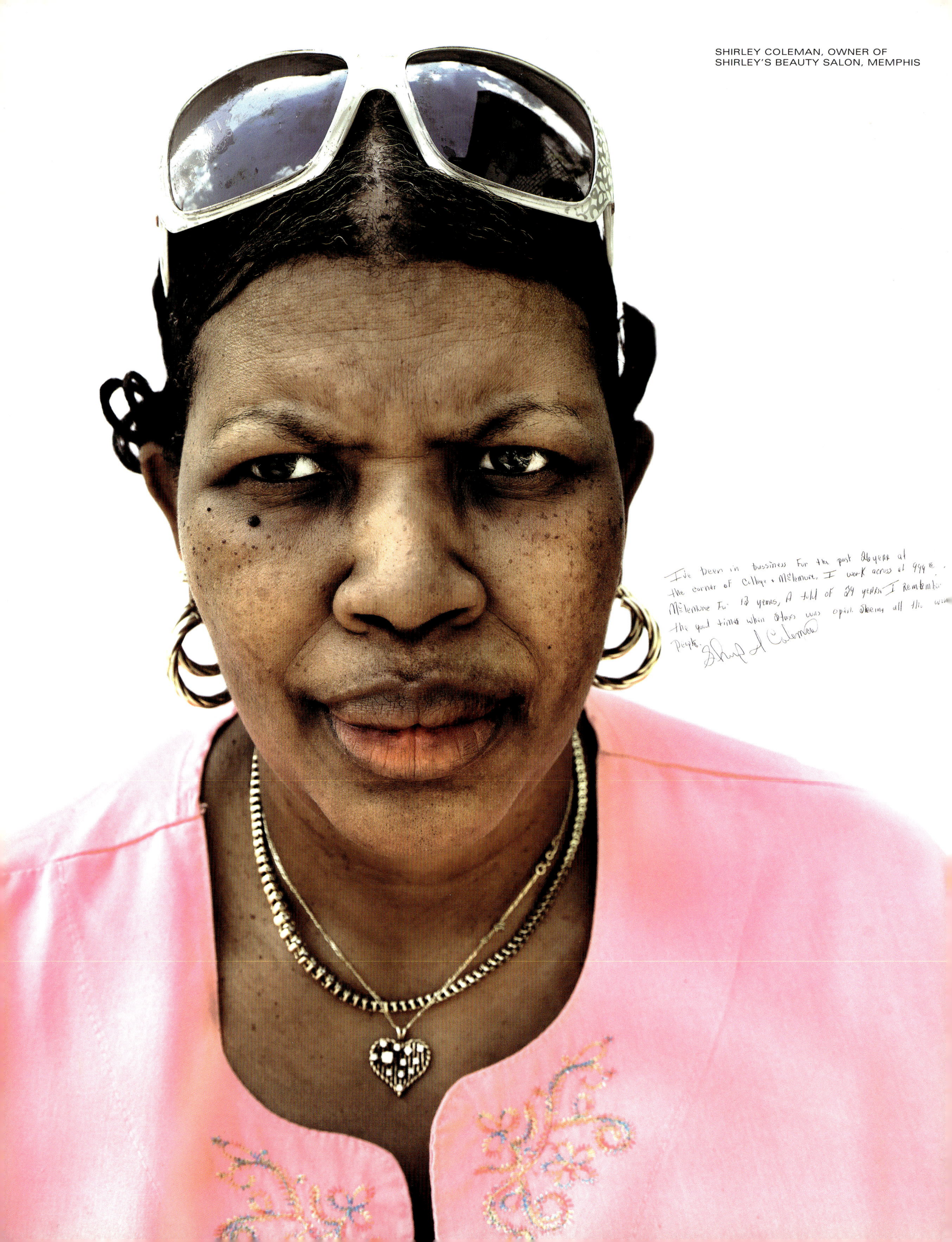


SHIRLEY COLEMAN, OWNER OF
SHIRLEY'S BEAUTY SALON, MEMPHIS

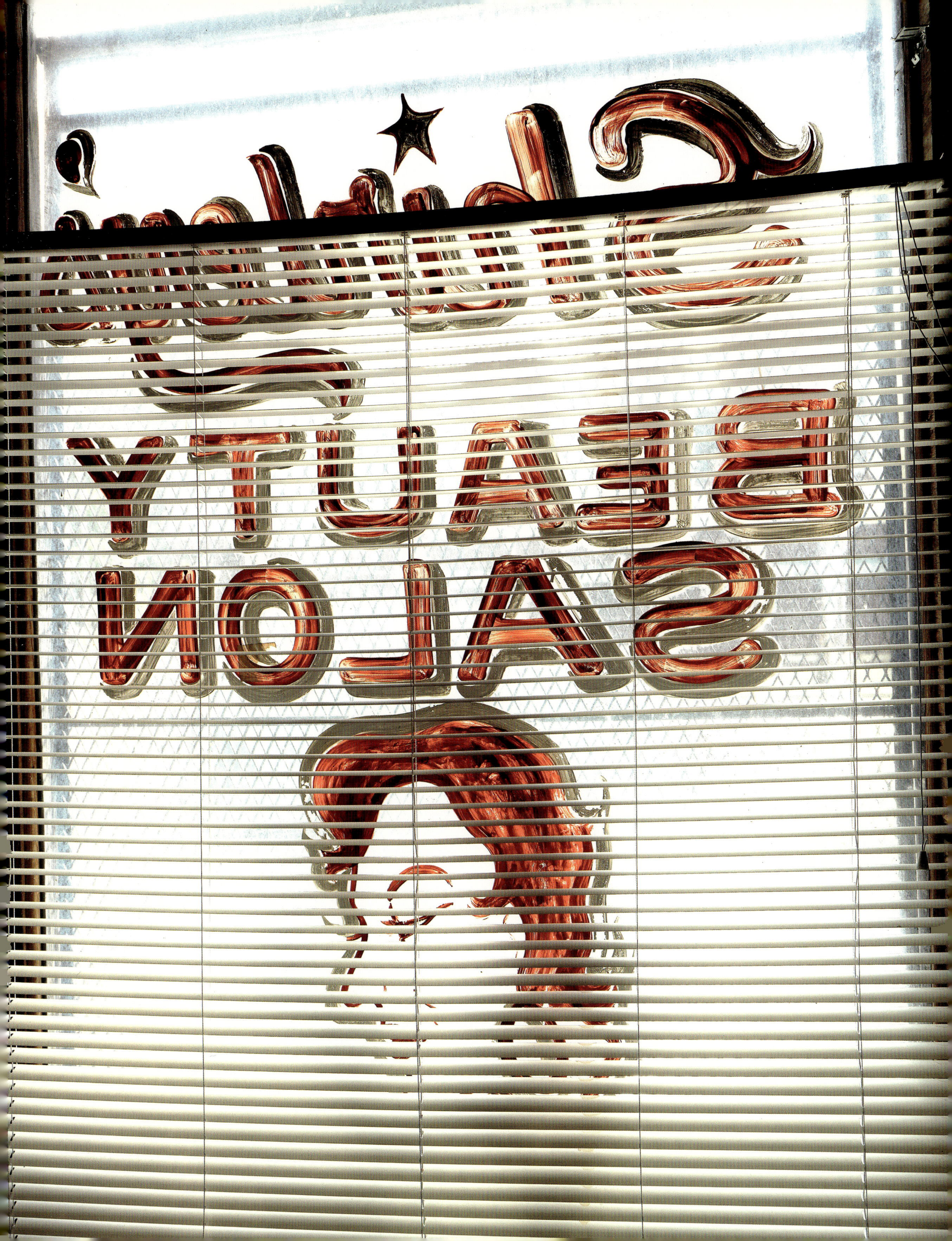
BEAUTY
SALON

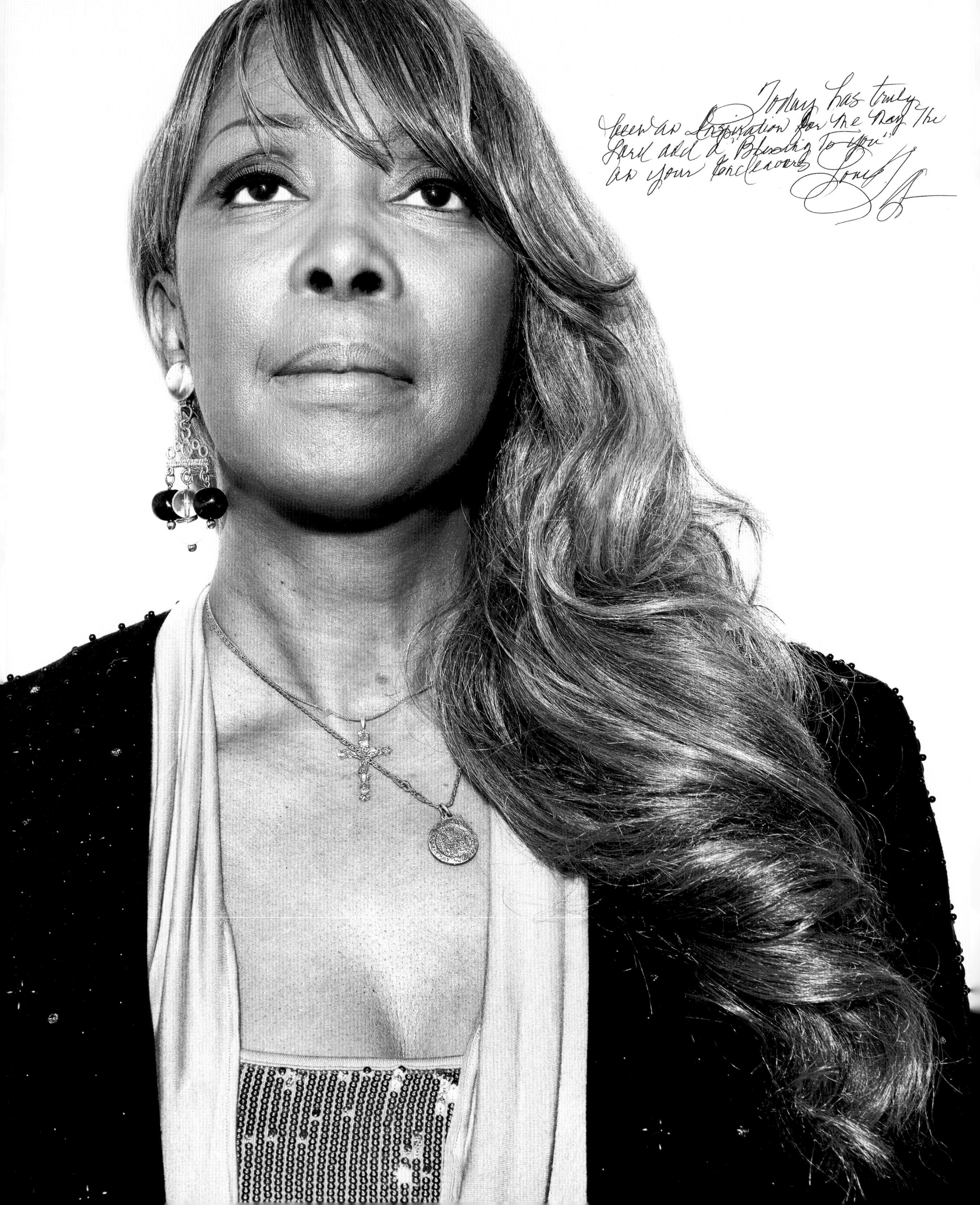
Today has truly
been an Inspiration for me May the
Lord add a "Blessing to you"
in your endeavors Toni G

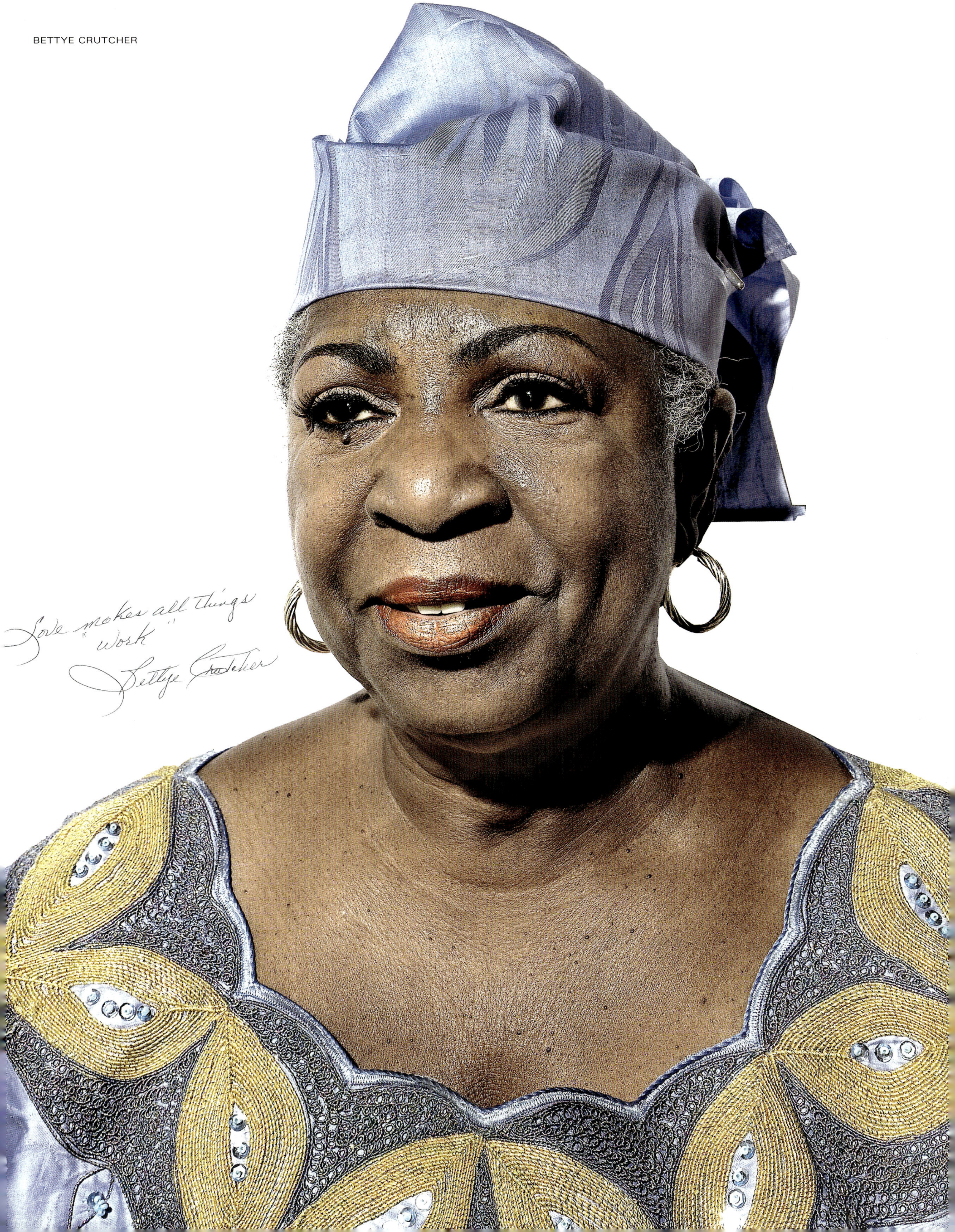
Love makes all things
"work"
Bettye Crutcher

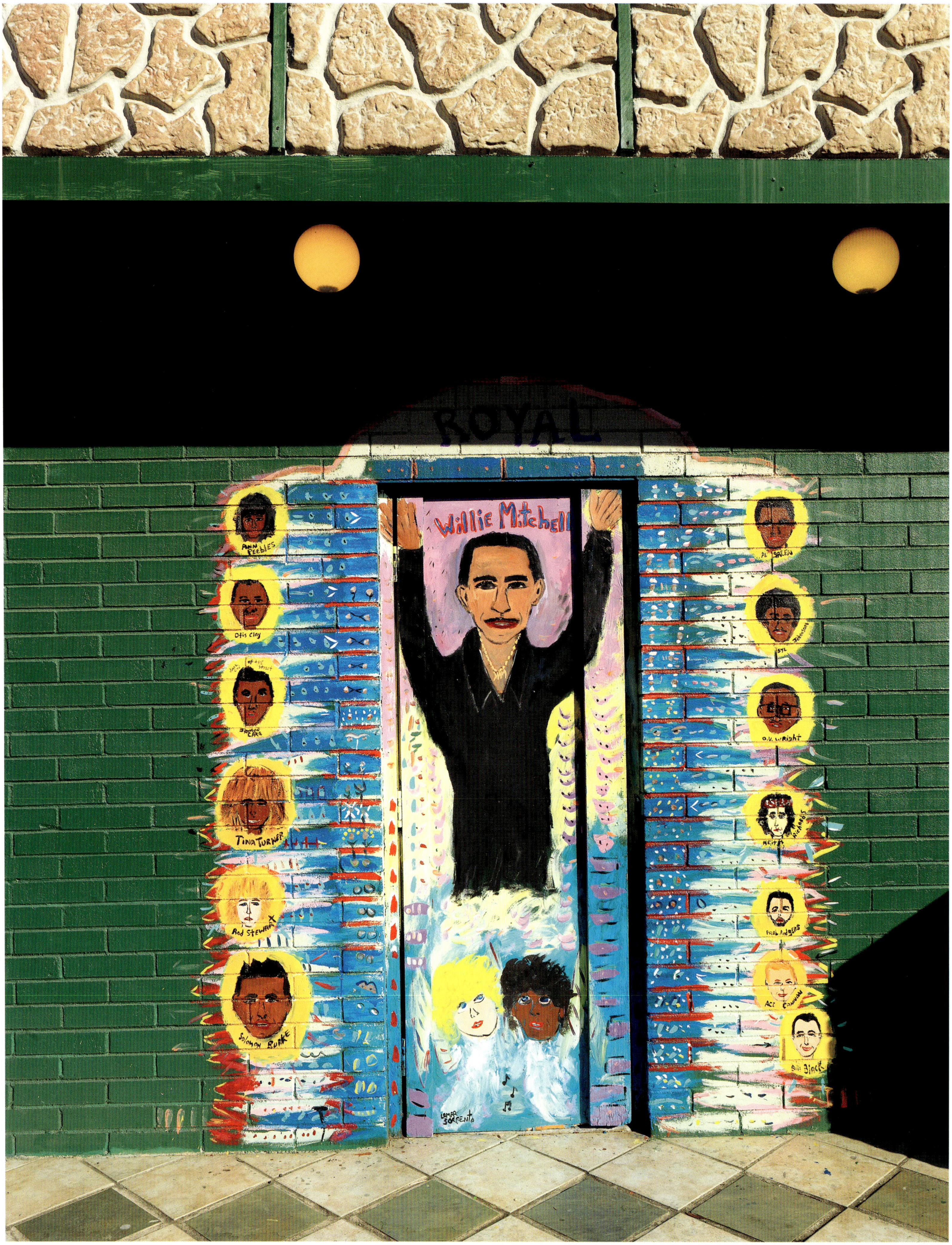
ROYAL
Willie Mitchell
ANN PEEBLES
Otis Clay
TINA TURNER
Rod STEWAR
Solomon BURKE
SYL JOHNSON
O.V. WRIGHT
RICHARDS
PAUL RodGERS
ACE CANNON
Bill BLACK

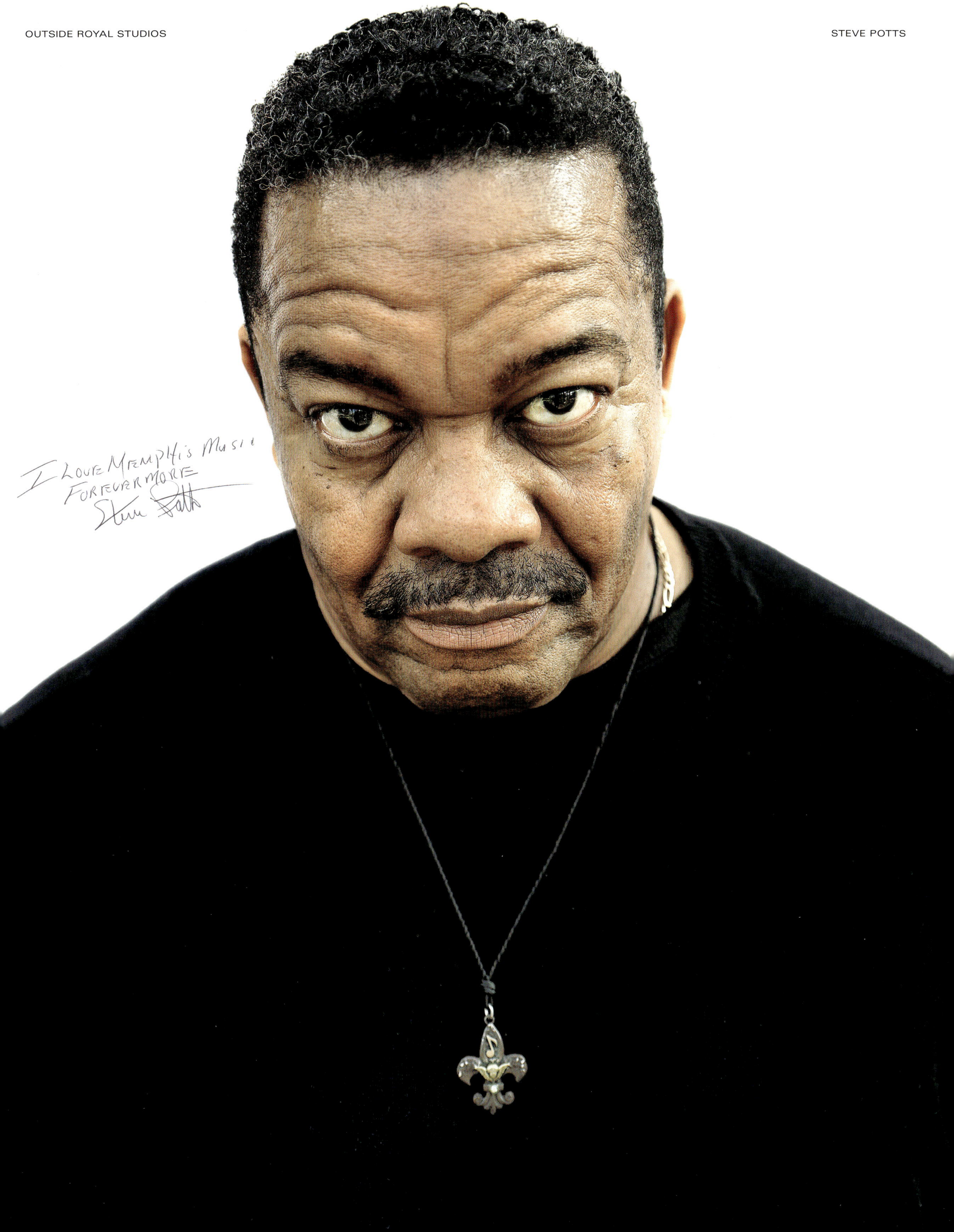
I Love Memphis Music
Forevermore
Steve Potts

EDDIE BRADDOCK

a blessing to work with the most wonderful and talented people in the World!!!

Eddie Braddock

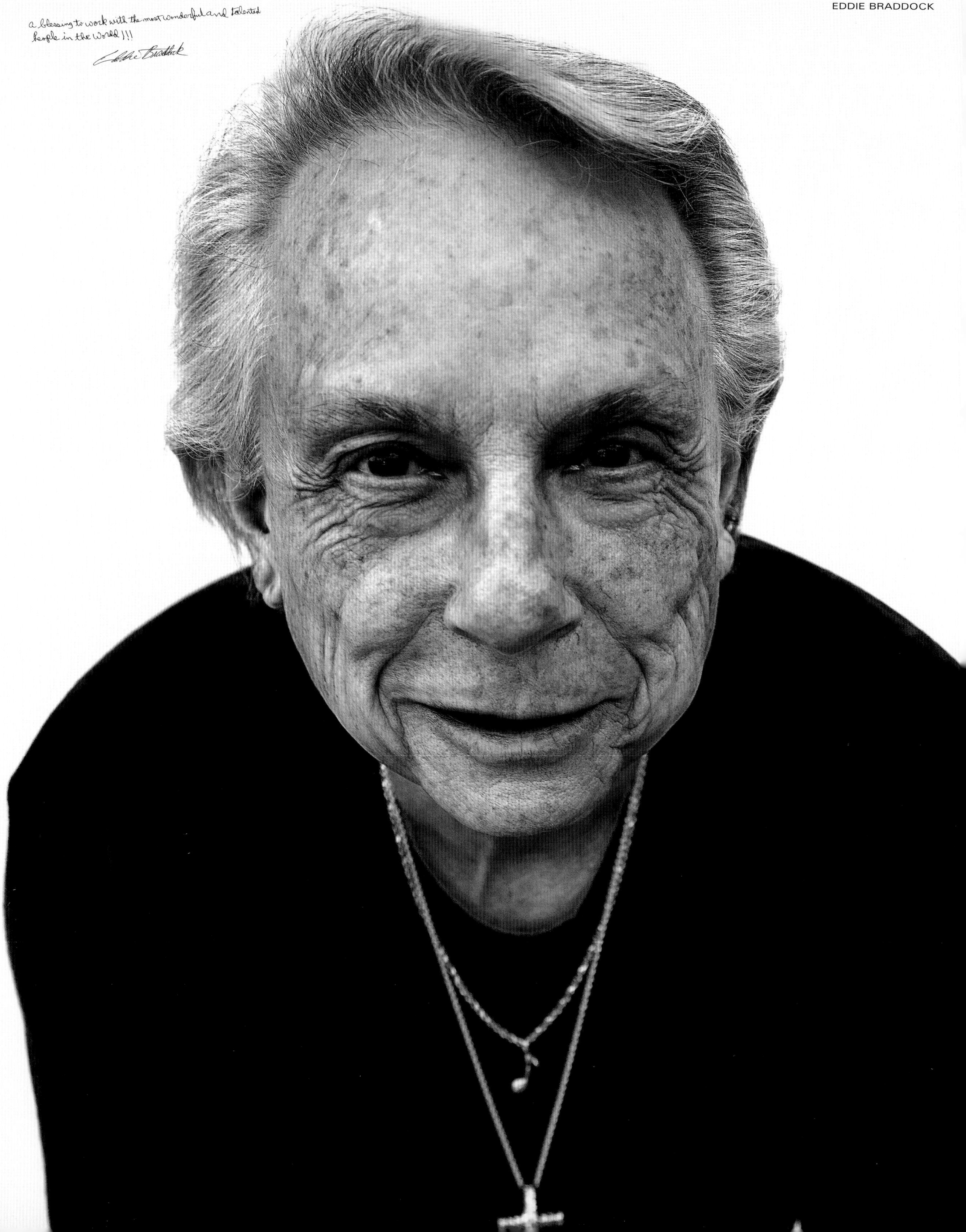

# Black on White

*Thom Gilbert interviews Eddie Braddock, former Director of Promotions for Stax Records.*

**Eddie Braddock:** I was working for a company called Memphis Delta Distribution. Mrs. Axton [co-owner of Stax Records] sent me that job and Ewell Roussell was the guy that hired me. I was close to Jim [Stewart, co-owner of Stax Records] and of course I was close to Mrs. Axton [co-owner of Stax Records] because she lived one block over...we went to church together. "Packy" Axton [son of Mrs. Axton] and Mrs. Axton's daughter were in the first grade and all the way with me until they kicked me out. And so Jim told me one day—I'm up in his office and I'm working for Memphis Delta, and he said—"Hey nobody's playing my records; none of the White stations are playing my records, ya know?" and I said, "Well that can be fixed, man." And so I think it was "B-A-B-Y" by Carla Thomas, and I had a tape of it, and I took it to Johnny Dark [the radio DJ], my dear blood brother.

**Thom Gilbert:** By the way, why was that music not being played?

**EB:** Well, you know, you're not far out from when they used to call it "race music." Okay? And, so I took it to Johnny. Johnny became so powerful when he came here, but there were people, when he came here, some of the promotion guys told him, "We can't be friends with you man because George might get mad"—as in George Klein [radio DJ]. But, Johnny became huge, the highest ratings of any White man that's ever been in Memphis. And I guess that includes Dewey Phillips, who I love.

**TG:** What station was he on?

**EB:** WMPS. And Klein and all the other brothers were at WHBQ.

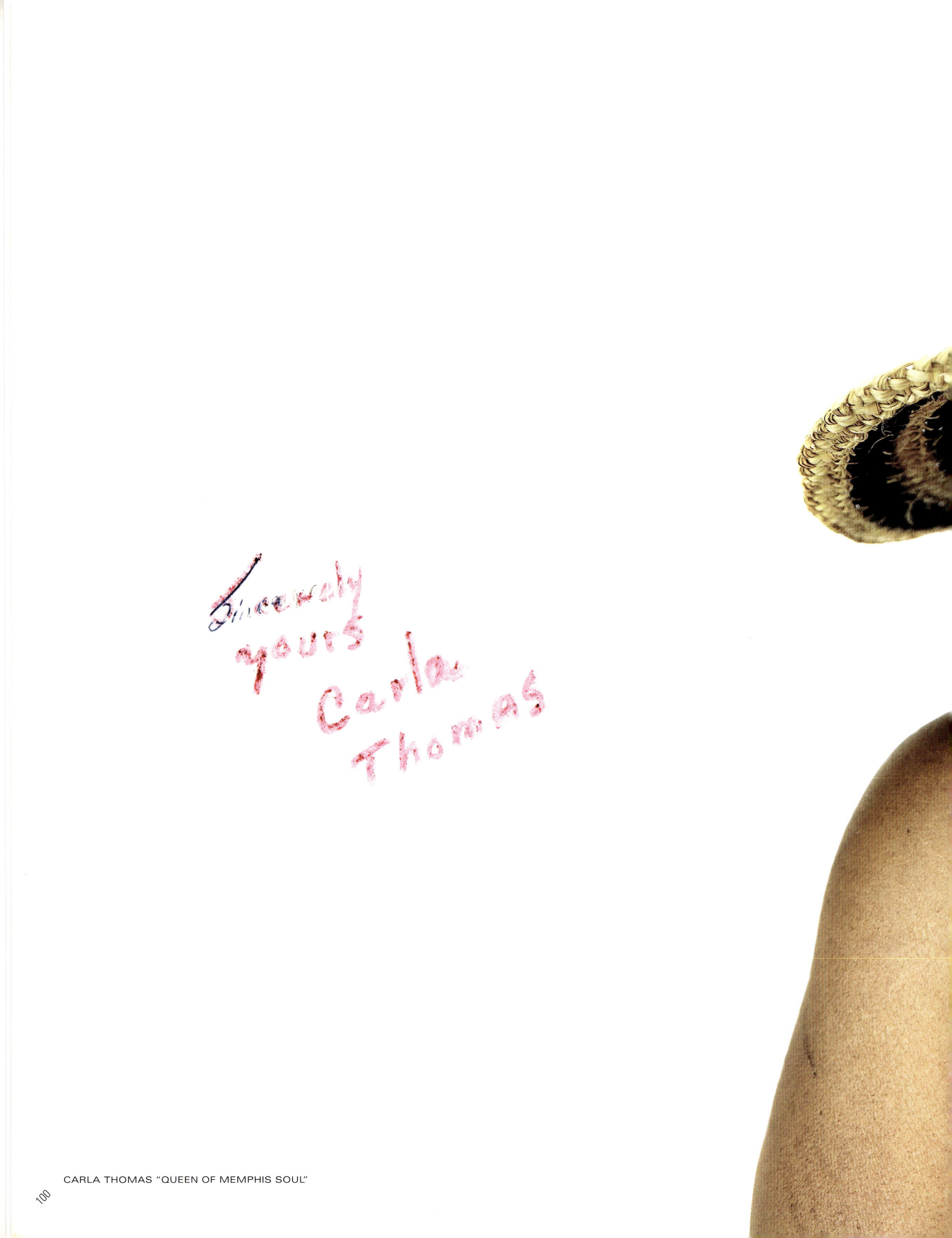


CARLA THOMAS "QUEEN OF MEMPHIS SOUL"

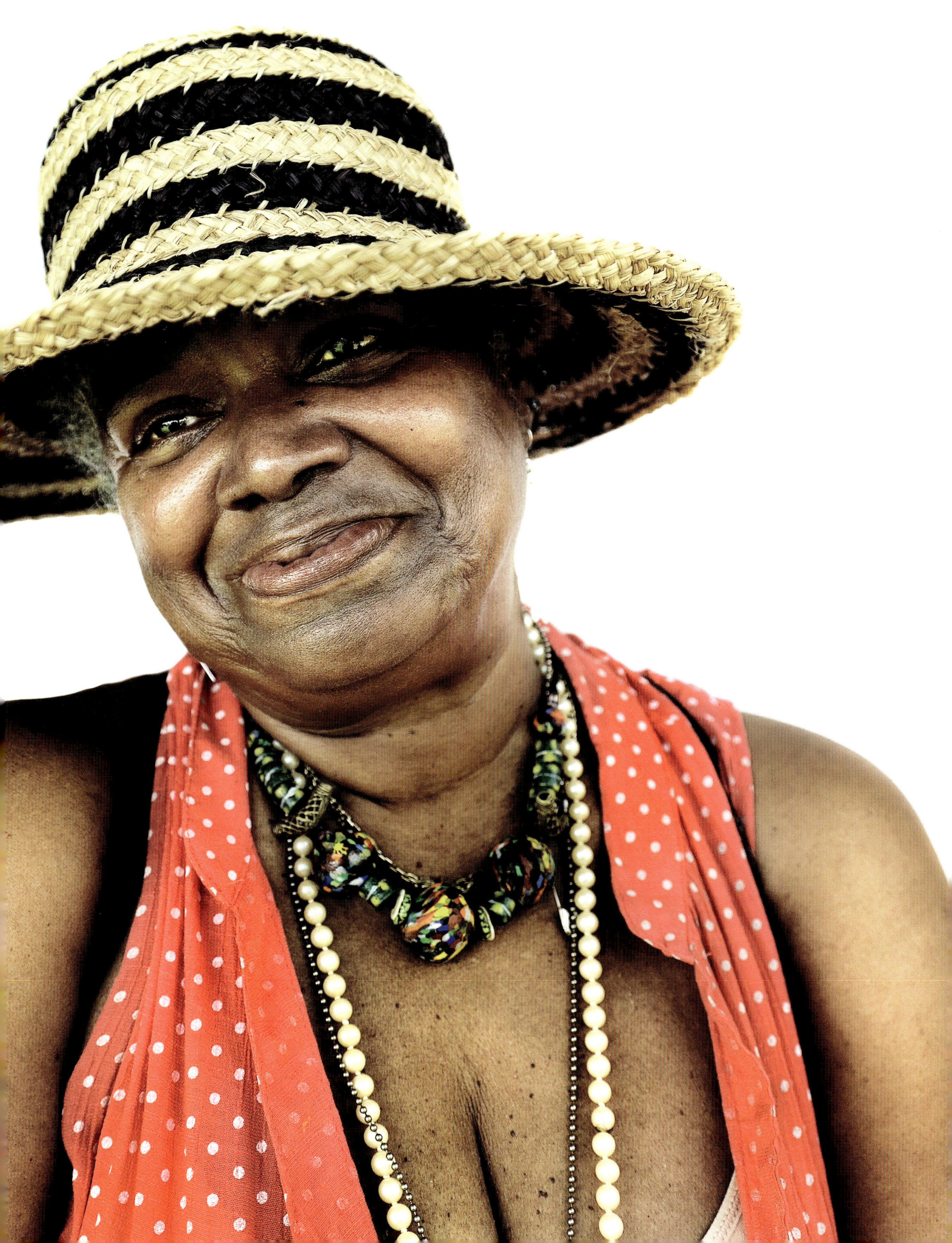

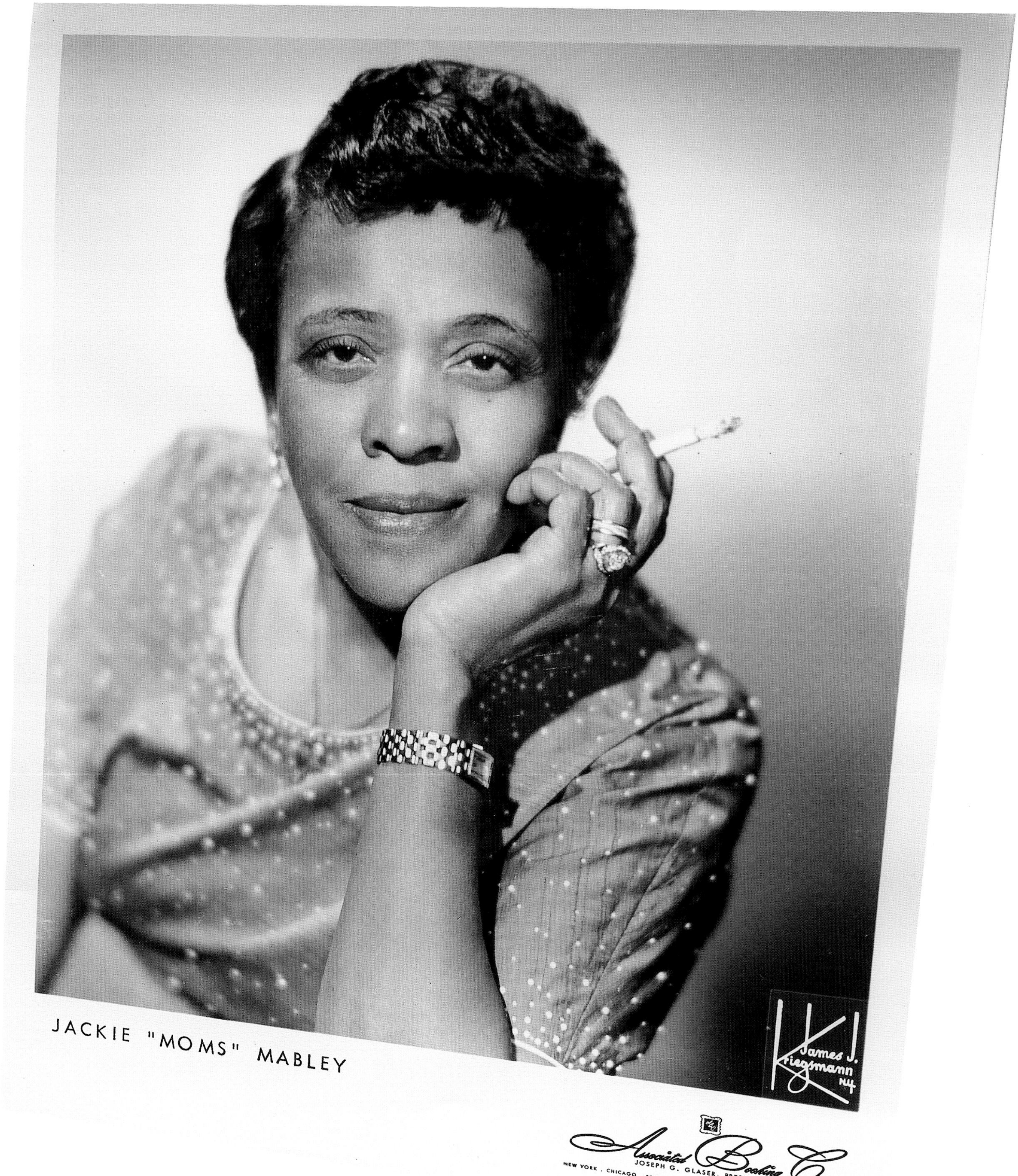


JACKIE "MOMS" MABLEY

1950s' PUBLICITY PHOTO

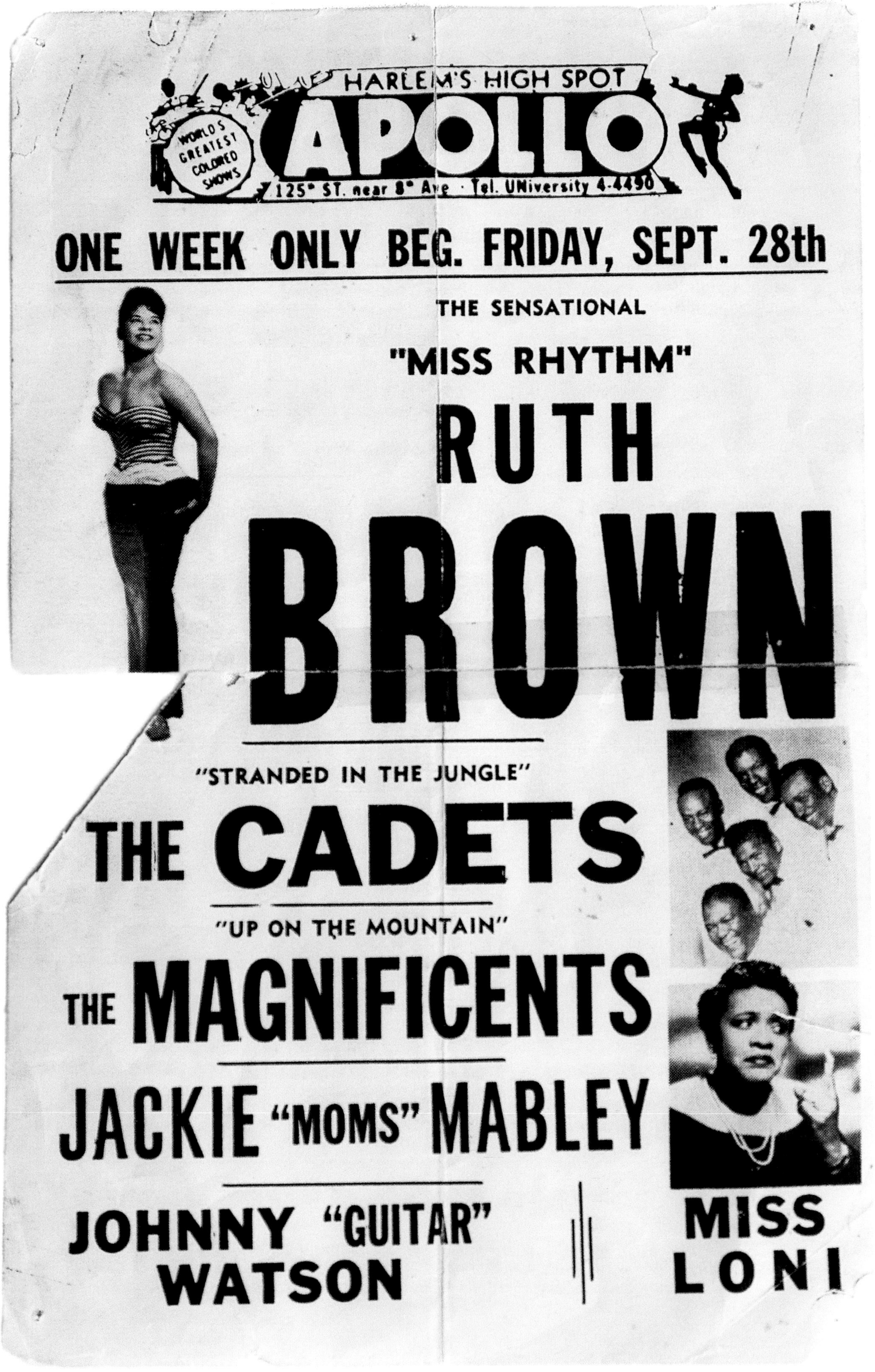
HARLEM'S HIGH SPOT
APOLLO
WORLD'S GREATEST COLORED SHOWS
125th ST. near 8th Ave · Tel. UNiversity 4-4490
ONE WEEK ONLY BEG. FRIDAY, SEPT. 28th
THE SENSATIONAL
"MISS RHYTHM"
RUTH
BROWN
"STRANDED IN THE JUNGLE"
THE CADETS
"UP ON THE MOUNTAIN"
THE MAGNIFICENTS
JACKIE "MOMS" MABLEY
JOHNNY "GUITAR" WATSON
MISS LONI

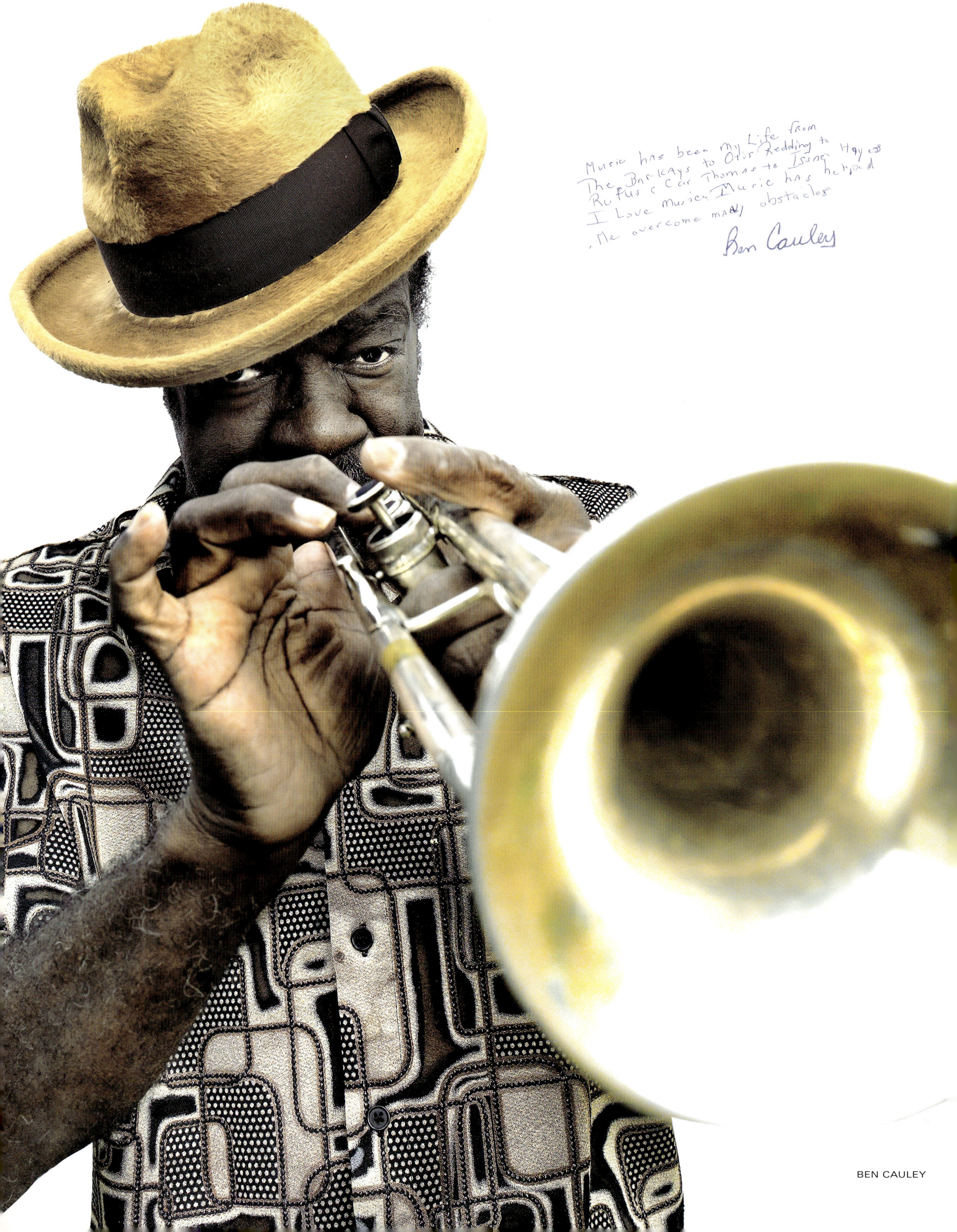

Music has been my Life from
The Bar-Kays to Otis Redding to
Rufus c Car Thomas to Issac Hayess
I Love music. Music has helped
. Me overcome many obstacles

Ben Cauley

BEN CAULEY

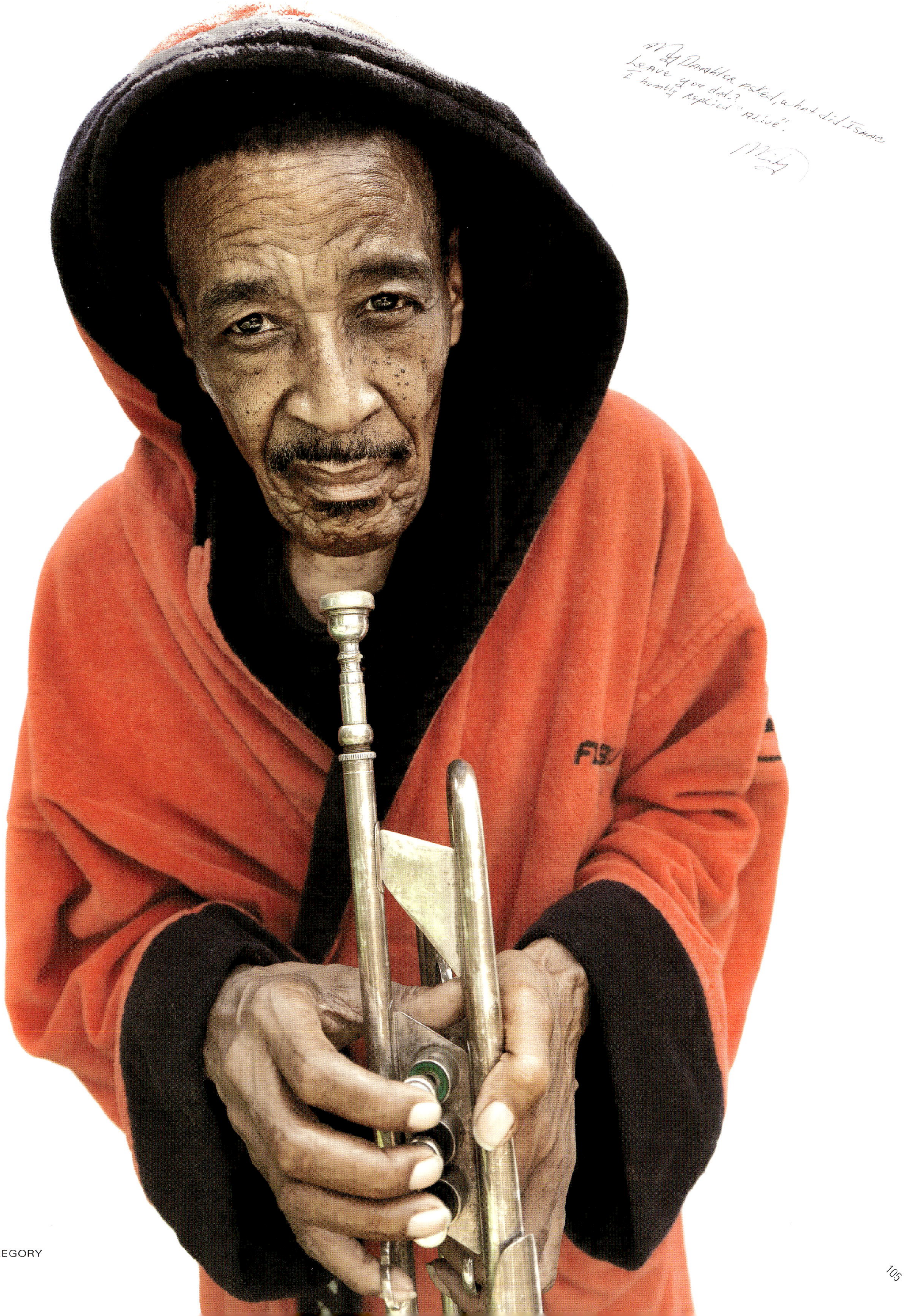


MICKEY GREGORY

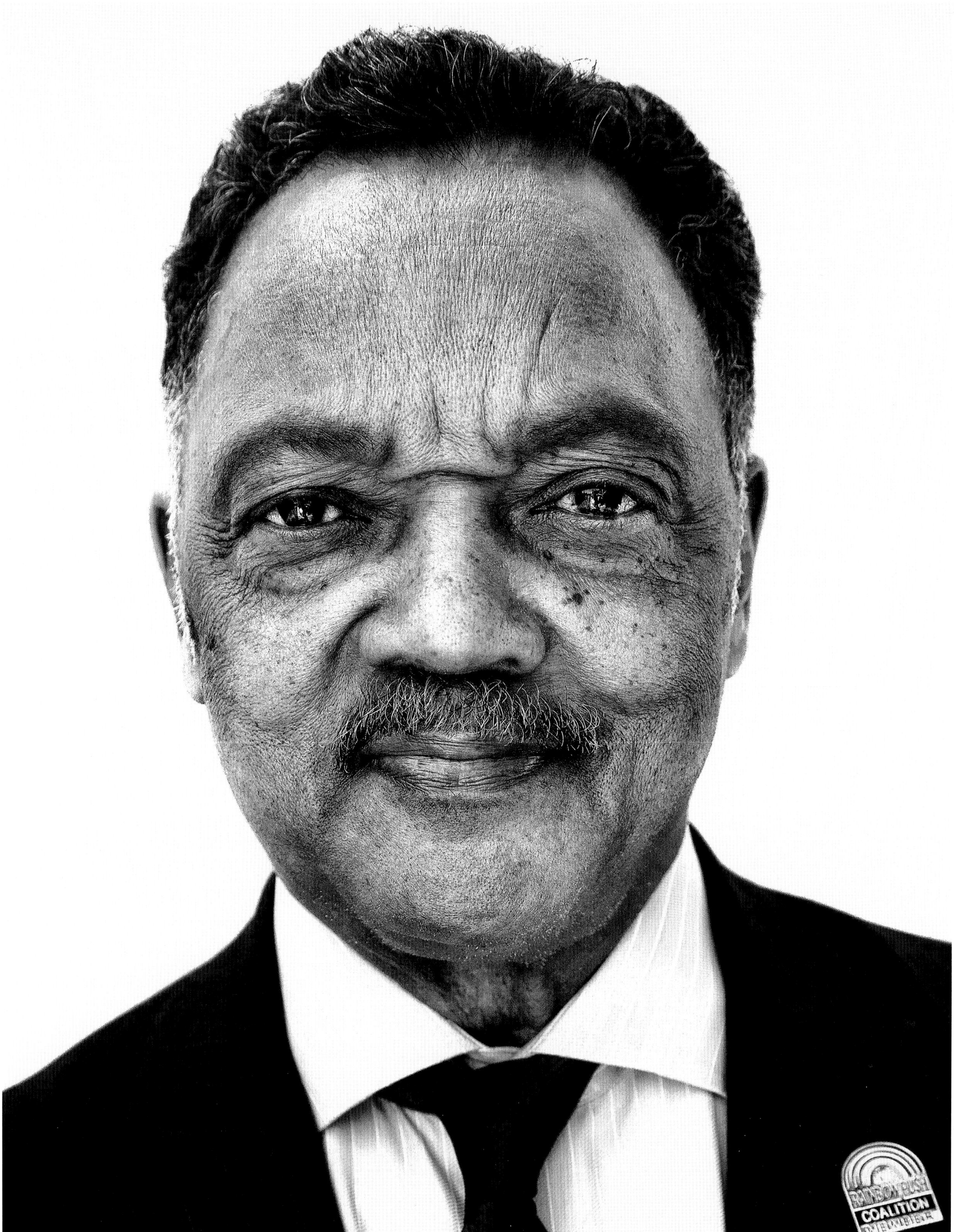
RAINBOW PUSH
COALITION

REV. JESSE JACKSON JR.

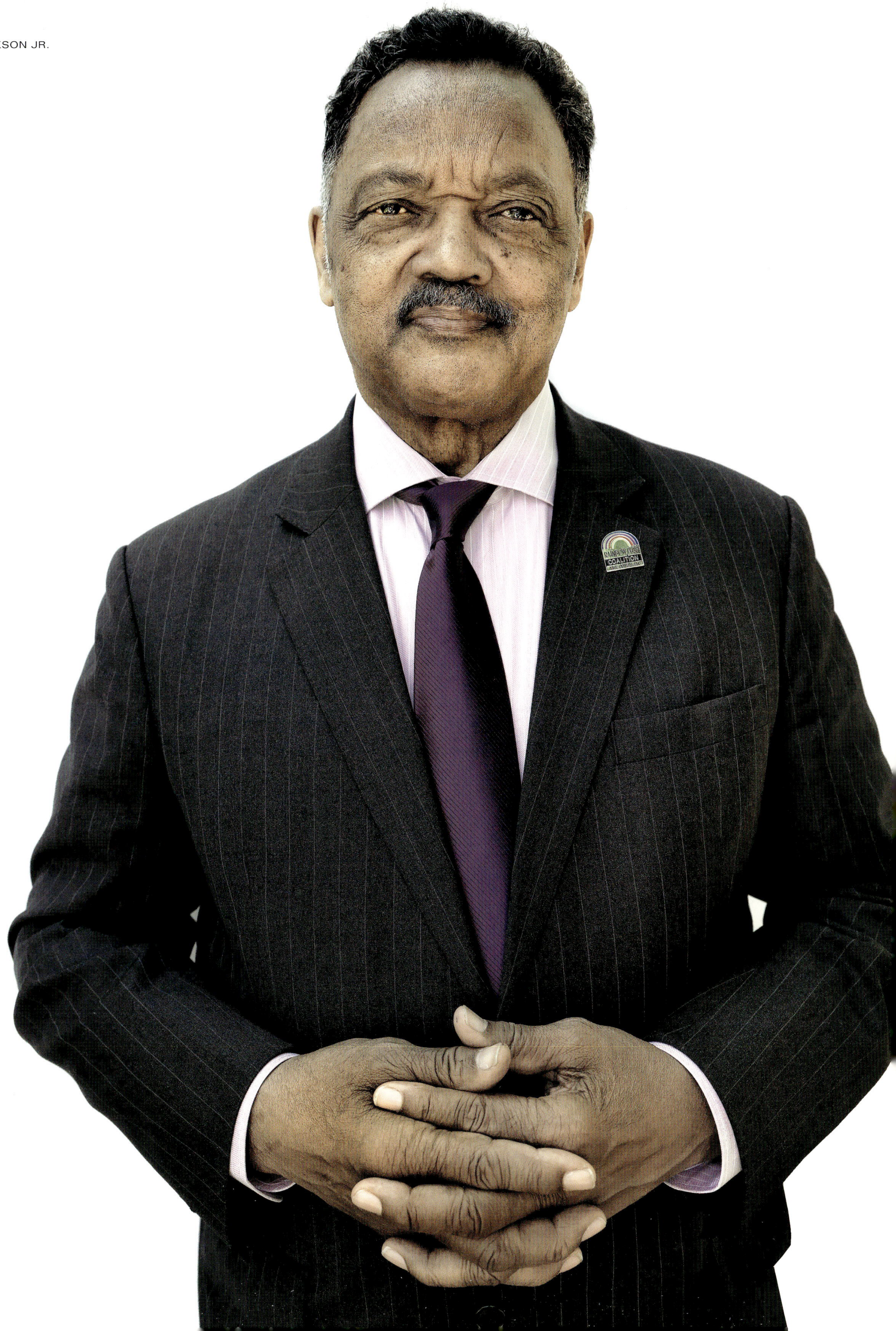

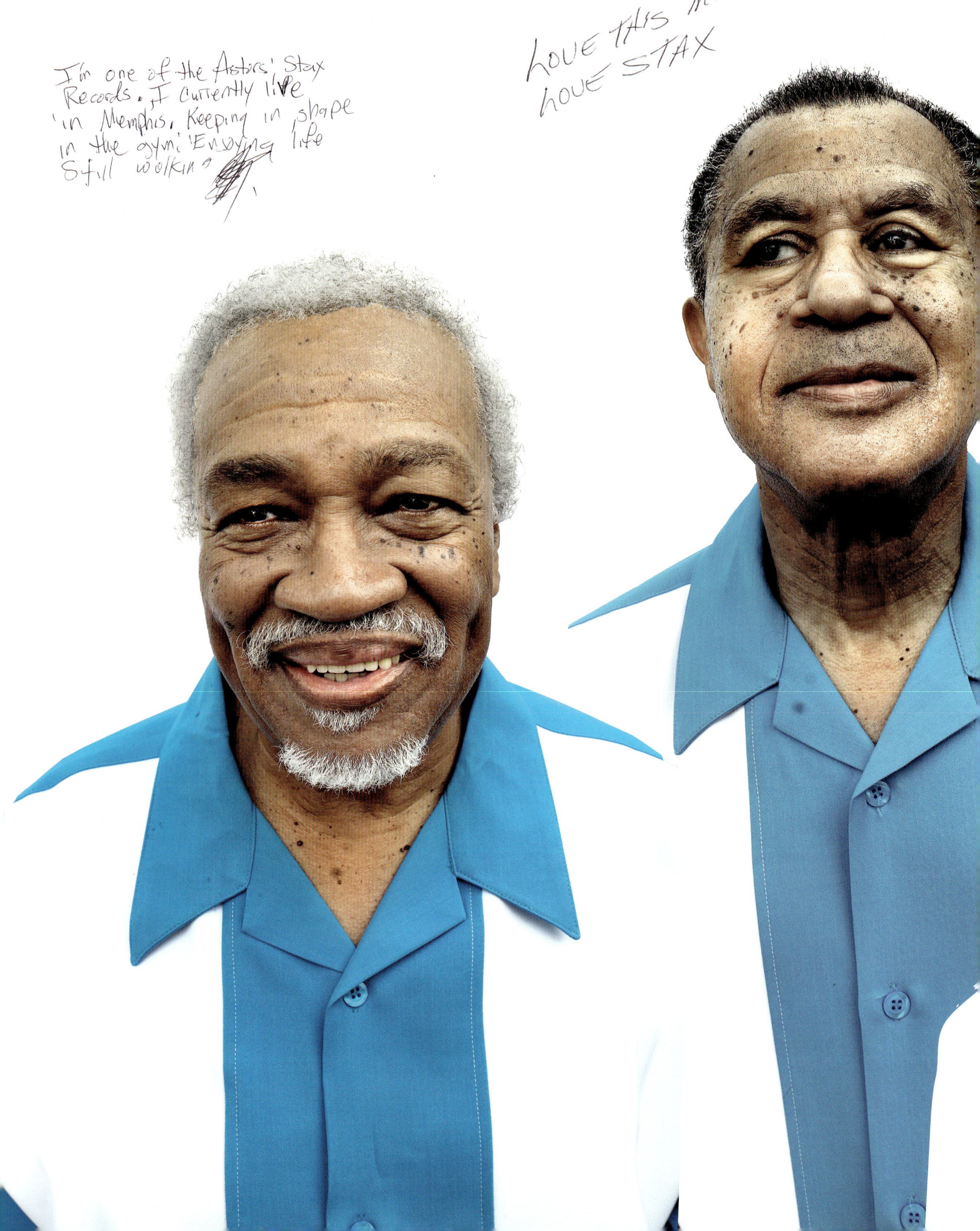
I'm one of the Astors' Stax
Records. I currently live
in Memphis, Keeping in shape
in the gym, Enjoying life
Still walking
Love this music
Love STAX

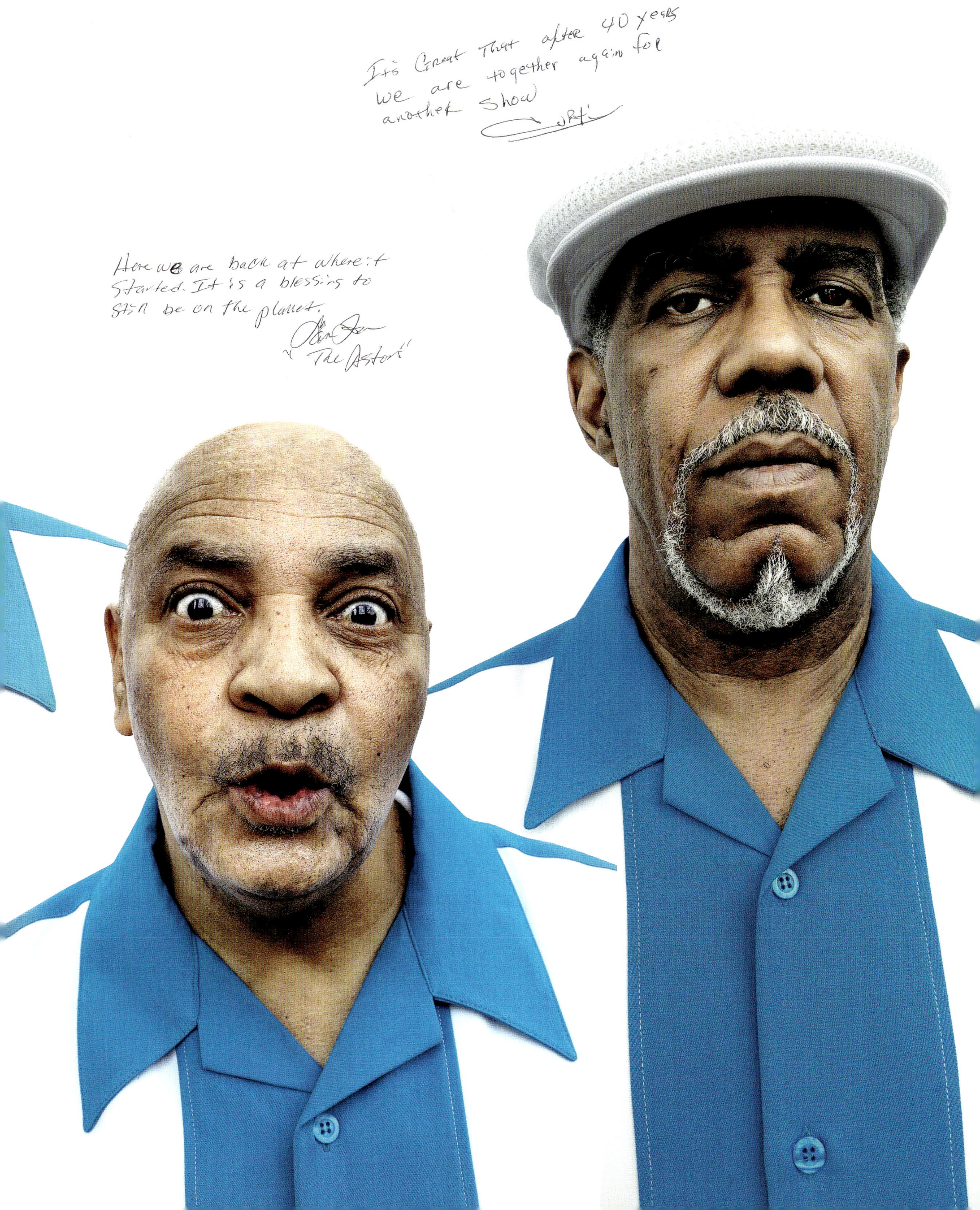
It's Great That after 40 years
we are together again for
another show
Here we are back at where it
Started. It is a blessing to
Still be on the planet.
"The Astors"

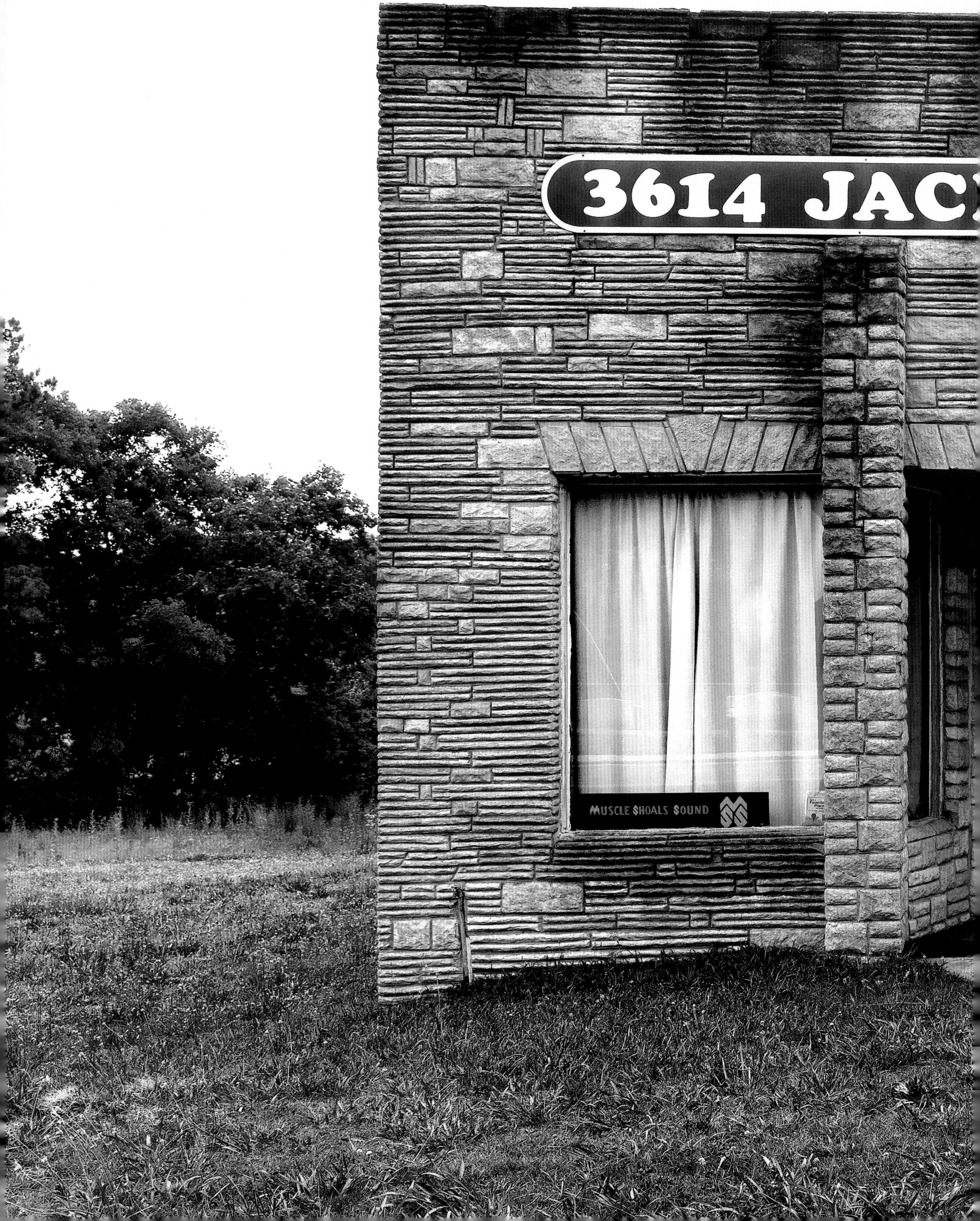
3614 JAC
MUSCLE SHOALS SOUND

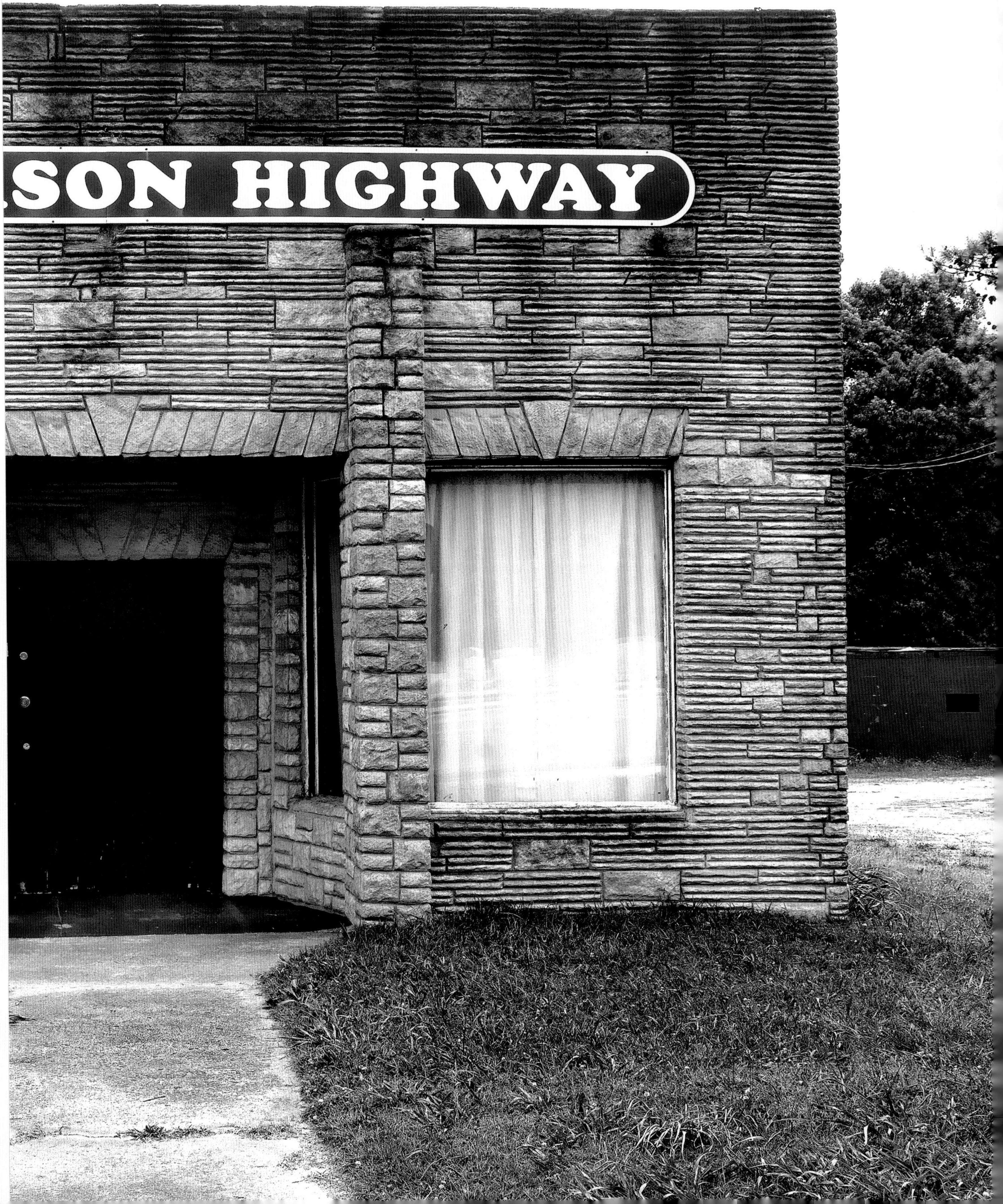
SON HIGHWAY

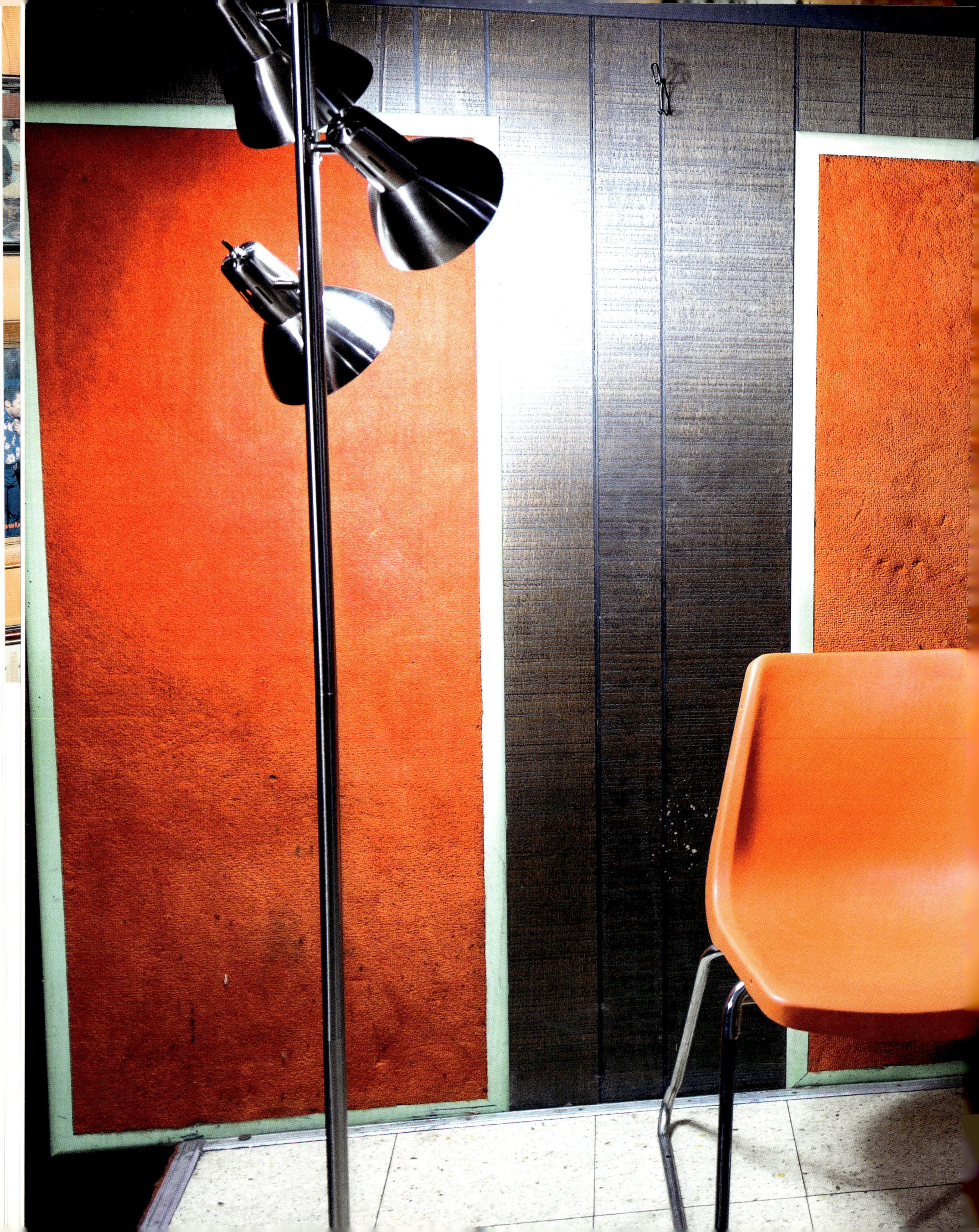

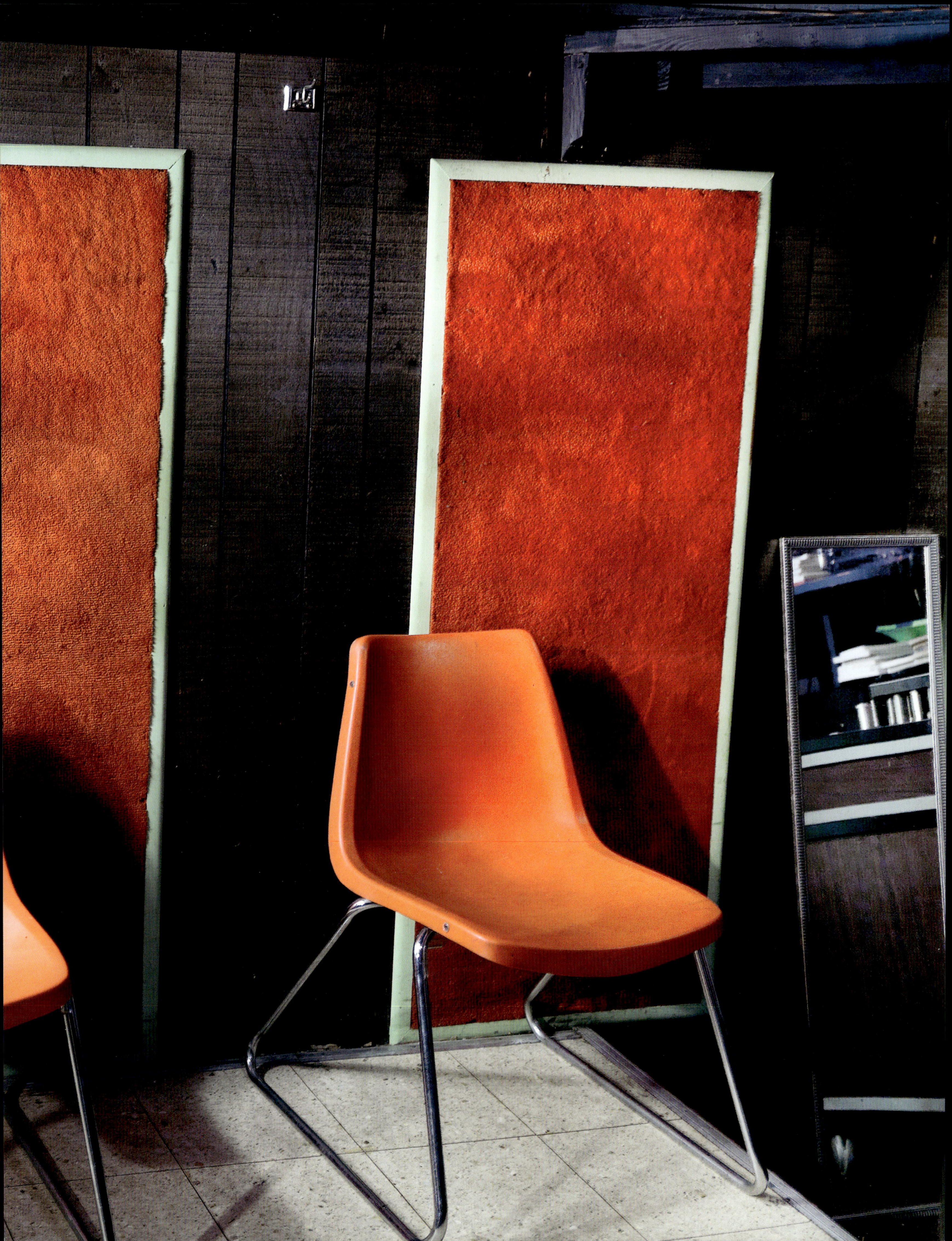

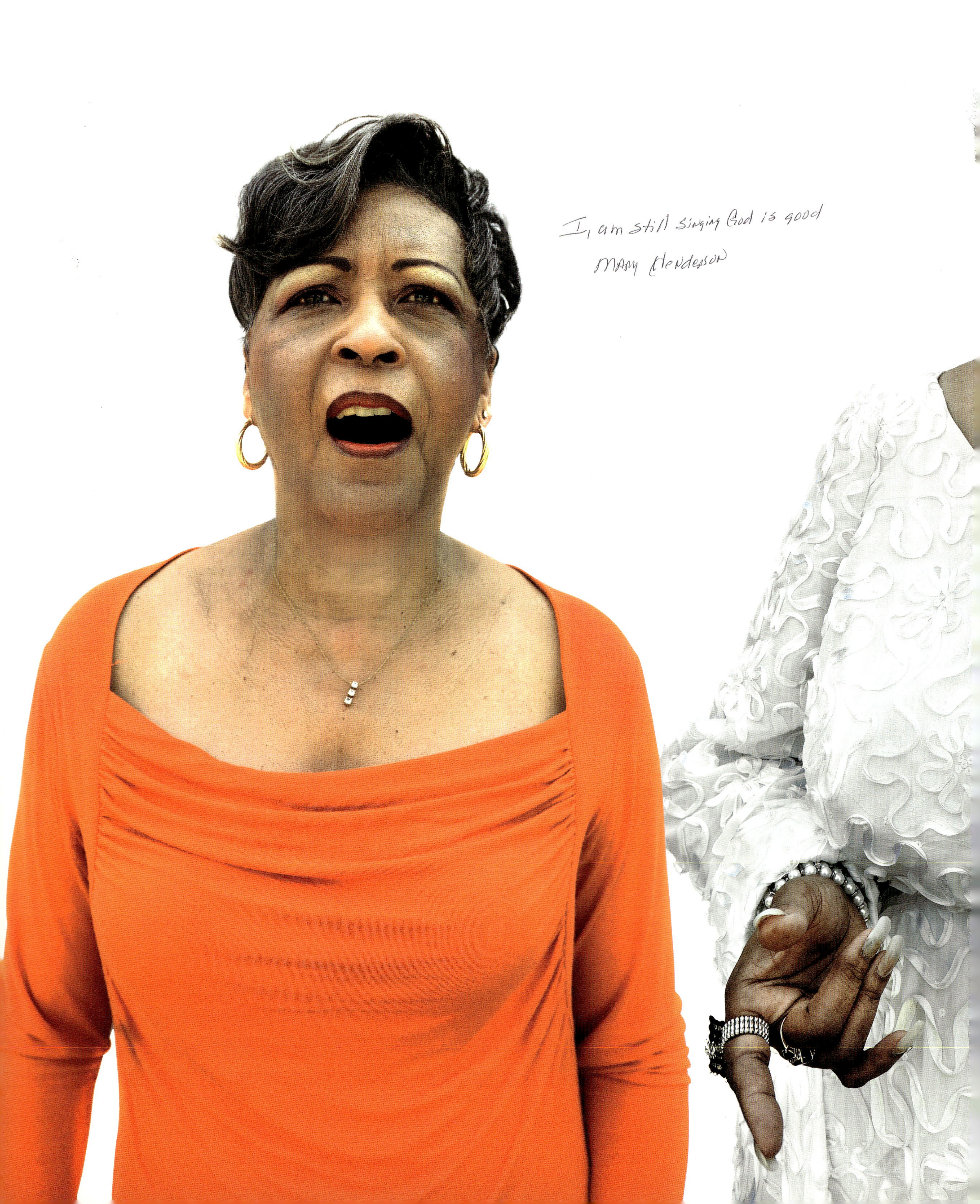
I, am still singing God is good
Mary Henderson

Singing has been an awesome time for me now and then.
Bonnie R. Bradshaw

The journey is equally as important as the destination.
Barbara McCoy

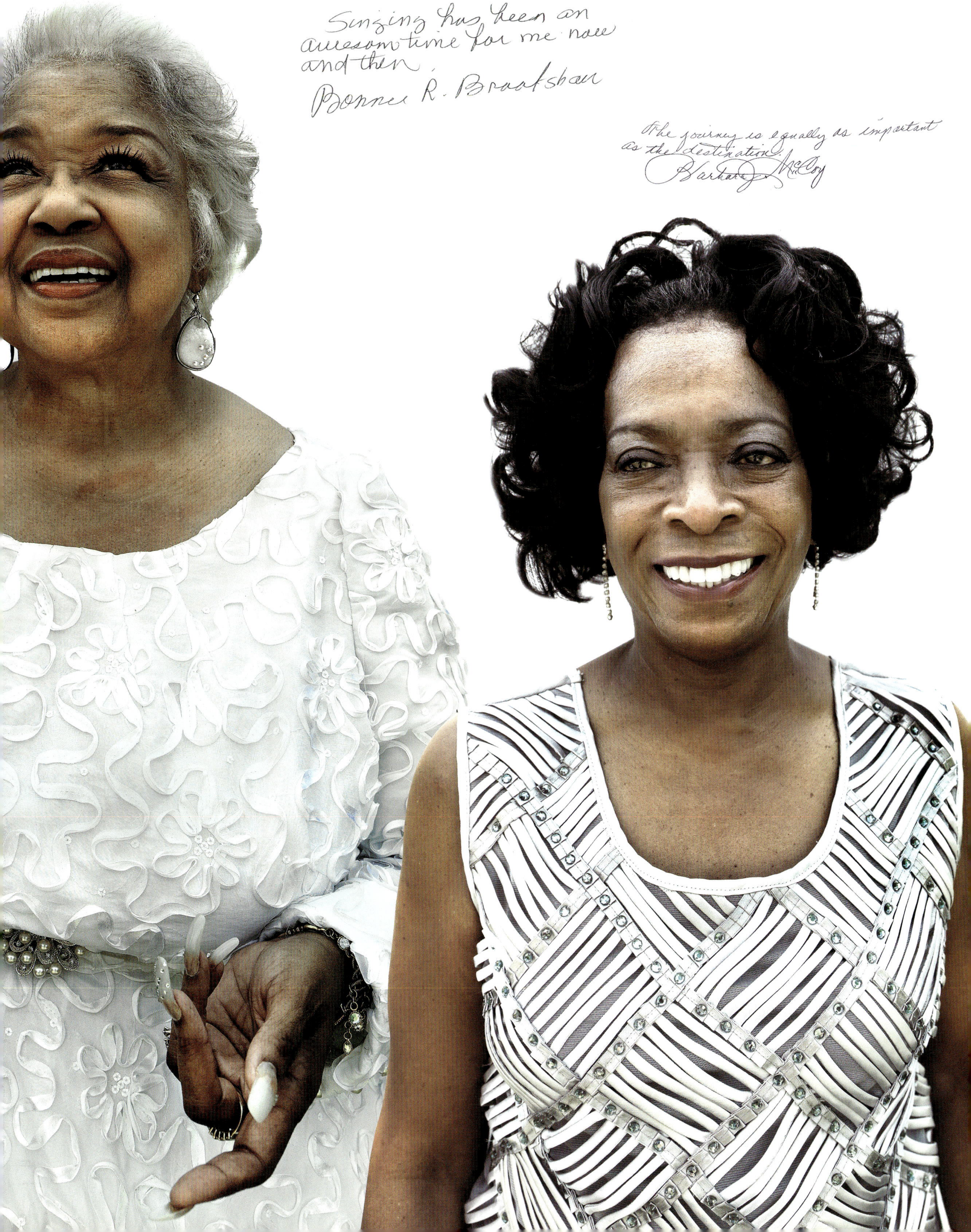

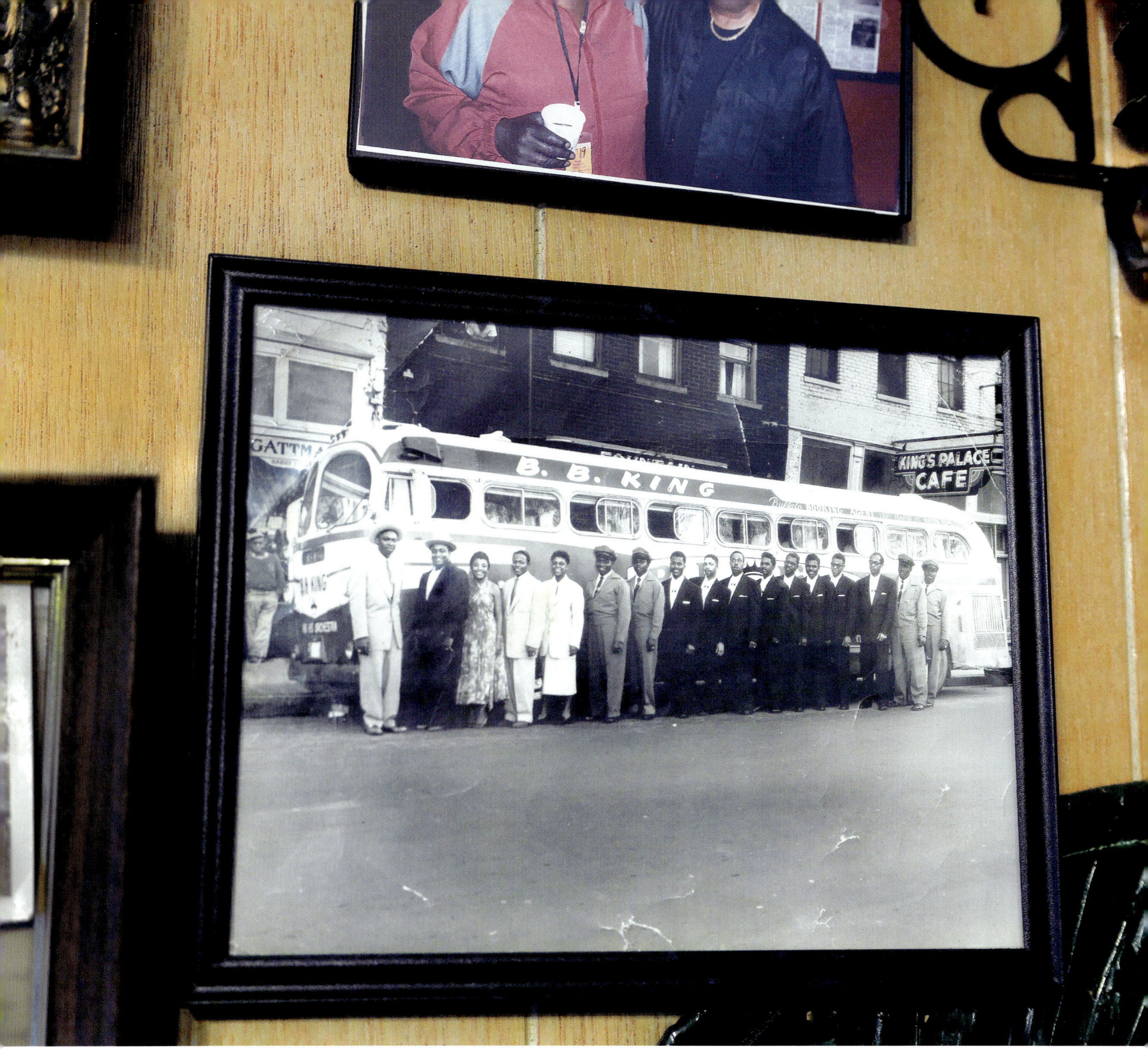


FLOYD AT B. B. KING'S TOUR BUS

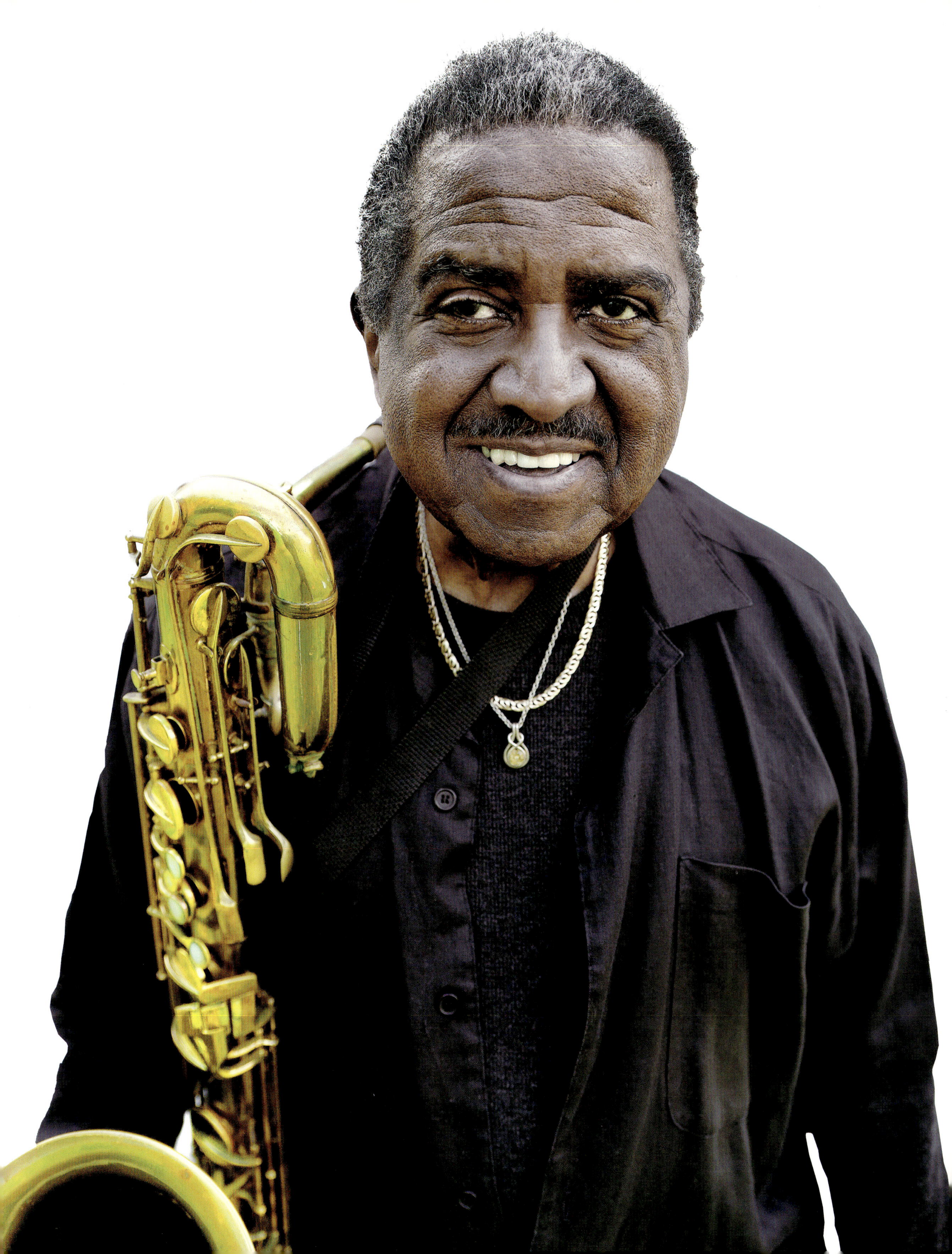

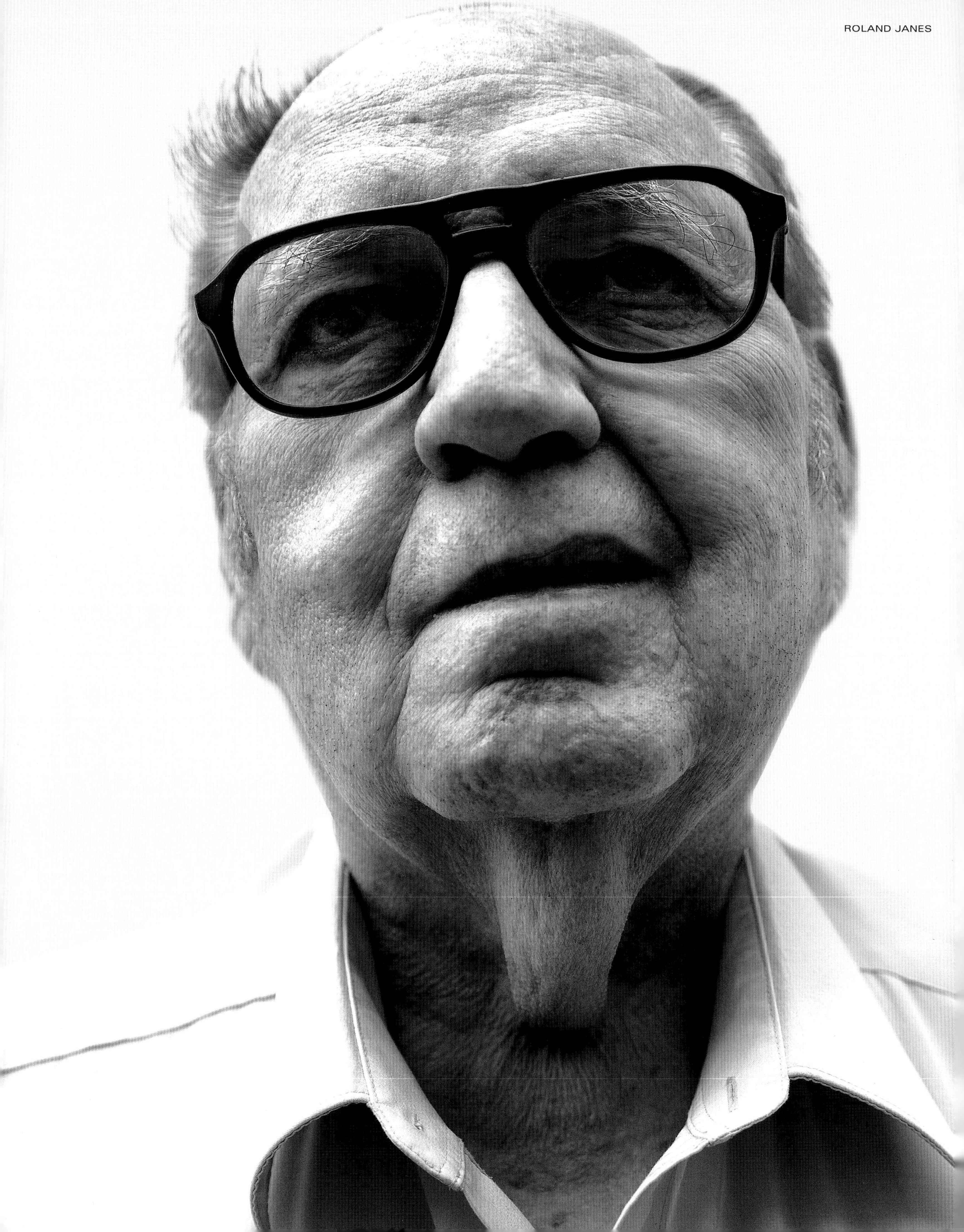

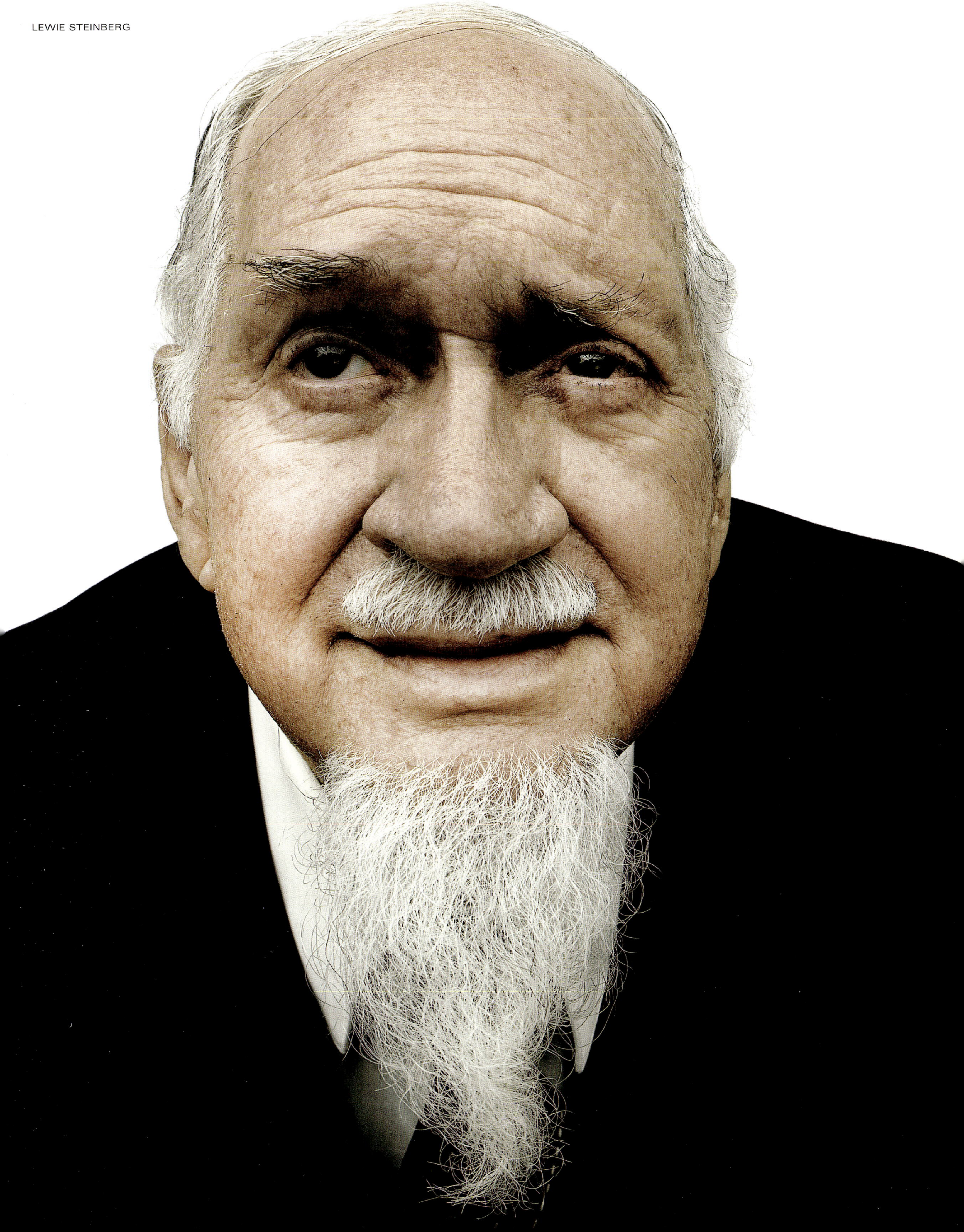

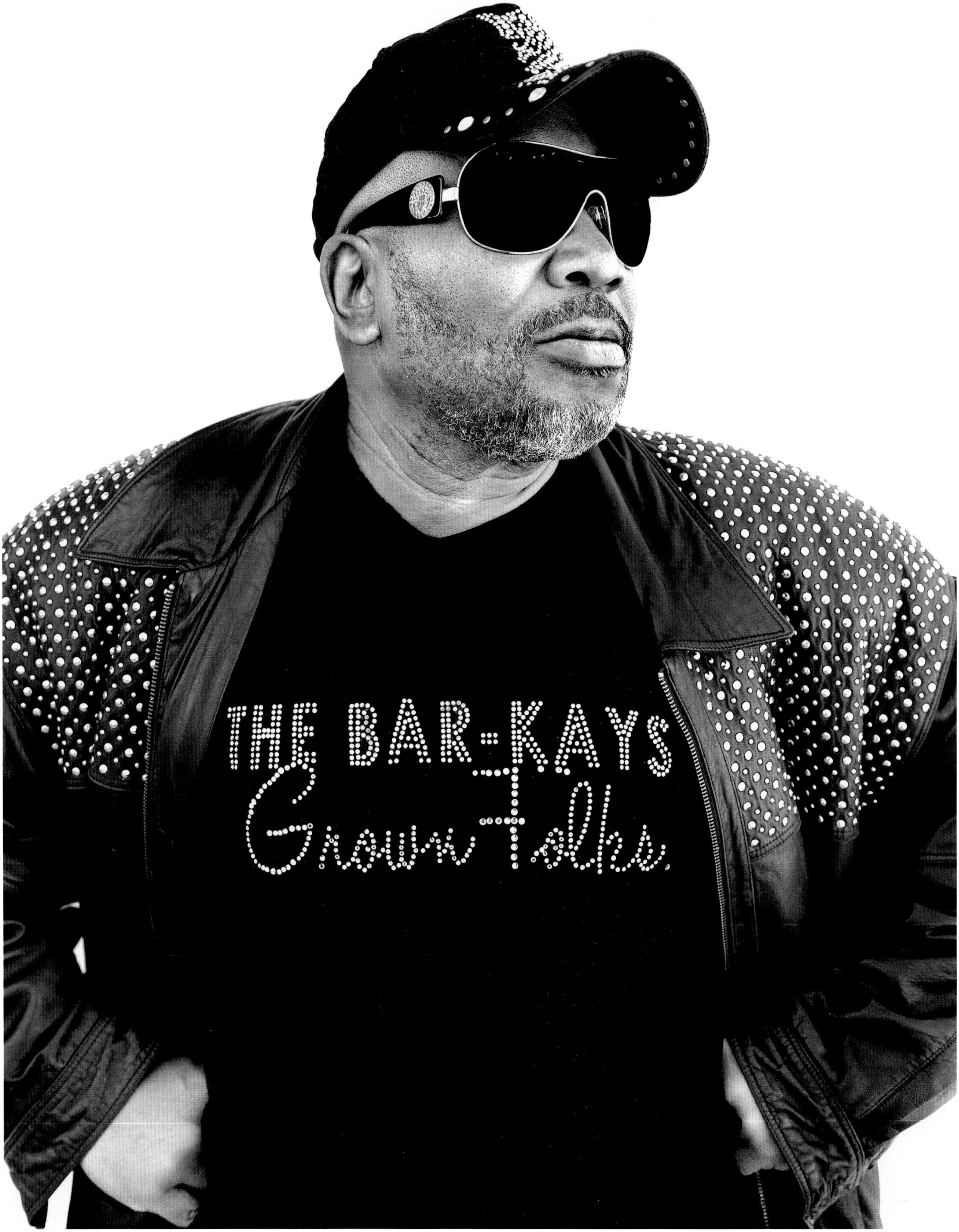
THE BAR-KAYS
Grown Folks

RANDY HODGES

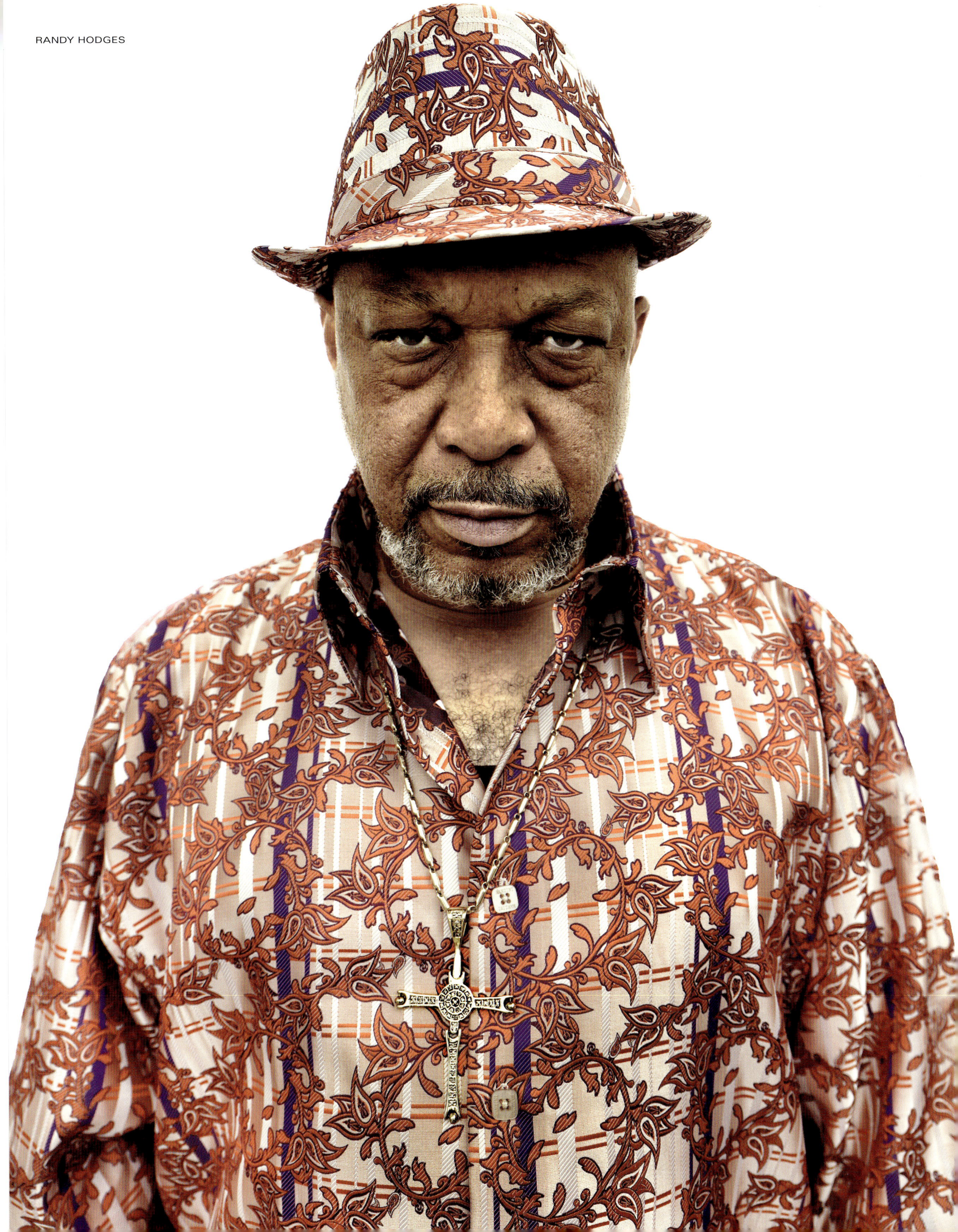

By far my years at Stax Records were the best of my life. Larry T [signature]

As a little boy, my mother took me to Handy Park in the 50's on Beale St. in Memphis, Tn to see Bobby "Blue" Bland and B.B. King perform on a flat bed truck. Life has never been the same!!! James Alexander

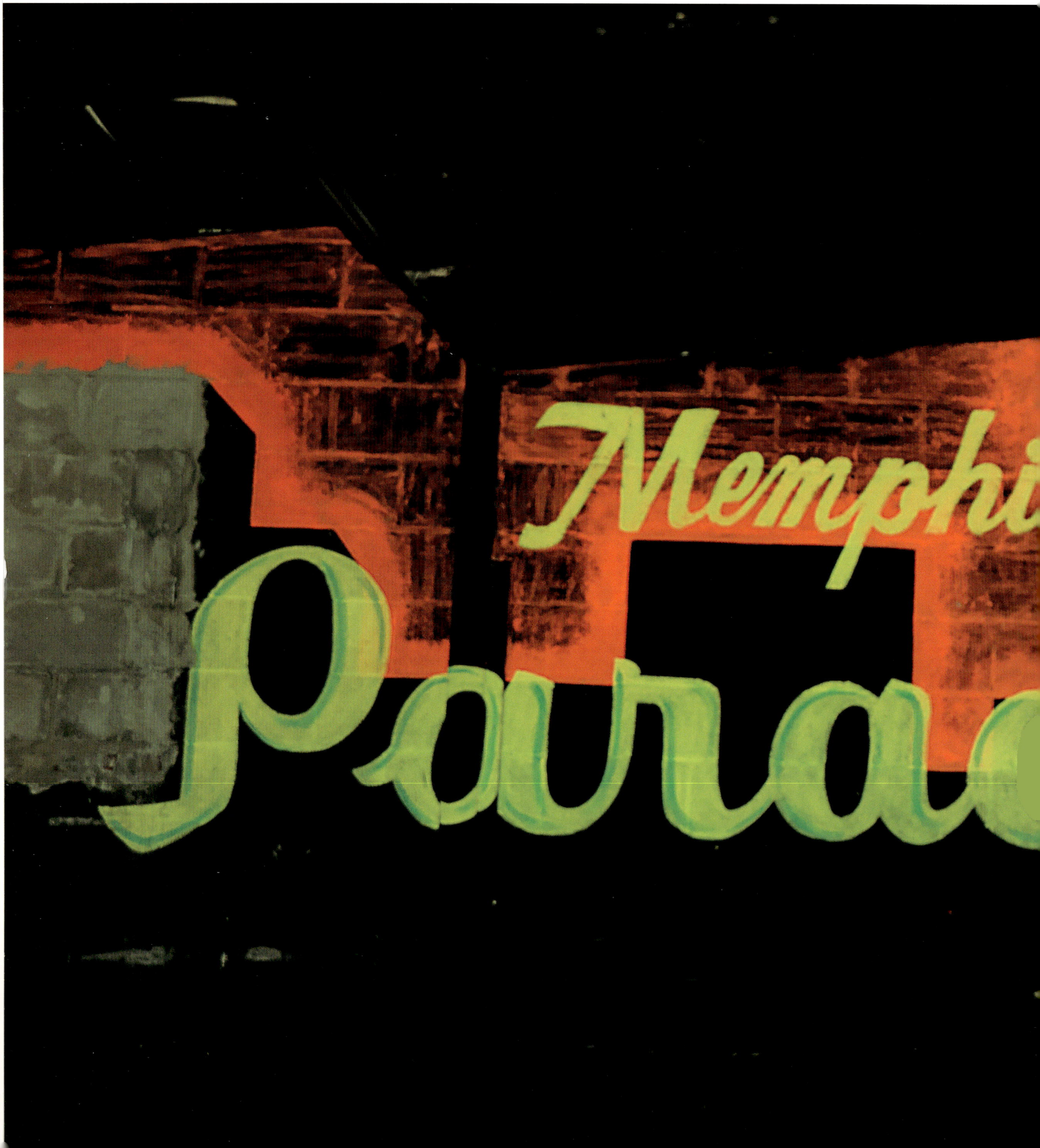

Robert L Jackson

I like to know what I need to know when I need to know it and when I need to know it

Lewie Steinberg

Road Manager for the S.O.S. Band
Road Manager for the Shirley Brown Band
Tour Manager for the Mighty Bar-Kays
To Tom it is a honor to work with you,
Thank you,
Randy Hodges

LIKE THE MISSISSIPPI RIVER
MEMPHIS MUSIC IS
FOREVER. ALWAYS GREAT
AND ROLLING ON.

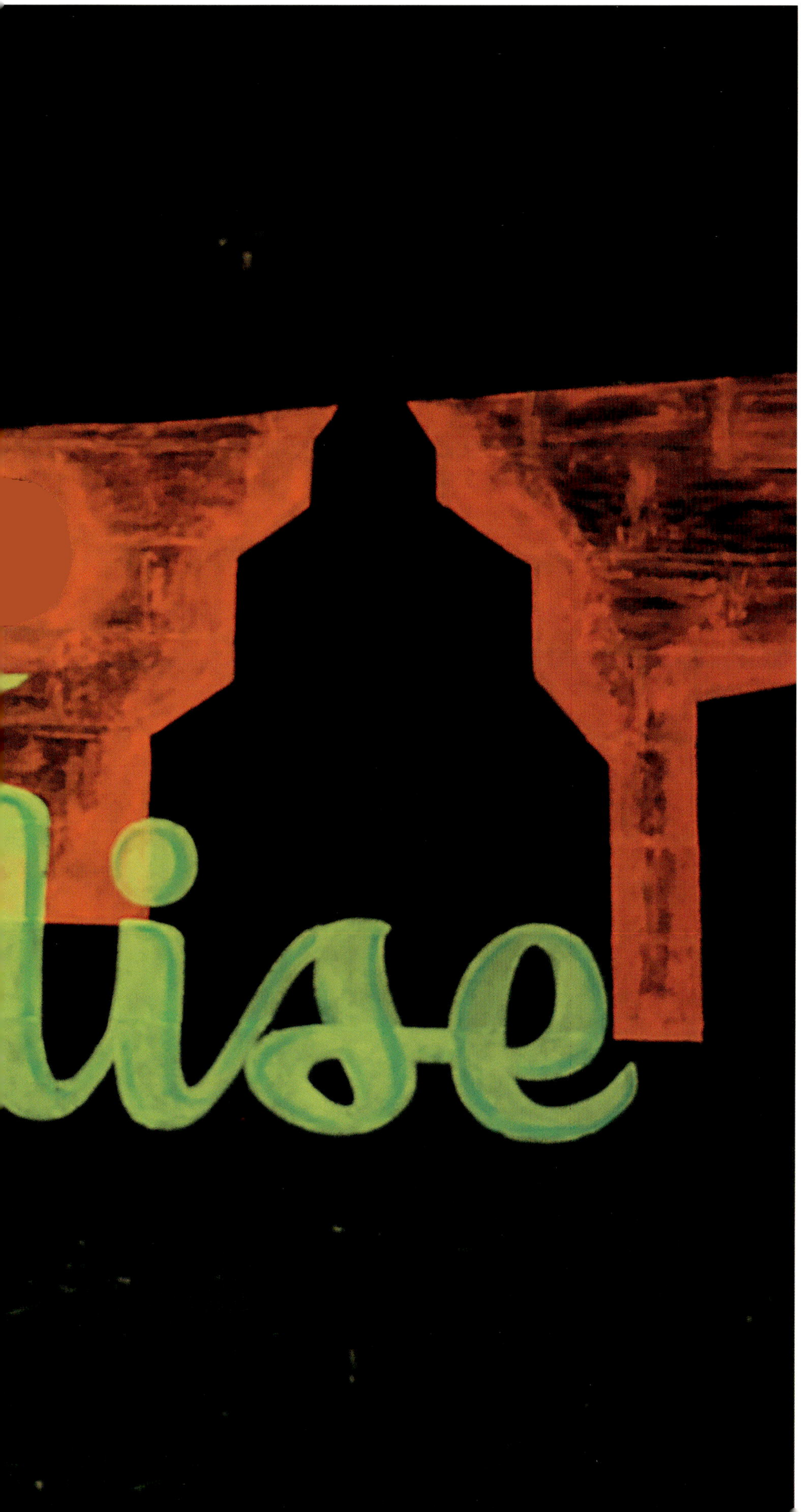


ON-STAGE MURAL AT CLUB PARADISE, MEMPHIS

What I'm doing this for?

Eddie Floyd

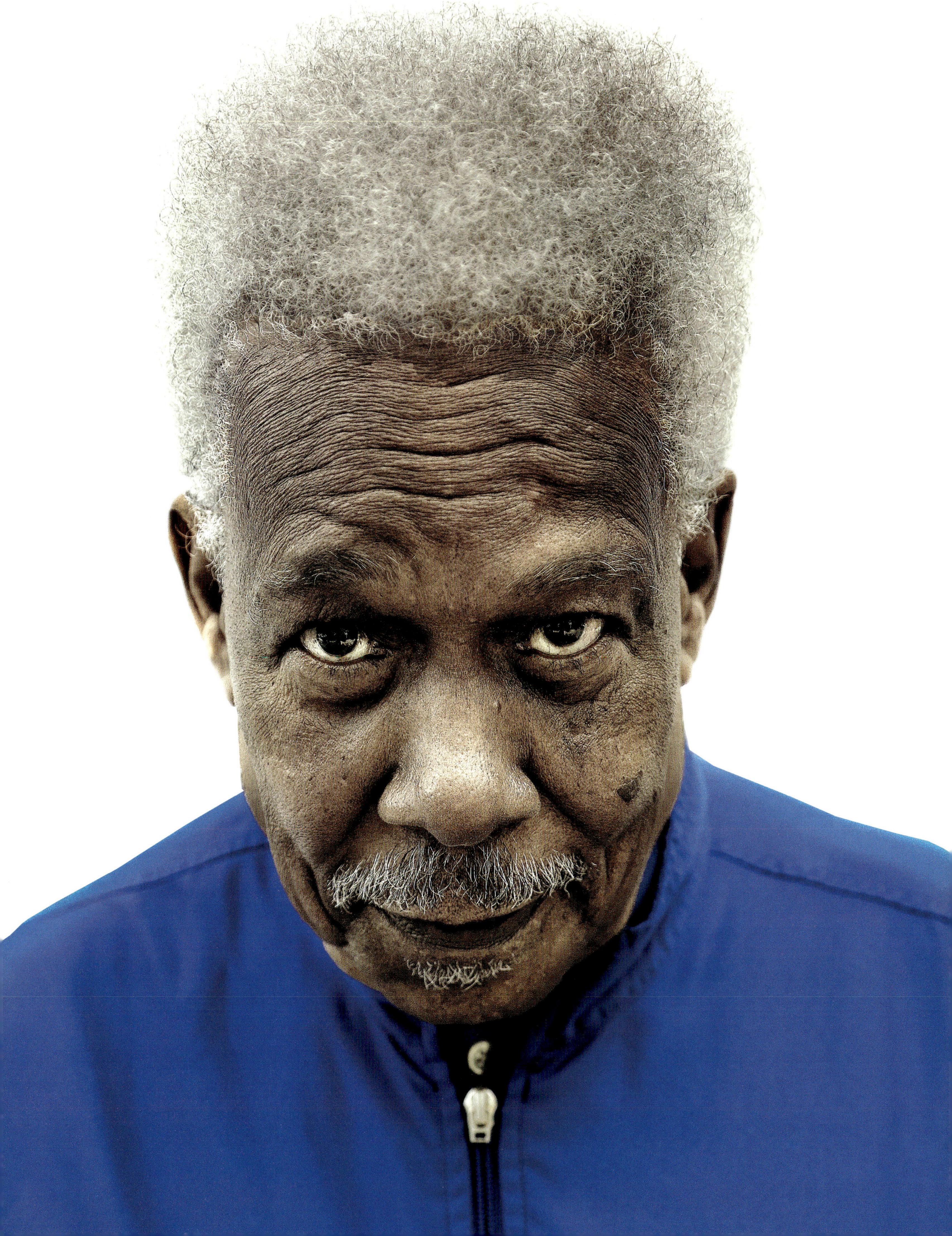

My Greates supperters are—
my fans and students
George Coleman

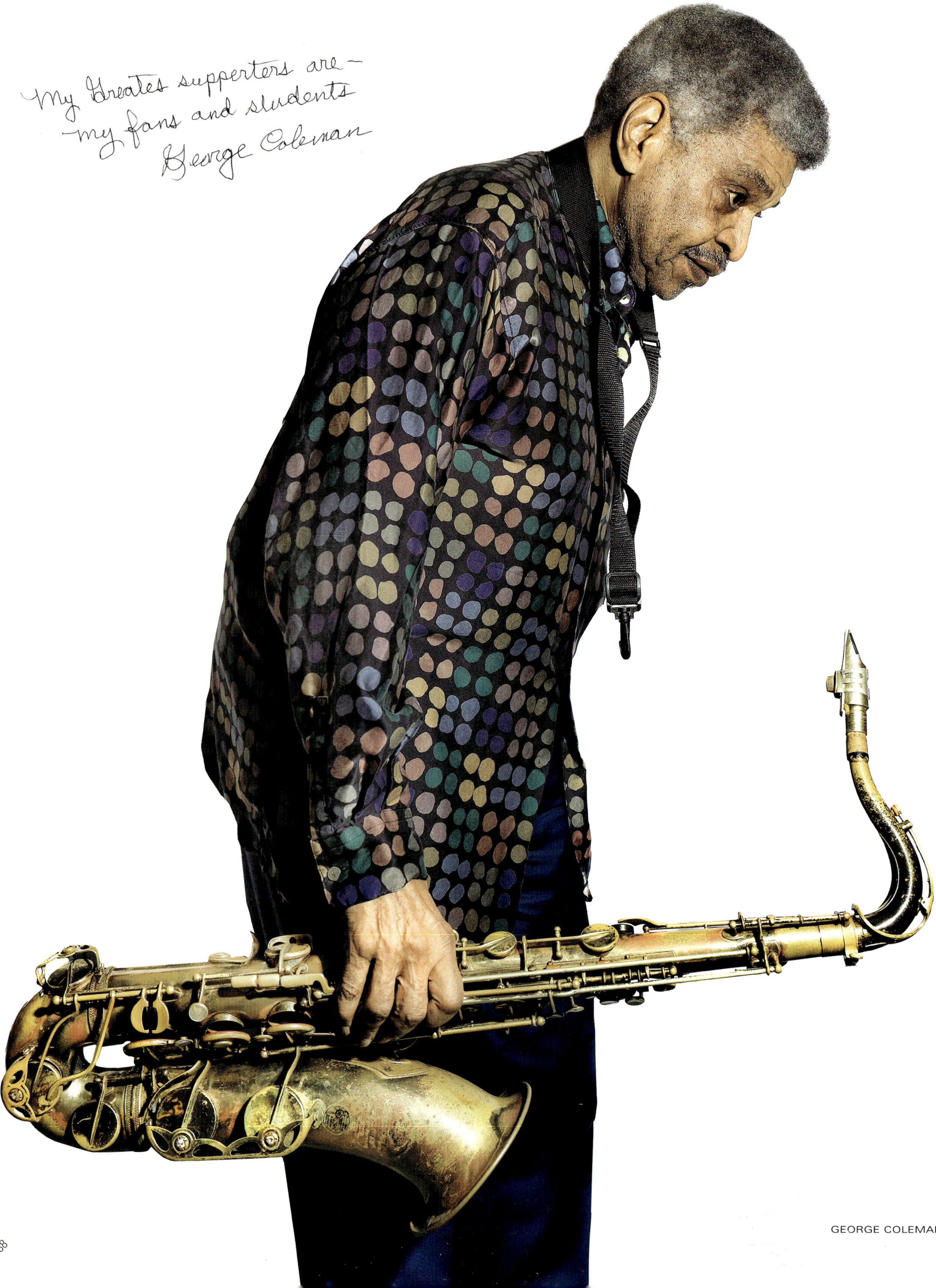

GEORGE COLEMAN

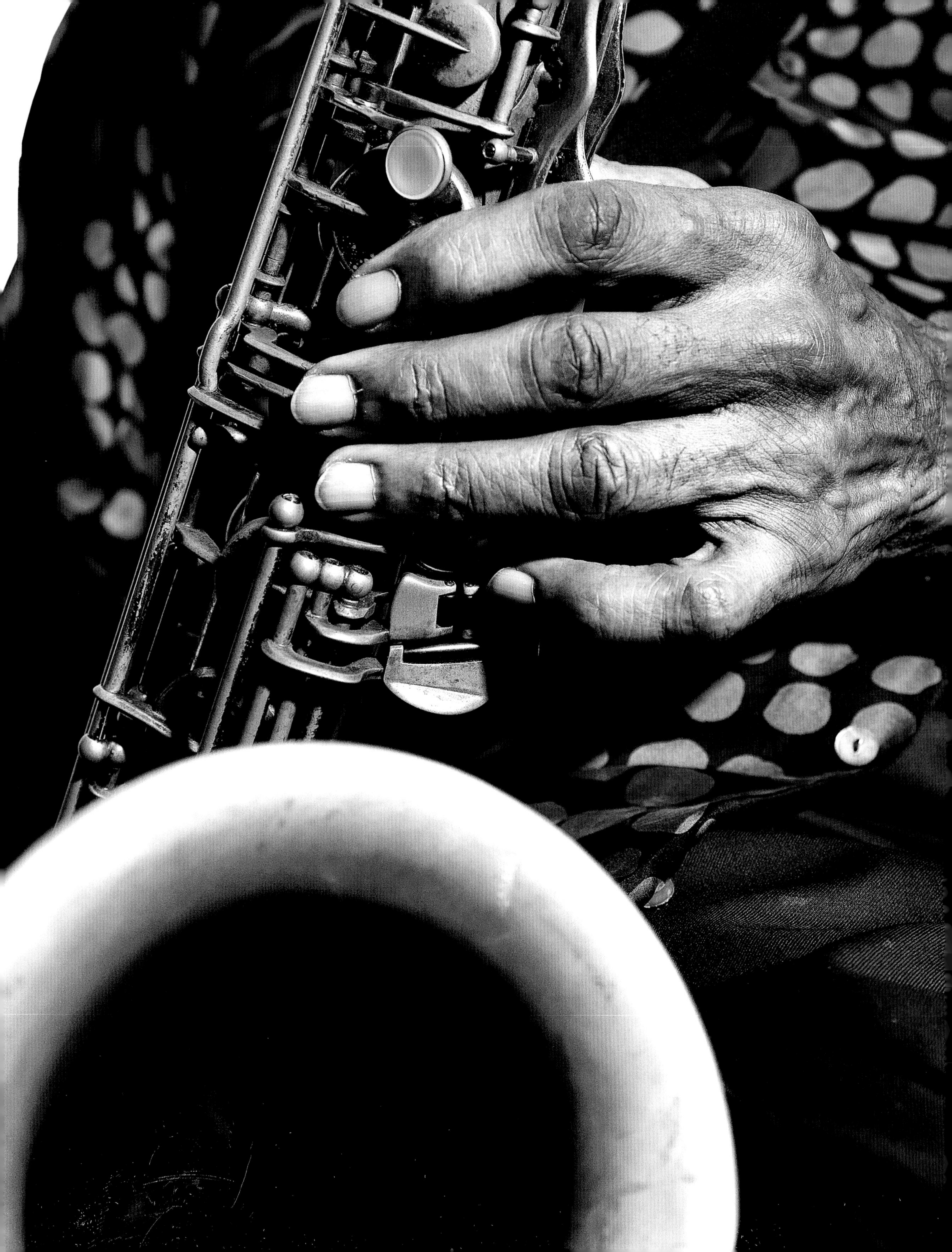

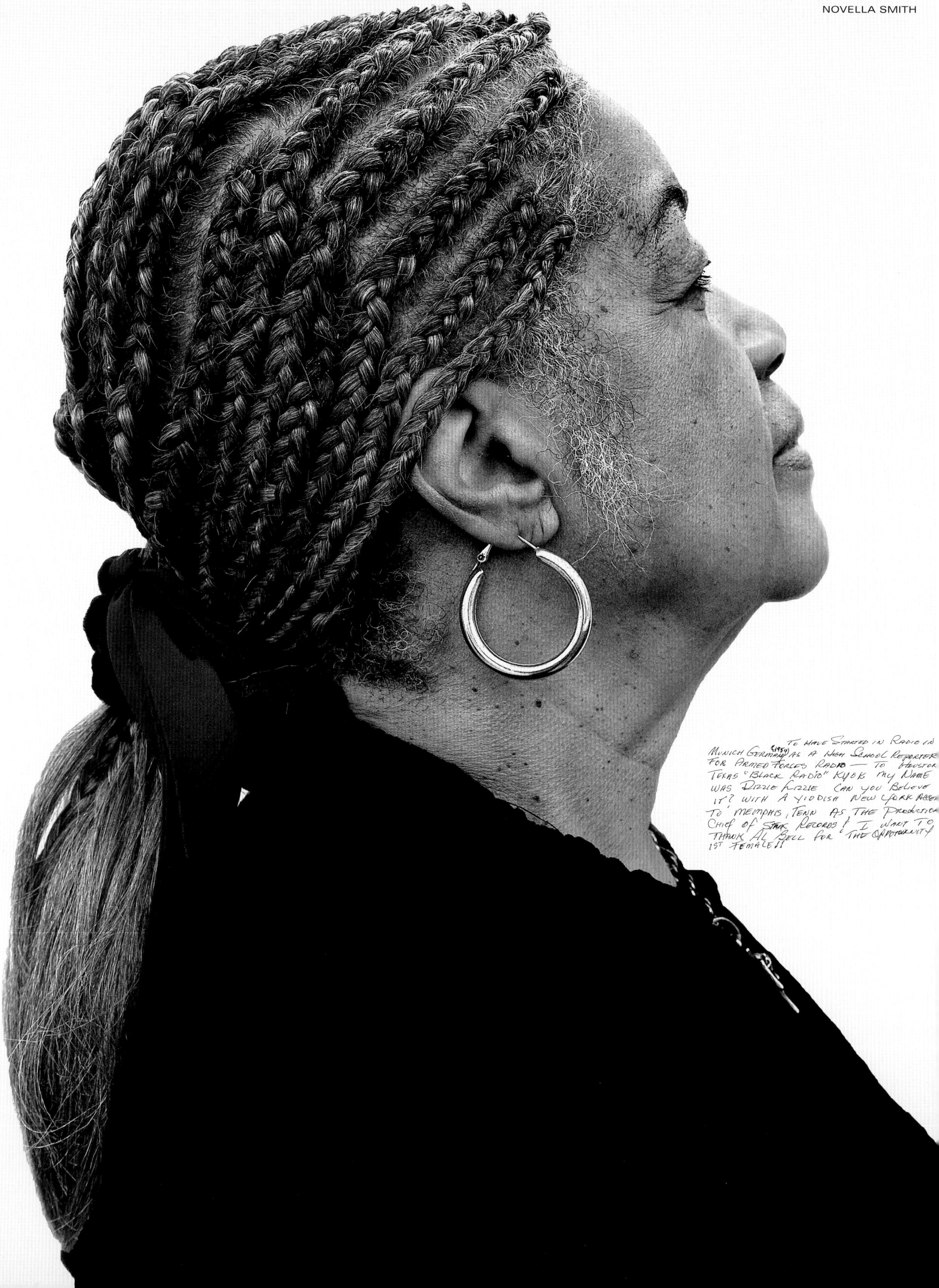

TO HAVE STARTED IN RADIO IN
MUNICH GERMANY (1954) AS A HIGH SCHOOL REPORTER
FOR ARMED FORCES RADIO — TO HOUSTON
TEXAS "BLACK RADIO" KYOK MY NAME
WAS DIZZIE LIZZIE CAN YOU BELIEVE
IT? WITH A YIDDISH NEW YORK ACCENT
TO MEMPHIS, TENN AS THE PRODUCTION
CHIEF OF STAX RECORDS! I WANT TO
THANK AL BELL FOR THE OPPORTUNITY
1ST FEMALE!!

JUDY (WILLIAMS) LOVE

As a teenager, I was signed, along with Sandra and Kay, to be part of the Hip Label. We were known as the Goodees. This relationship with Stax and the wonderful people I came in contact with will live forever in my heart, along with the music. Long live Stax!

Judy Williams Love

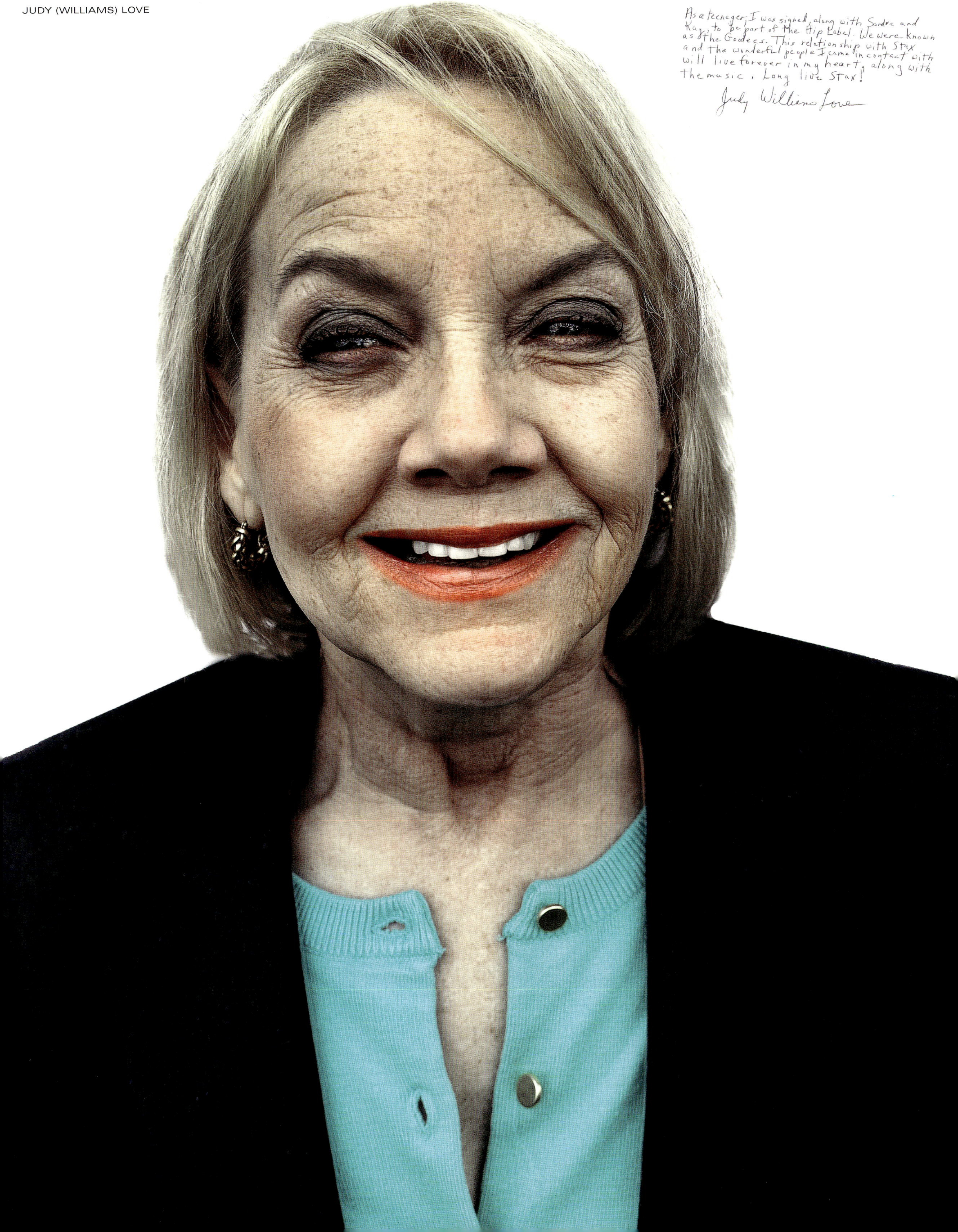

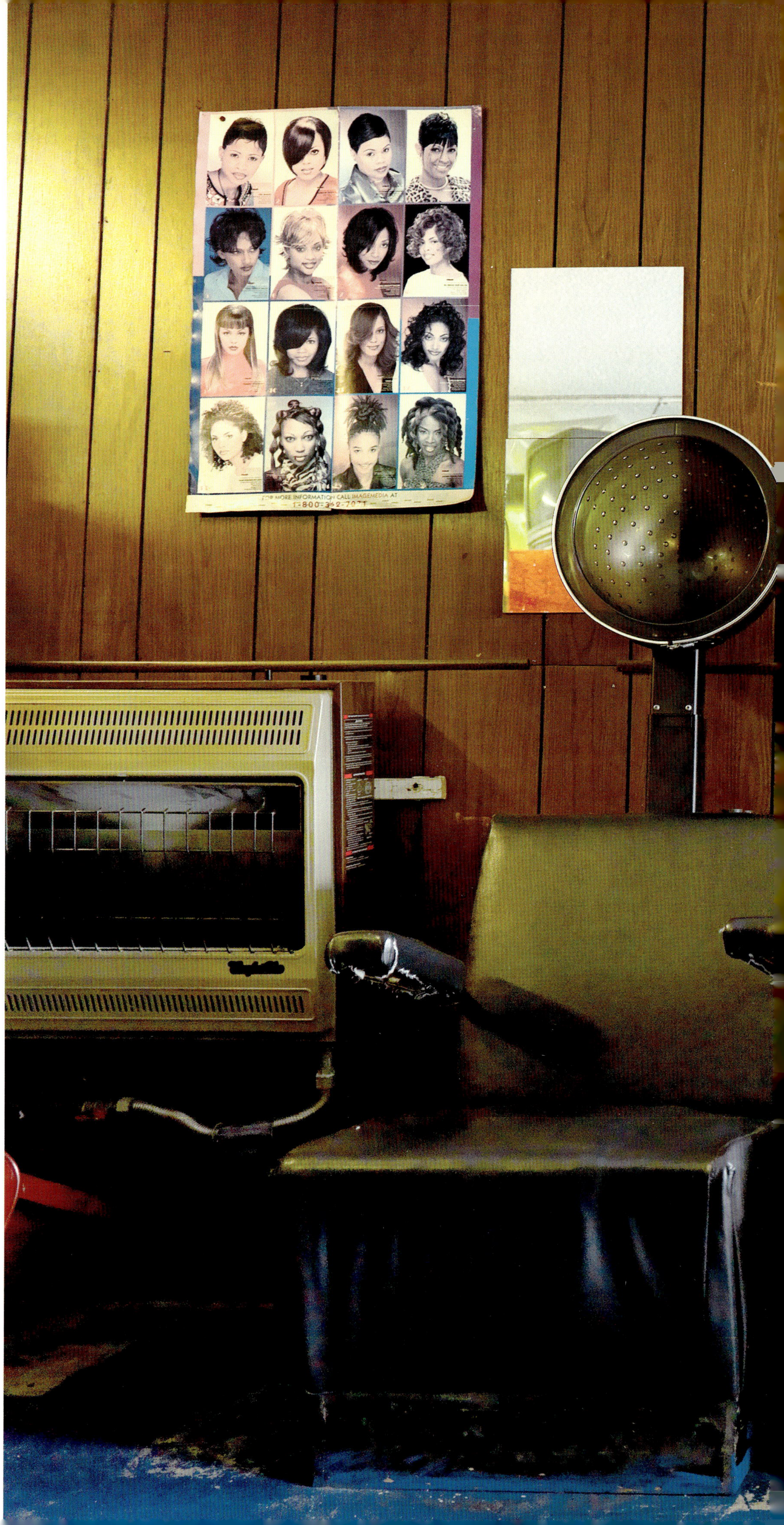


SHIRLEY'S BEAUTY SALON, MEMPHIS

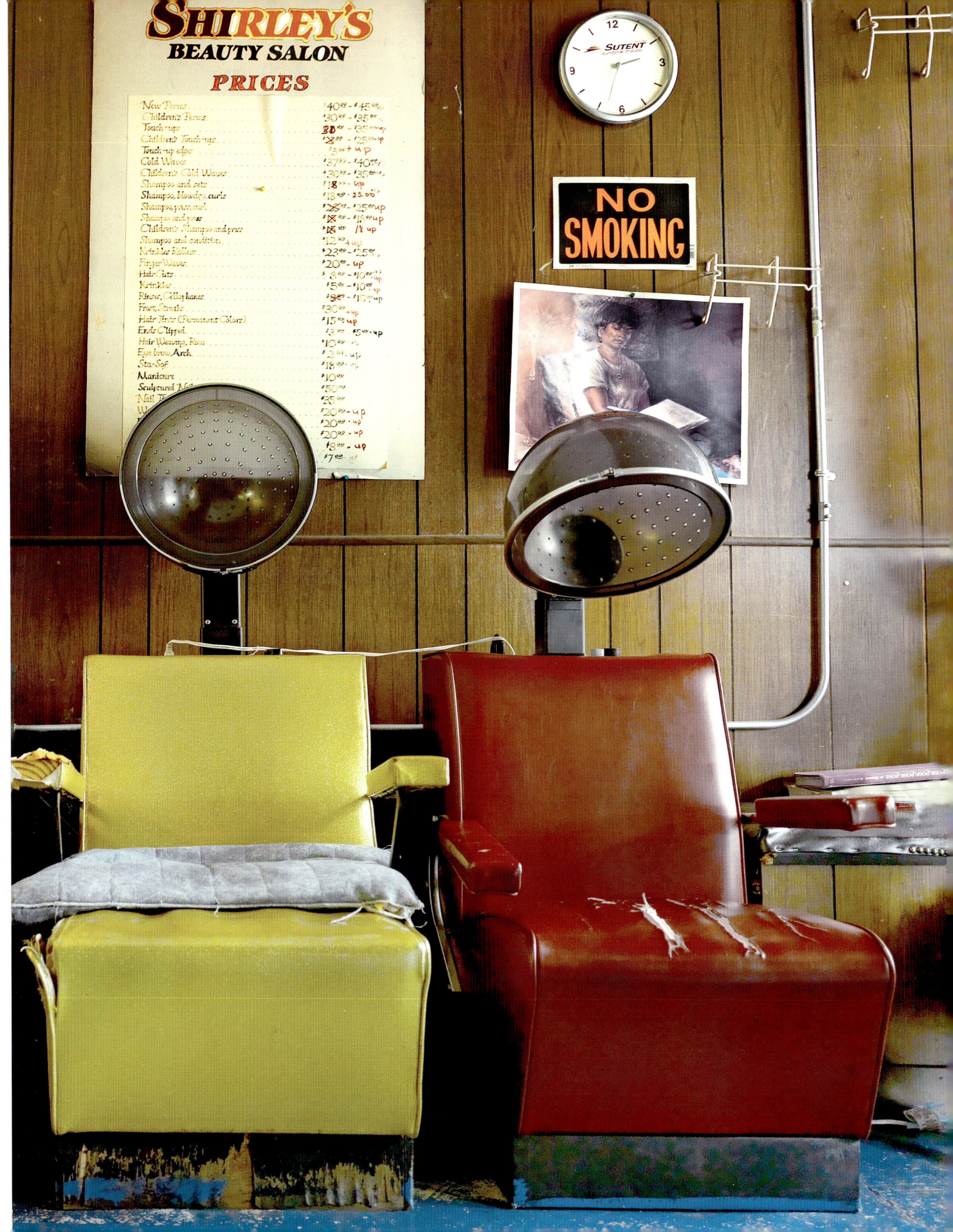
SHIRLEY'S
BEAUTY SALON
PRICES
New Perms $40.00 - $45.00
Children's Perms $30.00 - $35.00
Touch-ups $35.00 up
Children's Touch-ups $25.00 up
Touch-up edges $3.00 + up
Cold Waves $37.00 - $40.00
Children's Cold Waves $30.00 - $35.00
Shampoo and sets $18.00 + up
Shampoo, blowdry, curls $18.00 - 25.00
Shampoo, press, curl $25.00 up
Shampoo and press $18.00 up
Children's Shampoo and press 18 up
Shampoo and condition $12.00 + up
Krinkles Rollers $23.00 - $25.00
Finger Waves $20.00 - up
Hair Cuts $8.00 - $10.00 up
Krinkles $5.00 - $10.00 up
Rinses, Cellophanes $10.00 up
Frost, Streaks $30.00 + up
Hair Tints (Permanent Colors) $15.00 up
Ends Clipped $5.00 - up
Hair Weaving, Row $10.00
Eye brow Arch $2.00 up
Sta-Sof $18.00
Manicure $10.00
$50.00
$35.00
$20.00 - up
$20.00 - up
$20.00 - up
$8.00 - up
$7.00
NO SMOKING
12
3
6
9

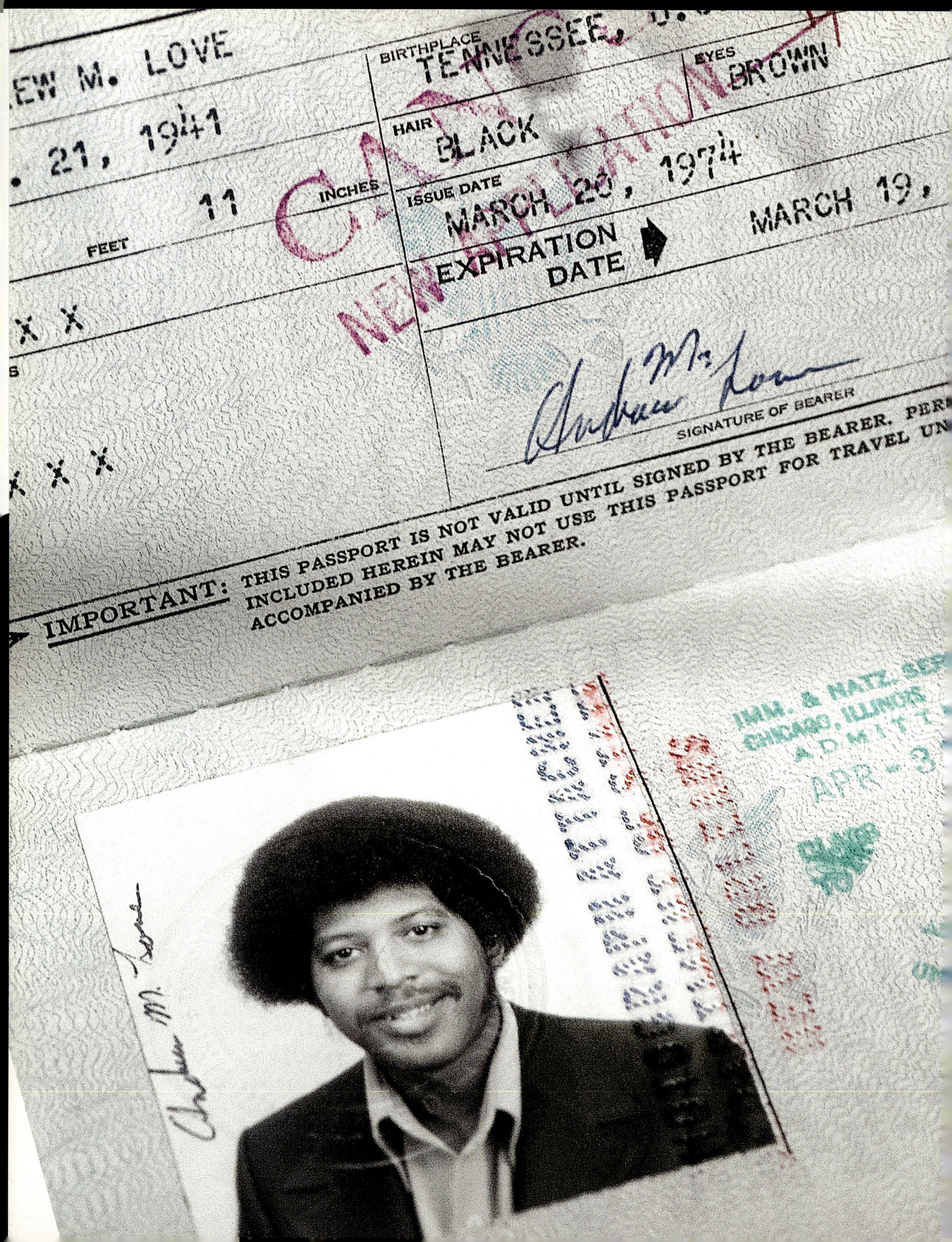

EW M. LOVE
BIRTHPLACE
TENNESSEE,
EYES
BROWN
. 21, 1941
HAIR
BLACK
INCHES
11
FEET
ISSUE DATE
MARCH 20, 1974
MARCH 19,
EXPIRATION DATE
CANCELLED
NEW APPLICATION
SIGNATURE OF BEARER
IMPORTANT: THIS PASSPORT IS NOT VALID UNTIL SIGNED BY THE BEARER. PER
INCLUDED HEREIN MAY NOT USE THIS PASSPORT FOR TRAVEL UN
ACCOMPANIED BY THE BEARER.
IMM. & NATZ. SER
CHICAGO, ILLINOIS
ADMITT
APR-3

ANDREW LOVE

BOBBY RUSH

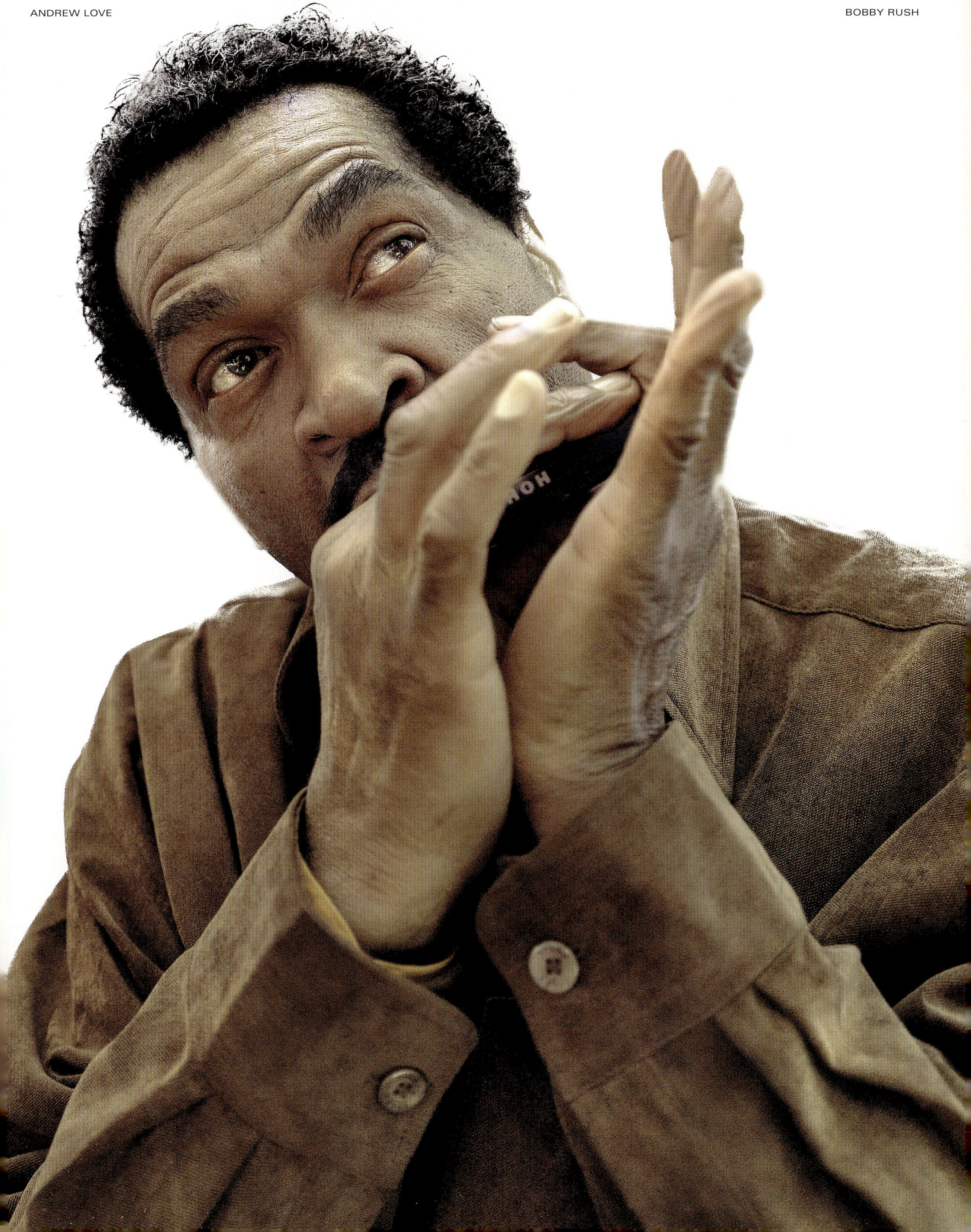

For So Many of Us, Stax
was the beginning of "Creation",
and there is no end of such
Music Forever, Rita Coolidge

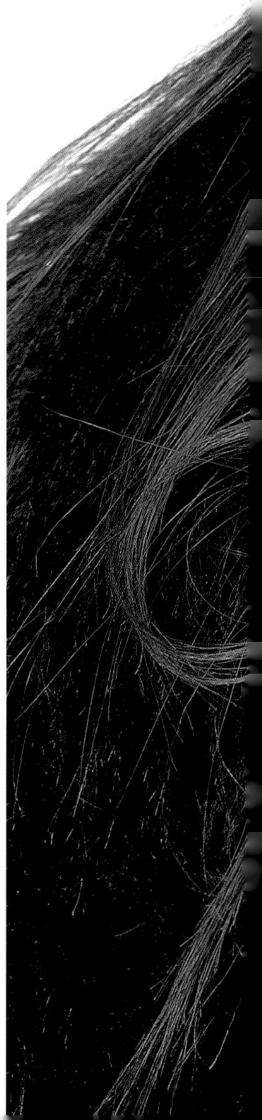

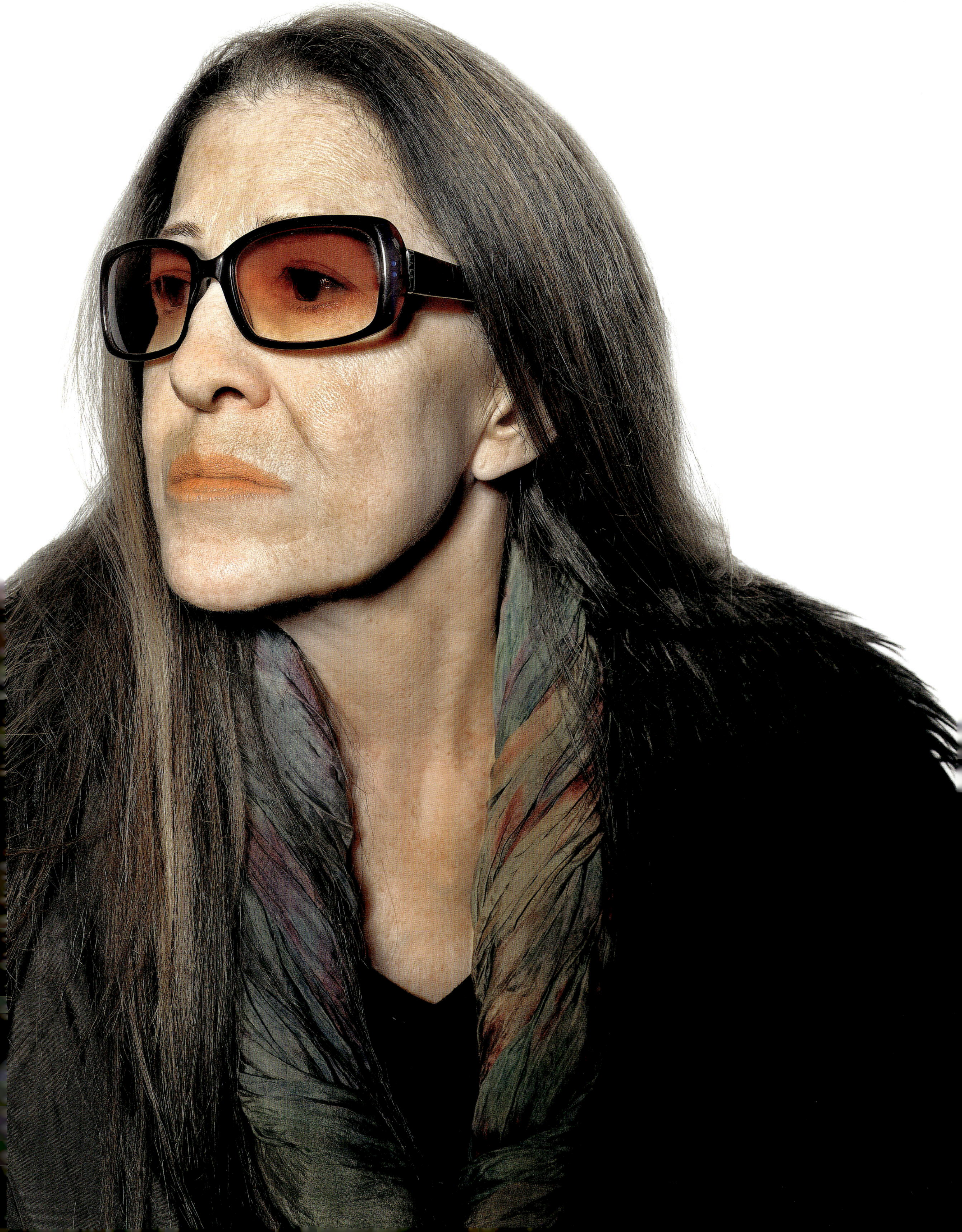

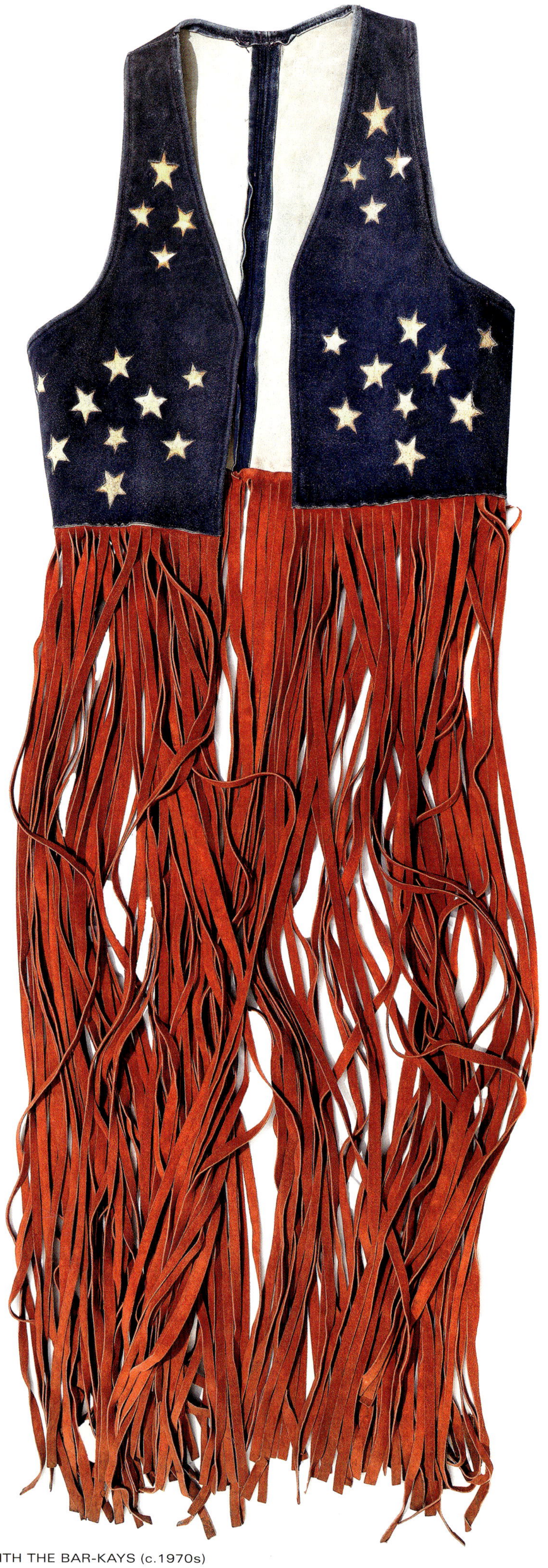

LARRY DODSON JR.'S STAGE VEST WORN WITH THE BAR-KAYS (c.1970s)

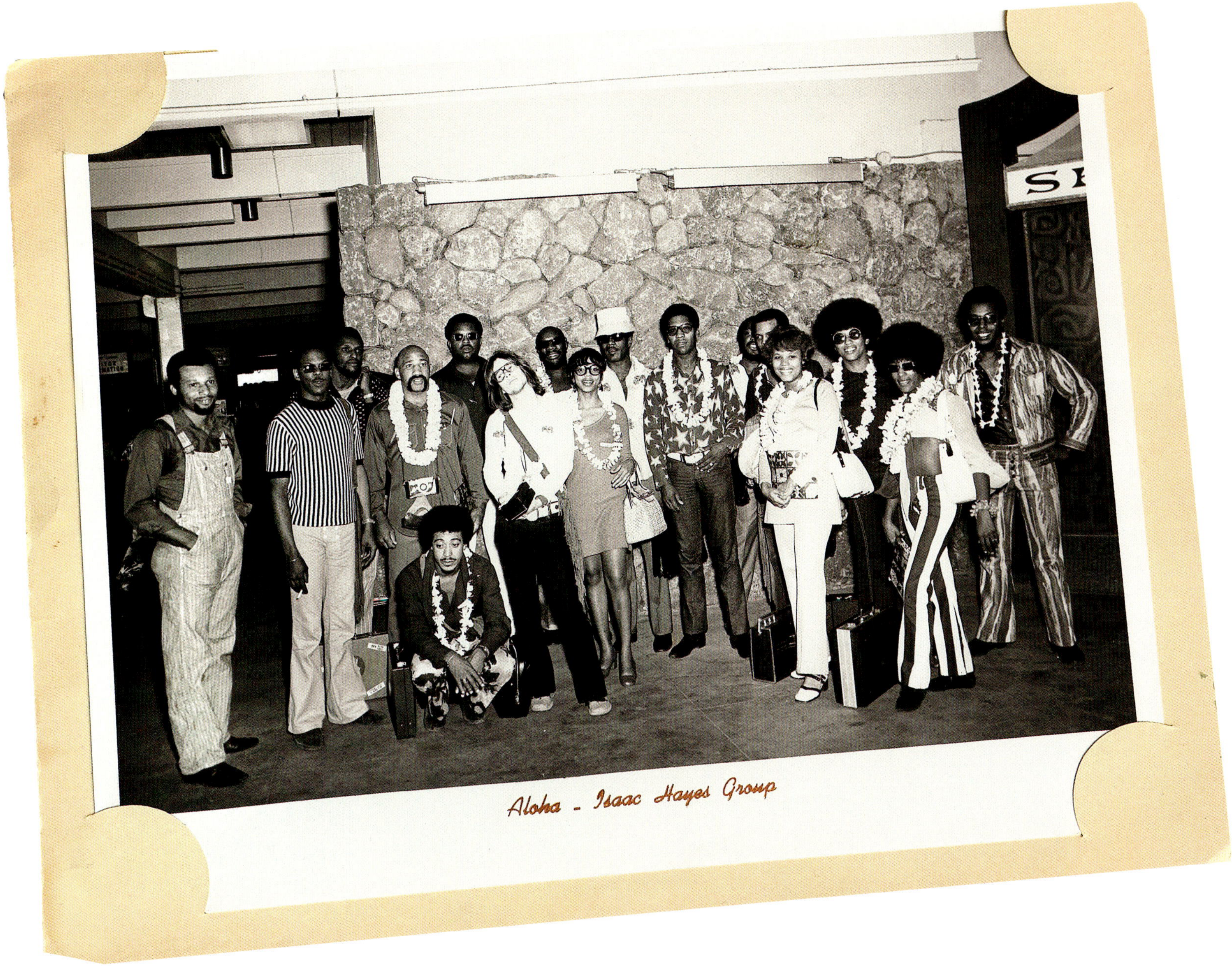




ISAAC HAYES'S BAND AND ENTOURAGE AT HAWAII AIRPORT (c.1970s)

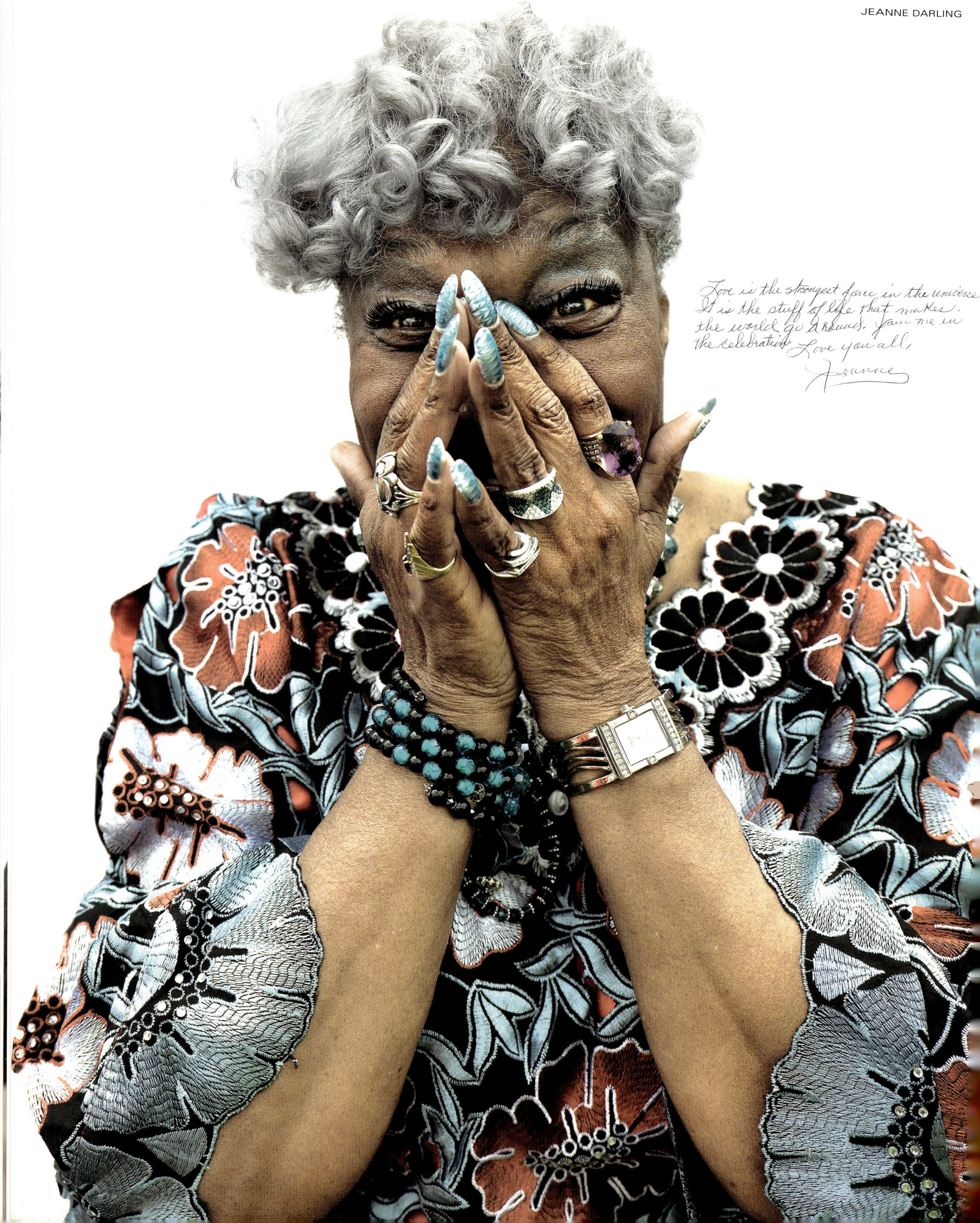

Love is the strongest force in the universe
It is the stuff of life that makes.
the world go around. Join me in
the celebration. Love you all,
Jeanne

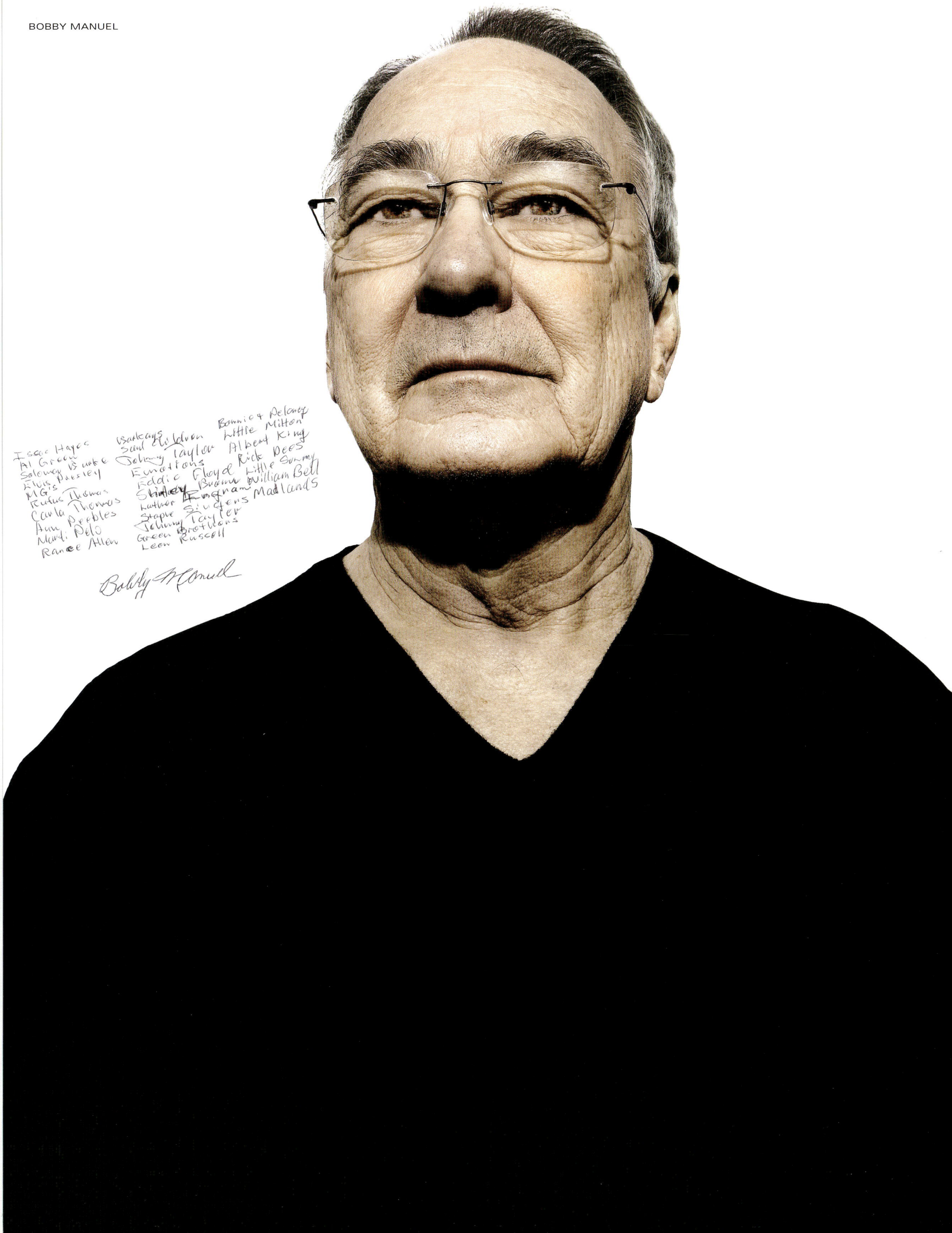
Isaac Hayes
Al Green
Elvis Presley
MG's
Rufus Thomas
Carla Thomas
Ann Peebles
Rance Allen
Barkays
Johnny Taylor
Emotions
Eddie Floyd
Luther Ingram
Staple Singers
Johnny Taylor
Leon Russell
Bonnie & Delaney
Little Milton
Albert King
Rick Dees
William Bell
Madlands

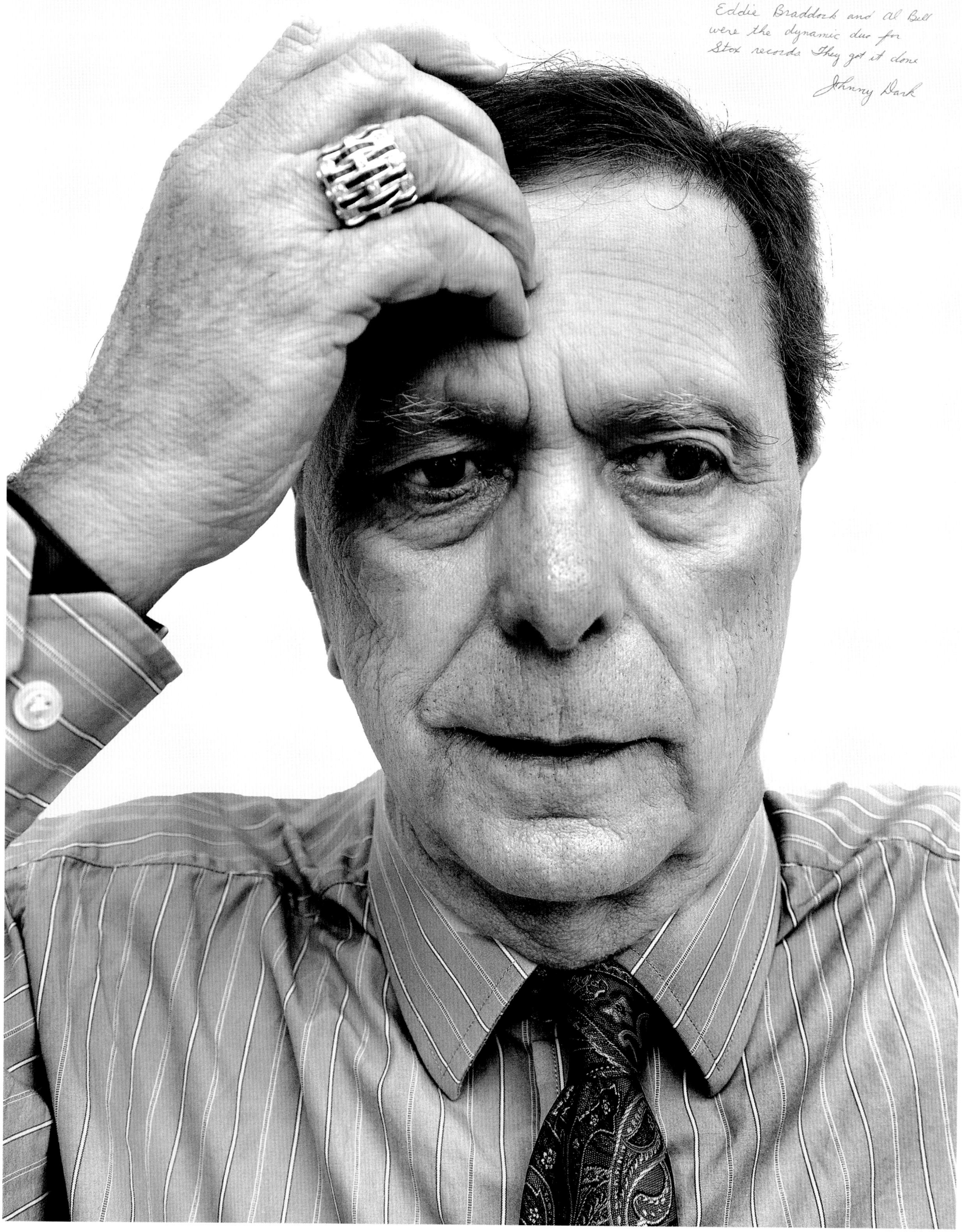
Eddie Braddock and Al Bell
were the dynamic duo for
Stax records They got it done
Johnny Dark

"SUNSHINE" SONNY PAYNE

Pass the Biscuits 'Tis King Biscuit time
over KFFA. Really no Kiddin'
Sunshine Sonny Payne

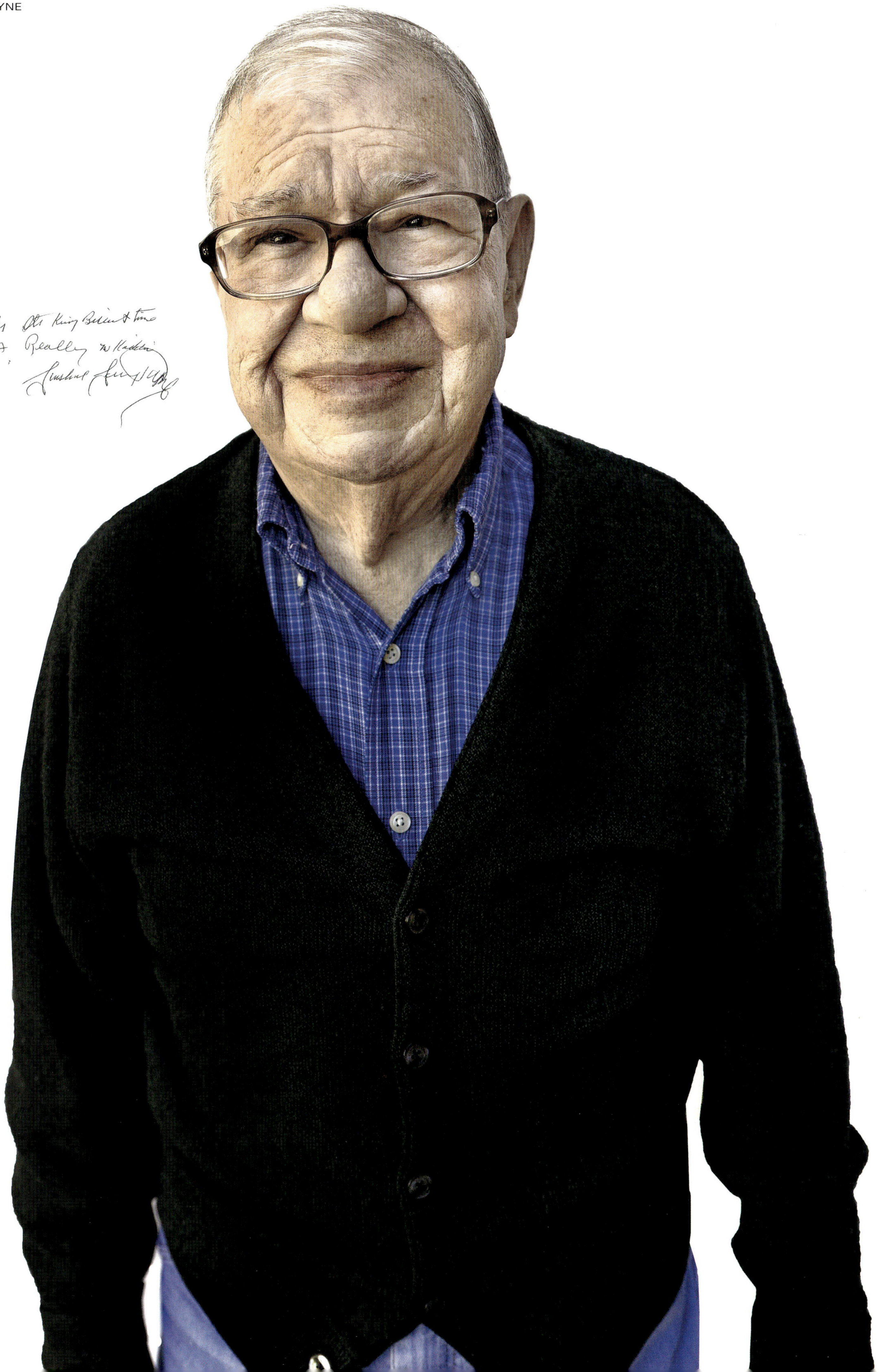

I staring playing at the age of 14 with Carl Perkins
have played with many different artist.
I have written a book on my life. also had a
million seller record for Stax Recording
Co. in 1961. So many songs So Little Time.
Music is my life

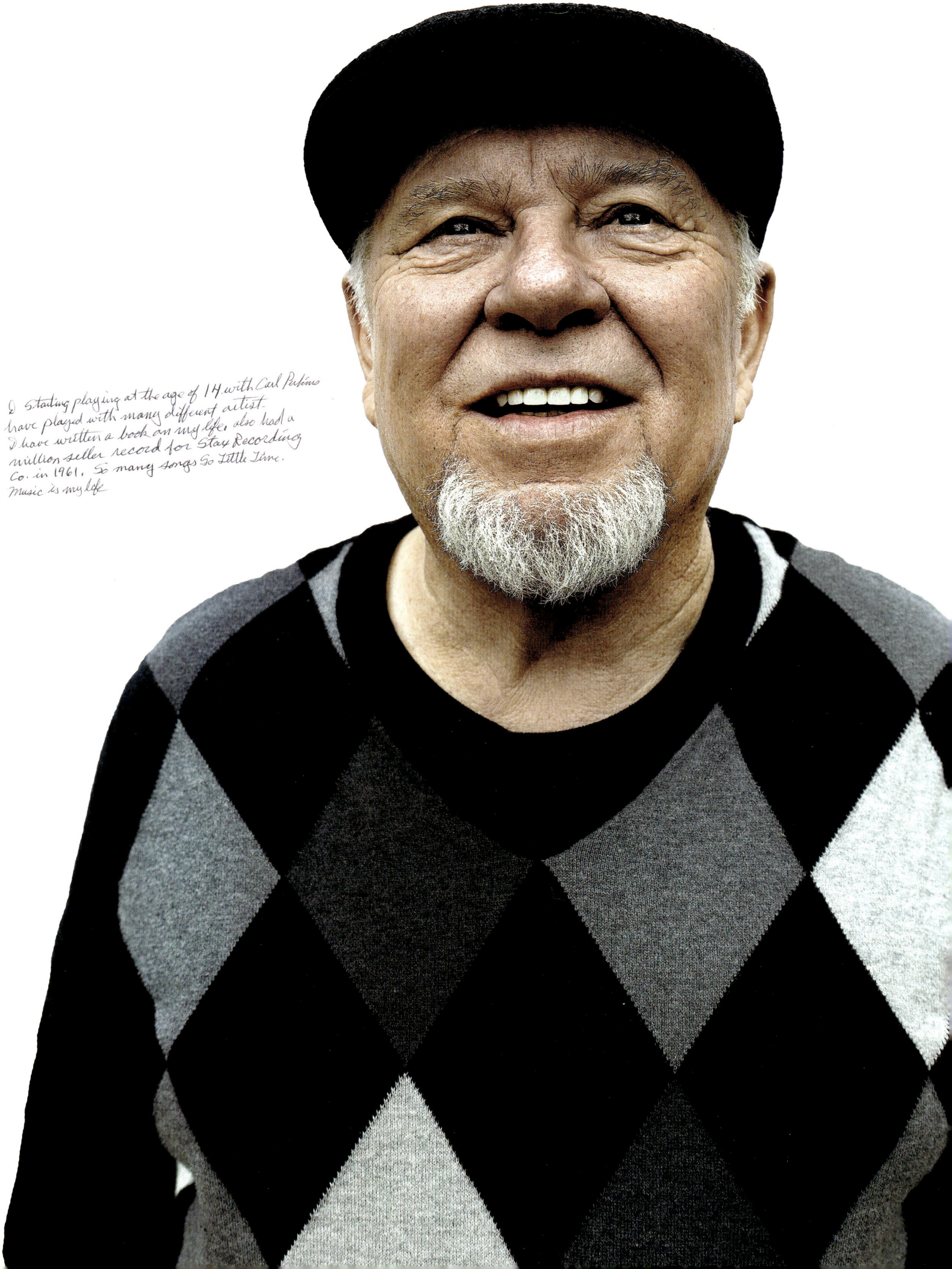

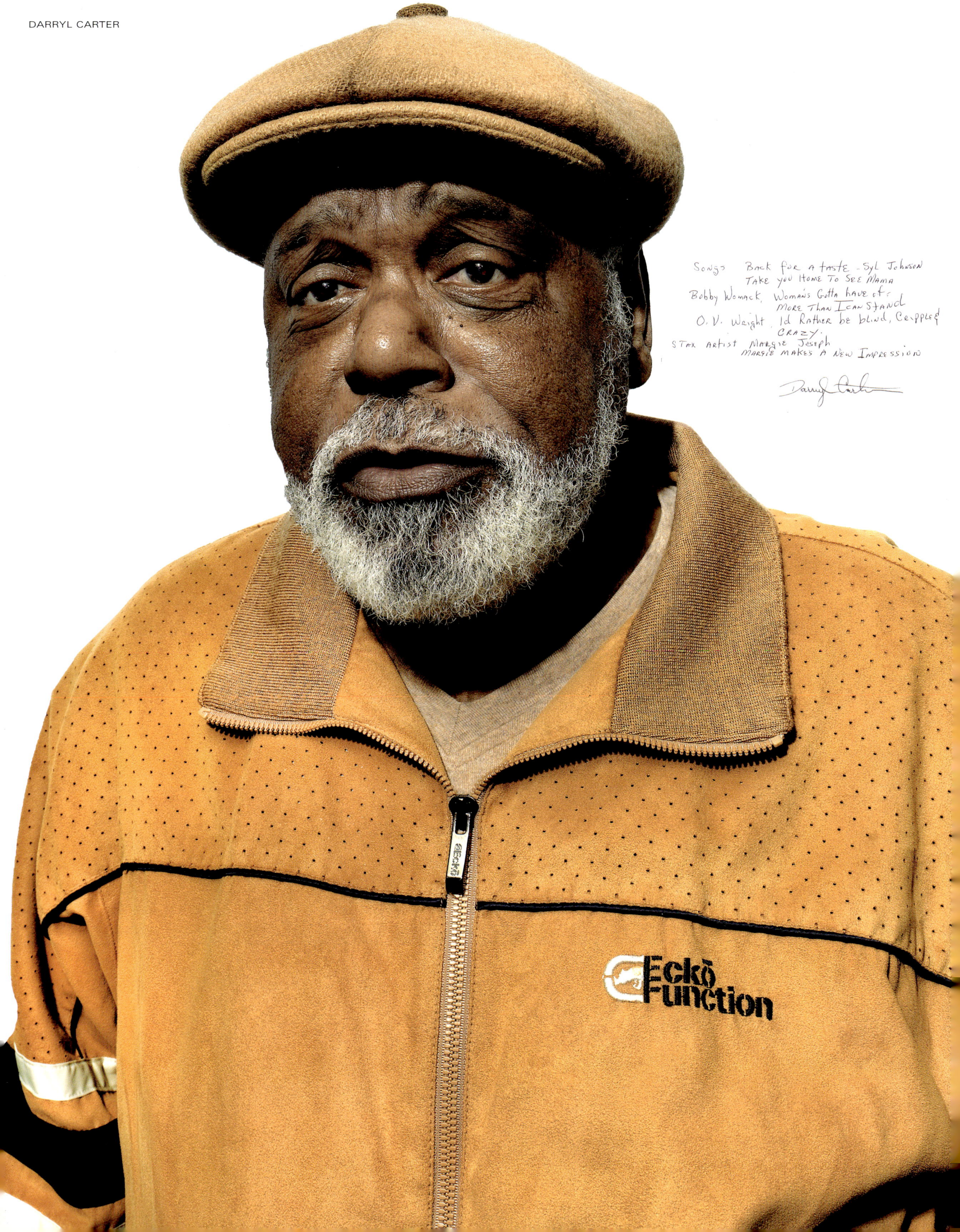


Songs Back for a taste - Syl Johnson
Take you Home To See Mama
Bobby Womack, Womans Gotta have it;
More Than I can Stand
O.V. Weight, Id Rather be blind, Crippled & Crazy.
Stax Artist Margie Joseph
Margie Makes A New Impression

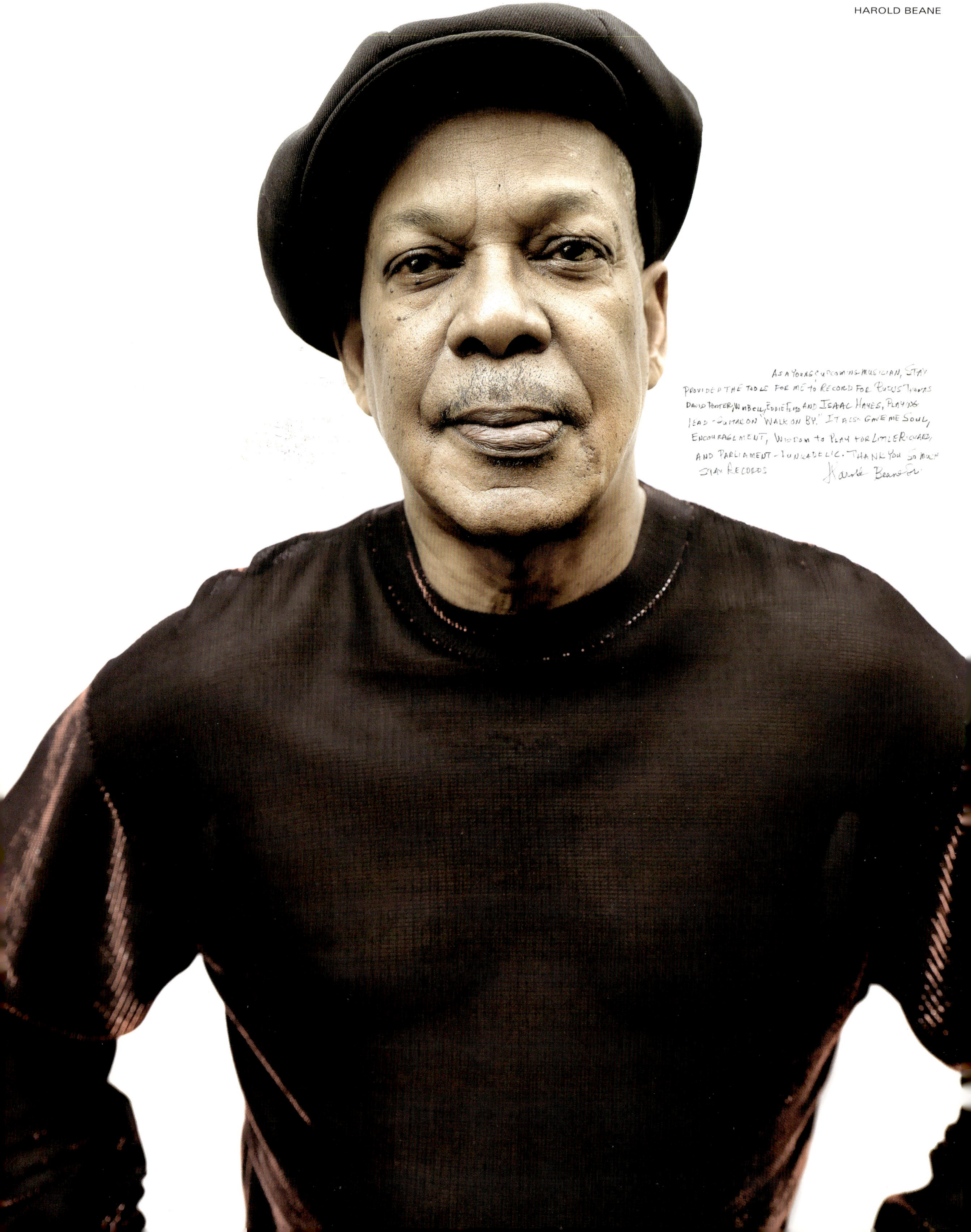
AS A YOUNG & UPCOMING MUSICIAN, STAX
PROVIDED THE TOOLS FOR ME TO RECORD FOR RUFUS THOMAS
DAVID PORTER, WM BELL, EDDIE FLOYD AND ISAAC HAYES, PLAYING
LEAD-GUITAR ON "WALK ON BY." IT ALSO GAVE ME SOUL,
ENCOURAGEMENT, WISDOM TO PLAY FOR LITTLE RICHARD,
AND PARLIAMENT-FUNKADELIC. THANK YOU SO MUCH
STAX RECORDS
Harold Beane Sr.

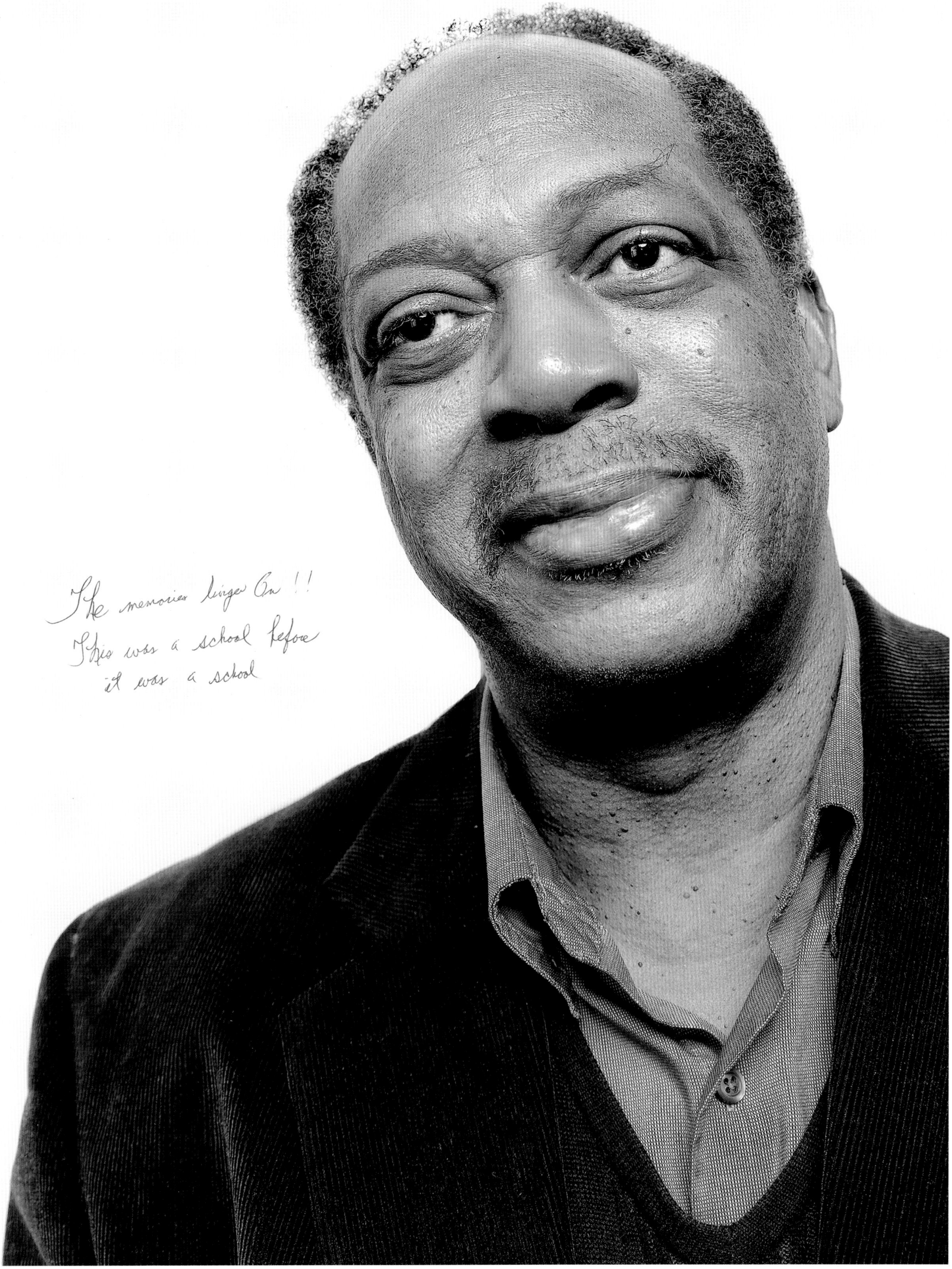
The memories linger On!!
This was a school before
it was a school

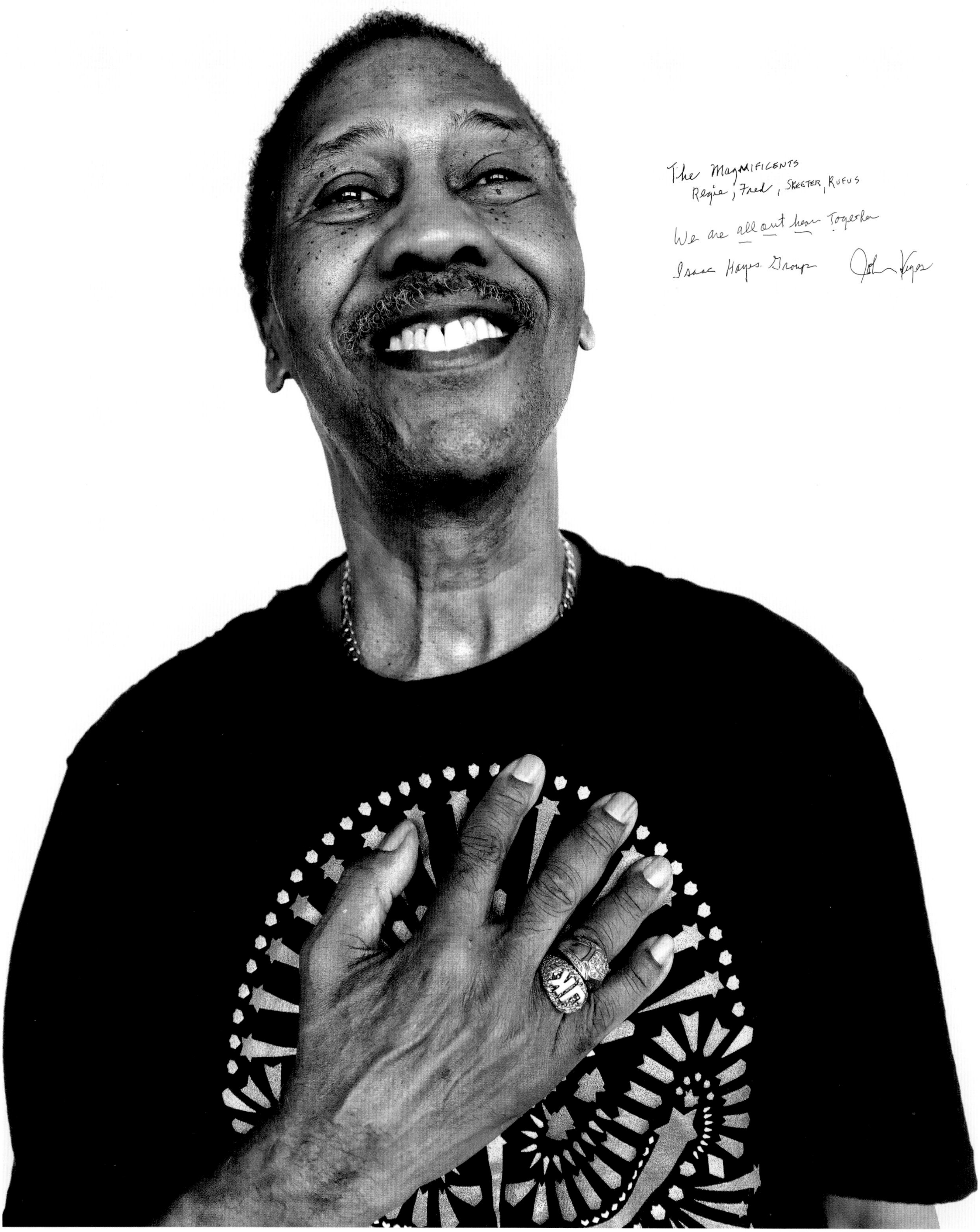
The MagMIFICENTS
Regie, Fred, SKEETER, RUFUS
We are all out hear Together
Isaac Hayes. Group
John Keyes

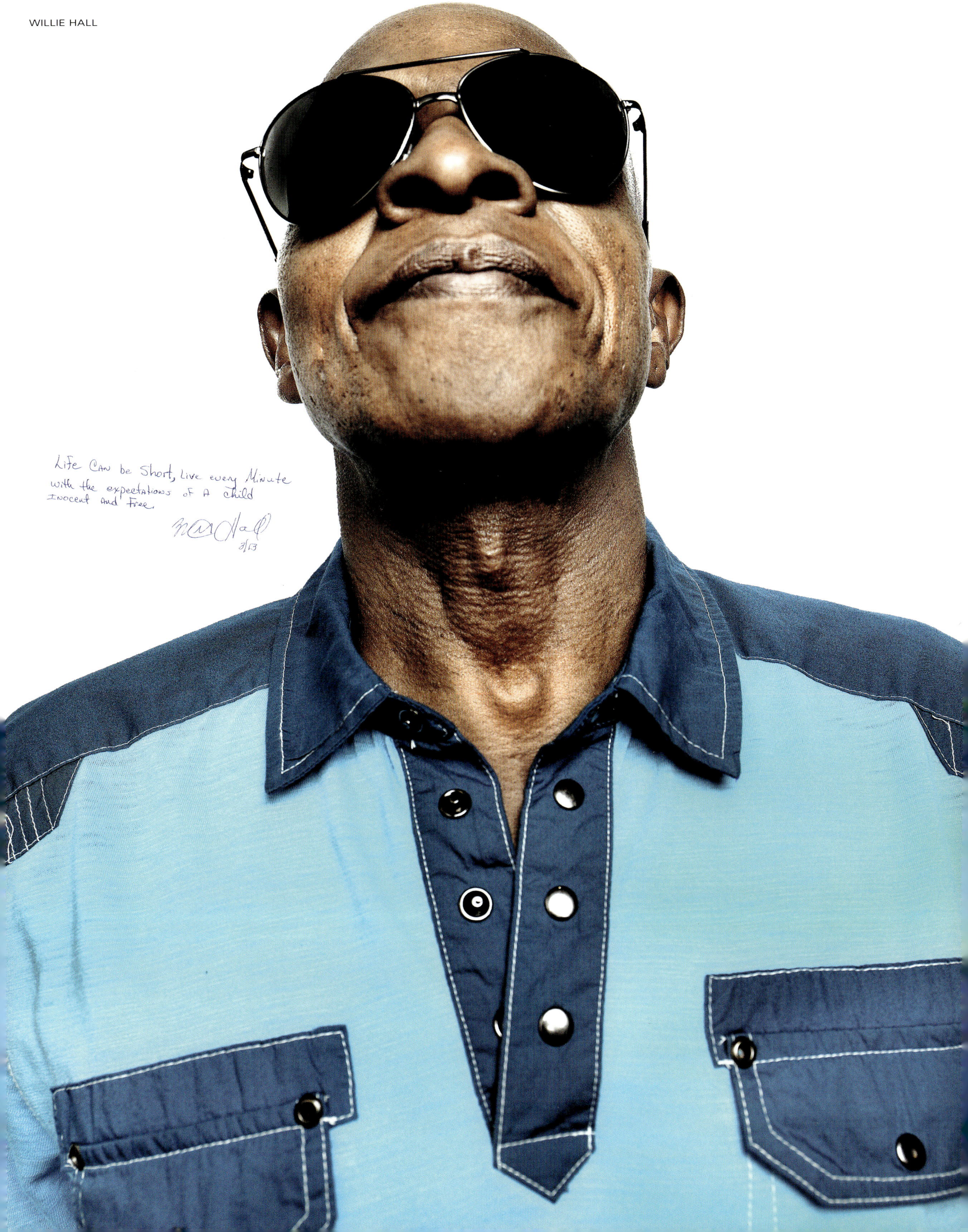
Life Can be Short, Live every Minute
with the expectations of A child
Inocent And Free.
8/13

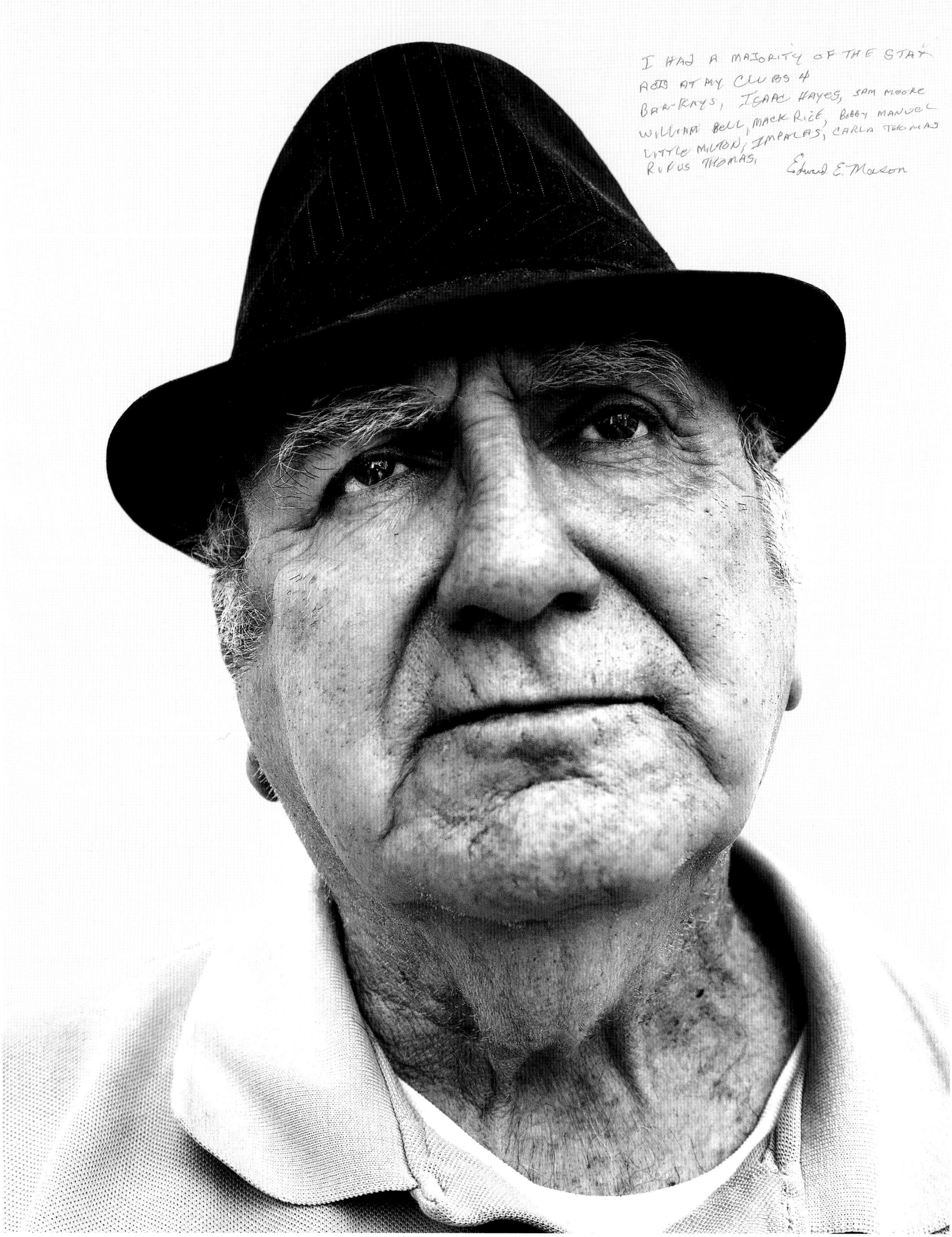
I HAD A MAJORITY OF THE STAX
ACTS AT MY CLUBS 4
BAR-KAYS, ISAAC HAYES, SAM MOORE
WILLIAM BELL, MACK RICE, BOBBY MANUEL
LITTLE MILTON, IMPALAS, CARLA THOMAS
RUFUS THOMAS,
Edward E. Mason

I am the Queen of Beale St. Been around the world
Seven Times. Closeup acroc. To Mr. B.B. King
done over 29 movies and memphis Is my
Home I Love It.

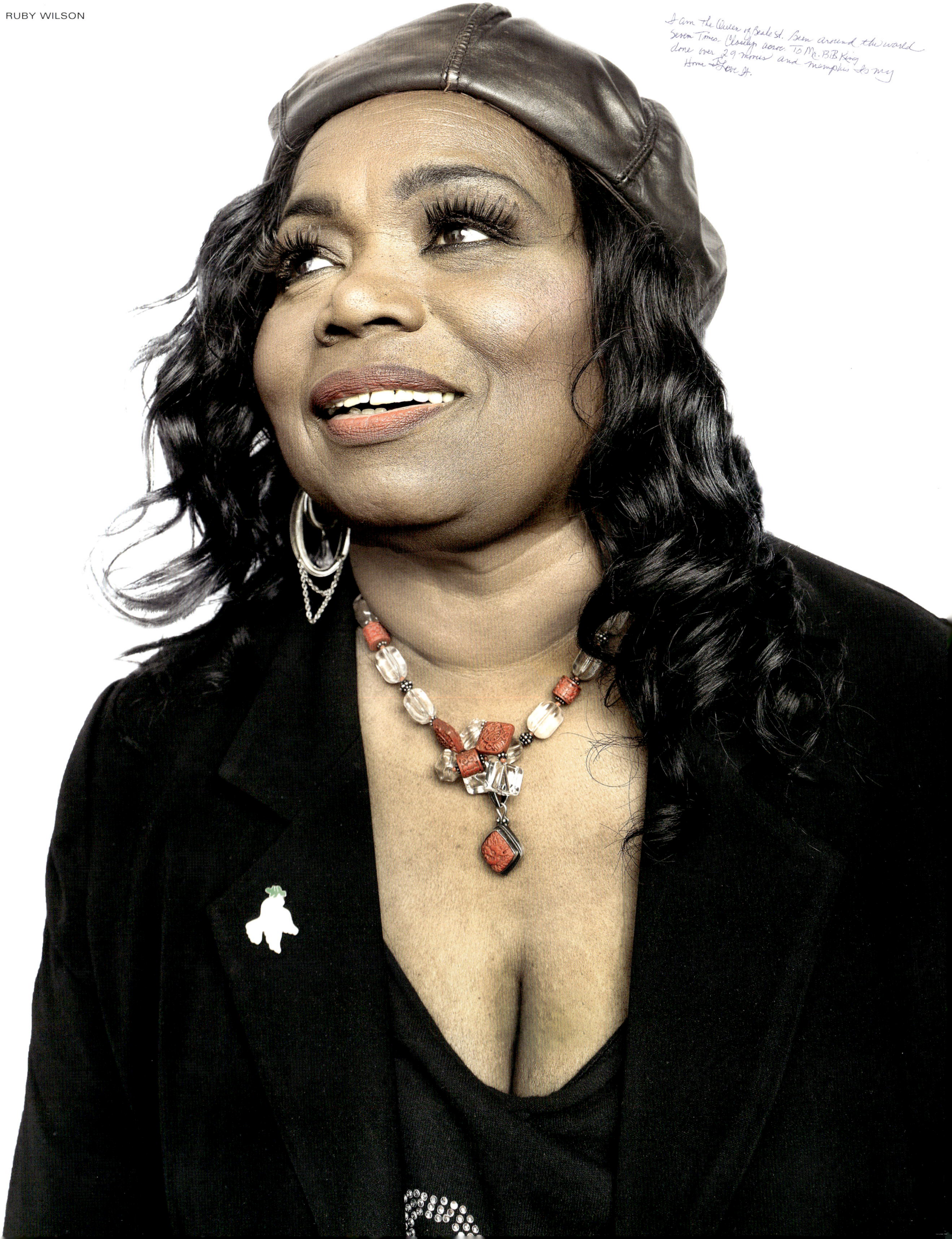

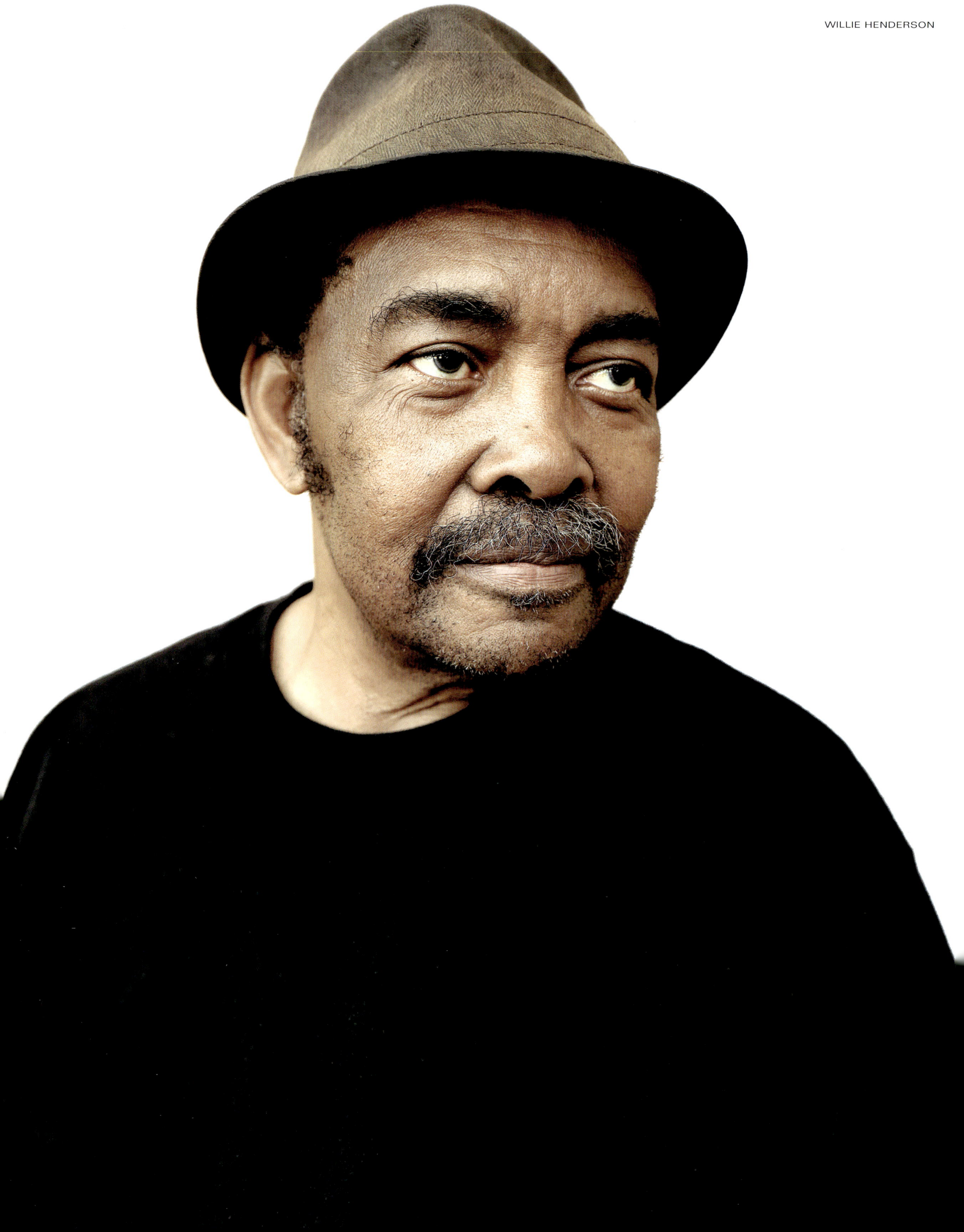

MARK BYRUM

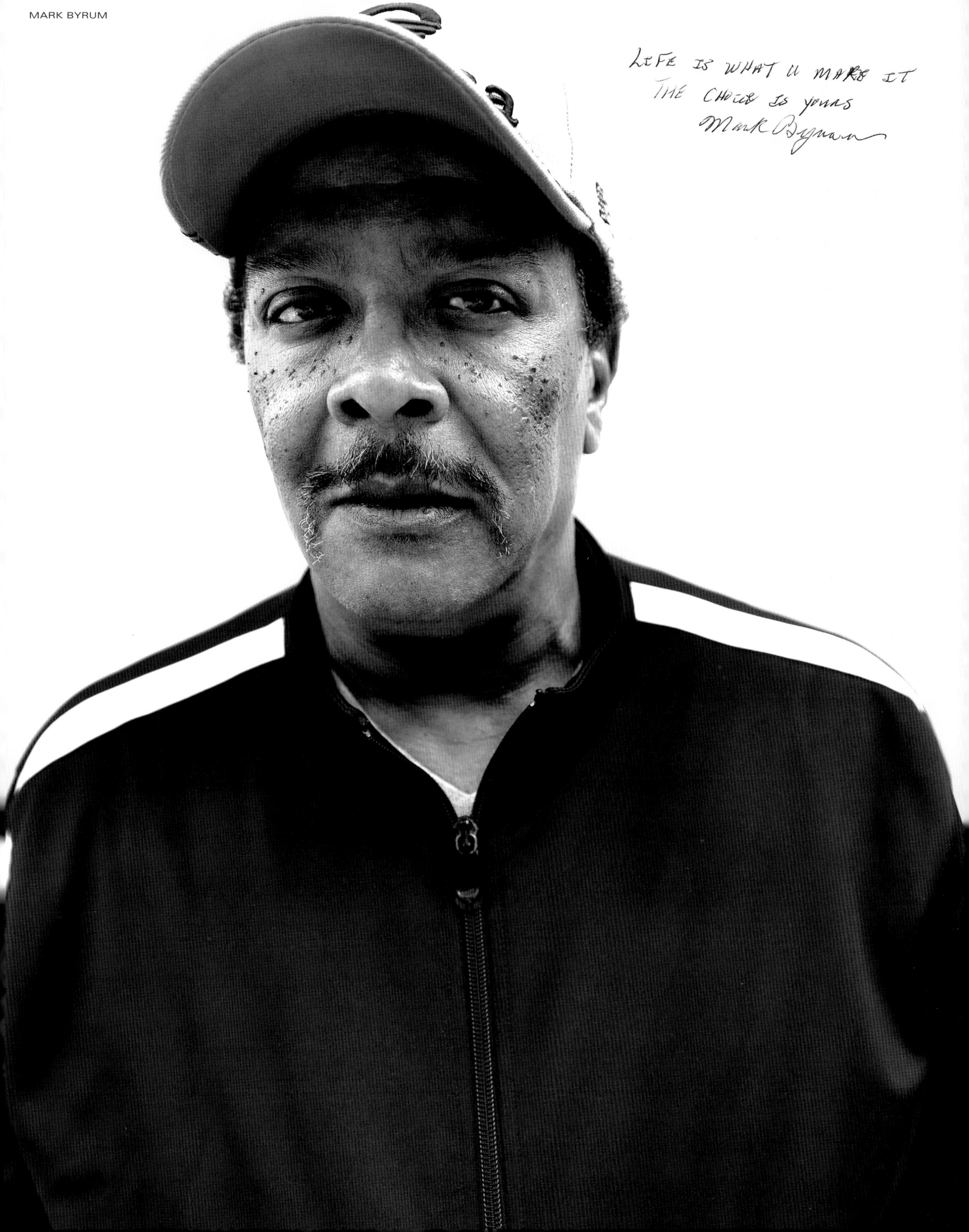

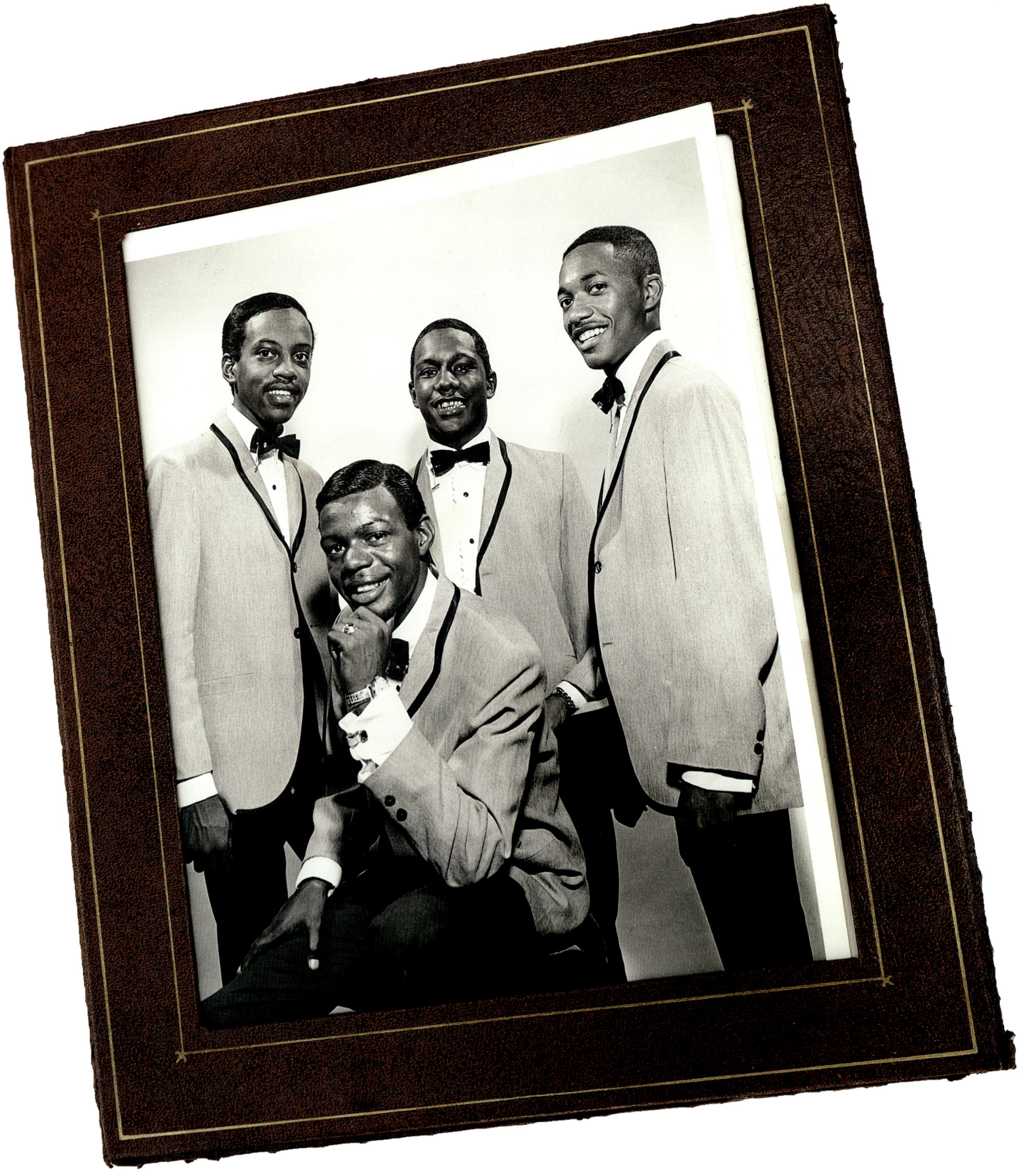

The Closest Star to the Earth
Shines the Brightest

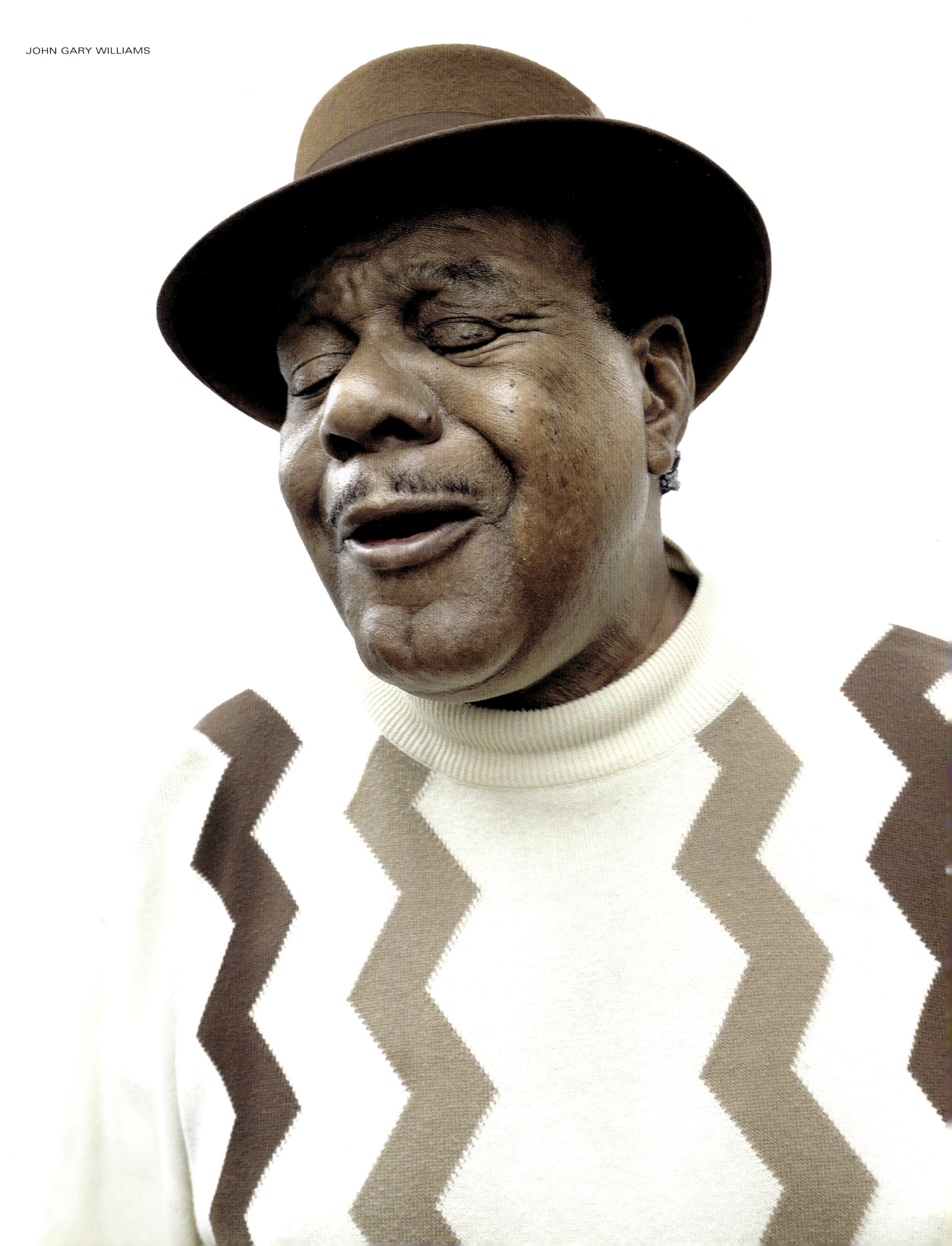

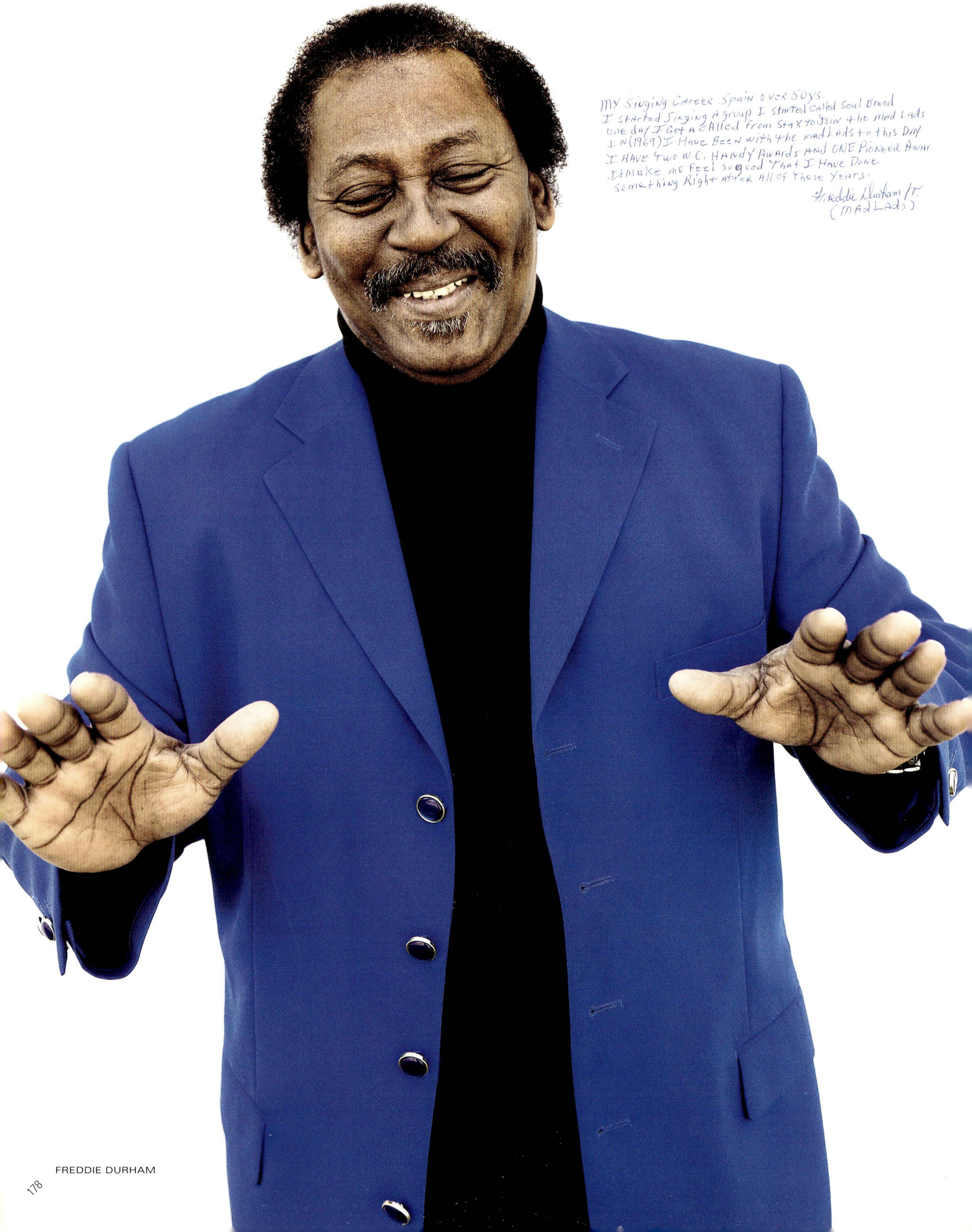


FREDDIE DURHAM

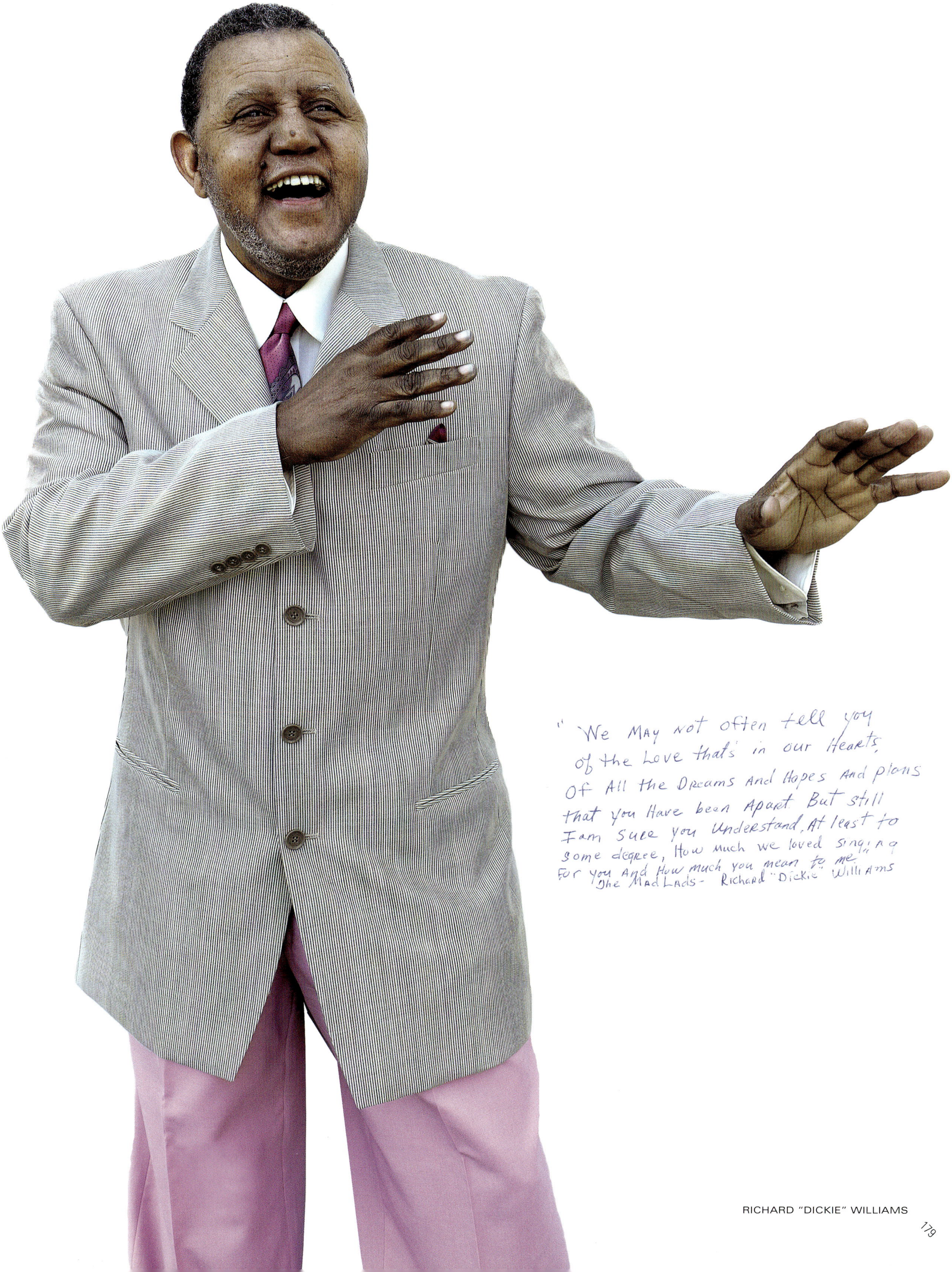

" We May not often tell you
of the Love that's in our Hearts,
Of All the Dreams And Hopes And plans
that you Have been Apart. But still
I am Sure you Understand, At least to
some degree, How much we loved singing
For you And How much you mean to me."
The Mad Lads - Richard "Dickie" Williams

RICHARD "DICKIE" WILLIAMS

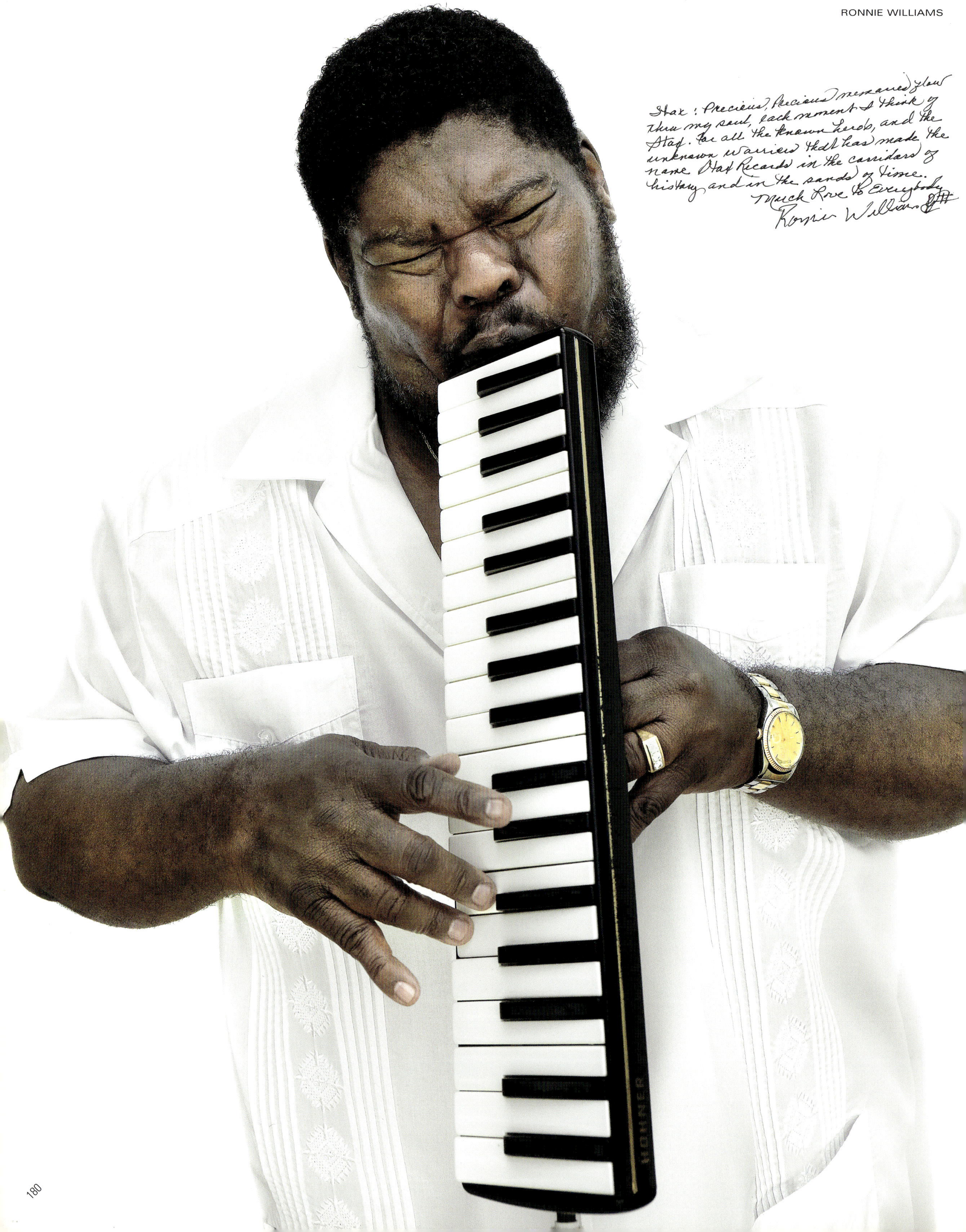


Stax: Precious, Precious memories flow
thru my soul, each moment I think of
Stax. For all the known heros, and the
unknown warriors that has made the
name Stax Records in the corridors of
history and in the sands of time.
Much Love to Everybody
Ronnie Williams

I Tried workin' for a living,
It didn't work out for me.. But I'm not
a strange to it....All you gotta do
is Do it......
Praise God.....
Sam The Sham (?)

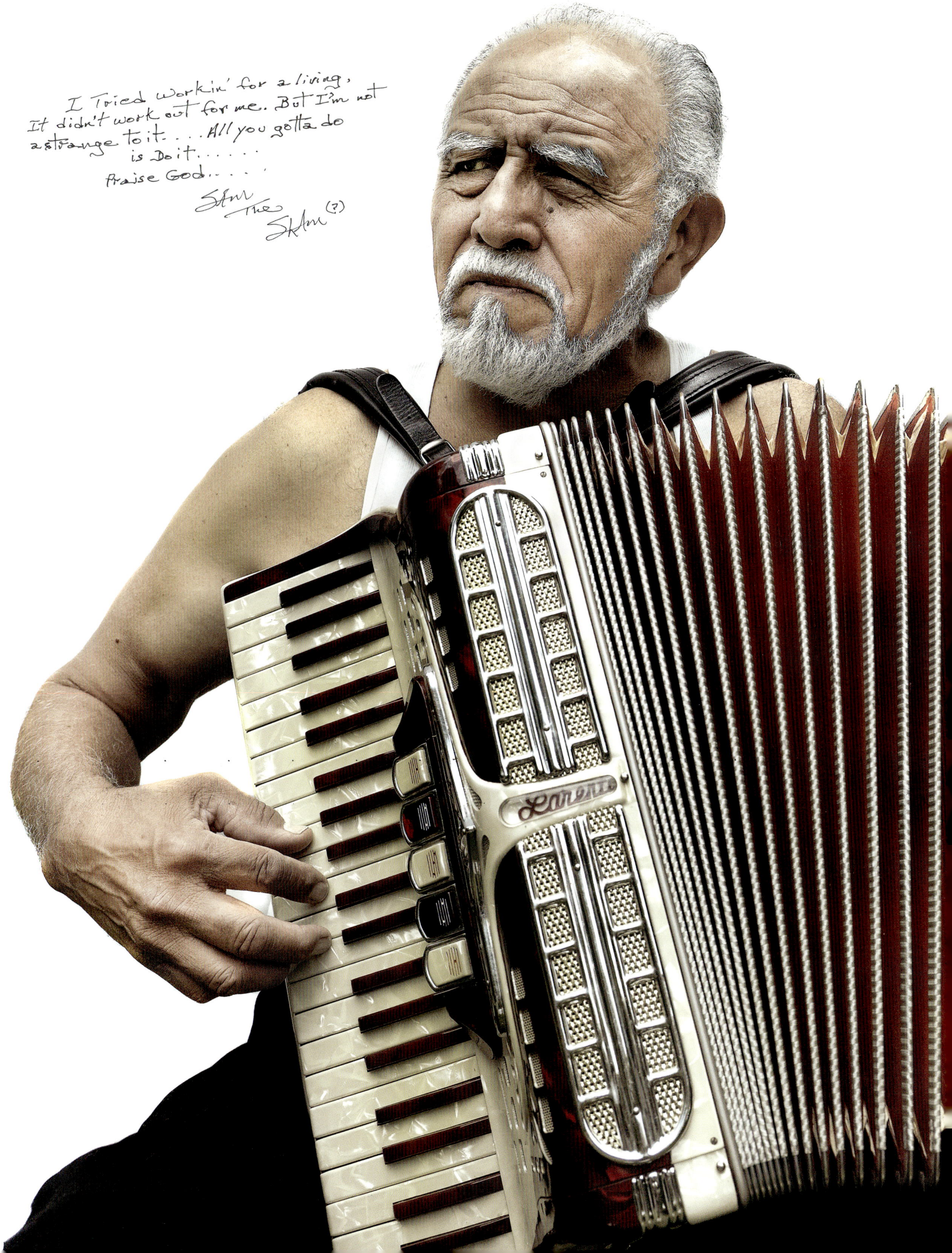

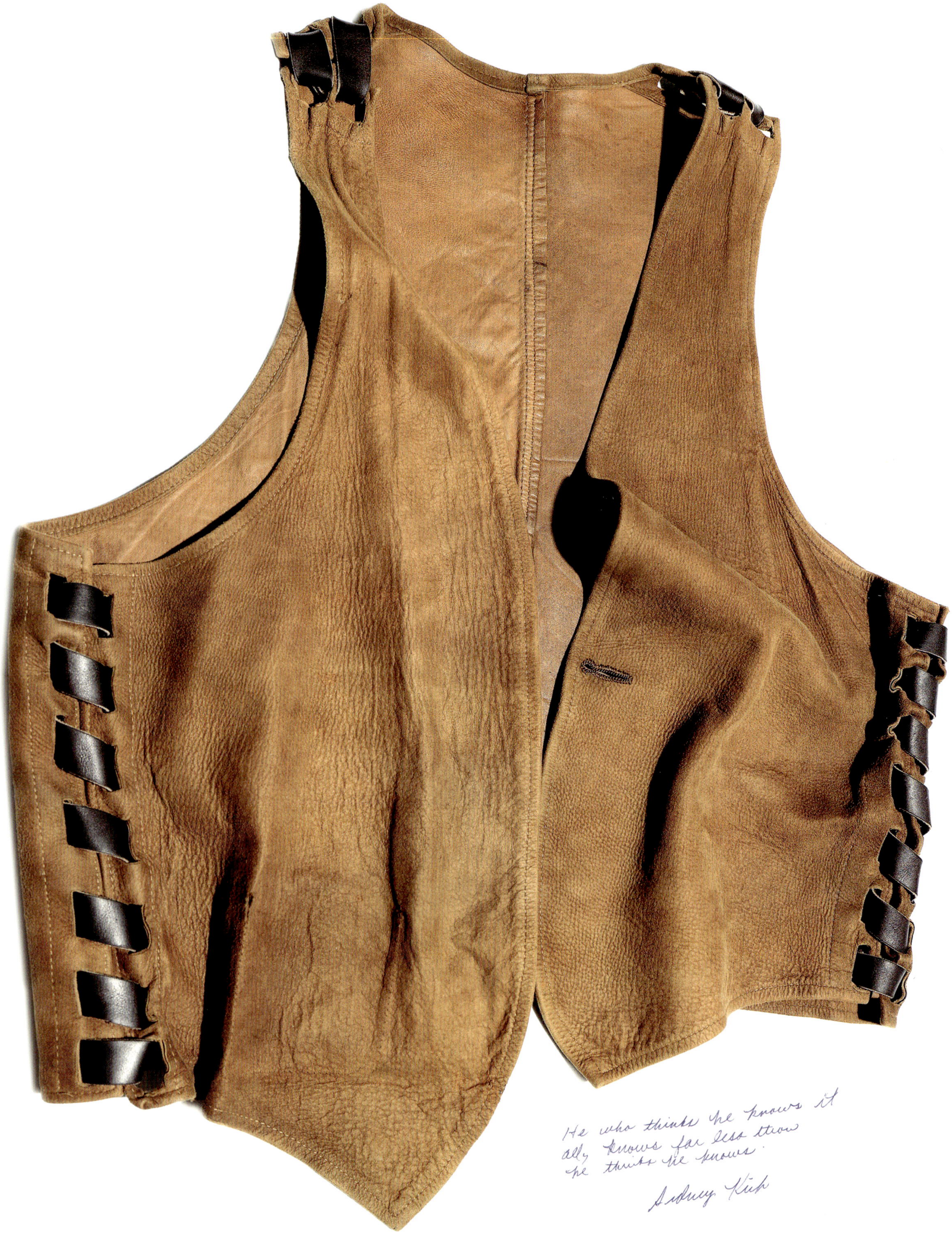


LUTHER INGRAM'S STAGE VEST (c.1970s)

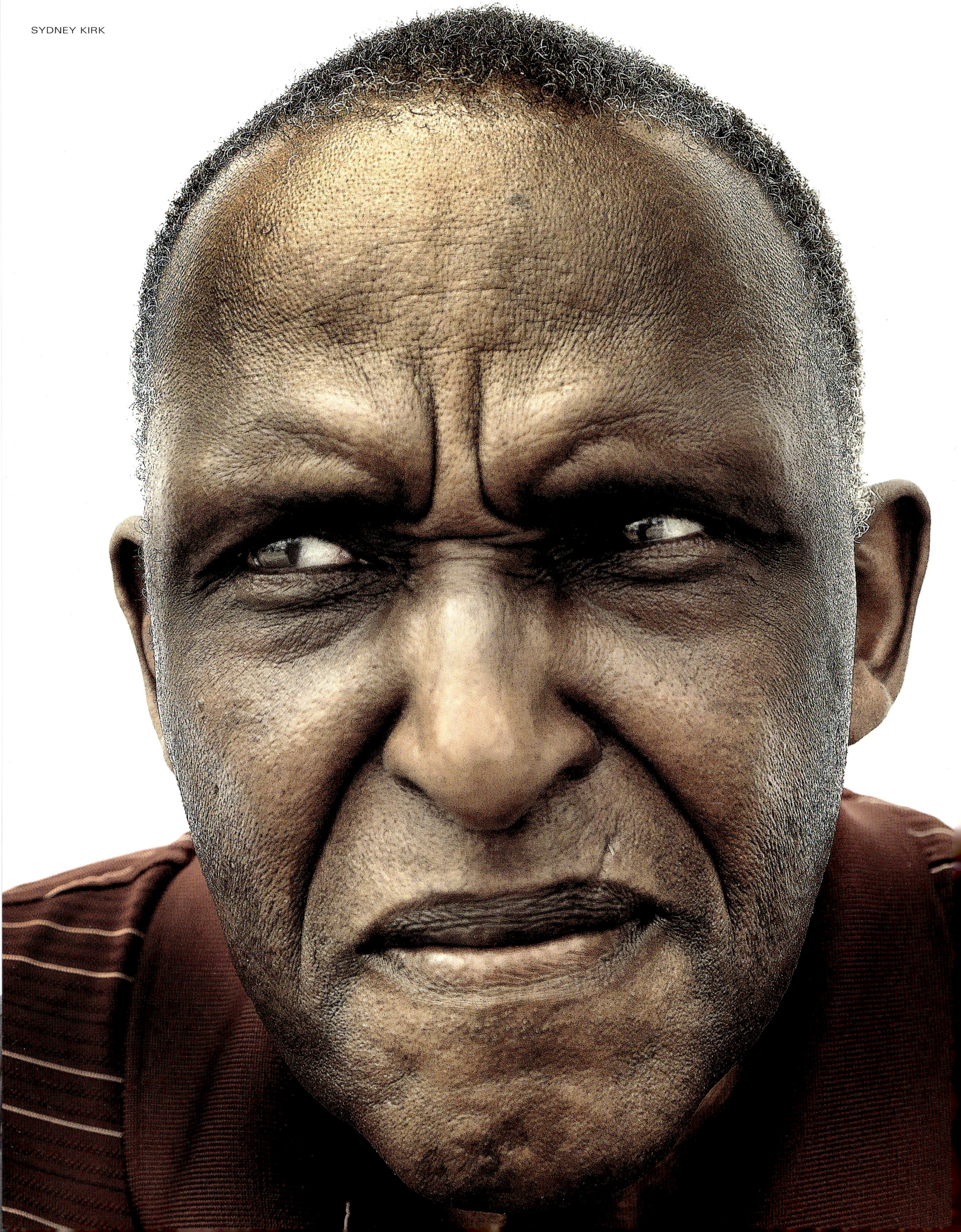

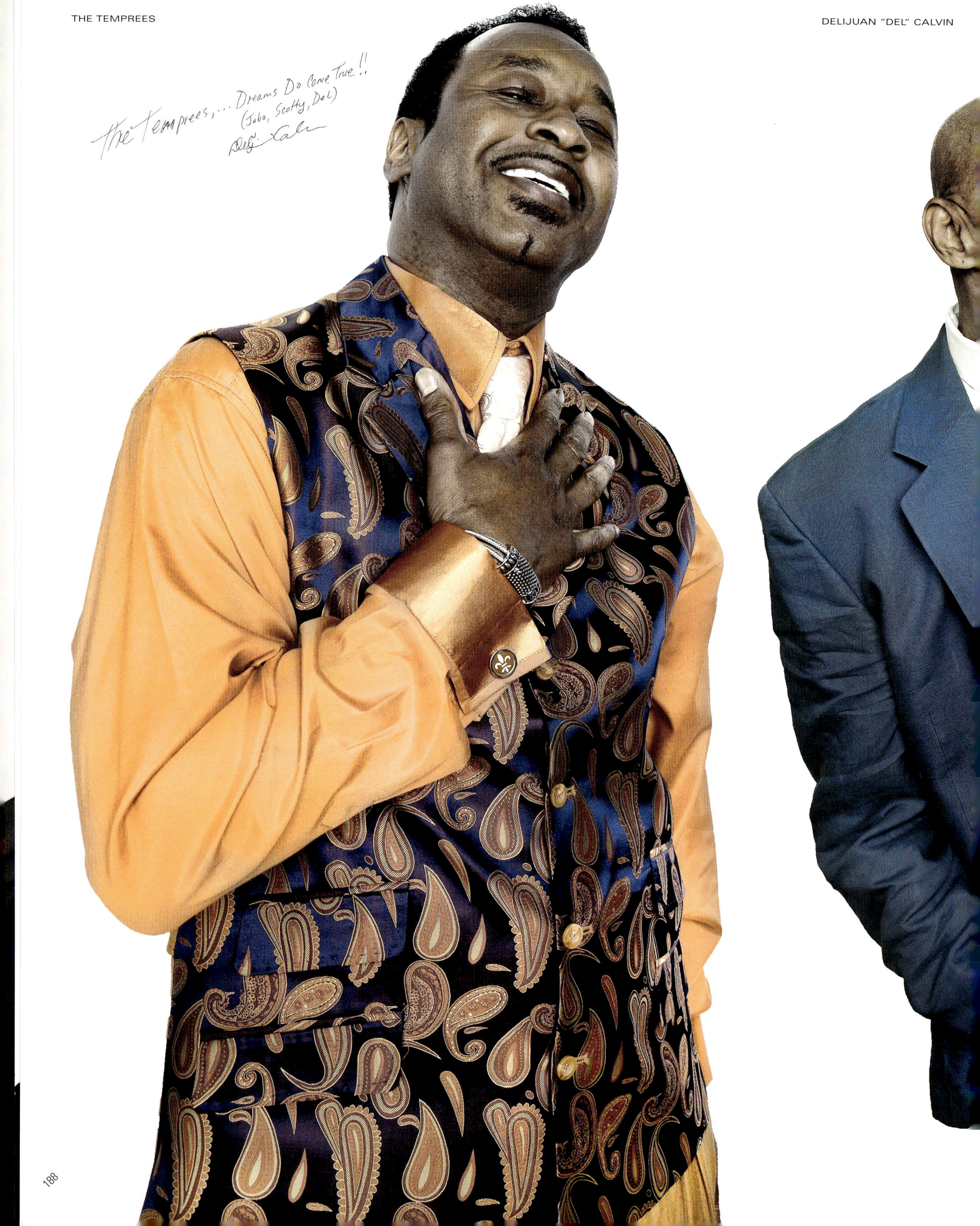
The Temprees,... Dreams Do Come True!!
(Jabo, Scotty, Del)

From the age of seven I began to sing in Jr high through High school from one group to the next now with the Tempress.

Solomon E Young

Been a member of the Tempreer for 40 yrs (since its inception) a school teacher, has my own interior decorating firm, and a professional entertainer for the Tempreer.

Harold Scott

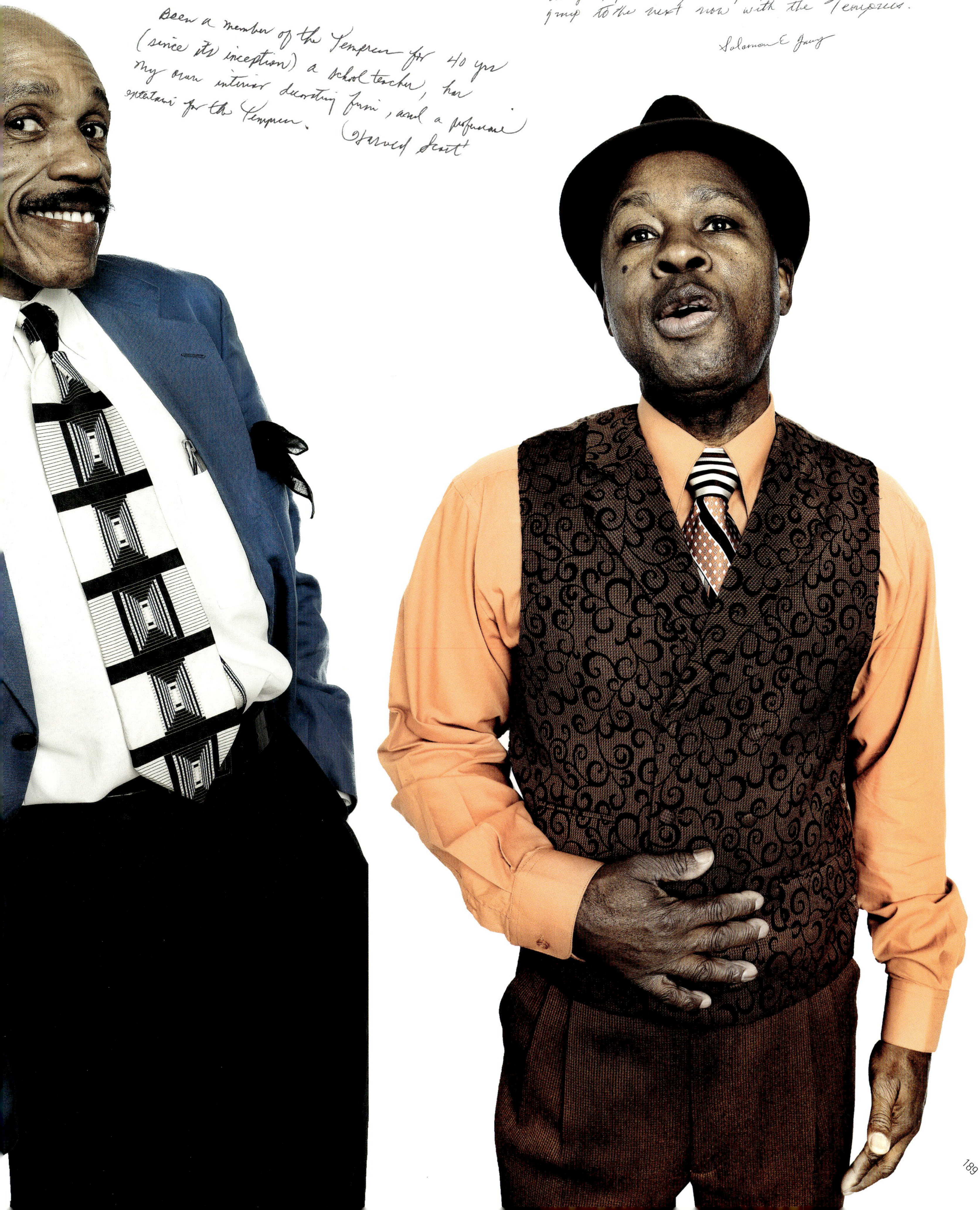

Music has been one of my Most Prize Possessions - it has been most Profittable for me & Family

Emerson R. Able

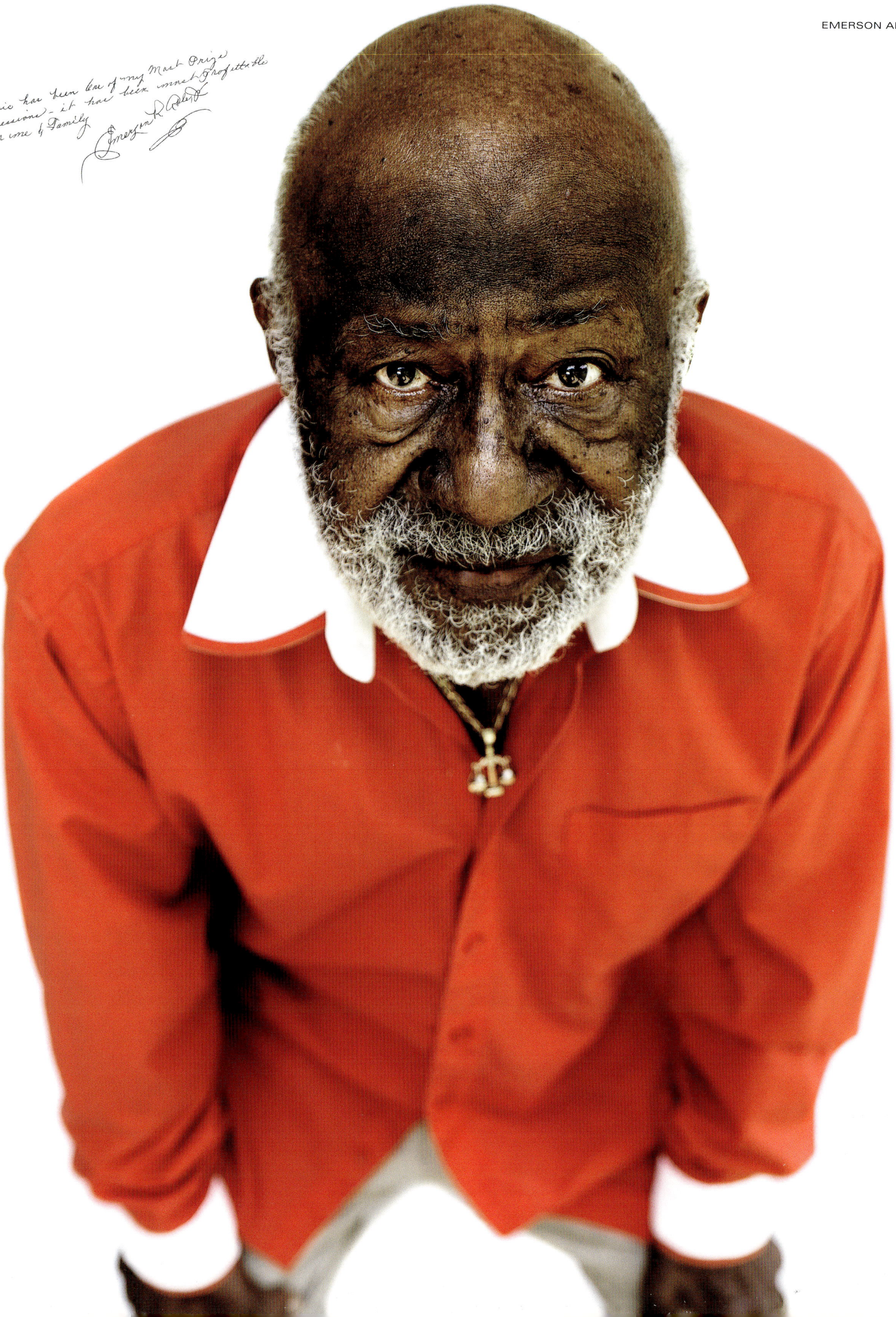

BERNIE HAYES

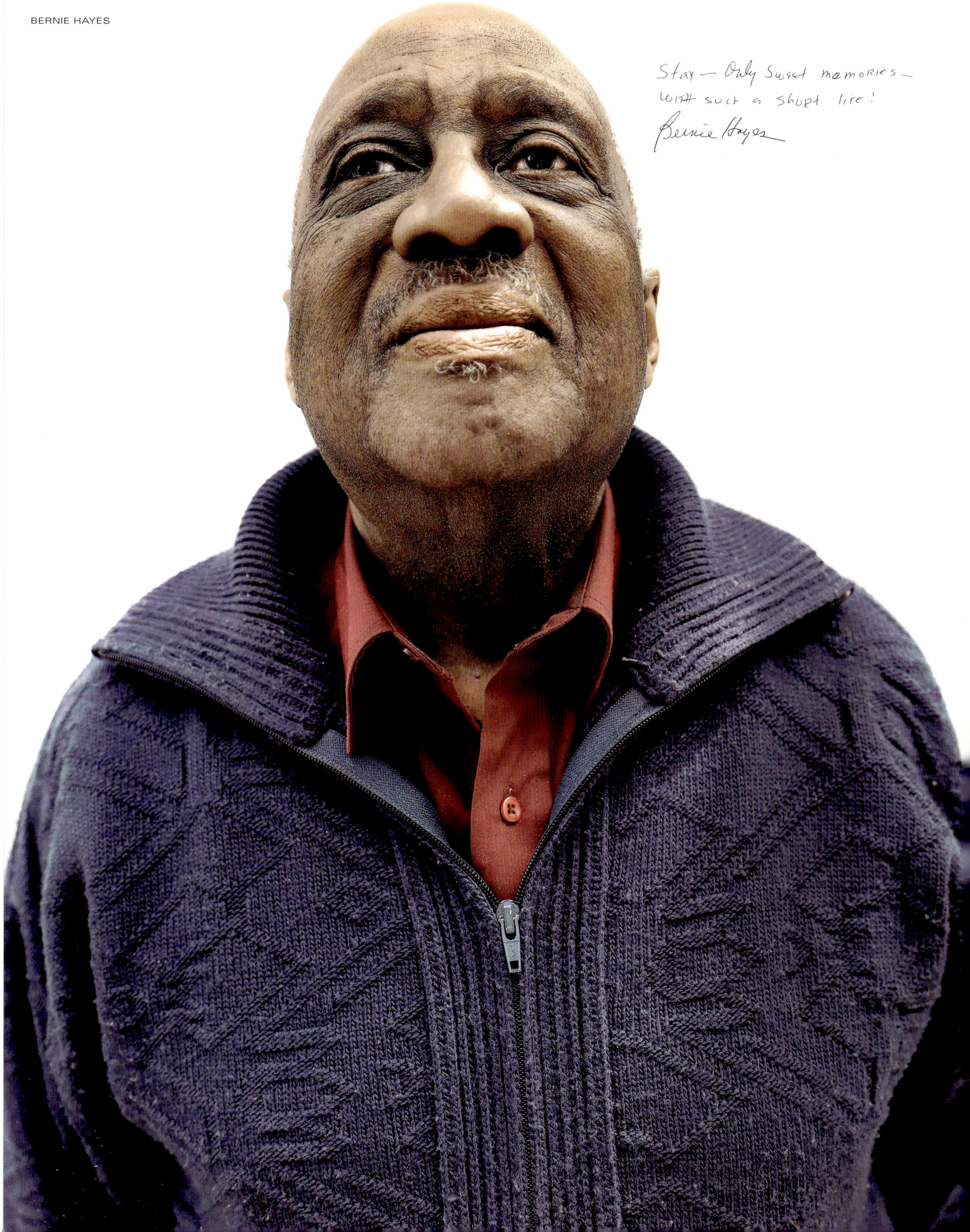

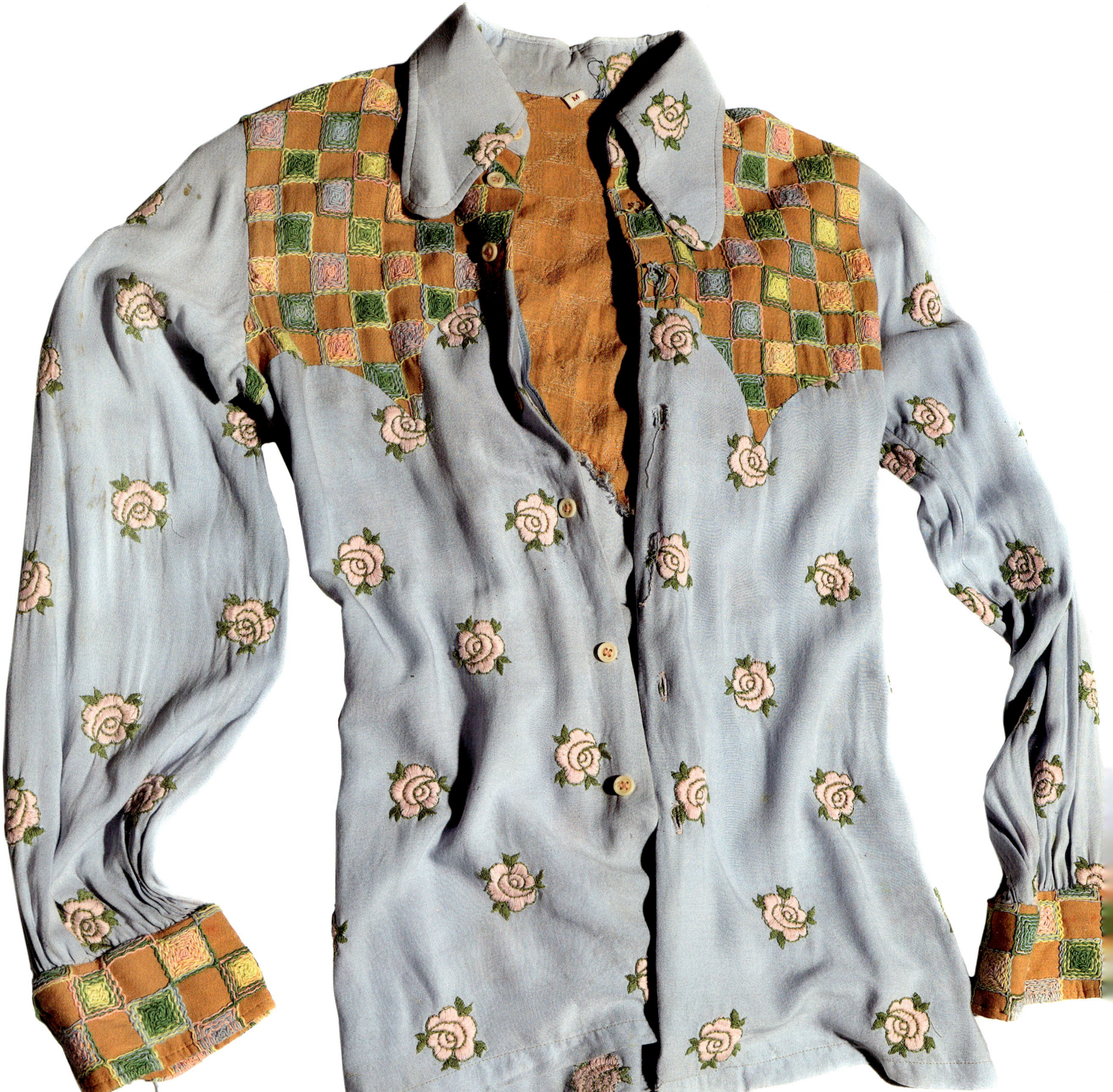

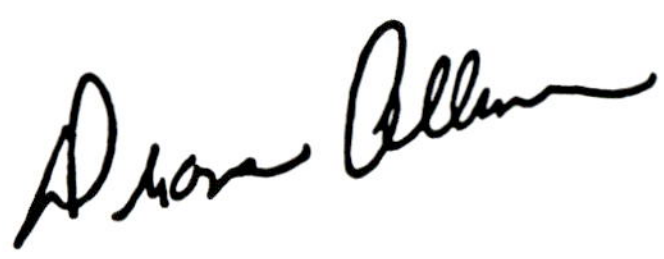

DUANE ALLMAN'S HAND-MADE, LATE 1960s' STAGE SHIRT & GIBSON 1957 LES PAUL GOLDTOP GUITAR

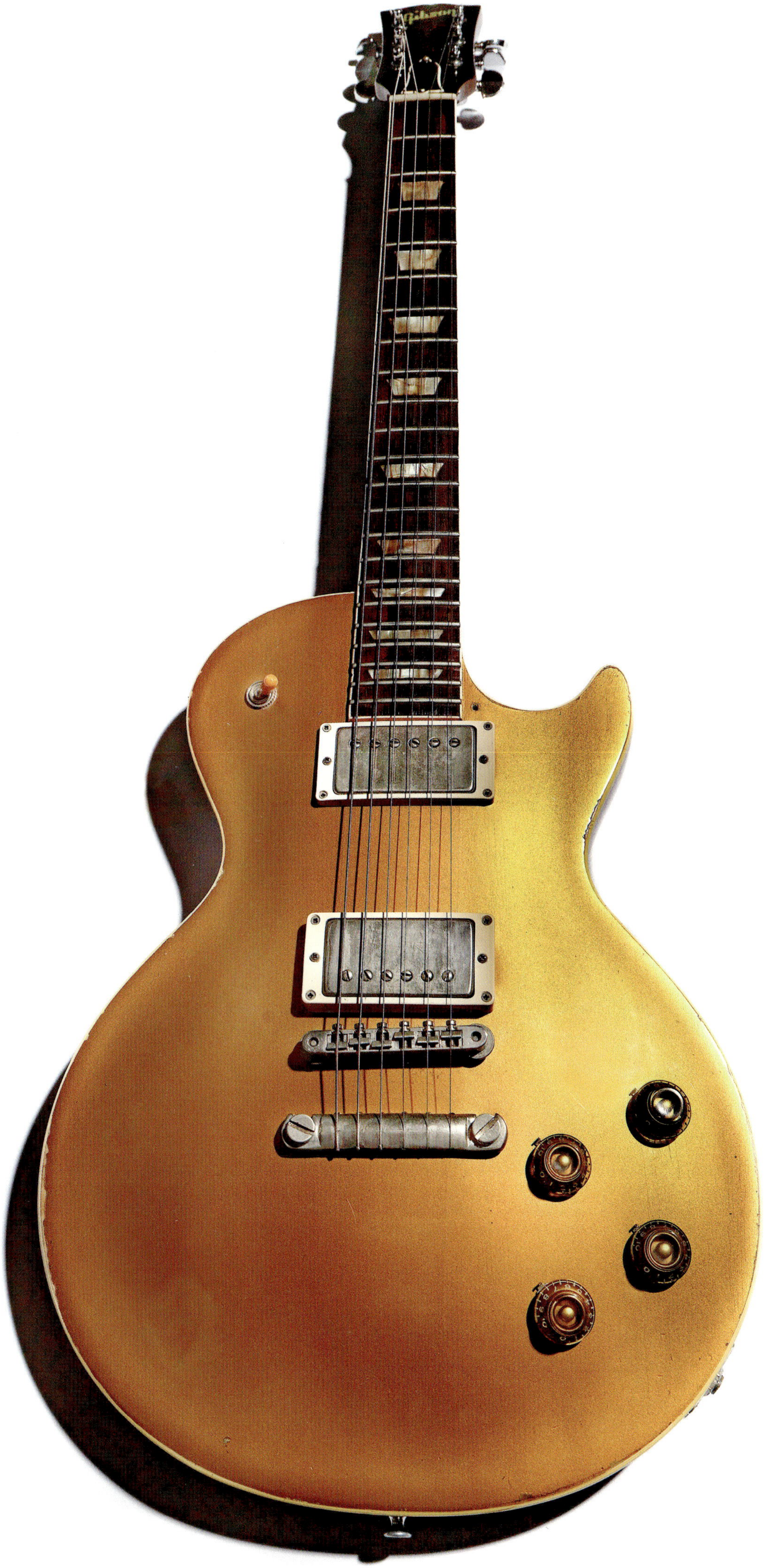

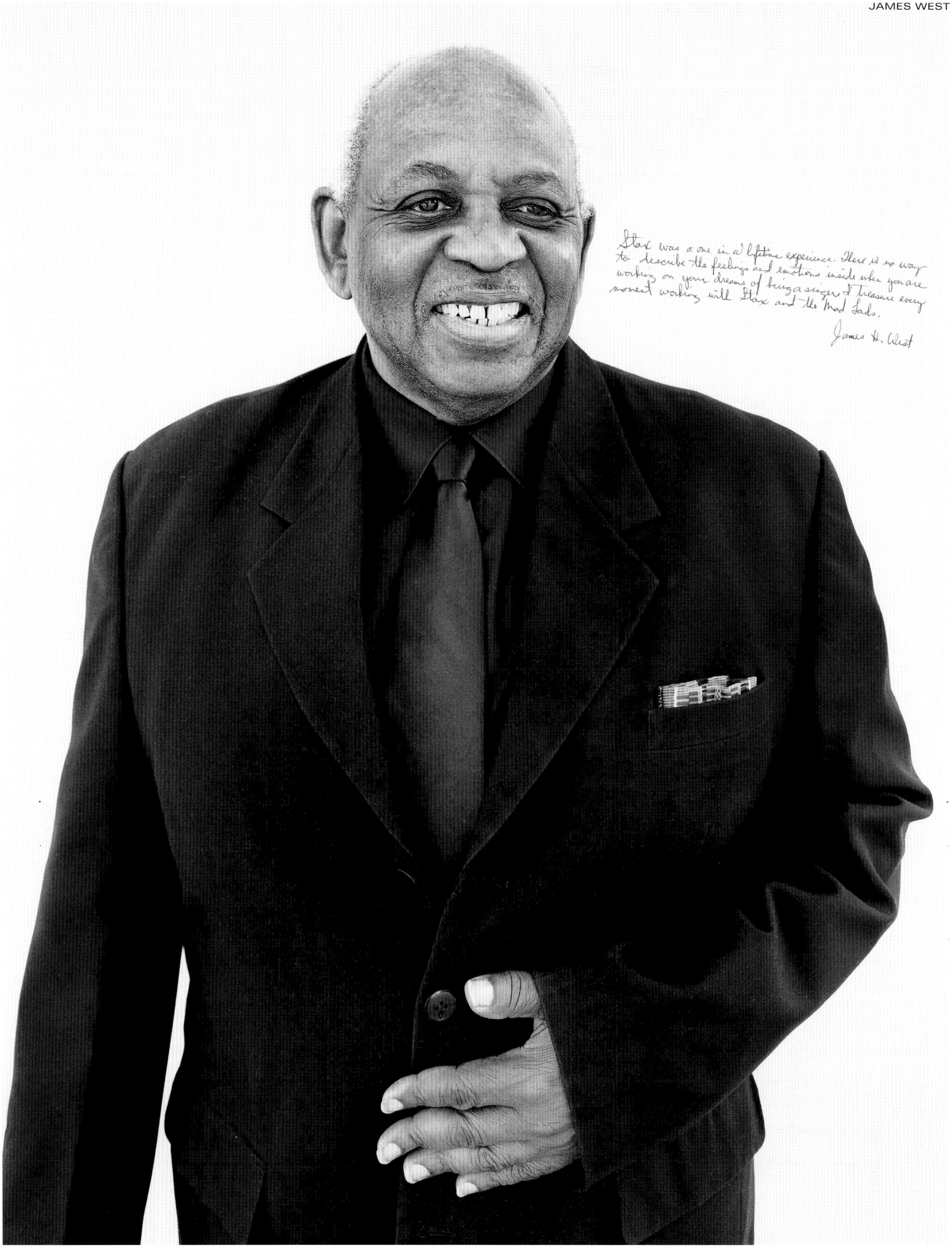
Stax was a one in a lifetime experience. There is no way
to describe the feelings and emotions inside when you are
working on your dreams of being a singer. I treasure every
moment working with Stax and the Mad Lads.
James H. West

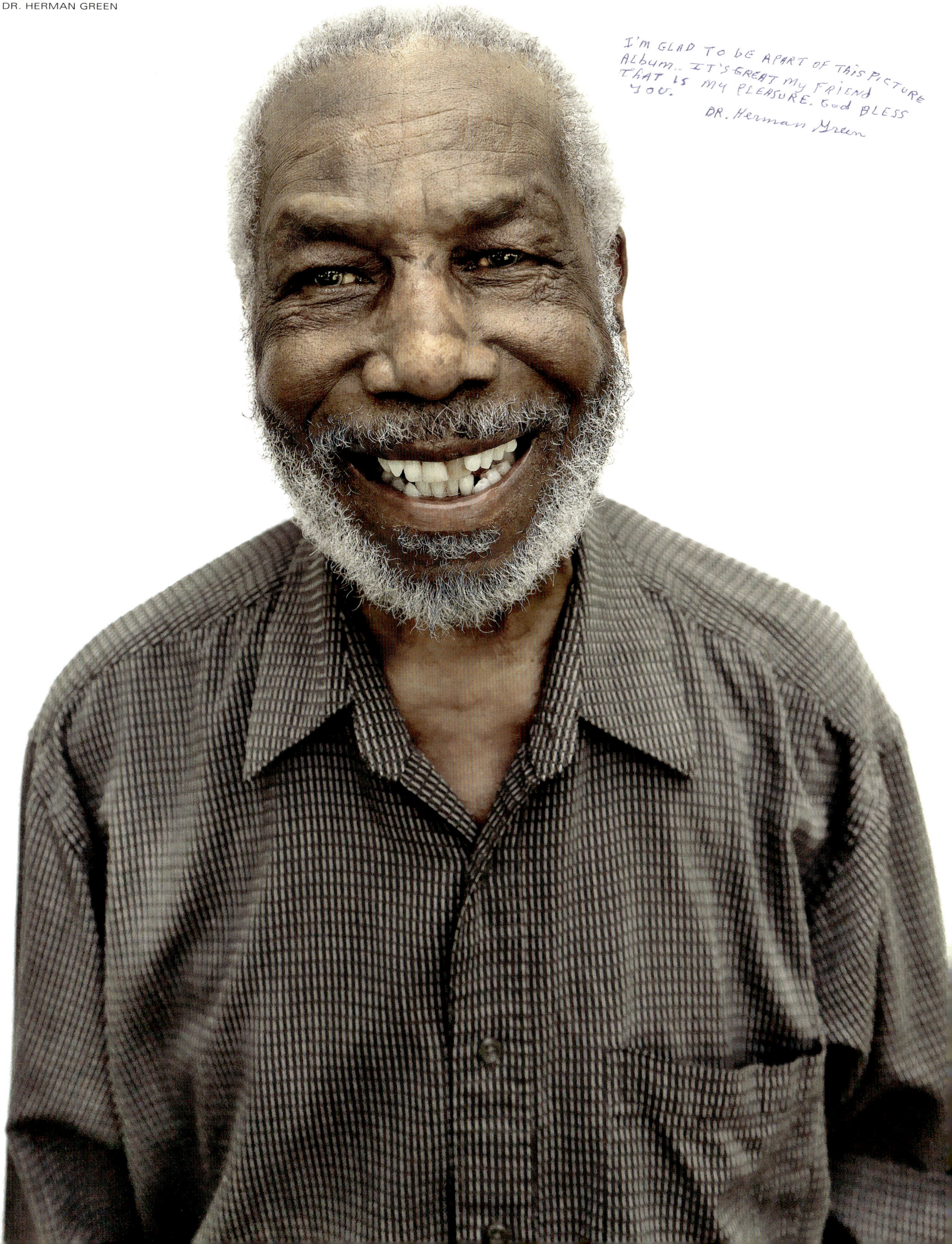
I'M GLAD TO BE APART OF THIS PICTURE
Album. IT'S GREAT my FRIEND
THAT IS MY PLEASURE. God BLESS
YOU.
DR. Herman Green

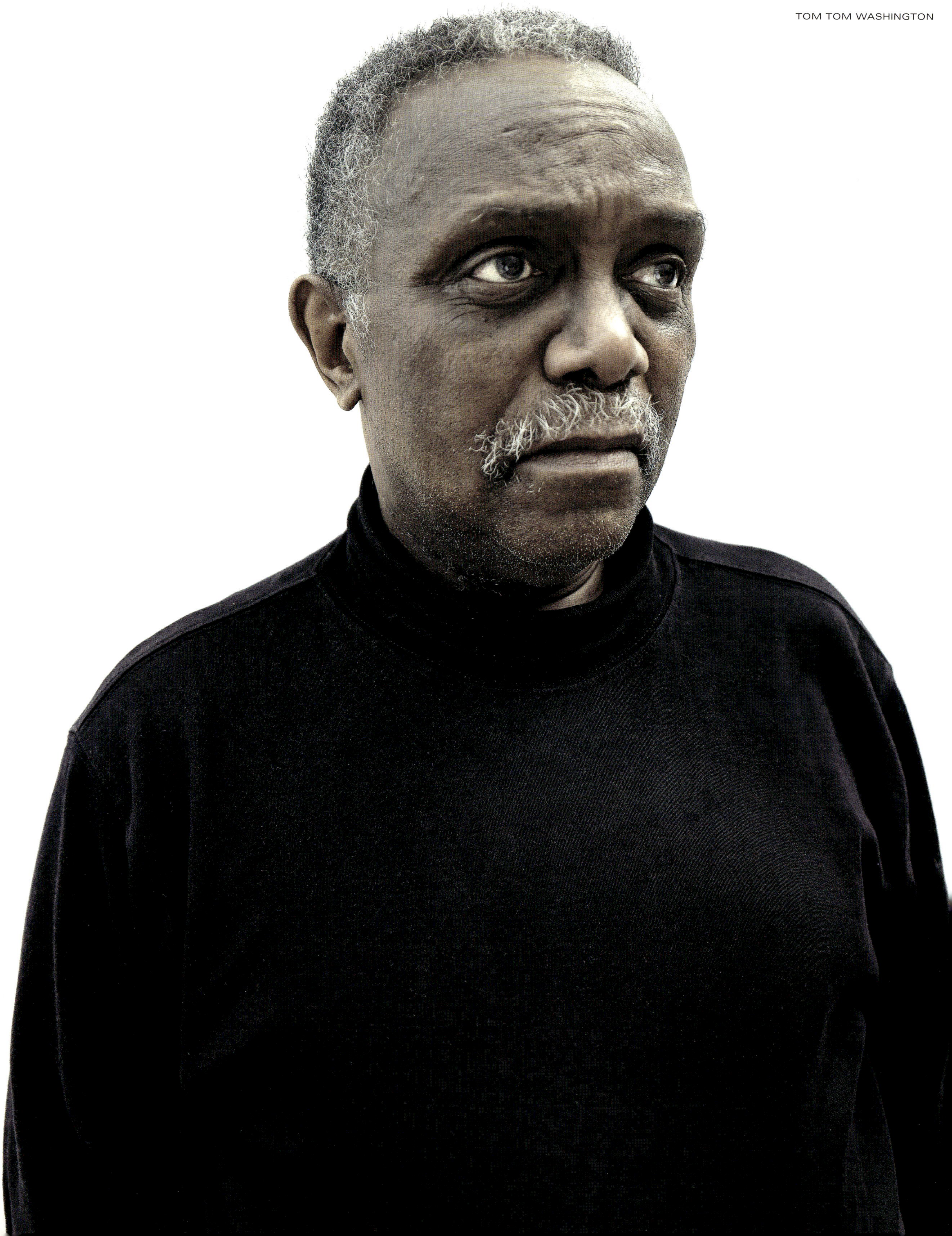

TOM PLEASANTS

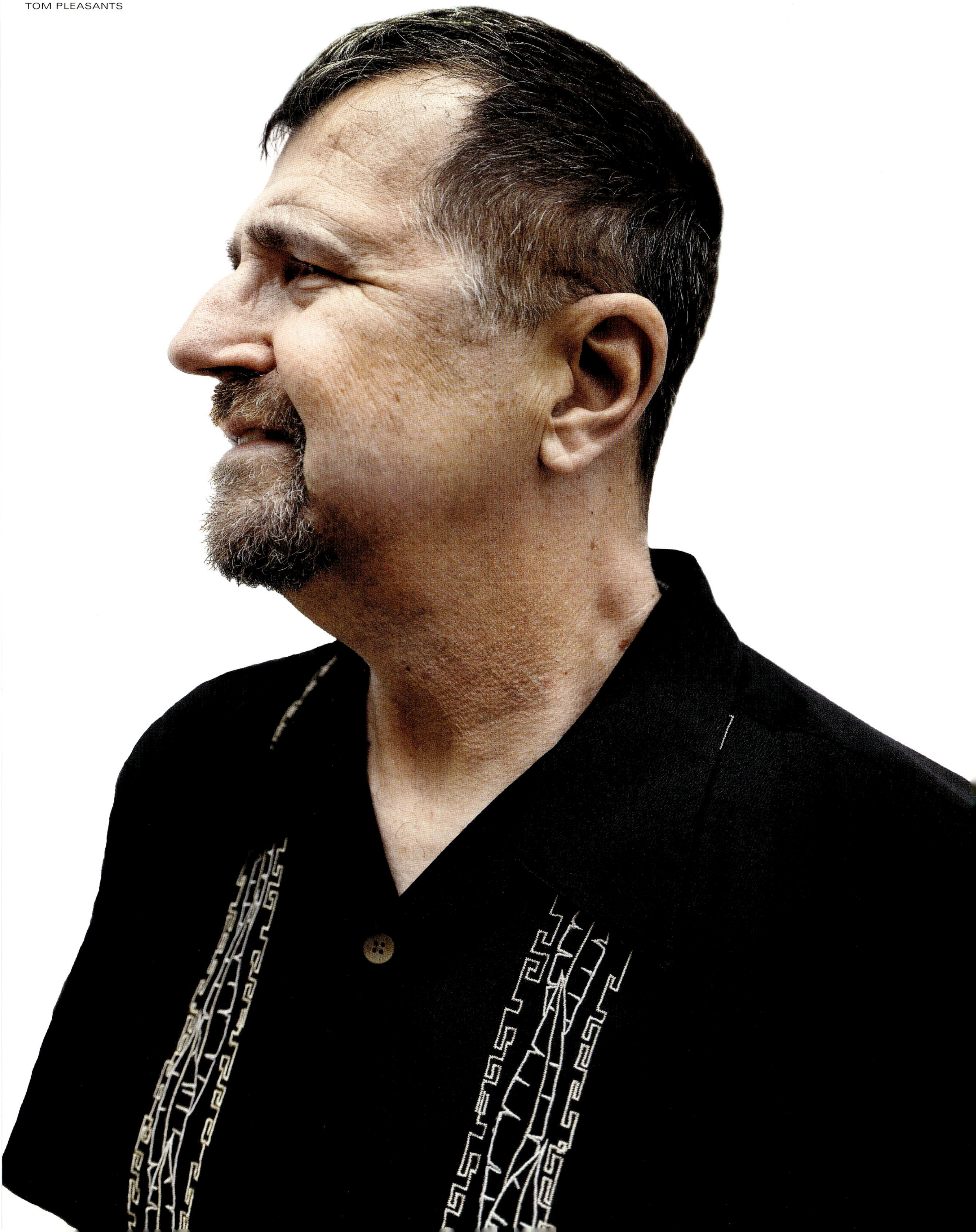

TO HAVE STARTED IN RADIO IN
MUNICH GERMANY (1954) AS A HIGH SCHOOL REPORTER
FOR ARMED FORCES RADIO — TO HOUSTON
TEXAS "BLACK RADIO" KYOK MY NAME
WAS DIZZIE LIZZIE CAN YOU BELIEVE
IT? WITH A YIDDISH NEW YORK ACCENT!
TO MEMPHIS, TENN AS THE PRODUCTION
CHIEF OF STAX RECORDS! I WANT TO
THANK AL BELL FOR THE OPPORTUNITY
1ST FEMALE!!

I'M GLAD TO BE APART OF THIS PICTURE
ALBUM.. IT'S GREAT MY FRIEND
THAT IS MY PLEASURE. God BLESS
YOU.
DR. Herman Green

I Love everyone
[illegible]

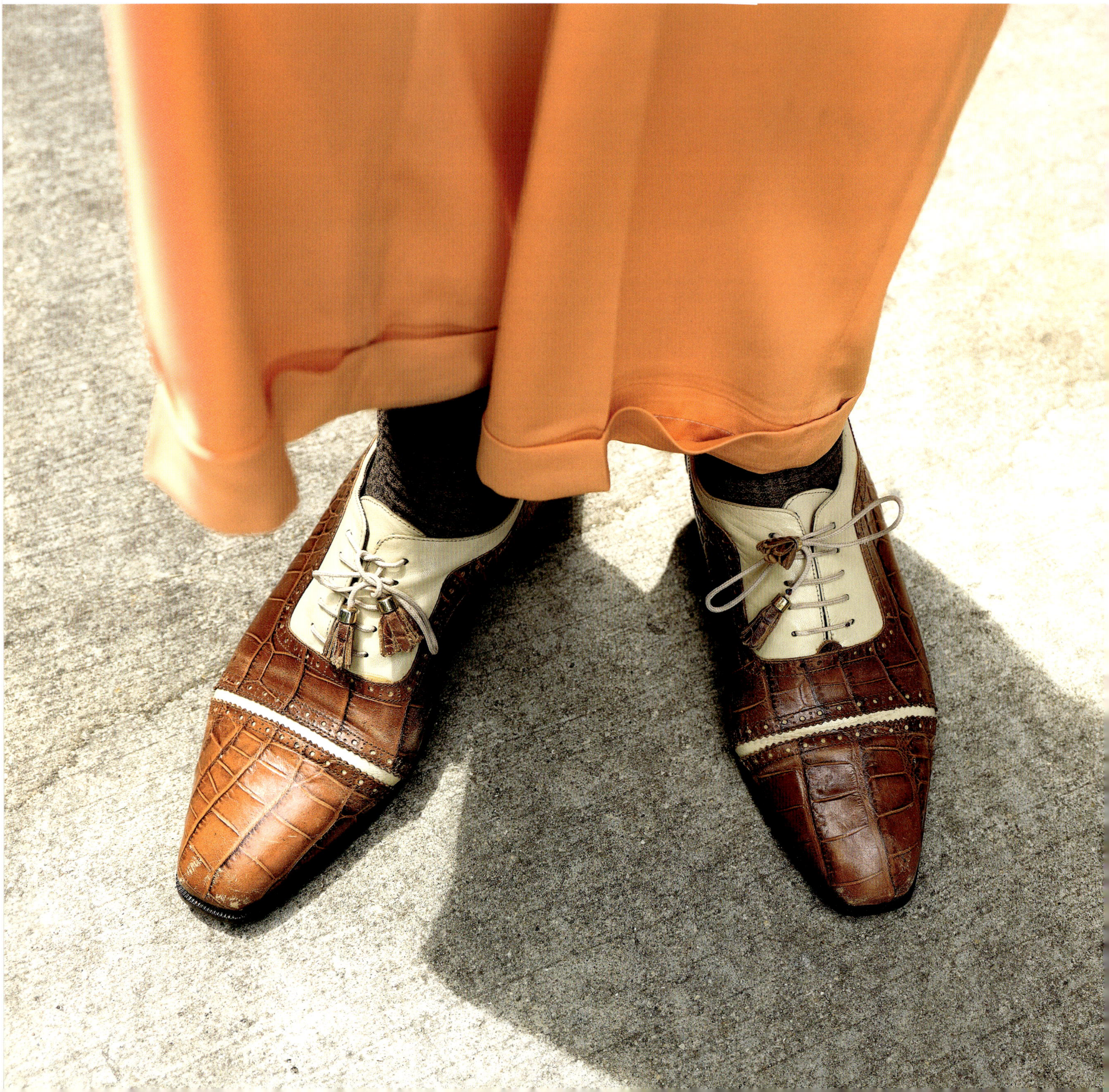

Memphis music is the Real Deal.
My Life Has been Good!

Hoft Campbell Jr.

I WAS THE IN HOUSE M.C.
FOR STAX Rec.
I AM THE MC, HEARd ON MOMS MABLEY ALBUM
+ DIONNE WARWICK + ISAAC HAYES ALBUM
I WAS ALSO WRITER, + PRODUCER FOR STAX RECORDS
ALL I GOT TO SAY, "WHAT A Ride
WHAT A Ride, WHAT A Ride"

Associate yourself with the best of
everything you can, for this is what you'll
be known by.

Carl Thomas

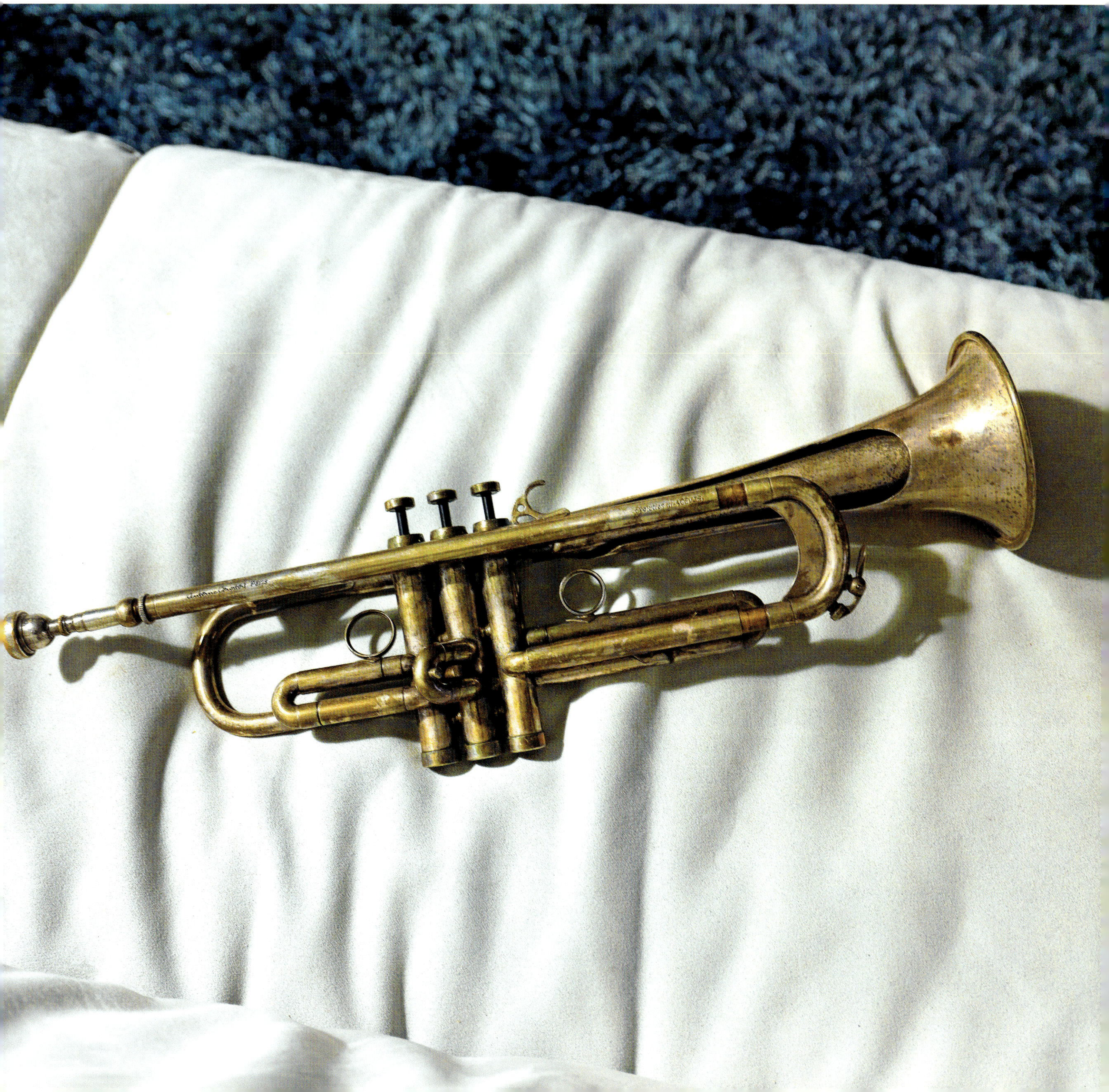

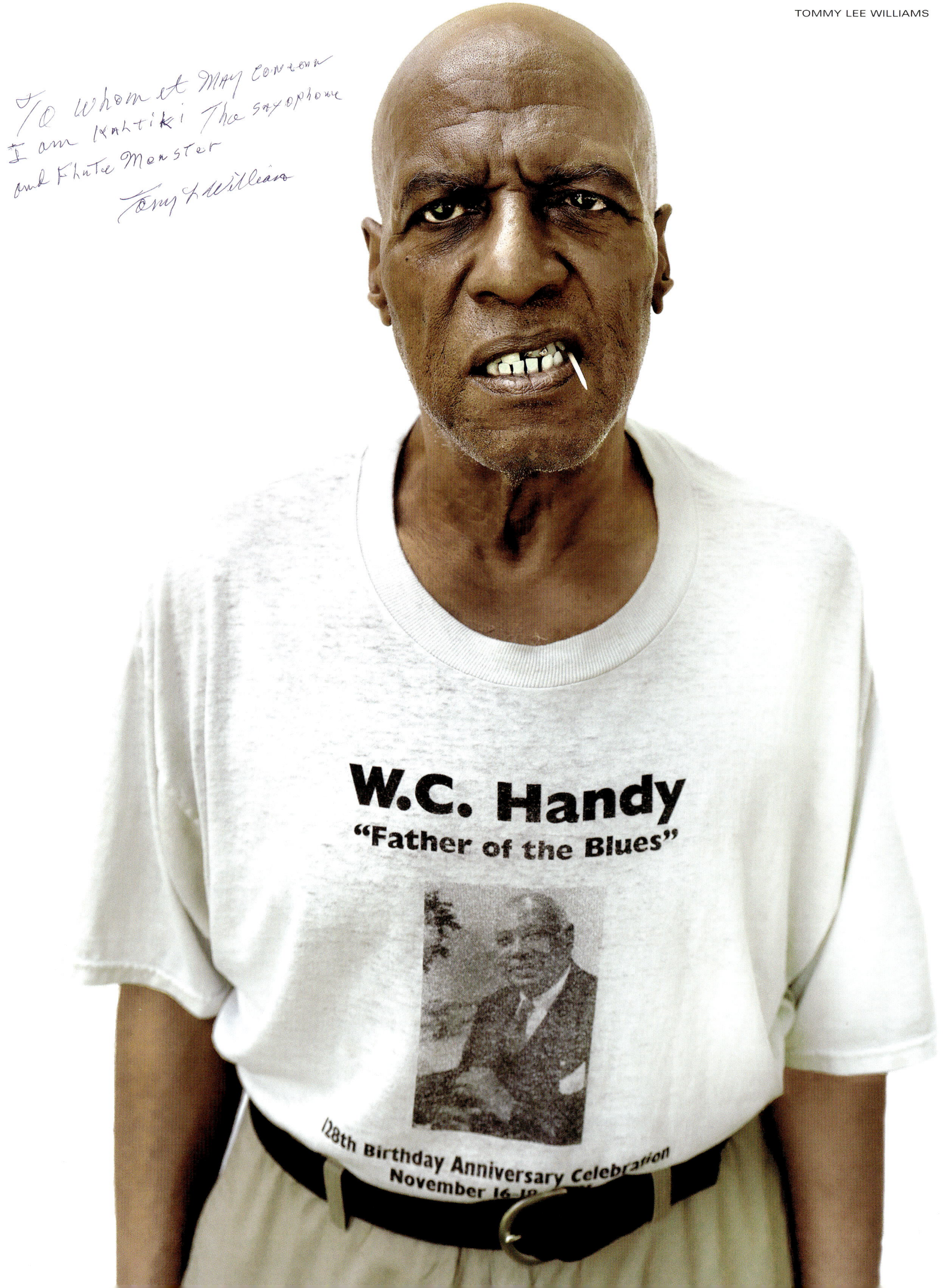
To whom it May concern
I am Kahtiki The saxophone
and Flute Monster
Tommy L Williams
W.C. Handy
“Father of the Blues”
128th Birthday Anniversary Celebration
November

IRMA THOMAS

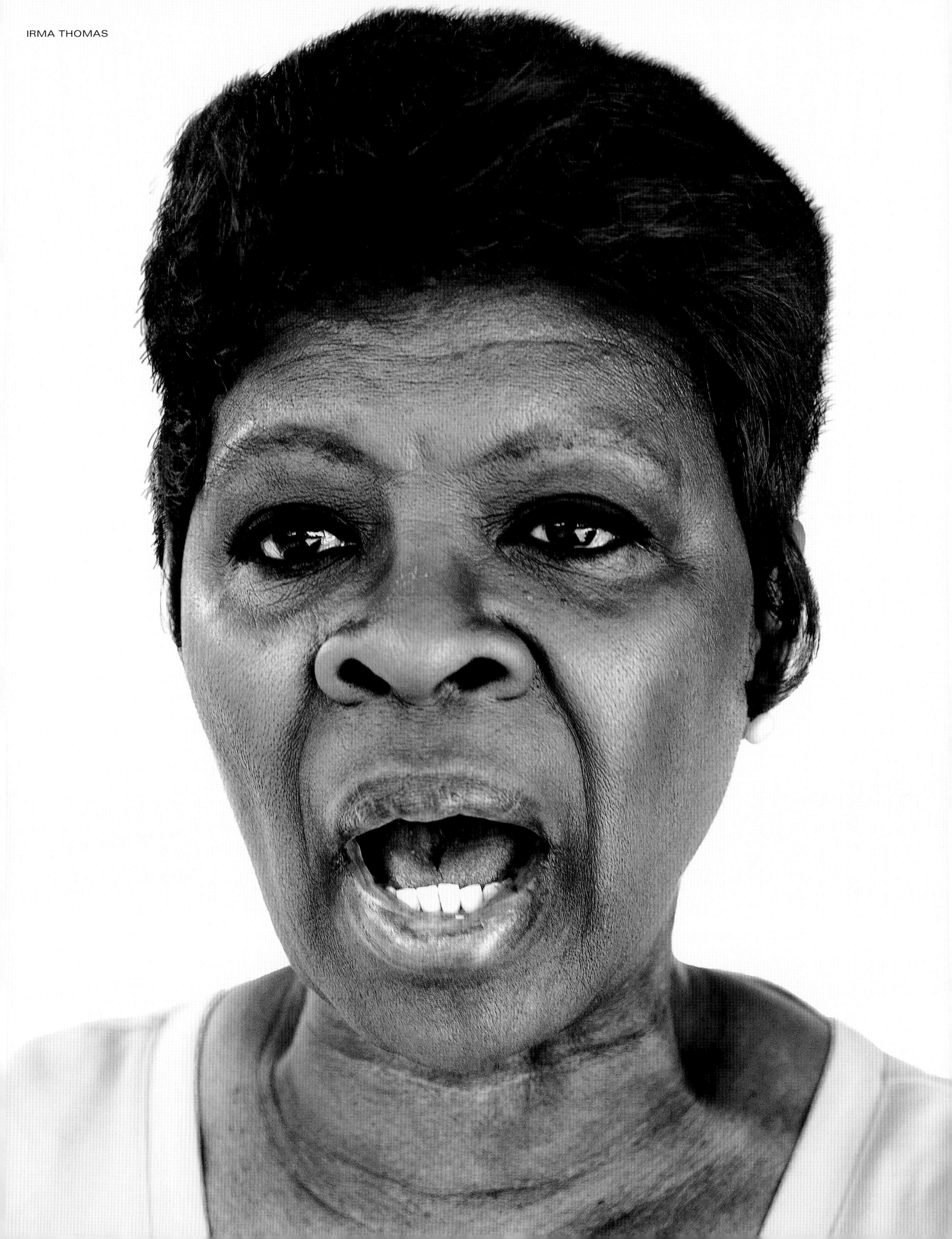

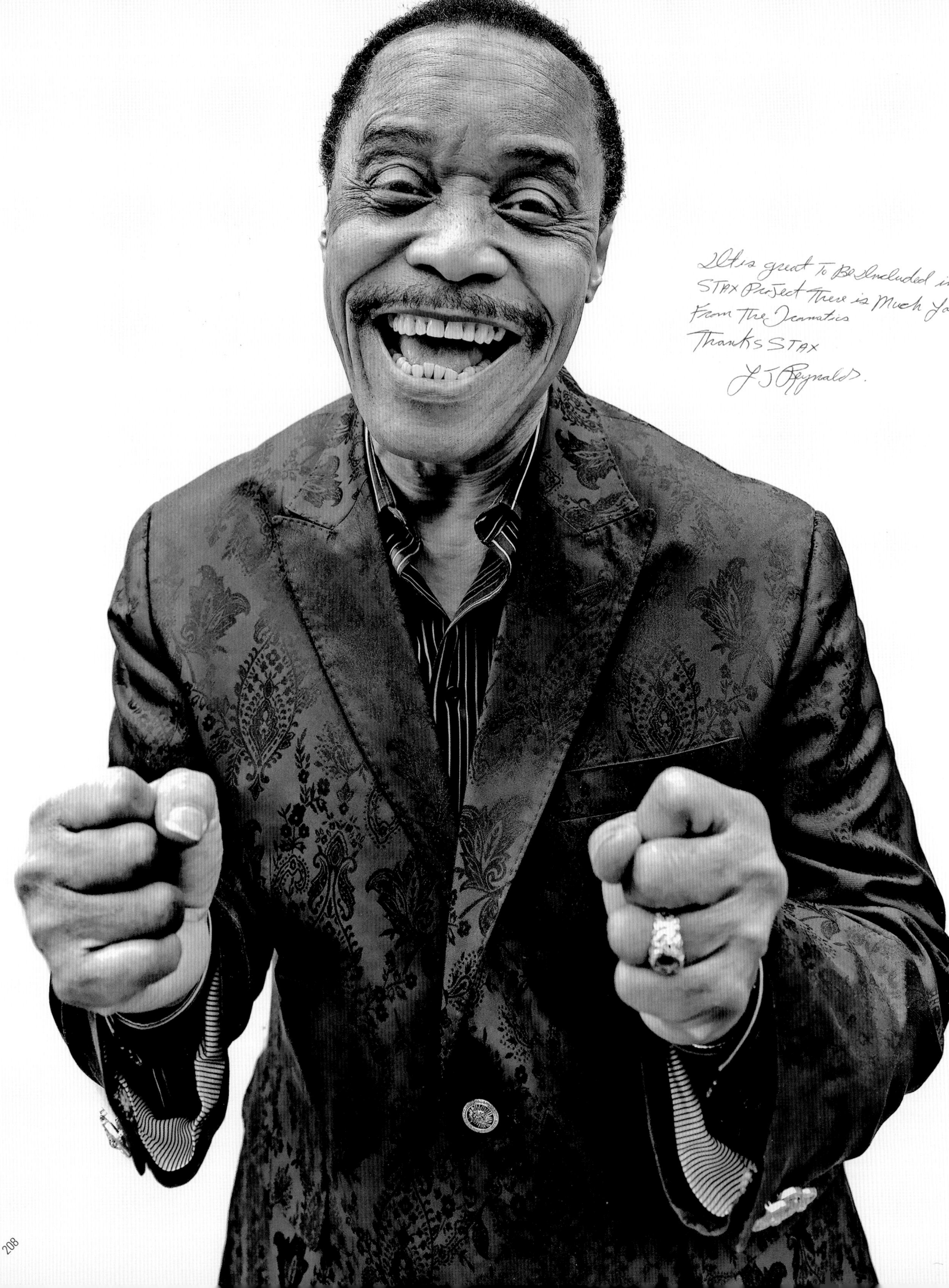

It's great To Be Included in The
STAX Project There is Much Love
From The Dramatics
Thanks STAX
L J Reynolds.

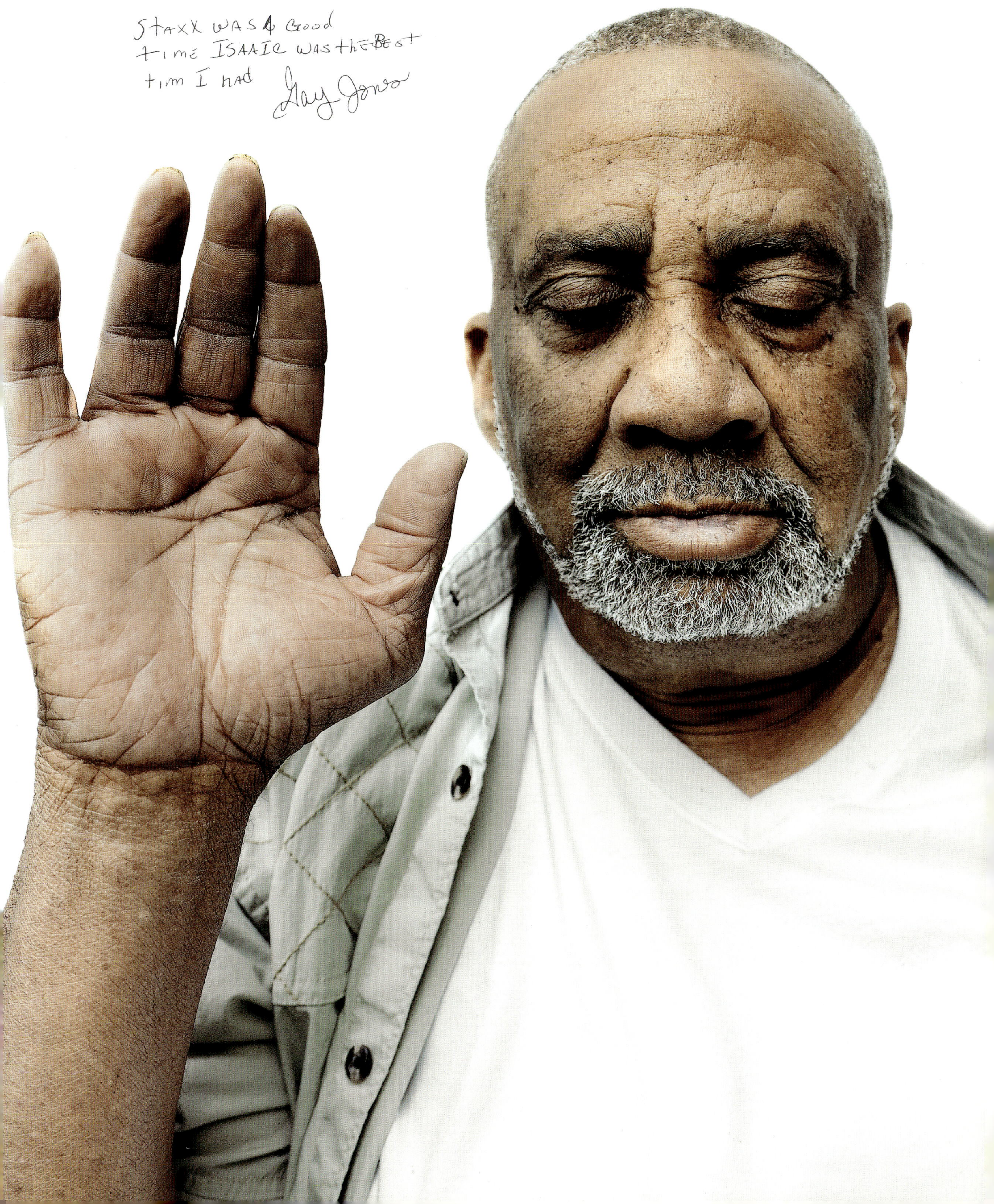
StAXX WAS A Good
time ISAAIC WAS the Best
tim I had
Gary Jones

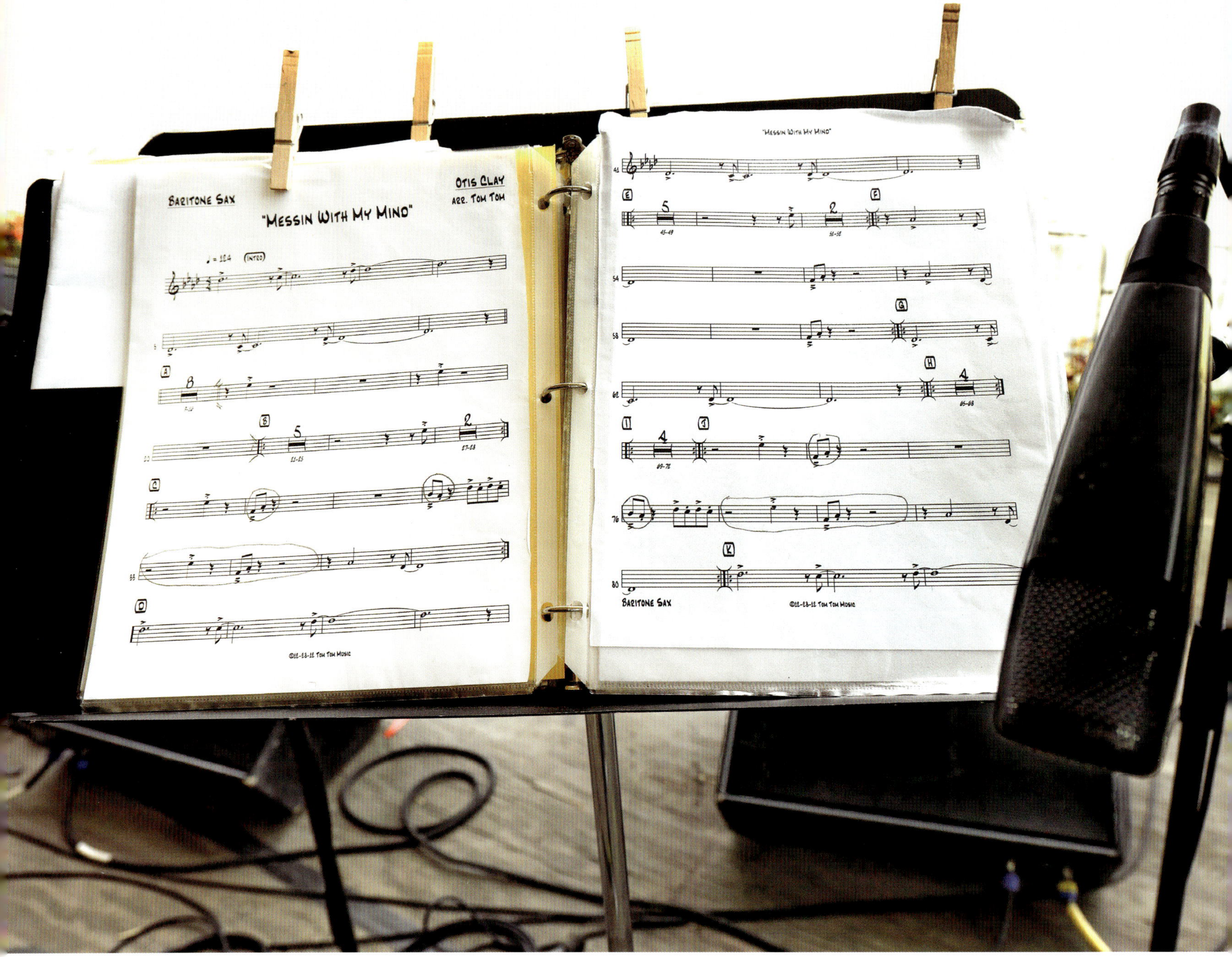


OTIS CLAY CONCERT, CHICAGO

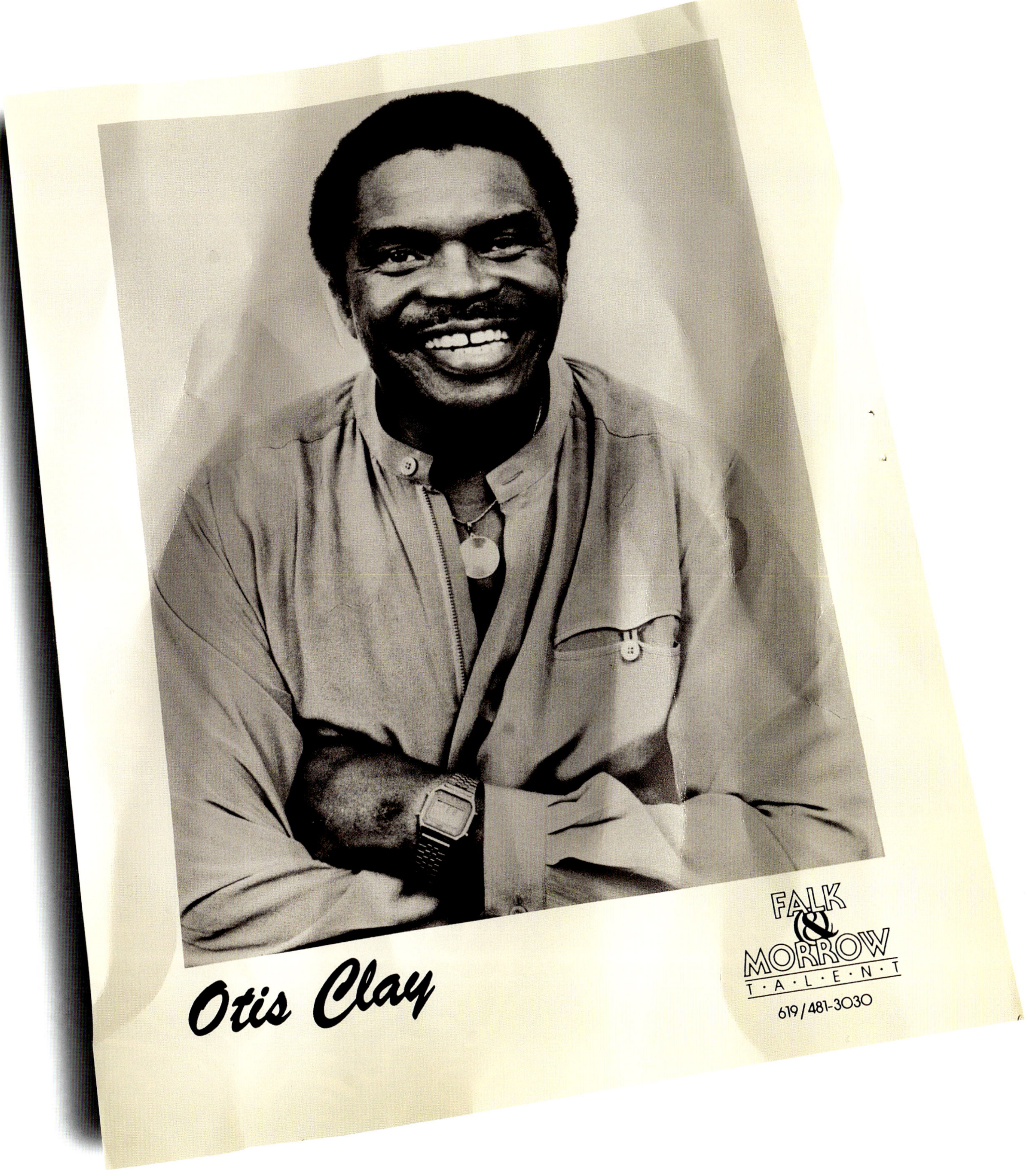


OTIS CLAY PRESS PHOTO

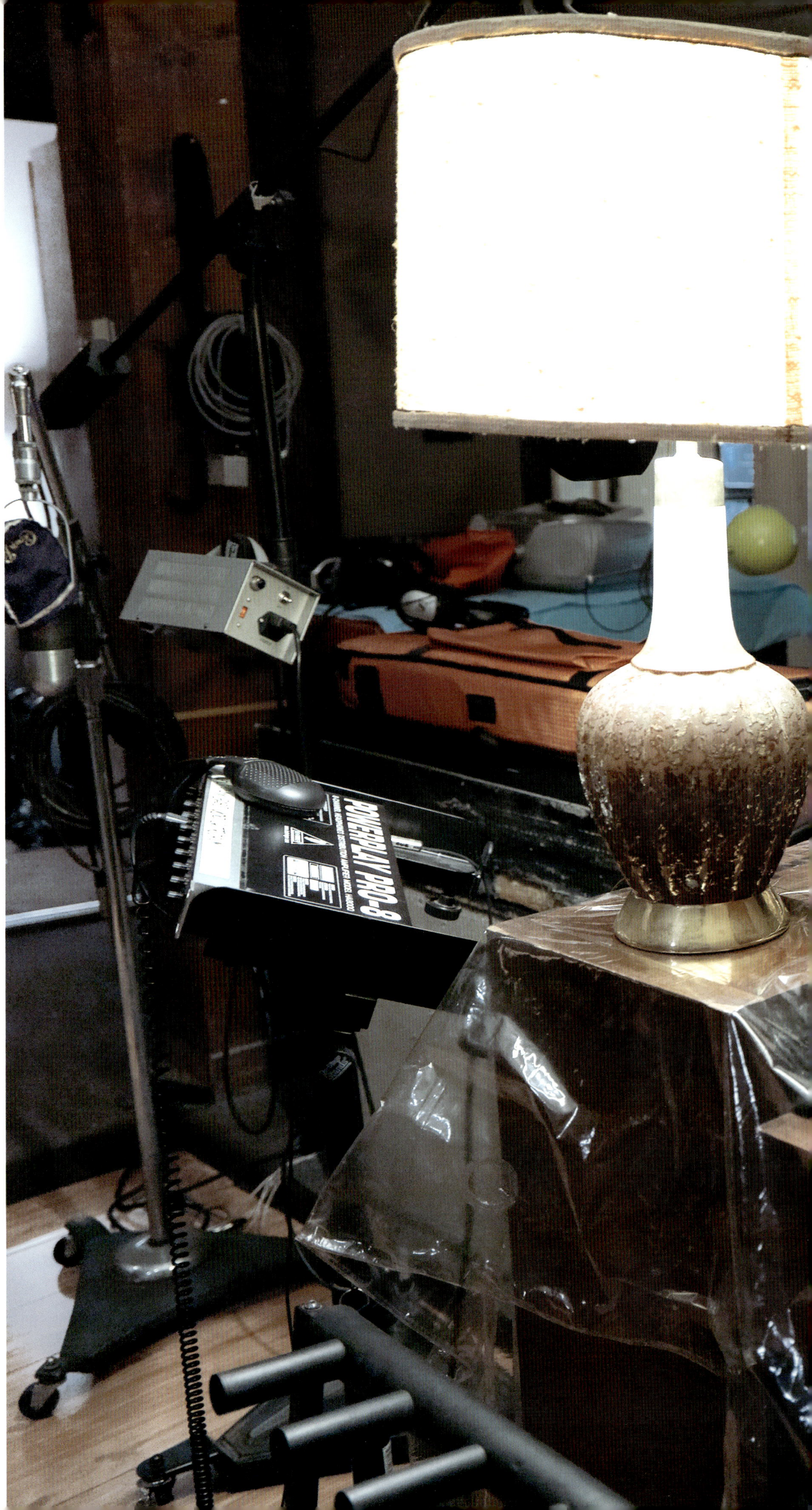


VINTAGE 1960s' INSTRUMENTS
AT ELECTRAPHONIC RECORDING
STUDIO, MEMPHIS

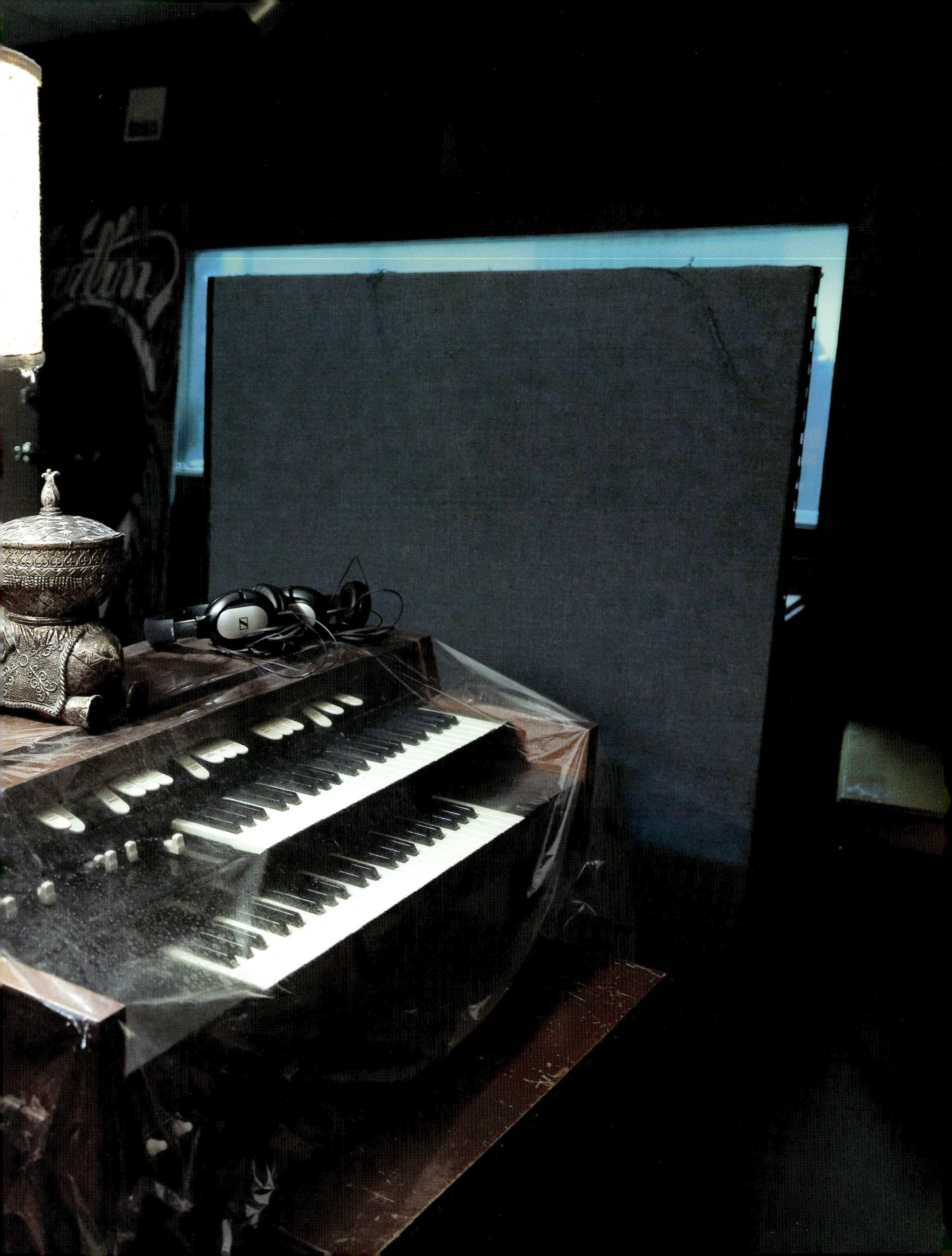

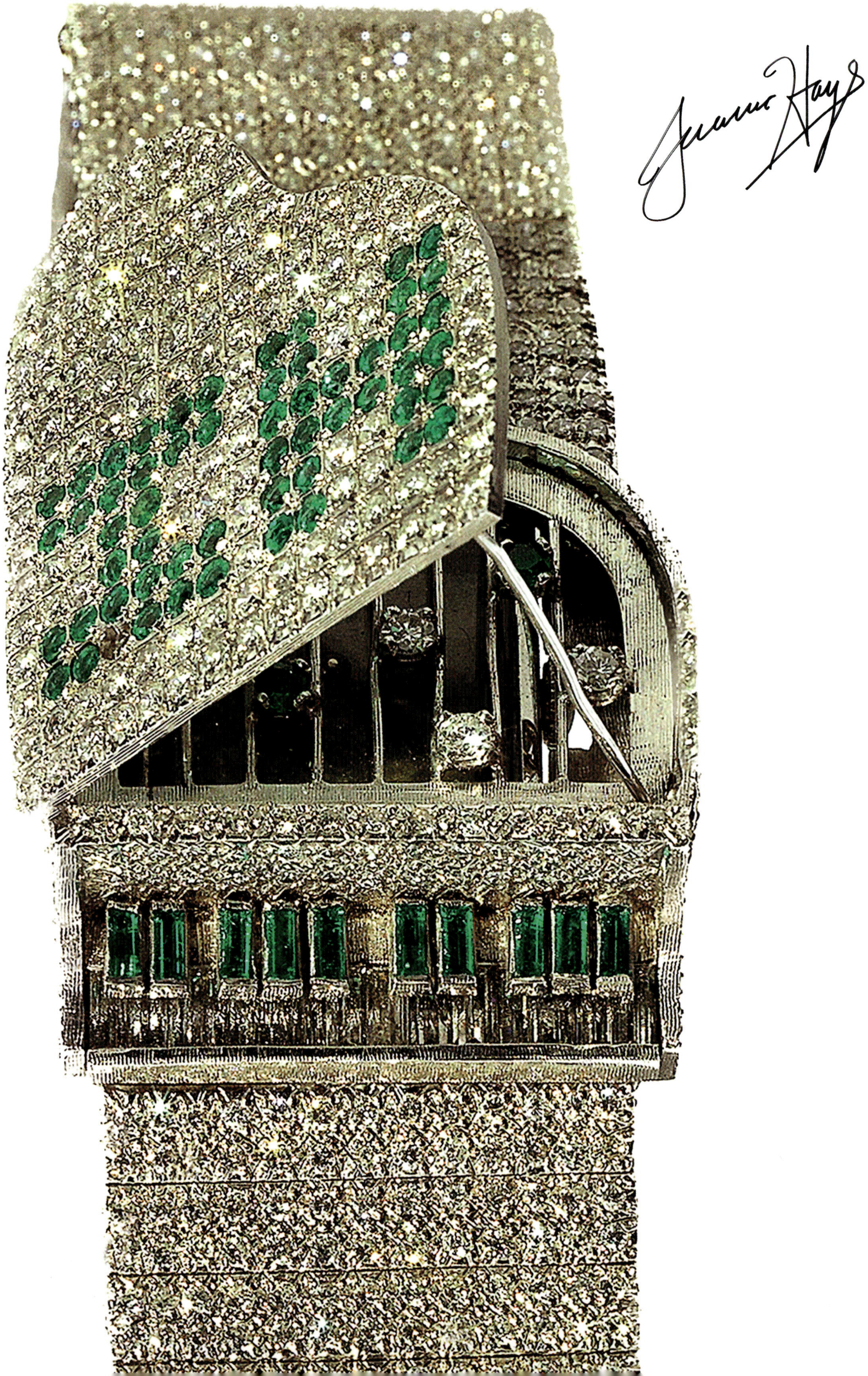

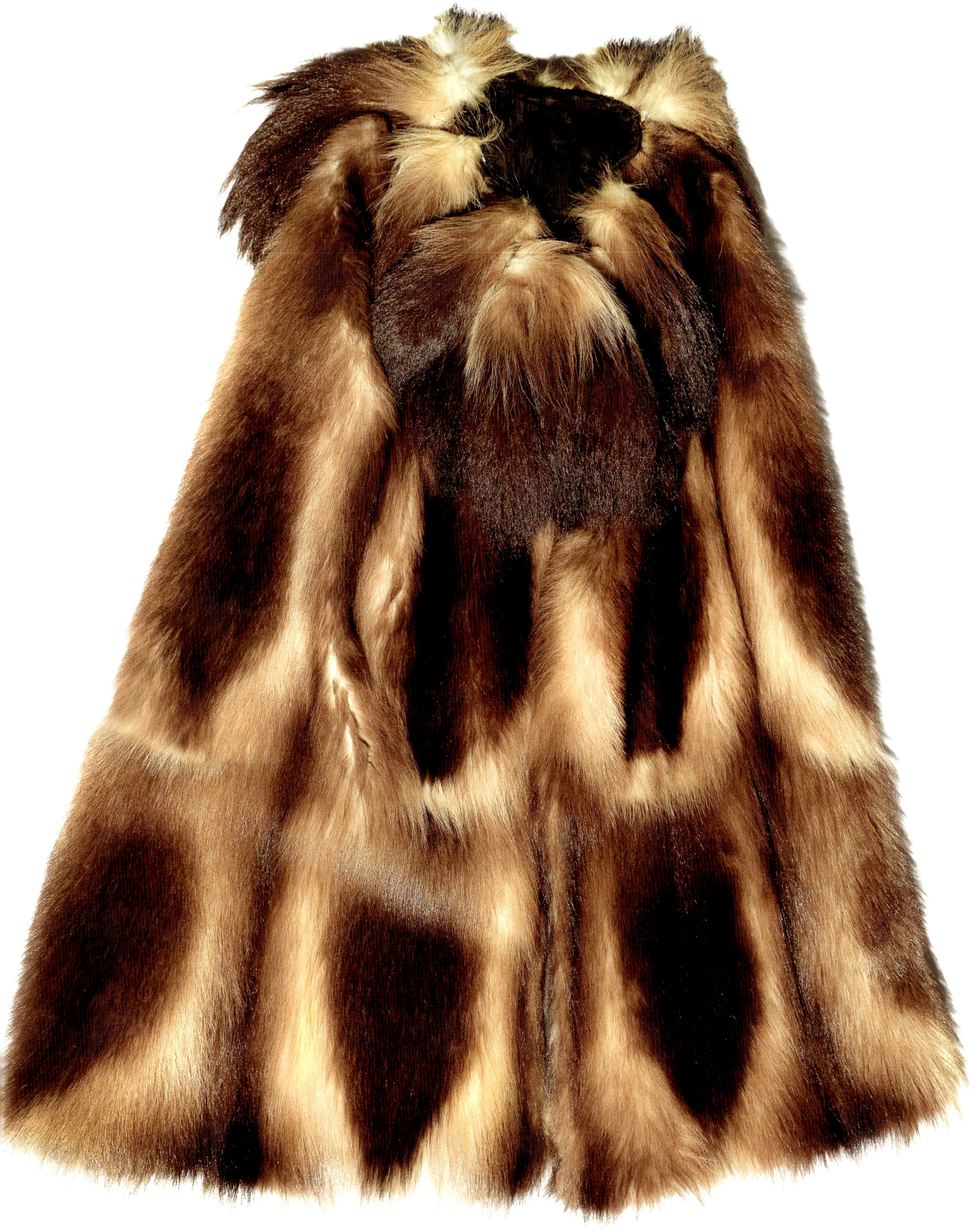

ISAAC HAYES'S CUSTOM-DESIGNED DIAMOND-AND-EMERALD "GRAND PIANO" WRISTWATCH & MINK COAT

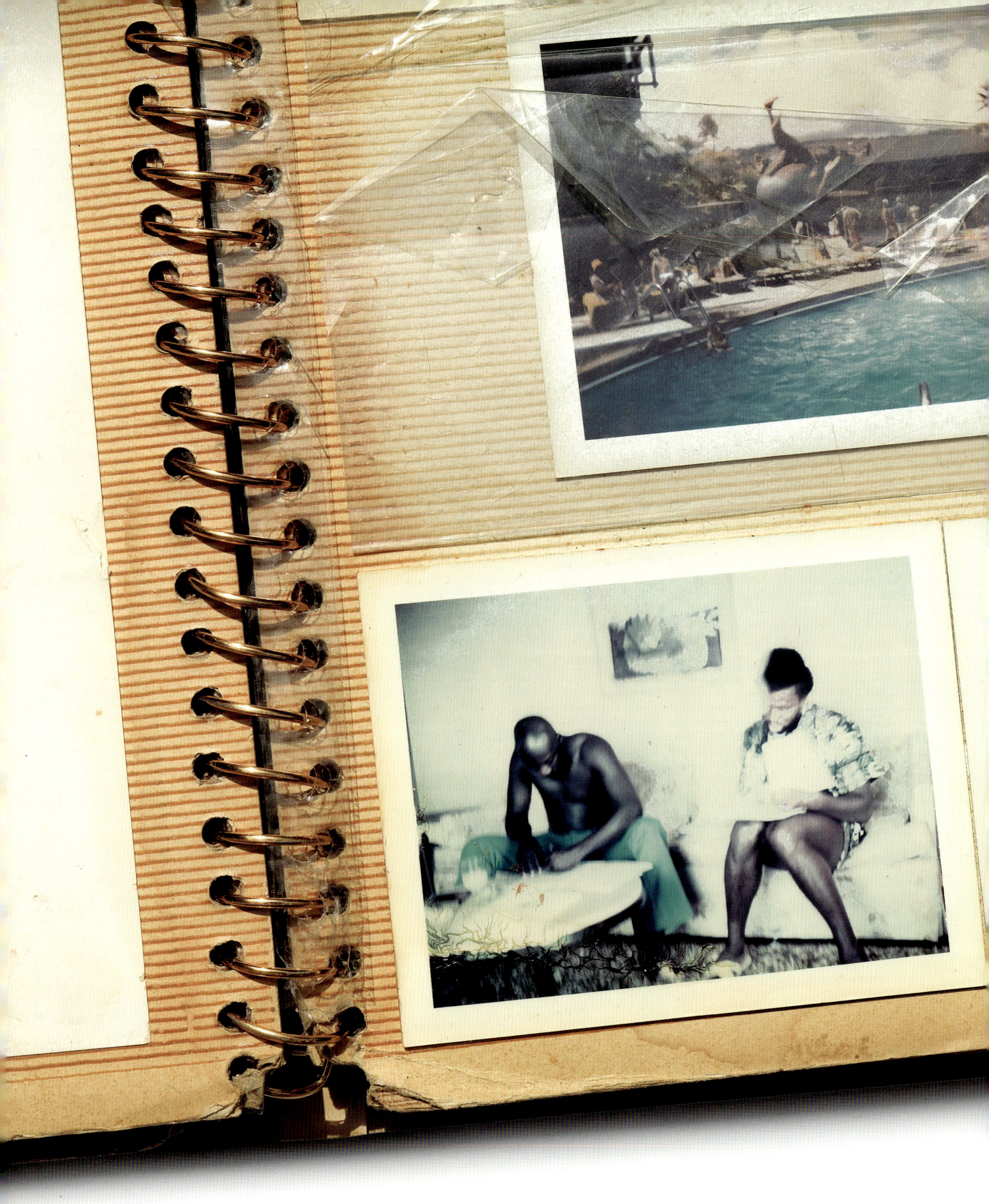

HAYES WITH HELEN WASHINGTON IN A HAWAII HOTEL ROOM (c.1972)

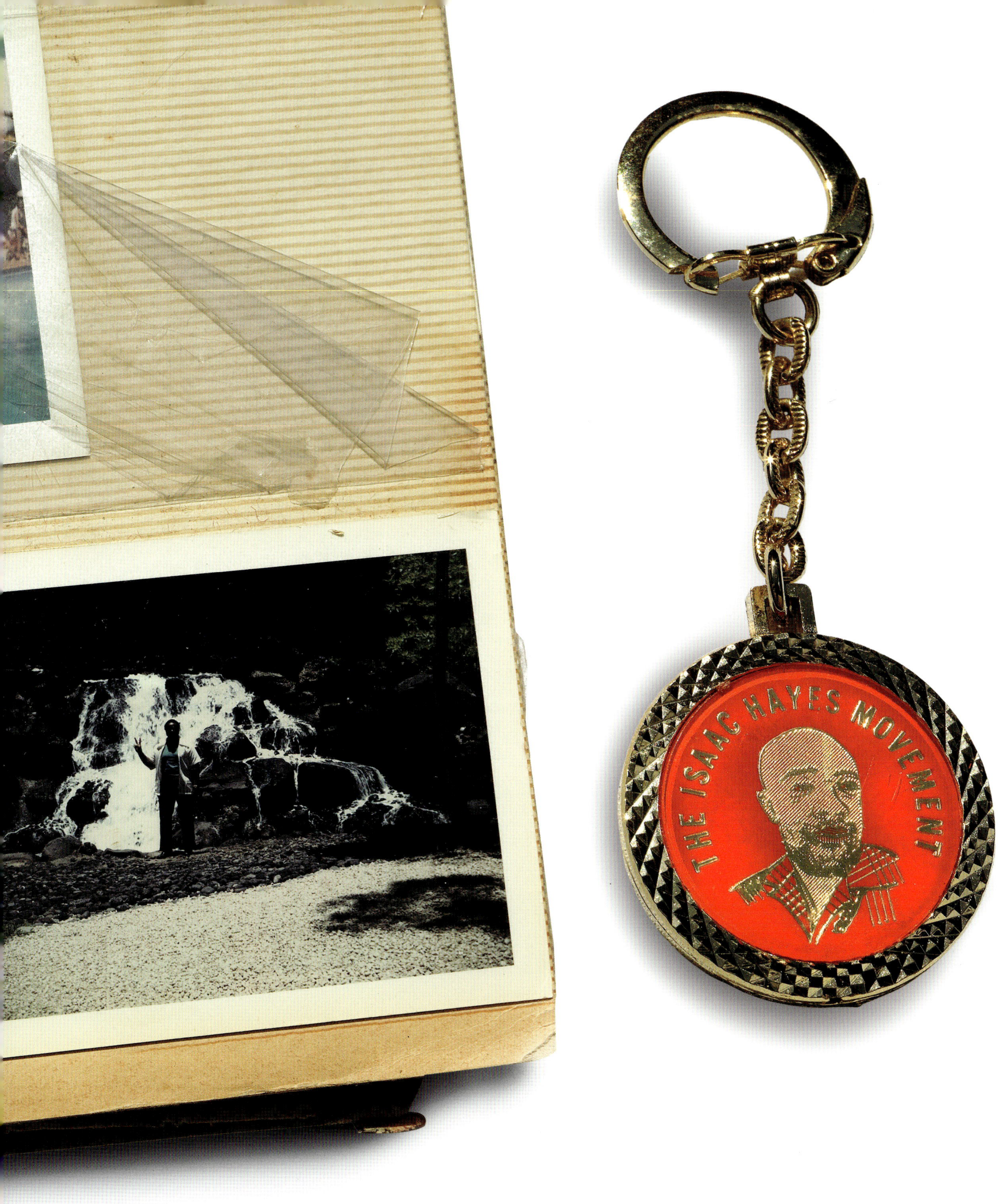


ISAAC HAYES MOVEMENT CONCERT GIVEAWAY KEY CHAIN

PRESTON SHANNON

IT WAS A pleasure TAKING this picture,
And MORE OF A pleasure spending time
on world FAMOUS STAX PARKING LOT.
Preston Shannon

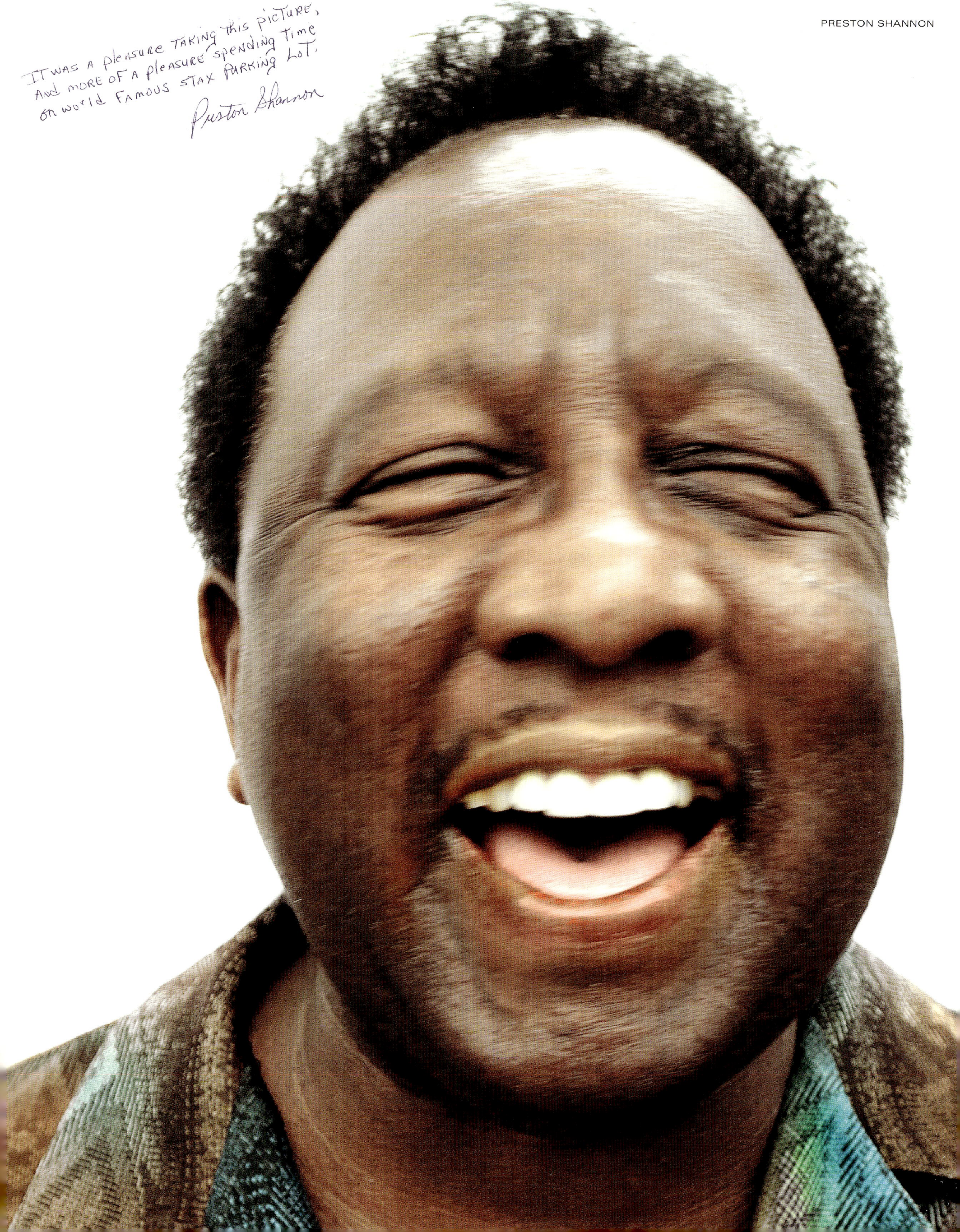

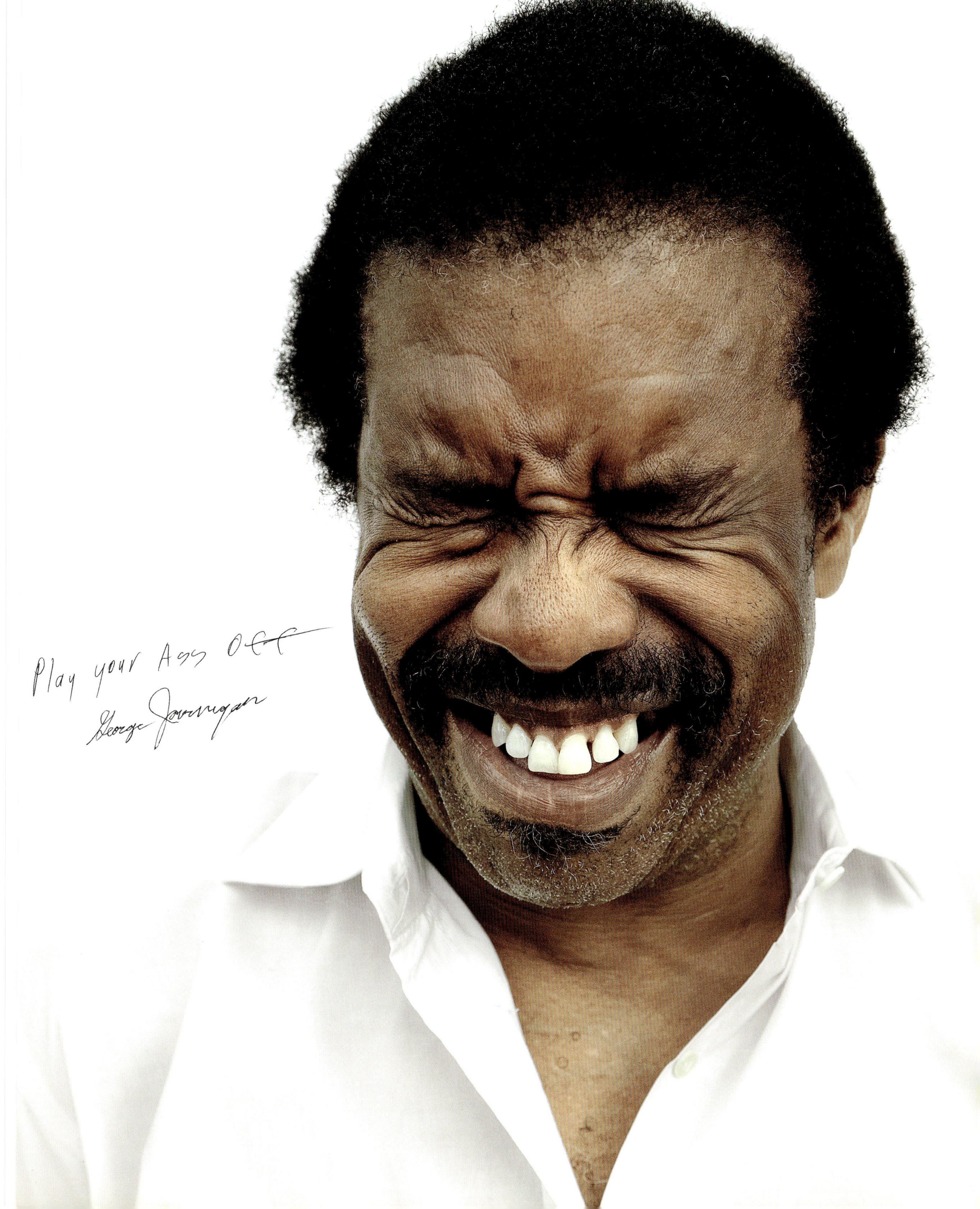
Play your Ass Off
George Journigan

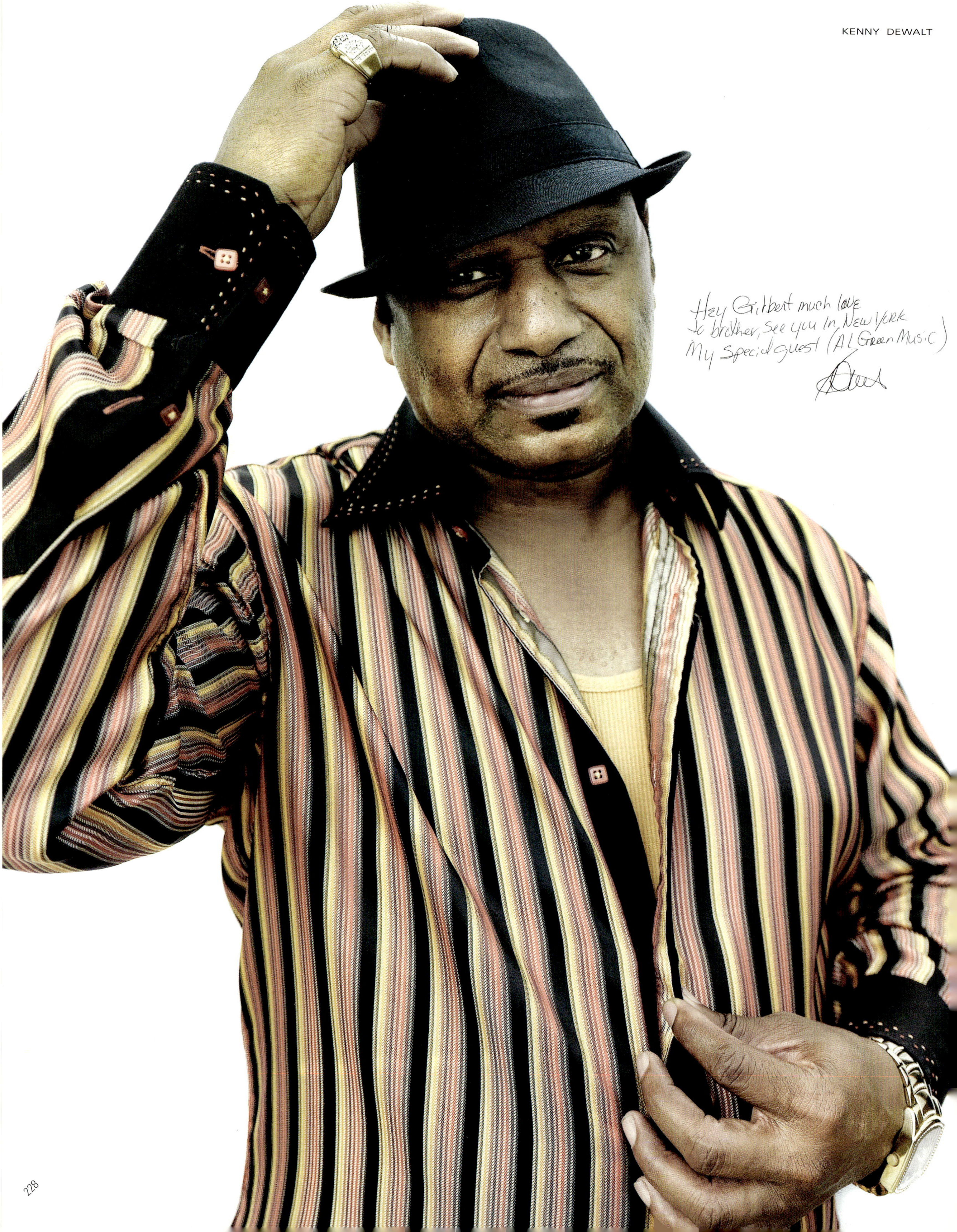
Hey Gilbert much love
to brother, see you in New York
My special guest (Al Green Music)

Born small town - Arlington Tn.
Memphis Blues Artist
traveled the world w/ Denise LaSalle
Shirley Brown, Jerry Lee Lewis
Beale Street Singer
Jewel J.

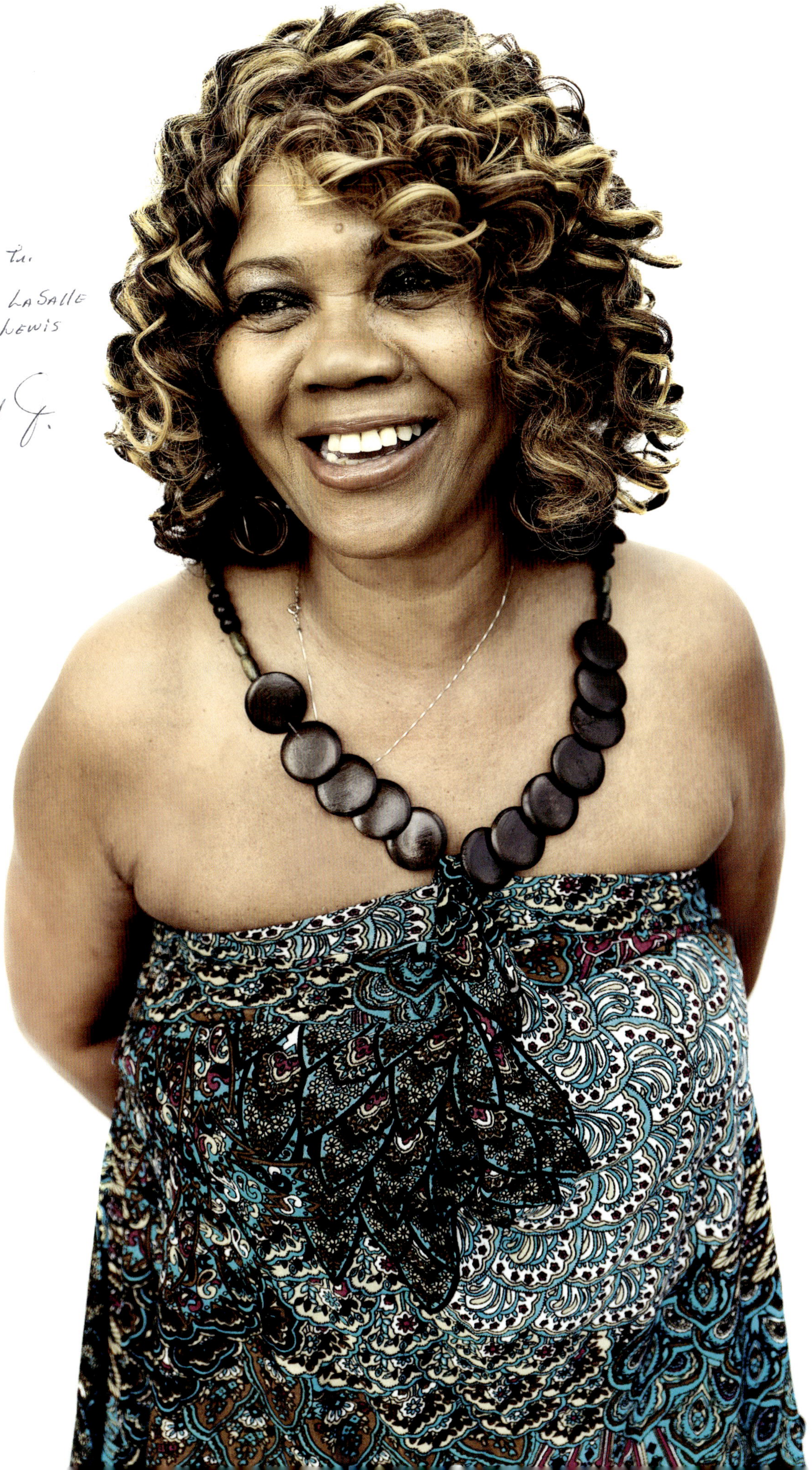

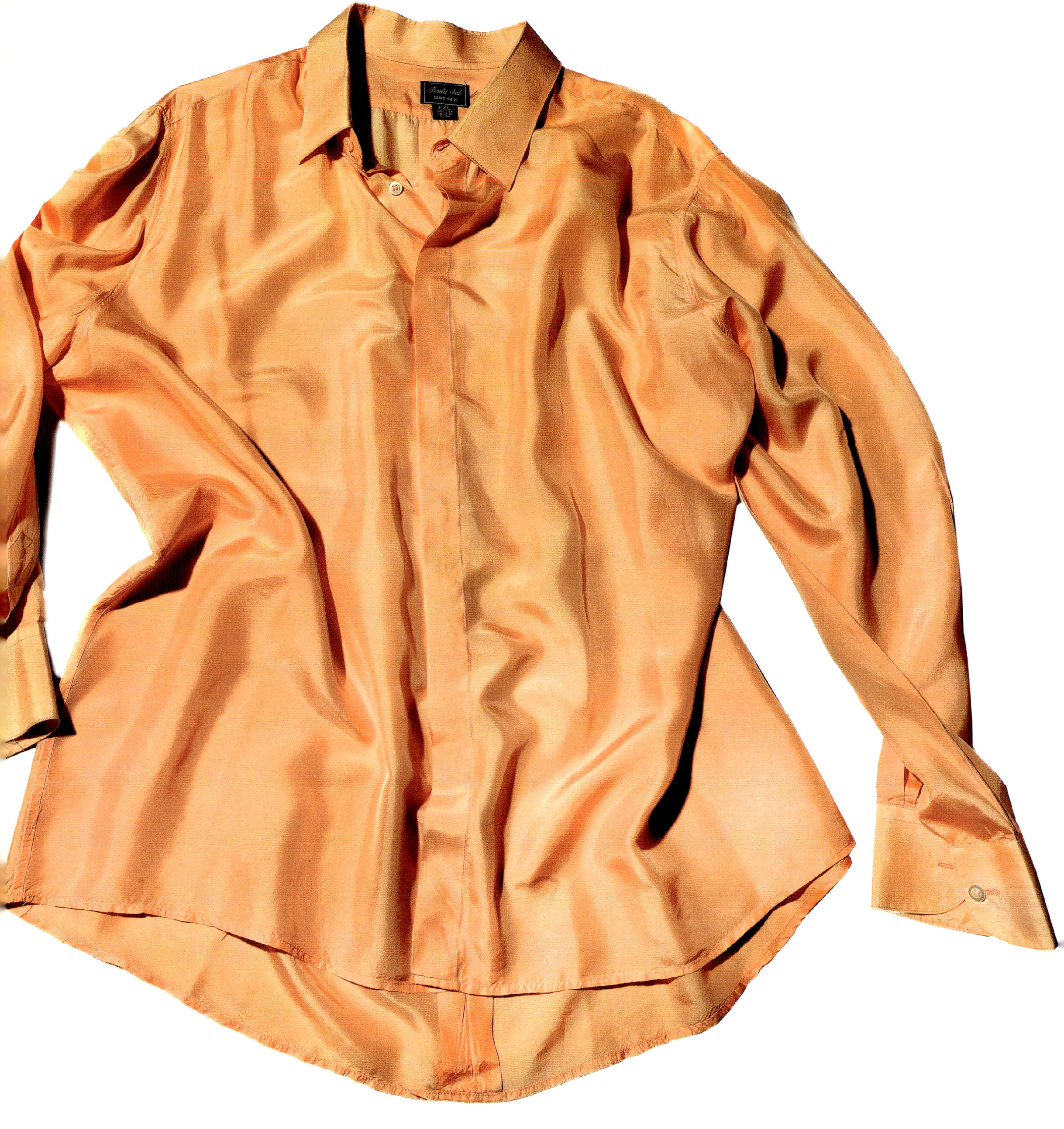


ALBERT KING'S 1960s' STAGE CLOTHES: PENTA CLUB SILK SHIRT & LANSKY BROS. JACKET

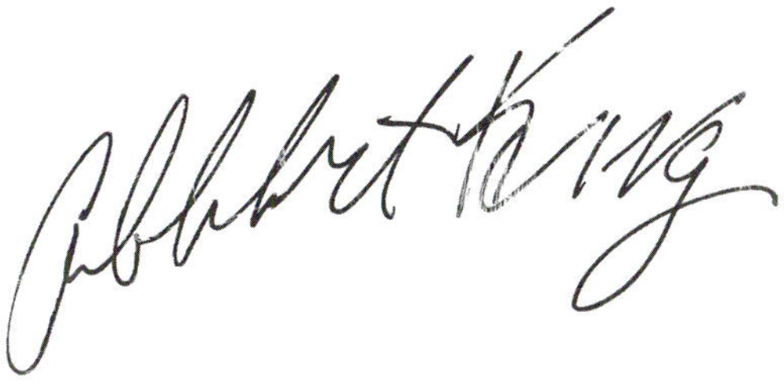

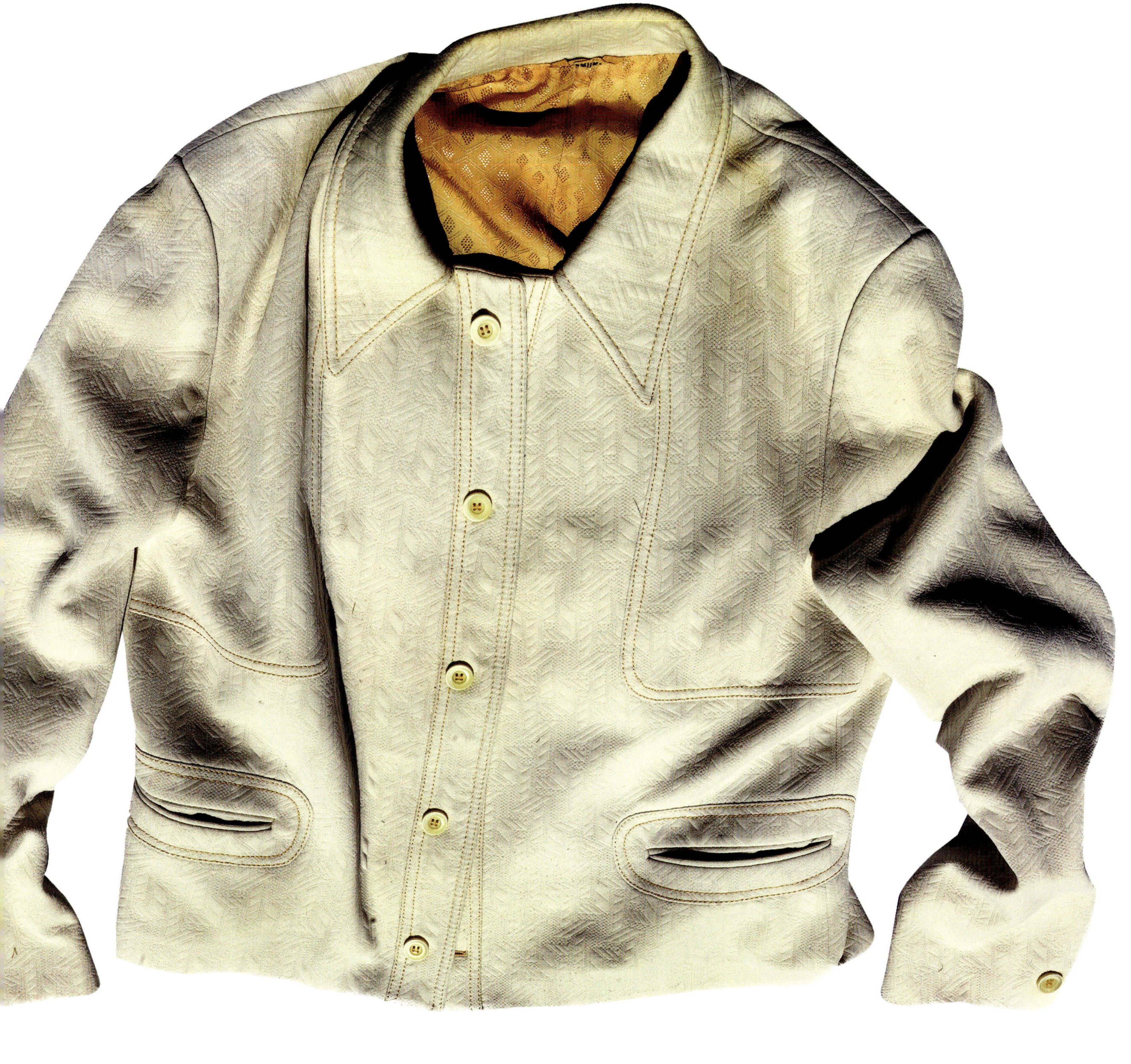

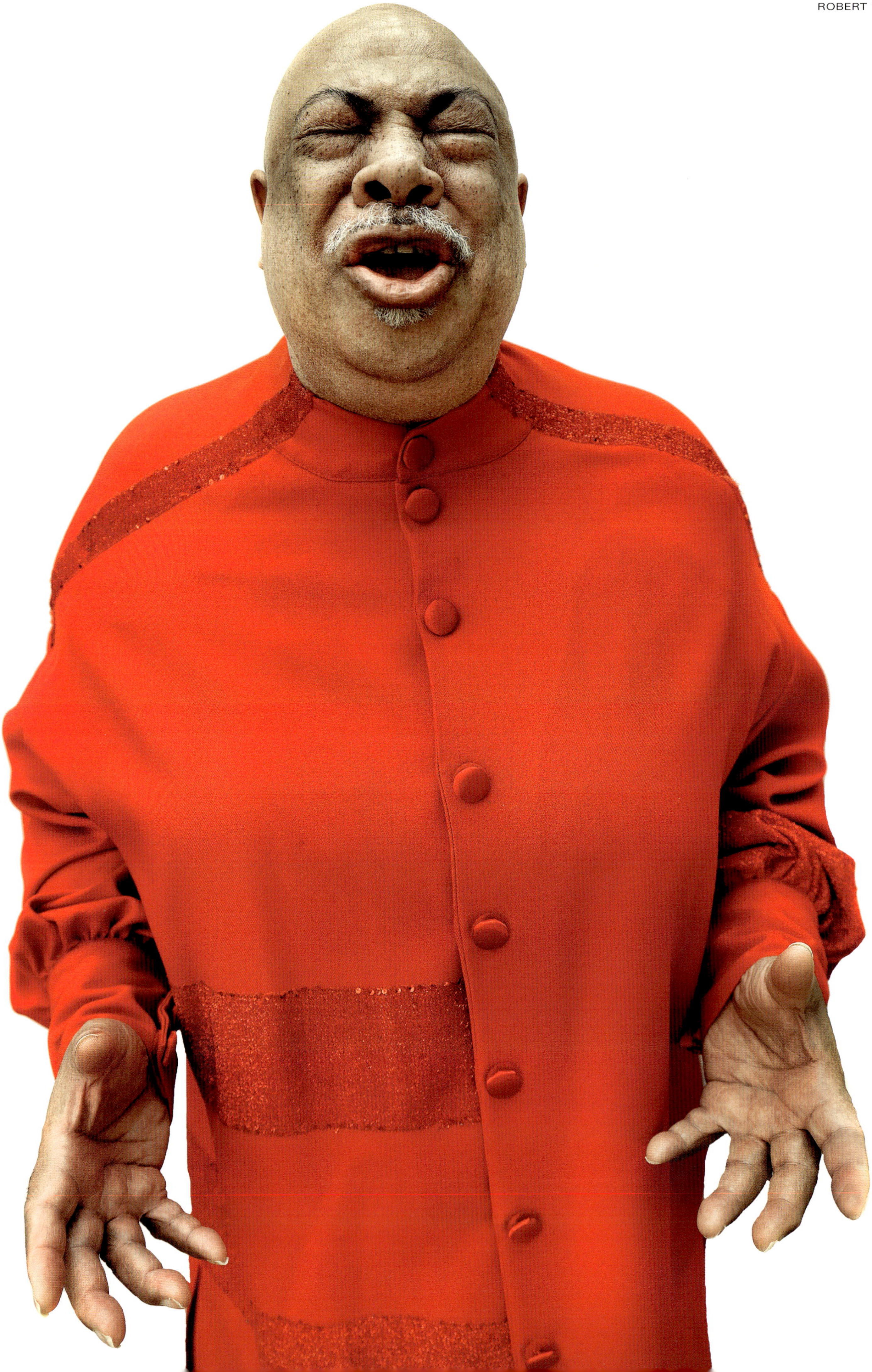

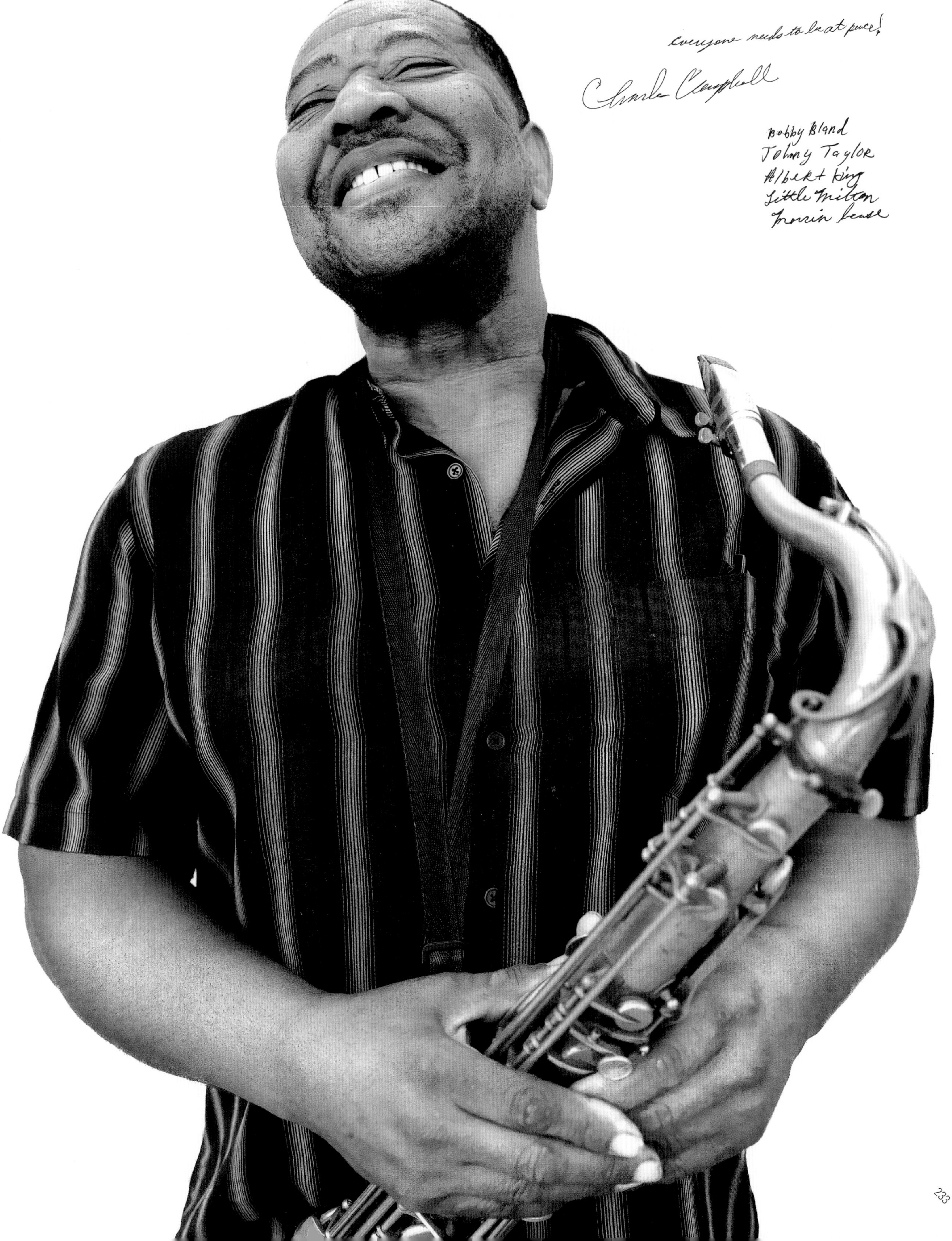
everyone needs to be at peace!
Charles Campbell
Bobby Bland
Johny Taylor
Albert King
Little Milton

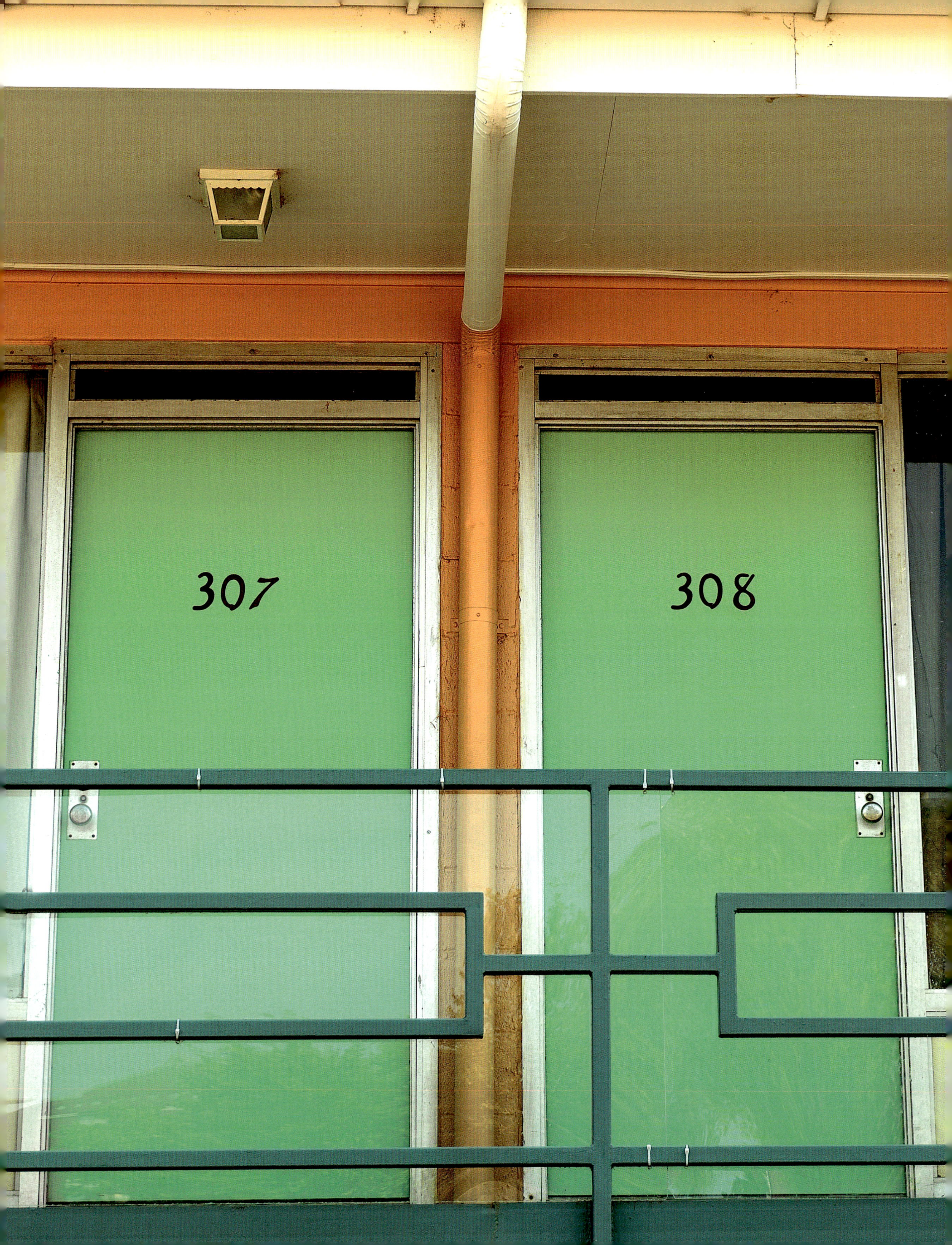
307
308

Behind the doors
of the
Lorraine Motel
songs were written...

"Knock on Wood"
"The Midnight Hour"
"Ninety-Nine and A Half
(Won't Do)"
"Things Get Better"
"634-5789"
"Your Good Thing is About
to Come to an End"

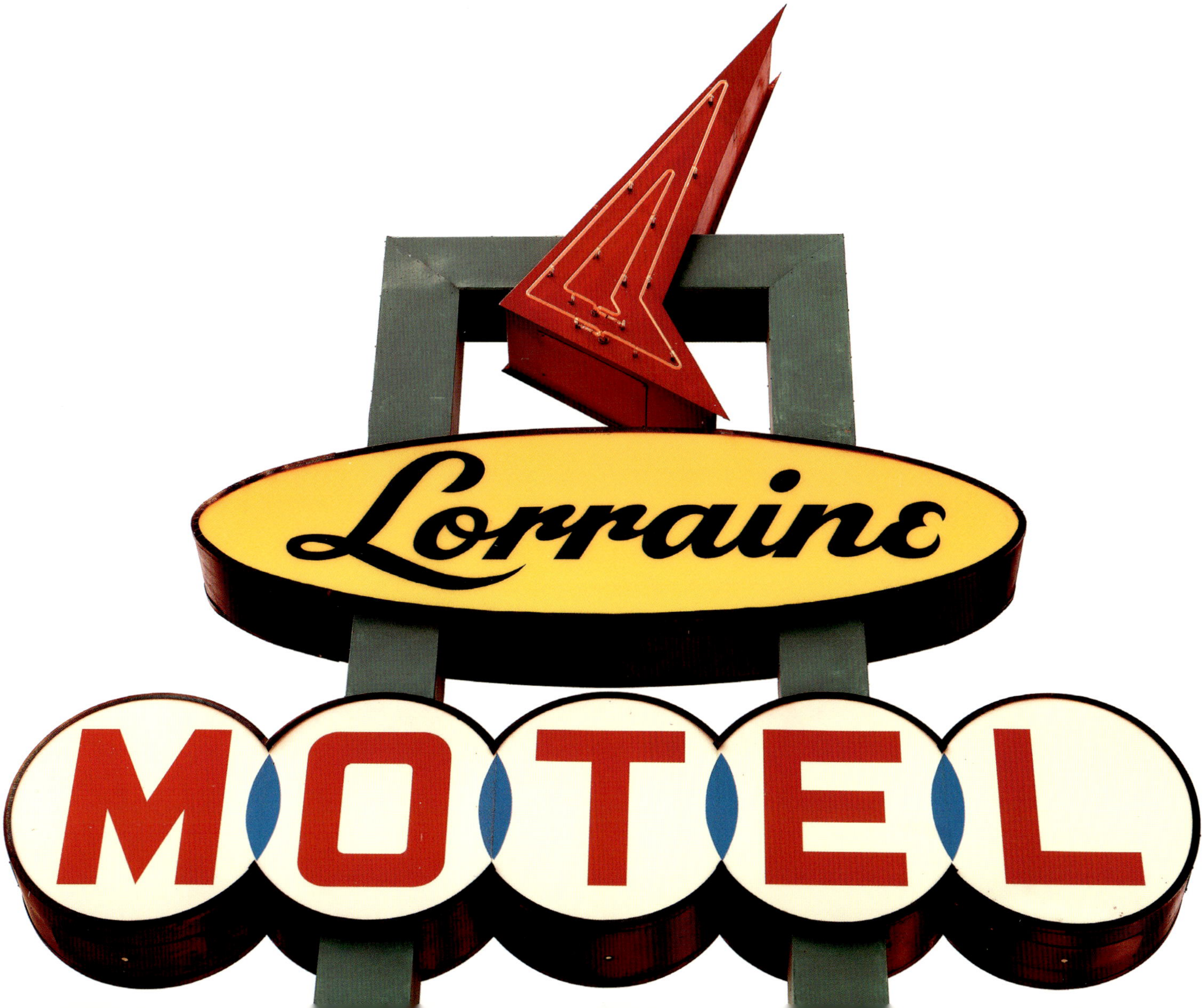

HARVEY HENDERSON

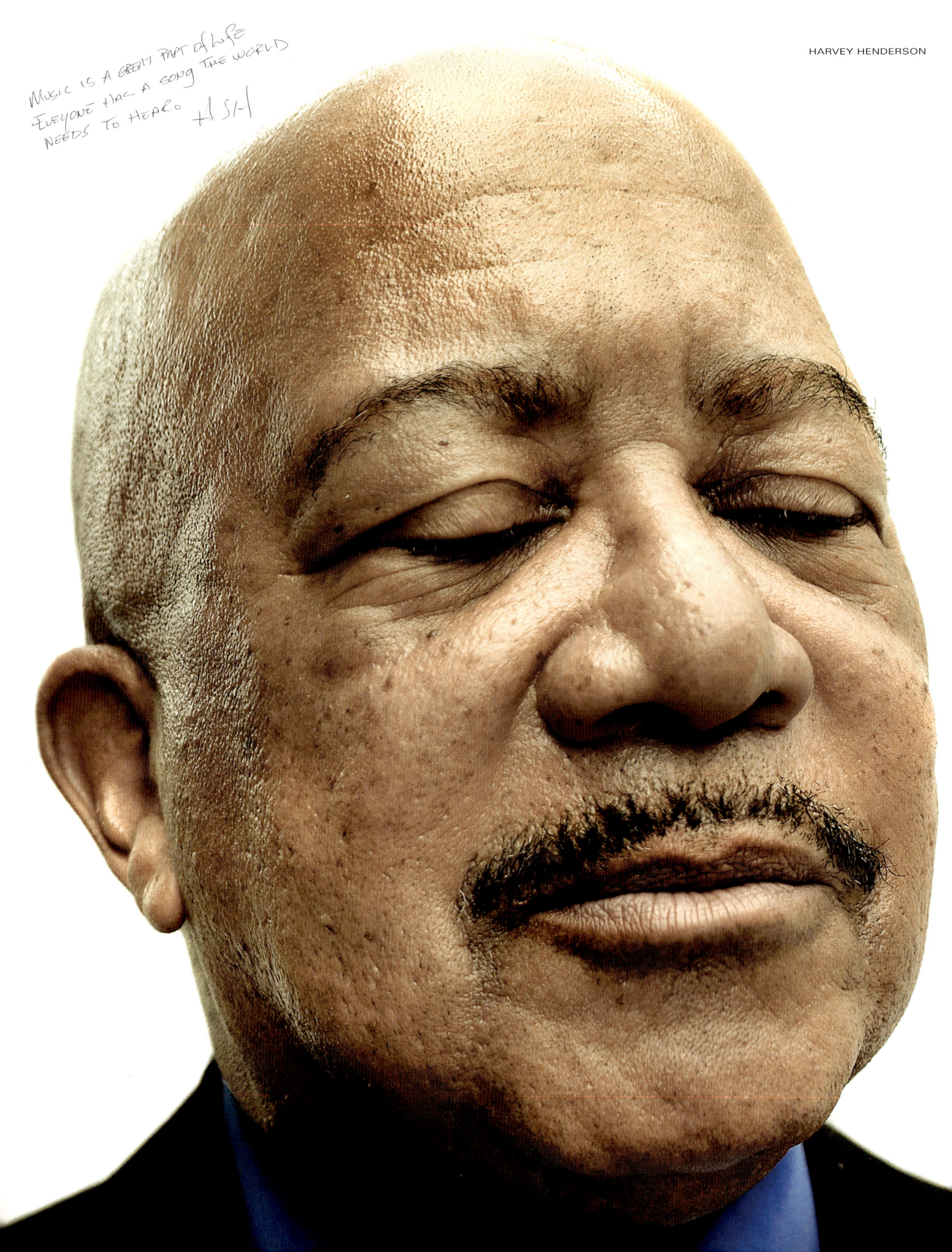

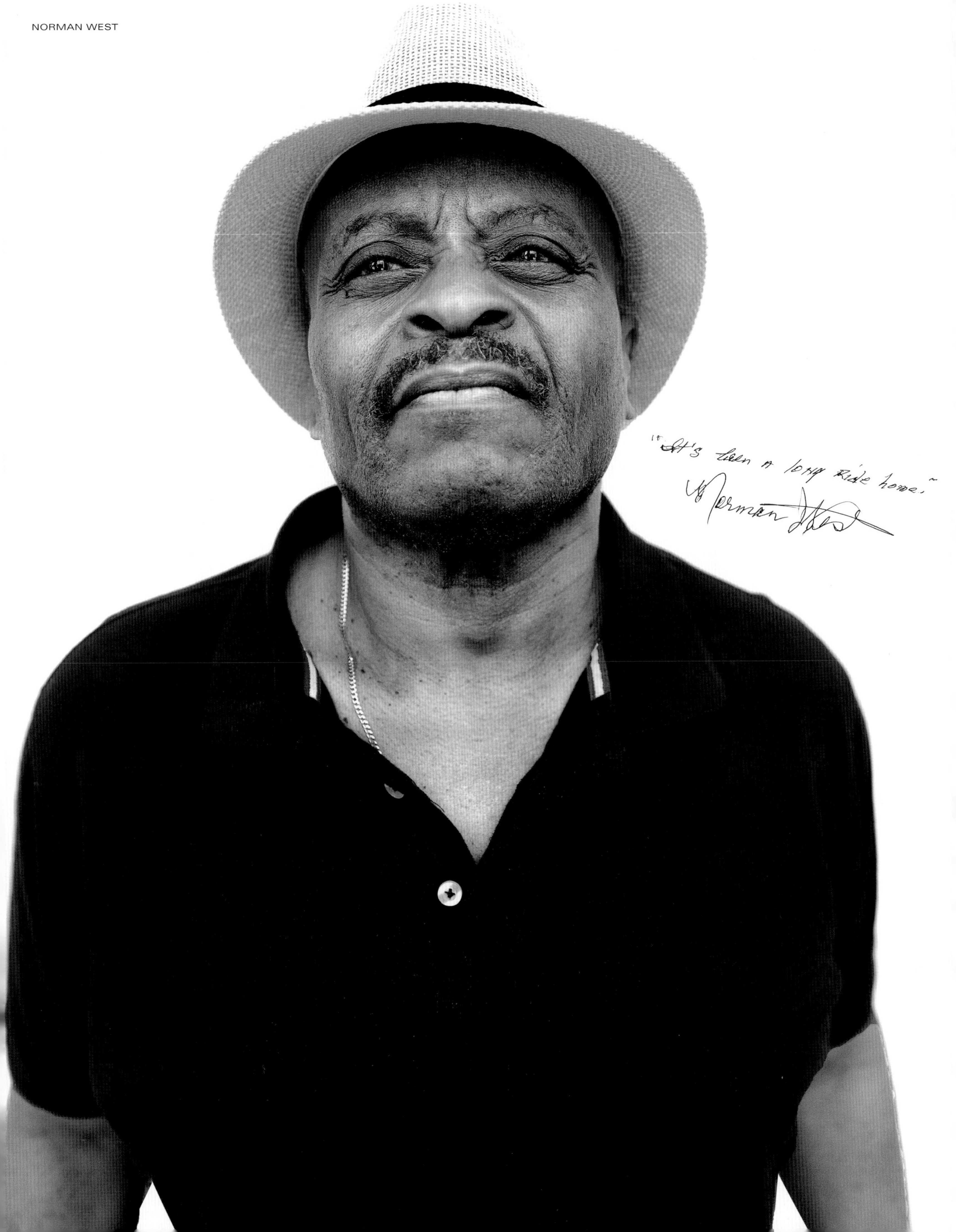
"It's been a long ride home."
Norman West

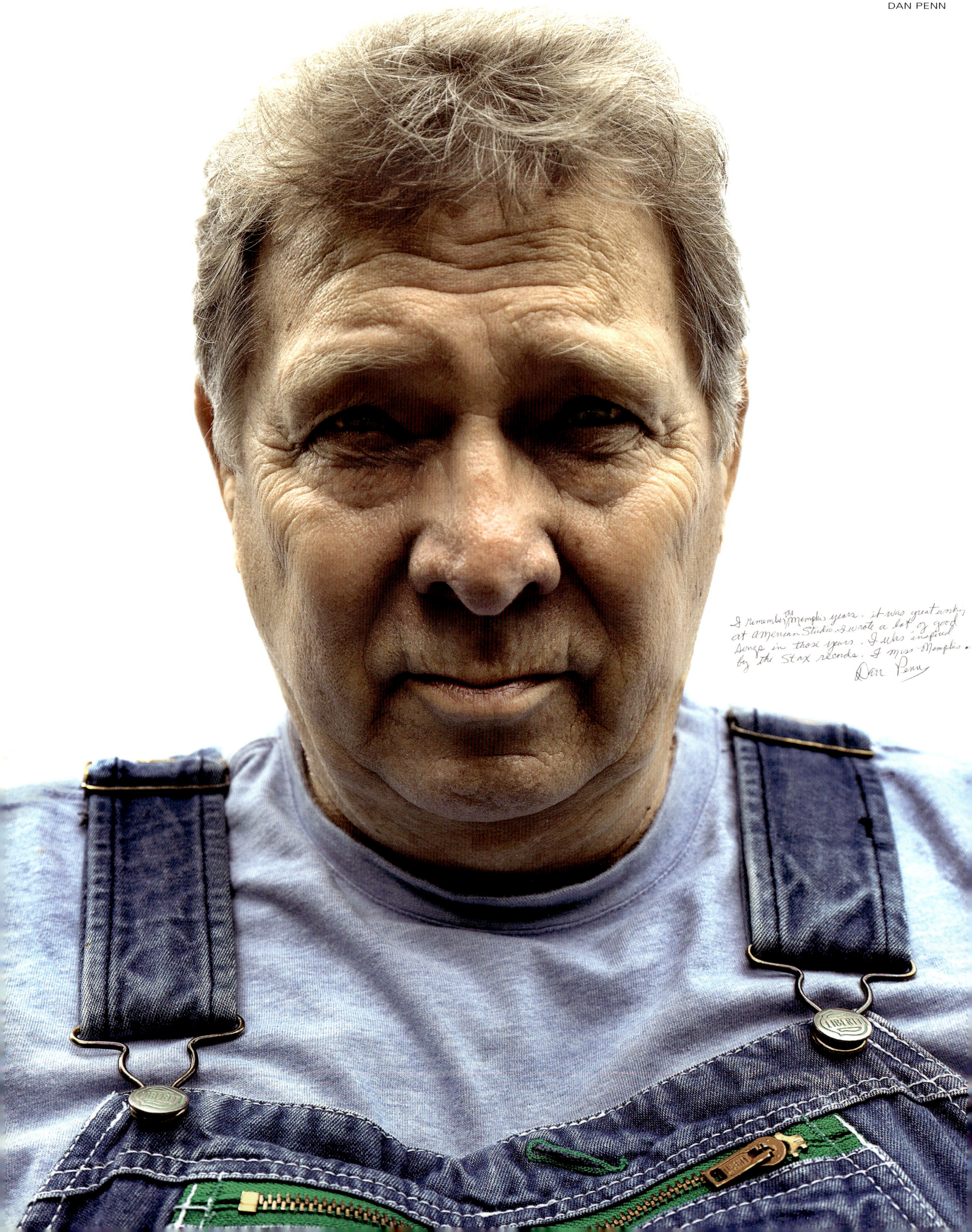

I remember the Memphis years. it was great working
at American Studio. I wrote a lot of good
songs in those years. I was inspired
by the Stax records. I miss Memphis.
Dan Penn

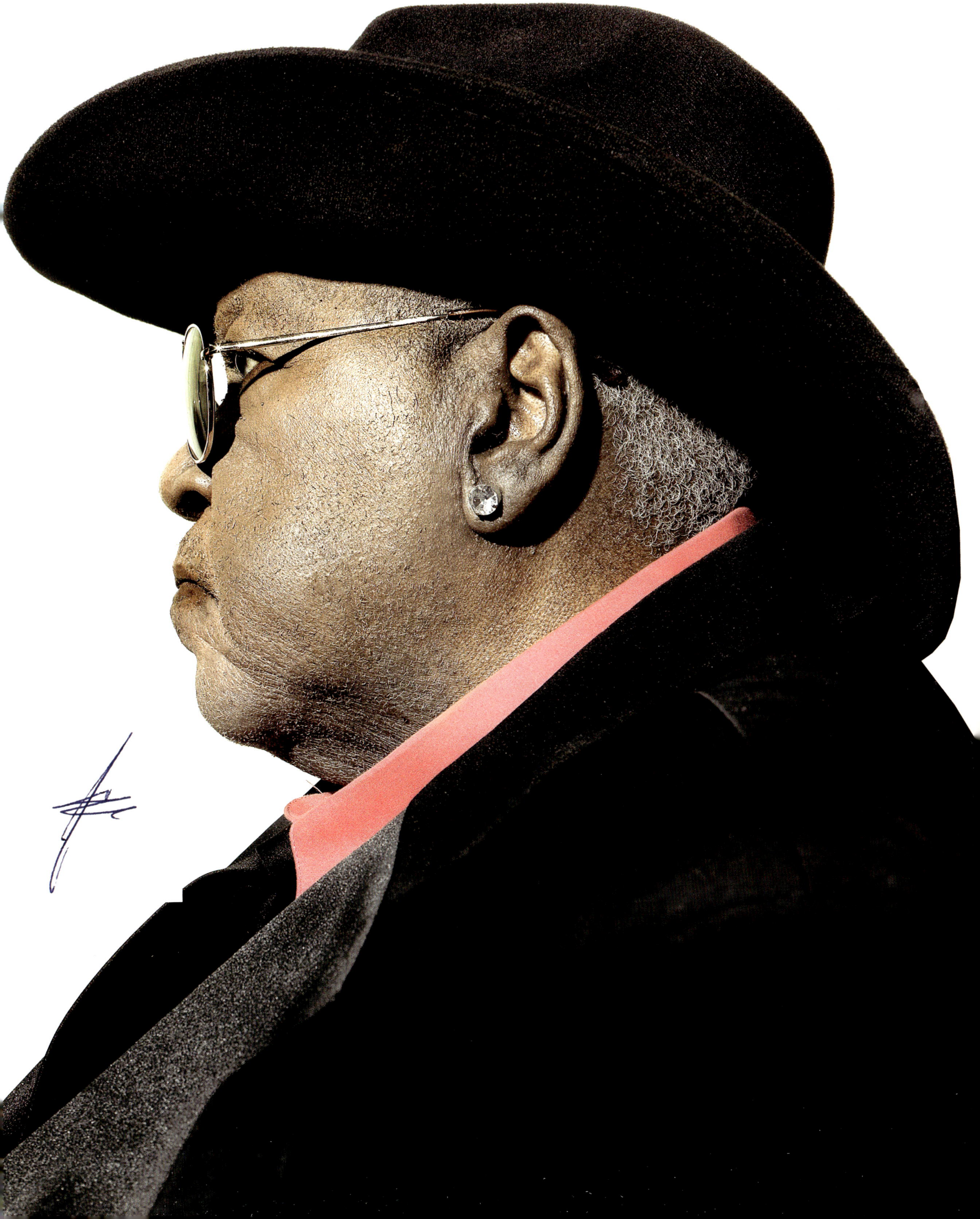

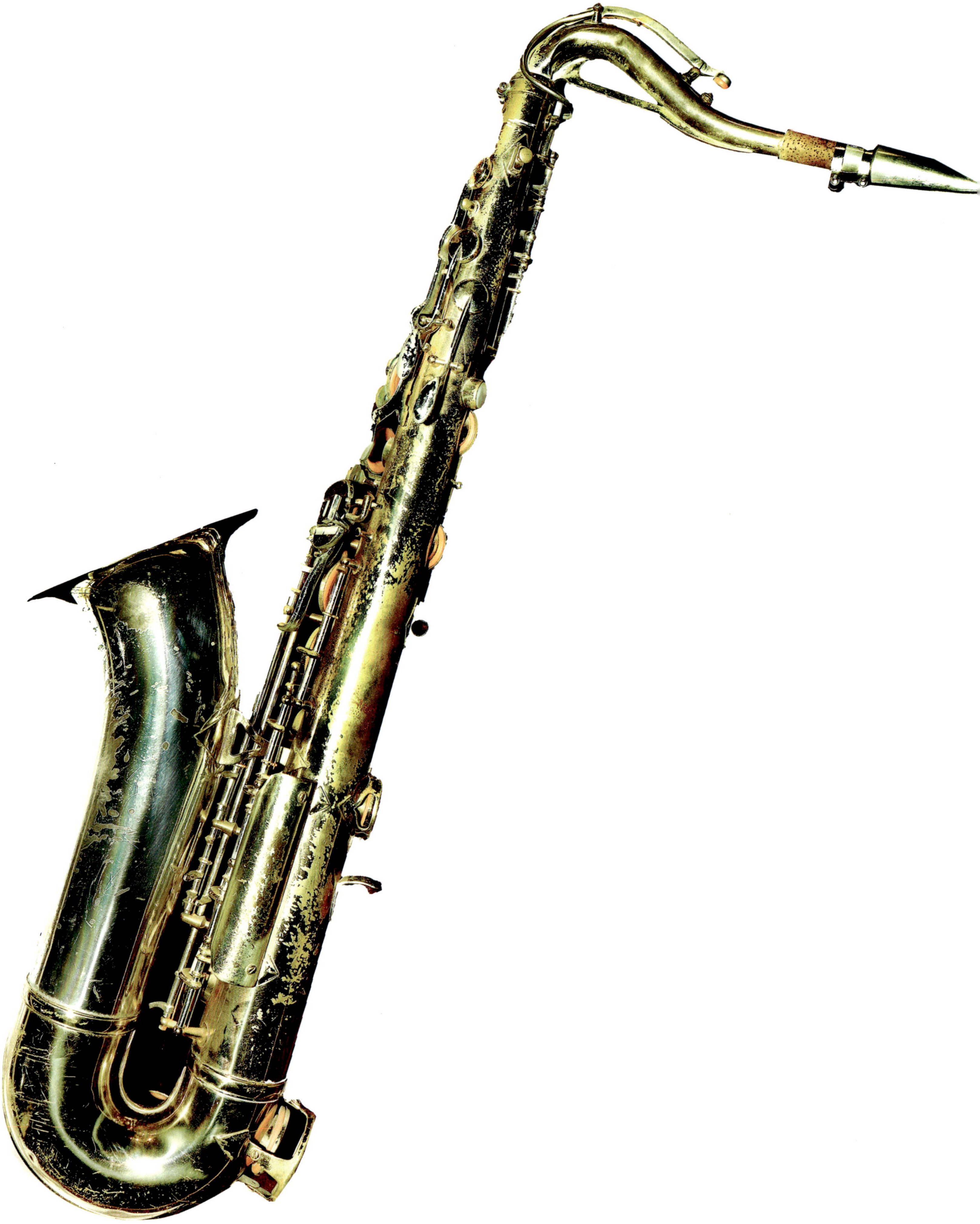

# History of Stax Records and the Stax Museum of American Soul Music*

Capitol Theater in the heart of Soulsville, USA, was transformed into Stax Records in 1959, it began launching the careers of unknowns who would become icons, cranking out a massive catalog of smash soul hits by the likes of Isaac Hayes, Otis Redding, the Staple Singers, Wilson Pickett, Luther Ingram, Albert King, the Bar-Kays, Booker T. & the MGs, Johnnie Taylor, Rufus and Carla Thomas, and dozens of other artists whose influence remains vital in the music of today.

**1957** First Tennessee banker Jim Stewart begins recording country music in his wife's uncle's garage in north Memphis. Satellite Records is launched.

**1958** Stewart moves his "recording studio" to Brunswick, Tennessee. Stewart's sister Estelle Axton, then employed by Union Planters Bank, mortgages her home to pay for recording equipment for the company.

**1959** Stewart and Axton move to the old Capitol Theater, currently abandoned on McLemore Avenue.

**1960** WDIA disc jockey Rufus Thomas hustles over to the studio with his daughter Carla and together they cut Satellite's first hit, "Cause I Love You."

**1961** Local high school R&B band the MarKeys cut the instrumental hit "Last Night" that sends Satellite Records soaring. Stewart takes the first two letters from his last name (ST) and adds the first two letters of his sister's last name (AX) to form the new label name: STAX RECORDS. For the next 14 years, the hits from the corner of McLemore and College cannot be stopped.

**1962** The MarKeys evolve into Booker T. and the MGs, forming the house band for the next eight years of Stax hits, beginning with a B-side, "Green Onions." Georgia crooner Otis Redding comes to the studio and begins a career that shoots straight to the top of the R&B charts and eventually crosses over into the pop world. William Bell hits with "You Don't Miss Your Water."

**1963** Rufus Thomas begins his dance-craze hit parade with "The Dog," "Walking the Dog," and "Can Your Monkey Do the Dog?"

**1965** Sam & Dave come on the Stax scene. Immediately, local musicians and Stax writers Isaac Hayes and David Porter take them under their wing and crank out a streak of hits, including "I Take What I Want," "Soul Man," "You Don't Know Like I Know," "Said I Wasn't Gonna Tell Nobody," "I Thank You," and "Hold On, I'm Coming." Well-known DJ Al Bell joins Stax Records as its first promotions man.

**1966** Eddie Floyd "Knocks on Wood," Carla Thomas hits on "B-A-B-Y," Albert King cuts the "Crosscut Saw," and Sam & Dave hit again with "You Got Me Hummin.'" Otis Redding performs in Europe for the first time on the popular television show *Ready, Steady, Go!*

**1967** Stax takes its show on the road to Europe, shaking the whole continent with Booker T. & the MGs, Carla Thomas, the MarKeys Horns, Sam & Dave, and then wiping the audience out with Otis Redding. Redding slays the hippies at the Monterrey Pop Festival in California. The Bar-Kays score with "Soul Finger." The year ends on a sour note as Otis Redding's plane goes down into Lake Monono, Wisconsin, killing Redding and most of the Bar-Kays who were touring with him. Stax loses all of its master tapes to Atlantic Records due to a fine-print clause in a contract.

**1968** "(Sittin' on) the Dock of the Bay," released posthumously, goes to no. 1 on both the pop and R&B charts. Martin Luther King is assassinated in Memphis in April. Film company Gulf & Western buys Stax from Jim Stewart, Estelle Axton, and Al Bell in exchange for stock.

**1969** In an effort to create a new catalog, Al Bell launches an aggressive release campaign, releasing 27 albums and 30 singles in one month. Stax hits hard with "Time is Tight" by Booker T. & the MGs as well as "Who's Making Love" by Johnnie Taylor. Isaac Hayes unleashes *Hot Buttered Soul*, his first of a string of million-selling long-form albums.

**1970** Stewart and Bell re-purchase Stax from Gulf & Western, expanding the label into jazz, comedy, country, spoken word, gospel, and rock.

**1971** Isaac Hayes becomes a mega-superstar with the release of the soundtrack to *Shaft*, which eventually wins Grammys and an Oscar.

**1972** The Staple Singers come on board with "I'll Take You There" and "Respect Yourself." Luther Ingram scores with "(If Loving You is Wrong) I Don't Want to be Right." Bell negotiates a lucrative deal for CBS to distribute Stax. Stax takes almost its entire current roster of artists to Los Angeles and puts on the Wattstax concert to raise money for Watts charities, and films a documentary not only of the concert, but also of everyday life for African Americans at the time.

**1975** A record pressing company sues Stax, and Stax cannot meet payroll. Stax owes millions to Union Planters and loses most of its artists. Al Bell is indicted by a federal grand jury for bank fraud and is acquitted on all charges. Isaac Hayes sues Stax. Al Jackson is murdered. Union Planters forecloses on the publishing arm of Stax. Three small creditors, encouraged by Union Planters, force Stax into involuntary bankruptcy December 19, 1975.

**1977** Stax's master tapes are sold at bankruptcy auction for a fraction of their value—$1.3 million. Fantasy Records in California buys the Stax catalog from Nassi & Assoc.

**1998** After years of discussions and various unrelated efforts at bringing Stax back, Memphis civic leaders form the nonprofit Ewarton Foundation (using the rest of the letters after ST in Jim Stewart's last name and AX in Axton) to rebuild the Capitol Theatre and create the Stax Museum of American Soul Music to serve as the anchor for a broader neighborhood revitalization. The vision is expanded to include the Stax Music Academy as a vehicle to mentor at-risk youth and honor the Stax legacy.

**1998** With $5 million in seed money from anonymous donors, Ewarton receives a $3 million challenge grant from the Plough

Foundation that is matched with $2.5 million grants each from the City of Memphis, Shelby County, and the United States Federal Government.

In addition to raising further capital, Ewarton acquires the original Stax Records site and roughly five acres of land from various owners, demolishes multiple neglected and/or abandoned buildings; obtains the critical intellectual rights necessary for using the Stax Museum and Stax Records names, builds neighborhood and community goodwill, and effectively promotes "Soulsville" as the appropriate neighborhood designator; designs and entitles the multi-building campus, including the Museum galleries; collects and acquires key memorabilia, oversees construction and exhibit installation, and begins building a world-class museum and music academy.

**2000** On February 8, Ewarton holds a press conference at nearby LeMoyne-Owen College to announce that the Stax Museum of American Soul Music and Stax Music Academy will be built at the original site of Stax Records.

**2001** On April 20, Ewarton hosts a "Ground Shakin' Ground Breakin'" ceremony at the site of the planned museum and thousands, including Rufus Thomas, who was the first to arrive at 5 a.m., attend it.

**2002** On July 24, the ribbon is cut during the grand opening ceremonies for the newly constructed Stax Music Academy.

**2003** On May 2, the Stax Museum opens its doors to the public to great international fanfare. In the previous days, other grand opening celebrations had taken place throughout the city, including Soul Comes Home at the Orpheum Theater, a Stax reunion concert featuring Booker T. & the MGs, Mavis Staples, the Rance Allen Group, Jean Knight, Eddie Floyd, William Bell, Carla Thomas, Ann Peebles, Al Green, Jimmie Vaughan, and others. There is also a concert at Gibson Lounge featuring Mable John, Big Star, and Linda Lyndell.

**2004** In January, Stax Museum kicks off a concert series, "Last Mondays in Studio A," which takes place on the last Monday evening of each month through December 2007 and featured live music by the likes of Eddie Floyd, William Bell, Sir Mack Rice, the Temprees, the Mad Lads, Wayne Jackson of the Memphis Horns with the Stax Music Academy; Linda Lyndell, Mable John, Ann Peebles and the 35th reunion of the Hi Rhythm Section, and dozens of other singers and musicians.

**2005** Ewarton changes its name to Soulsville Foundation.

**2008** *Time* magazine names Stax Museum "The most authentic American experience in Tennessee."

**2009** Stax Music Academy students opened for B.B. King at his annual B.B. King Homecoming Festival and Concert in his hometown of Indianola, Mississippi.

**2010** Stax Music Academy students were invited to perform at the national AARP convention in Orlando, Florida, with Stax legend William Bell. Other entertainers include Gladys Knight, Los Lobos, Gloria Gaynor, Judy Collins, and B.B. King.

**2011** Stax Museum adds new interactive exhibits, including listening stations with more than 300 Stax songs by some 85 Stax artists.

**2012** Stax Museum opens special Wattstax 40th Anniversary Exhibit and hosts panel discussion with those who performed at, planned, and attended the famed concert. Other special exhibits Stax Museum has hosted since opening include photographic exhibits highlighting Bob Dylan, the Beatles, Rolling Stones; an exhibit of Blaxploitation film posters; an exhibit about the surrounding neighborhood known as Soulsville, USA; exhibits honoring blues, hip hop, jazz, and gospel artists; two special Otis Redding exhibits; and many others.

**2013** PBS airs *In Performance at the White House: Memphis Soul* on April 16 featuring an 8-minute introduction by President Barack Obama (see page 000) about the importance of Memphis soul music, particularly that of the integrated Stax Records.

* Extracted from the Stax Museum of American Soul Music website. Available at http://www.staxmuseum.com/about/history (accessed October 11, 2013).

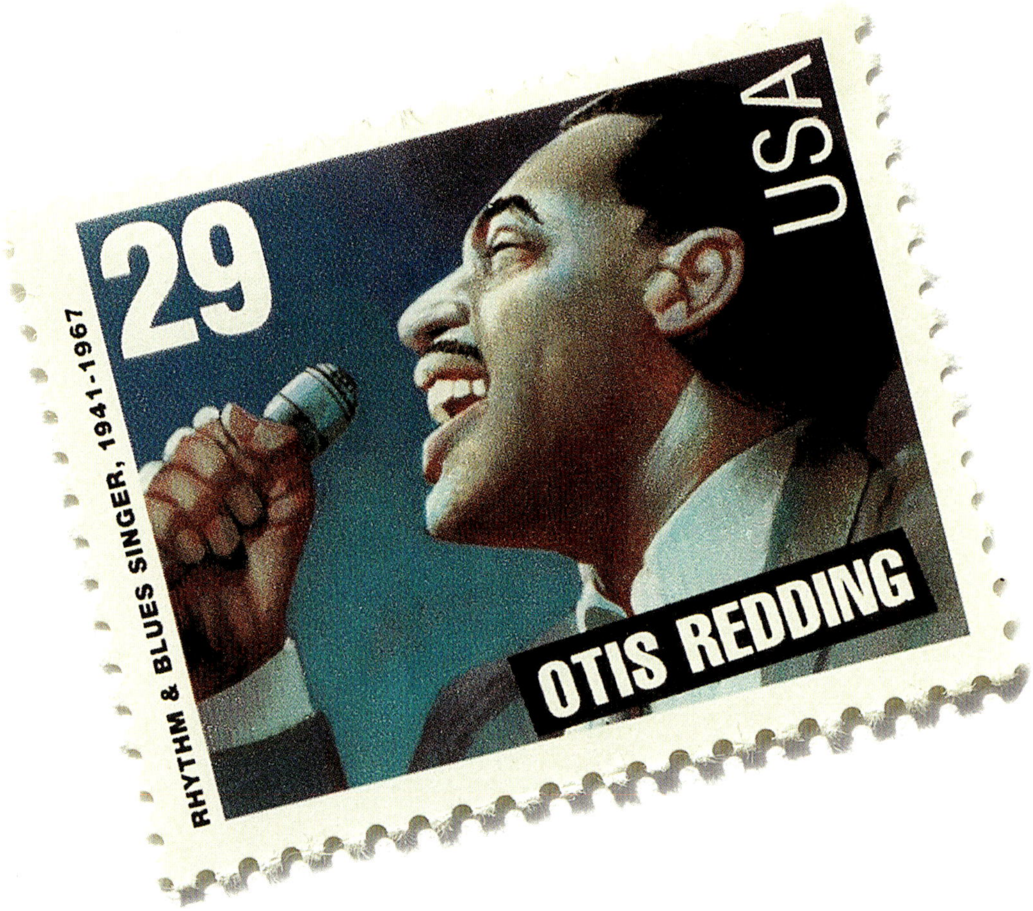


1993 U.S. POSTAL SERVICE COMMEMORATIVE STAMP HONORING OTIS REDDING

# Index of Artists*

** Asterisk against entry denotes a corresponding photograph*

## *Emerson Able

Saxophonist and former bandleader at Manassas High School, Memphis. Able recorded and traveled with the Isaac Hayes Movement, including at the great Wattstax Festival in 1972. Hayes is just one just one of his legendary students from Manassas High.

## *James Alexander

(born 1948) An American soul and rhythm and blues (R&B) musician, he is a longtime member of the band the Bar-Kays, for which he plays bass guitar. He was the bassist for the band when four of the six band members, including Phalon Jones, were killed in the same plane crash that claimed the life of soul singer Otis Redding. Alexander was the only Bar-Kays member not aboard that flight, as the plane, a Beechcraft owned by Redding, only held eight occupants (Redding, five of the Bar-Kays, the pilot, and Redding's road manager); it was Alexander's turn in the rotation to board a commercial flight to the next destination. He had the task of identifying the bodies of his bandmates, as well as that of Redding.

## Rance Allen

(born November 19, 1948) An American pastor and gospel musician, and the leader of the Rance Allen Group, which he founded in Detroit in 1969, joined by his brothers Thomas and Steve. In 1978, the group had a Top 30 R&B hit, "I Belong to You."

## *Duane Allman

(November 20, 1946–October 29, 1971) An American guitarist, session musician, and the co-founder and primary leader of the Allman Brothers Band until his death in a motorcycle accident at the age of 24. A sought-after session musician both before and during his tenure with the band, Duane performed with such established stars as King Curtis, Aretha Franklin, Wilson Pickett, and Herbie Mann. He also contributed heavily to the 1970 album *Layla and Other Assorted Love Songs* by Derek and the Dominos.

## Joe Arnold

Tenor sax player, and, from 1965 to 1967, a staff musician at Stax Records in Memphis. He has played with Otis Redding, Bobby "Blue" Bland, Booker T. & the M.G.s, and Sam & Dave, to name a few.

## *The Astors

Originally consisting of Curtis Johnson, Eliehue Stanback, Sam (Byrnes) Jones, and Richard Harris, they recorded their first release "You Make Me Feel So Good" in 1961. Initially, they provided backing vocals for Carla and Rufus Thomas and other artist recording at a new studio then called Satellite Records and later renamed Stax.

## *Charles "Packy" Axton

(February 17, 1941–January 1974) An American R&B tenor saxophone player and bandleader who was a member of the MarKeys and, later, the Packers. He was born in Memphis, Tennessee, the son of Everett and Estelle Axton. Estelle Axton and her brother Jim Stewart were the founders of Stax Records.

## *Estelle Axton

(September 11, 1918–February 25, 2004) Co-founder, with her brother Jim Stewart, of Stax Records.

## Homer Banks

(August 2, 1941–April 3, 2003) An African American songwriter, singer, and record producer, best known for his songs for Stax Records in the 1960s and 1970s. Many of the songs he wrote have become contemporary classics. His co-writer was Allen Jones.

## Homer Banks, Carl Hampton, and Raymond Jackson

The writing team for several hits, including their biggest "(If Loving You Is Wrong) I Don't Want to Be Right," performed by Luther Ingram. A ballad about marital infidelity, it was Ingram's most successful hit, and was released on KoKo Records (Stax was the distributor).

## Johnny Baylor

Record producer, artist manager, and owner of the KoKo record label.

## *Harold Beane

An American funk guitarist who worked for 15 years with the group Funkadelic. He has also worked with Stax composer David Porter, Little Richard, Isaac Hayes ("Walk on By"), Eddie Floyd ("Knock on Wood"), Otis Redding, Al Green, and William Bell, to name few.

## *Al Bell

(born Alvertis Isbell; March 15, 1940; Brinkley, Arkansas) An American record producer, songwriter, and record executive. Bell is best known as one of the key figures and co-owner of Memphis-based Stax Records, during the latter half of the label's 19-year existence. A former disc jockey in his hometown of Little Rock, Arkansas, Bell was vital to the careers of Stax's soul stars such as the Staples Singers and Isaac Hayes, the Emotions, the Dramatics, and Mel and Tim. Bell's promotional efforts drove the "Memphis sound" internationally, and made Stax the second-largest African American-owned business in the 1970s. In 2009, the BBC profiled Bell as "one of the icons of soul music" and "the driving force behind Stax Records."

## *William Bell

(born July 16, 1939) An American soul singer and songwriter, and one of the architects of the Stax/Volt sound. As a performer, he is probably best known for 1961's "You Don't Miss Your Water" (his debut single); 1968's "Private Number" (a duet with Judy Clay, and a top 10 hit in the UK); and 1976's "Tryin' To Love Two," Bell's only U.S. top 40 hit, which also hit no. 1 on the R&B chart. Upon the death of Otis Redding, Bell released the well-received memorial song "A Tribute to a King." As a songwriter, Bell co-authored the Chuck Jackson hit "Any Other Way" (itself a cover, since Bell issued it first, as a follow-up to "You Don't Miss Your Water"), Billy Idol's 1986 hit "To Be a Lover" (first a hit for Bell under its original title "I Forgot to Be Your Lover"), and the blues classic "Born Under A Bad Sign," popularized by both Albert King and Cream.

## *Bobby "Blue" Bland

(January 27, 1930–June 23, 2013) An American singer of blues and soul, Bland developed a sound that mixed gospel with the blues and R&B. Sometimes referred to as the "Lion of the Blues" or the "Sinatra of the Blues," his music was also influenced by Nat King Cole. His first

## *Sir Mack Rice

(born November 10, 1933; Clarksdale, Mississippi) An American songwriter whose compositions have been performed by many well-known artists, including the Staple Singers, Ike and Tina Turner, Albert King, Johnnie Taylor, Shirley Brown, Rufus Thomas, Etta James, Billy Eckstine, Eddie Floyd, Buddy Guy, the Rascals, Wilson Pickett, Albert Collins, Busta Rhymes, Lynyrd Skynyrd, Otis Clay, and the Blues Brothers (in *Blues Brothers 2000*). Some of his better-known songs include "Respect Yourself," "Betcha Can't Kiss Me (Just One Time)," "Cheaper to Keep Her," "Cadillac Assembly Line," "Money Talks," "Cold Women With Warm Hearts," "Do the Funky Penguin, Pt. 1," "It Sho Ain't Me," "Santa Claus Wants Some Lovin'," among others. His best-known composition and only hit as a solo performer is "Mustang Sally."

## Bernard Roberson

Head of promotion at Stax Records.

## Ewell Roussell

Head of the sales department at Stax Records.

## *Royal Studios

A recording studio located in Memphis, Tennessee. Established in 1956, it is one of the oldest continuously operated music recording studios in the world. It is widely known for producer, recording artist, and owner, Willie Mitchell (1928–2010), and for notable productions of Al Green, Chuck Berry, John Mayer, Buddy Guy, My Morning Jacket, Robert Cray, De La Soul, Otis Rush, Keith Richards, Solomon Burke, the Bo-Keys, Bobby "Blue" Bland, Ann Peebles, Ike and Tina Turner, Tom Jones, Anthony Hamilton, and Rod Stewart.

## *Bobby Rush

(born November 10, 1935; Homer, Louisiana) An American blues and R&B musician, composer, harmonica player, and singer. His style incorporates elements of soul, blues, rap, and funk. It was in the early 1970s that his self-penned "Chicken Heads" cracked the *Billboard* R&B chart on Galaxy, after being picked up from a small label started by former Vee-Jay Records producer, Calvin Carter (no. 34, 1971). He later recorded with leading black music label Philadelphia International, releasing his first album, *Rush Hour*, produced by Leon Huff, with one track, "I Wanna Do The Do," also charting in 1979 (no. 75).

## Harvey Scales

An American R&B singer, songwriter, and producer. Scales has been active in the music industry since the 1960s, and has composed songs for groups such as the Dells, the Dramatics, and the O'Jays. He is particularly notable for his co-authorship of the songs "Love-Itis" and "Disco Lady."

## *Preston Shannon

Memphis-based guitarist, singer, and songwriter. Hailed as the reigning "King of Beale Street" in Memphis.

## Larry Shaw

Head of advertising and marketing at Stax Records. He developed the Stax brand internationally through logo development, album covers, advertising, and marketing promotions. *Vanity Fair* has listed his work as encompassing the best album cover designs of all times. Additionally, he was head of the Stax's film division; Shaw, with Stax owner Al Bell, conceived and produced the movie *Wattstax*.

## *Jerry Lee "Smoochie" Smith

A self-taught pianist and vocalist. At Stax Records, Smoochie recorded with the MarKeys and was co-writer of their 1961 million-seller hit "Last Night." He also played on Carla Thomas's first album *Gee Whiz*, among many others to his credit.

## *Novella Smith

In 1973, Smith came to Memphis as production chief at Stax Records and stayed till they closed their doors.

## *Lester Snell

Pianist/keyboardist, songwriter, and producer. A veteran Stax Records session man and member of the Isaac Hayes Movement from 1971 until the late 1970s, Snell's record credits are legendary.

## The Soul Children

An American vocal group who recorded soul music for Stax Records in the late 1960s and early 1970s. They had three top ten hits on the U.S. *Billboard* R&B chart—"The Sweeter He Is" (1969), "Hearsay" (1972), and "I'll Be The Other Woman" (1973)—all of which crossed over to the Hot 100. The group was formed in 1968 by Isaac Hayes and David Porter of Stax Records in Memphis, Tennessee, after one of the label's top acts, Sam & Dave, left Stax to join the Atlantic label. As leading songwriters and producers for Stax, Hayes and Porter decided to put together a vocal group with two male and two female singers, all of who sang lead on some of the group's recordings. The original members were Norman West, John Colbert (a.k.a. J. Blackfoot), Anita Louis, and Shelbra Bennett.

## The Staple Singers

An American gospel, soul, and R&B singing group. Roebuck "Pops" Staples (1914–2000), the patriarch of the family, formed the group with his children Cleotha (1934–2013), Pervis (born 1935), Yvonne (born 1936), and Mavis (born 1939). They are best known for their 1970s' hits "Respect Yourself," "I'll Take You There," "If You're Ready (Come Go with Me)," and "Let's Do It Again."

## Stax Records

An American record label, originally based in Memphis, Tennessee. Founded in 1957 as Satellite Records, the name Stax Records was adopted in 1961. The label was a major factor in the creation of the Southern soul and Memphis soul music styles, also releasing gospel, funk, jazz, and blues recordings. While Stax is renowned for its output of African American music, the label was founded by two White businesspeople, Jim Stewart and his sister Estelle Axton (with the first two letters from each of their surnames forming the label's name), and featured several popular ethnically integrated bands, including the label's house band, Booker T. & the M.G.s. Following the death of Stax's biggest star, Otis Redding, in 1967, and the severance of the label's distribution deal with Atlantic Records in 1968, Stax continued primarily under the supervision of a new co-owner, Al Bell. Over the next five years, Bell expanded the label's operations significantly, in order to compete with Stax's main rival, Motown Records in Detroit. During the mid-1970s, a number of factors, including a problematic distribution deal with CBS Records, caused the label to slide into insolvency, resulting in its forced closure in late 1975. In 1977, Fantasy Records acquired the post-1968 Stax catalog, as well as selected pre-1968 recordings. Beginning in 1978, Stax (now owned by Fantasy) began signing new acts and issuing new material, as well as re-issuing previously recorded Stax material. However, by the early 1980s, no new material was being issued on the label, and, for the next two decades, Stax was strictly a re-issue label. After Concord Records acquired Fantasy in 2004, the Stax label was reactivated, and is today used to issue both the 1968–1975 catalog material and new recordings by current R&B and soul performers. Atlantic Records continues to hold the rights to the vast majority of the 1959–1968 Stax material.

## *Lewie Steinberg

(born September 13, 1933; Memphis, Tennessee) An American musician best known as the original bass guitar player for soul music group Booker T. & the M.G.s. Steinberg was in the group from 1962 to 1965. He is featured on "Green Onions," its B-side, "Behave Yourself," and the *Green Onions* album. He recorded one more album with the band, *Soul Dressing*, in 1965. Unlike the first album, every song but one on *Soul Dressing* was an original. When Steinberg stepped aside, Donald "Duck" Dunn took over on bass.

## *Jody Stevens

(born October 4, 1952; Memphis, Tennessee) An American drummer, who has played in Big

Star (with Alex Chilton of the Box Tops) and Golden Smog (with members of the Jayhawks and Soul Asylum). When not on tour with Big Star, he works at Ardent Studios, where Big Star has recorded all of their albums.

## *Jim Stewart

(born July 29, 1930) Former record company executive and producer who co-founded Stax Records. Some of the more well-known acts with Stax were Isaac Hayes, David Porter, Eddie Floyd, Johnnie Taylor, the Rance Allen Group, the Soul Children, the Staple Singers, the Temprees, the Emotions, the Dramatics, Mel and Tim, the Bar-Kays, Linda Lyndell, Richard Pryor, Bill Cosby, William Bell, Little Milton, Jesse Jackson, Big Star, Otis Redding, Sam & Dave, Carla Thomas Rufus Thomas, Booker T. & the M.G.s, and Albert King.

## *Randy Stewart

A former member of the 1960s' soul group the Fiestas and a Stax/Volt recording engineer. He also later road-managed for Isaac Hayes.

## Bob Talley

Pianist.

## Johnnie Taylor

(May 5, 1934–May 31, 2000) An American vocalist in a wide variety of genres, from rhythm and blues, soul, blues, and gospel to pop, doo-wop, and disco. In 1966, Taylor moved to Stax Records in Memphis, Tennessee, where he was dubbed the "Philosopher of Soul." Whilst there, he recorded with the label's house band, Booker T. & the M.G.s. His hits included "I Had a Dream," "I've Got to Love Somebody's Baby" (both written by the team of Isaac Hayes and David Porter), and, most notably, "Who's Making Love," which reached no. 5 on the *Billboard* Hot 100 chart and no. 1 on the R&B chart in 1968. "Who's Making Love" sold over one million copies, and was awarded a gold disc. During his tenure at Stax, he became an R&B star, with over a dozen chart successes, such as "Jody's Got Your Girl and Gone," which reached no. 23 on the Hot 100 chart; "Cheaper to Keep Her" (Mack Rice); and record producer Don Davis's penned "I Believe in You (You Believe in Me)," which reached no. 11 on the Hot 100 chart. "I Believe in You (You Believe in Me)" also sold in excess of one million units, and was awarded gold disc status by the RIAA in October 1973.

## *Nokie Taylor

Memphis trumpet player. Played with Alex Chilton, Herman Green, Big Star, and many others.

## *The Temprees

An American soul vocal trio from Memphis, Tennessee, most popular during the 1970s. The band released several albums under We Produce records, an offshoot of Stax Records. In 1972, they performed in front of more than 100,000 fans at the famous Wattstax festival in Los Angeles. Originally formed as the Lovemen, the trio were Jasper "Jabbo" Phillips, Harold "Scotty" Scott, and Deljuan "Del" Calvin. Lead singer Jasper "Jabbo" Phillips died on February 21, 2001. He was replaced by Del's brother Jerry "JC" Calvin. The band released four albums *Lovemen*, *Love Maze*, *Temprees*, and *Because We Love You*.

## *Carla Thomas

(born December 21, 1942; Memphis, Tennessee) An American singer often referred to as the "Queen of Memphis Soul." She is the daughter of Rufus Thomas, and is best known for the work she completed for Atlantic Records and, most notably, Stax Records in the 1960s. Her most famous single is "Gee Whiz (Look at His Eyes)." During this time, Thomas also released what is now considered to be one of the finest "Northern soul" records of all time, "I'll Never Stop Loving You." Her album of duets with Otis Redding was a big hit in Great Britain.

## *Elmo Lee Thomas

Popular front man for Elmo and the Shades in Memphis. The band featured some of the greats from the early years of Stax and Memphis music of the 1960s and 1970s, including Mickey Gregory, Tommy Lee Williams, and Melvin Robinson, to name but a few.

## *Errol Thomas

Bass guitar player for Isaac Hayes, Tommy Smiley, Al Green and Jerry Butler, Rufus Thomas, and the Temprees, to name just a few.

## *Irma Thomas

(born February 18, 1941; Ponchatoula, Louisiana) An American singer known as the "Soul Queen of New Orleans." She recorded for Chess Records in 1967 and 1968 with some success, the Otis Redding song "Good To Me" reaching the R&B chart. She then relocated to California, releasing records on various small labels, before returning to Louisiana, and, in the early 1980s, opened her own club, the Lion's Den.

## *Marvell Thomas

An American keyboardist known for his work in Memphis soul. His studio career started at the age of 17, and he was the first piano player to punch the clock at Stax Records. He played on the label's earliest national hits, including "Burnt Biscuits" (by the short-lived group the Triumphs, and later covered by Booker T. & the M.G.s), childhood friend William Bell's "You Don't Miss Your Water," and the company's very first hit "Cause I Love You" (featuring a 16-year-old Booker T. Jones on saxophone), a duet by Rufus and Carla Thomas. He also played on some of the legendary Wilson Pickett sessions at Stax and at Muscle Shoals. Other sessions at Muscle Shoals included Clarence Carter, Eddie Hinton, and Denise LaSalle. Thomas worked frequently as keyboardist and arranger, appearing on albums by Johnnie Taylor, the Staple Singers, Little Milton, the Emotions, Albert King, Mavis Staples, Yvonne Elliman, and Etta James. Thomas co-produced and handled the keys on the multi-platinum Isaac Hayes album *Hot Buttered Soul*.

## *Rufus Thomas

(March 26, 1917–December 15, 2001) An American R&B, funk, and soul singer and comedian from Memphis, Tennessee, who recorded on Sun Records in the 1950s and on Stax Records in the 1960s and 1970s. He was the father of soul singer Carla Thomas and keyboard player Marvell Thomas. A third child, Vaneese, has a solo career and sings backup for Aretha Franklin. The prime of Rufus's recording career came in the 1960s and early 1970s, when he was on the roster of Stax, having one of the first hit sides at the historic soul and blues label, "Walking the Dog" (no. 5, R&B; no. 10, pop), in 1963. Rufus is thus the first, and still the only, father to debut in the Hot 100's Top 10 after his daughter debuted there. (Rufus's daughter Carla also reached no. 10, with "Gee Whiz (Look At His Eyes)," on 27 March 1961.) At Stax, Rufus was often backed by Booker T. and the M.G.s or the Bar-Kays. The early 1970s brought him three major hits, including "(Do The) Push and Pull" in 1970, his only no. 1 R&B hit (no. 25, pop). Earlier that year, "Do the Funky Chicken" had reached no. 5 (R&B chart) and no. 28 (pop). A third, dance-oriented release in 1971, "The Breakdown," climbed to no. 2 (R&B) and no. 31 (pop), respectively.

## *Vaneese Thomas

From a very talented family, her father Rufus Thomas, brother Marvell, and sister Carla have all achieved iconic status during Memphis soul's heyday in the 1960s and 1970s. Vaneese is an A-list background singer and performs with Aretha Franklin as well as having her own solo career.

## Michael Tolles

Member of the Bar-Kays from 1968 until the early 1970s, after which he joined Isaac Hayes' band.

## *Archie Turner

Pianist from Memphis, Tennessee, and part of the regular recording backing group the Hi Rhythm Section at Willie Mitchell's Royal Studios. He has recorded and sometimes preformed with Al Green, Ann Peebles, O. V. Wright, and Albert King, to name a few.

## *Ike Turner

(November 5, 1931– December 12, 2007) An American musician, bandleader, songwriter, arranger, talent scout, and record producer. He is most popularly known for his 1960s work with his then wife, Tina Turner, in the Ike and Tina Turner Revue. His first recording, "Rocket 88," with the Kings of Rhythm, credited to "Jackie Brenston and his Delta Cats," in 1951, is considered a contender for "first rock and roll song."

## *Tom Tom Washington

(born 1944; Chicago, Illinois) Pianist, arranger, and producer. Worked with such artists as Jackie Wilson, Willie Henderson, Tyrone Davis, Mary Wells, and Otis Clay.

## Wattstax

On August 20, 1972, the Stax label presented a major concert, Wattstax, featuring performances by the label's music recording artists as well as humor from rising young comedian Richard Pryor. Known as the "Black Woodstock," Wattstax was hosted by Reverend Jesse Jackson and drew a crowd of more than 100,000 people, most of them African American. The festival was filmed by motion picture director Mel Stuart, and a concert film of the event was released to theaters by Columbia Pictures in February 1973.

## We Produce Records

Stax parent label.

## *James West

Vocalist for the Mad Lads, an American rhythm and blues group who recorded on Stax's label Volt in the 1960s.

## *Norman West

Founding member of the group Soul Children (and formerly of the Del-Rios), which also included John Colbert (a.k.a. J. Blackfoot), Anita Louis, and Shelbra Bennett. The group was formed by Isaac Hayes and David Porter in order to fill the gap that Sam & Dave had left after Stax's parting from Atlantic Records ended Stax's association with the popular duo. The Soul Children scored 15 R&B hits between 1968 and 1978.

## Jerry Wexler

(January 10, 1917–August 15, 2008) A music journalist turned music producer, and regarded as one of the major record industry players from the 1950s through the 1980s. He coined the term "rhythm and blues," and was integral in signing and/or producing many of the biggest acts of the last 50 years, including Ray Charles, the Allman Brothers, Chris Connor, Aretha Franklin, Led Zeppelin, Wilson Pickett, Dire Straits, Dusty Springfield, and Bob Dylan. He also cultivated a tight relationship with Stax Records and was an important proponent of the then-developing Muscle Shoals sound, founding the fortunes of Muscle Shoals Sound Studio and the Muscle Shoals Rhythm Section. Wexler was inducted in the Rock and Roll Hall of Fame in 1987.

## *Kirk Whalum

(born July 11, 1958) An American smooth jazz saxophonist and songwriter. He toured as Whitney Houston's opening act for several years and soloed in her single "I Will Always Love You." Ranging from pop to R&B to smooth jazz, his musical accomplishments have brought him a total of 12 Grammy nominations. He has, in addition, been the chief creative officer at the Soulsville Foundation.

## *Bobby Whitlock

(born March 18, 1948; Memphis, Tennessee) An American singer, songwriter, and musician, he is best known for being a member of blues–rock band Derek and the Dominos with Eric Clapton in 1970 to 1971. His musical career began with Memphis soul acts such as Sam & Dave and Booker T. & the M.G.s before he joined Delaney & Bonnie and Friends in 1968. His association with Delaney & Bonnie bandmate Clapton led to Whitlock participating in sessions for George Harrison's *All Things Must Pass* triple album (1970), in London, and the formation of Derek and the Dominos that year. On the band's sole studio album, the critically acclaimed *Layla and Other Assorted Love Songs* (1970), Whitlock wrote or co-wrote a number of songs, including "Tell the Truth," "Anyday," and "Why Does Love Got to Be So Sad?"

## Tim Whitsett

(born 1943; Jackson, Mississippi) An American music publisher, musician, songwriter, producer, author, and consultant. Whitsett headed up Stax Record's music publishing division, East/Memphis Music Corp., which included works written or recorded by Otis Redding, Sam & Dave, Al Green, Isaac Hayes, Rufus Thomas, and Booker T. & the M.G.s. During his years with Stax, Whitsett was the motivating force behind the releases of million sellers, such as "I've Been Lonely For So Long" (Frederick Knight), "I'll Play the Blues For You" (Albert King), and "Mr. Big Stuff" (Jean Knight).

## *Percy Wiggins

Lead vocalist for the Bo-Keys.

## *John Gary Williams

Lead vocalist for the Mad Lads.

## *Judy Love (Williams)

Part of the Stax female vocal group the Goodees, with other members Sandra Jackson and Kay Evans. Their first single, "For A Little While," was written and produced by Isaac Hayes and David Porter, and was one of the last recordings to feature the original Bar-Kays before all of them (except two) died in a plane crash with Otis Redding on December 10, 1967. It was followed by their only charting hit, "Condition Red," also written by the Hayes/Porter team. It is now a cult classic among girl group aficionados, due, in large part, to the "raunchy Southern girl" feel that many believe it has.

## *Richard "Dickie" Williams

Vocalist and member of the Mad Lads; brother of the group's original lead singer John Gary Williams. The Mad Lads made their recording debut on the Stax subsidiary label Volt in 1964 with "The Sidewalk Surf." Their biggest hits were "Don't Have to Shop Around" (1965) and "I Want Someone" (1966).

## *Ronnie Williams

Organist; played his first gig when he was just 16 years old. At Stax, Williams played on, wrote, and produced dozens of notable tracks. The list reads like a "who's who" of soul and includes Rufus Thomas, Carla Thomas, David Porter, Sir Mack Rice, the Bar-Kays, Johnny Taylor, the Staple Singers, Johnny London and the Rockets, the Rance Allen Group, and Ben Cauley.

## *Tommy Lee Williams

A sax player who was a member of house bands at both the legendary Stax Recording and Hi Records. Played for legendary artists such as Otis Redding and Isaac Hayes.

## *Ruby Wilson

Known as "the Queen of Beale Street," a singer who has recorded more than ten albums and has performed with other artists such as B.B. King, Isaac Hayes, and Ray Charles.

## *Carl "Blue" Wise

Producer, songwriter, and owner of Blueboy Records in Memphis, Tennessee.

## *Dino Woodward

Stax Records security. Now a pastor in NYC.

## *Overton Vertis "O. V." Wright

(October 9, 1939–November 16, 1980) An American singer who is generally regarded as a blues artist, and also considered to be one of Southern soul's most authoritative and individual artists. His best-known songs include "That's How Strong My Love Is" (1964), "You're Gonna Make Me Cry" (1965), "Nucleus of Soul" (1968), "A Nickel and a Nail" (1971), "I Can't Take It" (1971), and "Ace of Spades" (1971). His son Overton is a performing singer as well.

## *Domingo "Sam" Zamudio

(born 6 March 1937; Dallas, Texas). An American rock and roll singer also known by the stage name "Sam the Sham." As the front man for the Pharaohs, he sang on several Top 40 hits in the mid-1960s, notably "Wooly Bully" and "Li'l Red Riding Hood."

Other significant and notable artists that should be mentioned as part of the Stax Recording catalog are Big Nasty, Barbara Stevens, the Epsilons, Gus Cannon, Lee Sain, Mel and Tim, Margie Joseph, Little Sonny, Kim Weston, Jimmy Hughes, Inez Foxx, Ollie and the Nightingales, and Eric Mercury.

* The official Stax Museum of American Soul Music website provides definitive, illustrated insight into the work and lives of numerous Stax/Volt artists. Available at: www.staxmuseum.com/about/artists (accessed October 2013). In addition, numerous artists' discographies are detailed at http://staxrecords.free.fr, an independent Stax Records website created and maintained by Patrick Montier.
Thom Gilbert also gratefully acknowledges the authors of the respective Wikipedia articles used in the preparation of several of these biographical listings. *Wikipedia, The Free Encyclopedia*, http://en.wikipedia.org (accessed October 2013).
Finally, the author also wishes to note that he has taken every effort to include all who made up this vast and rich part of musical history, and apologizes for any unintentional omissions. Long may their contributions live on.

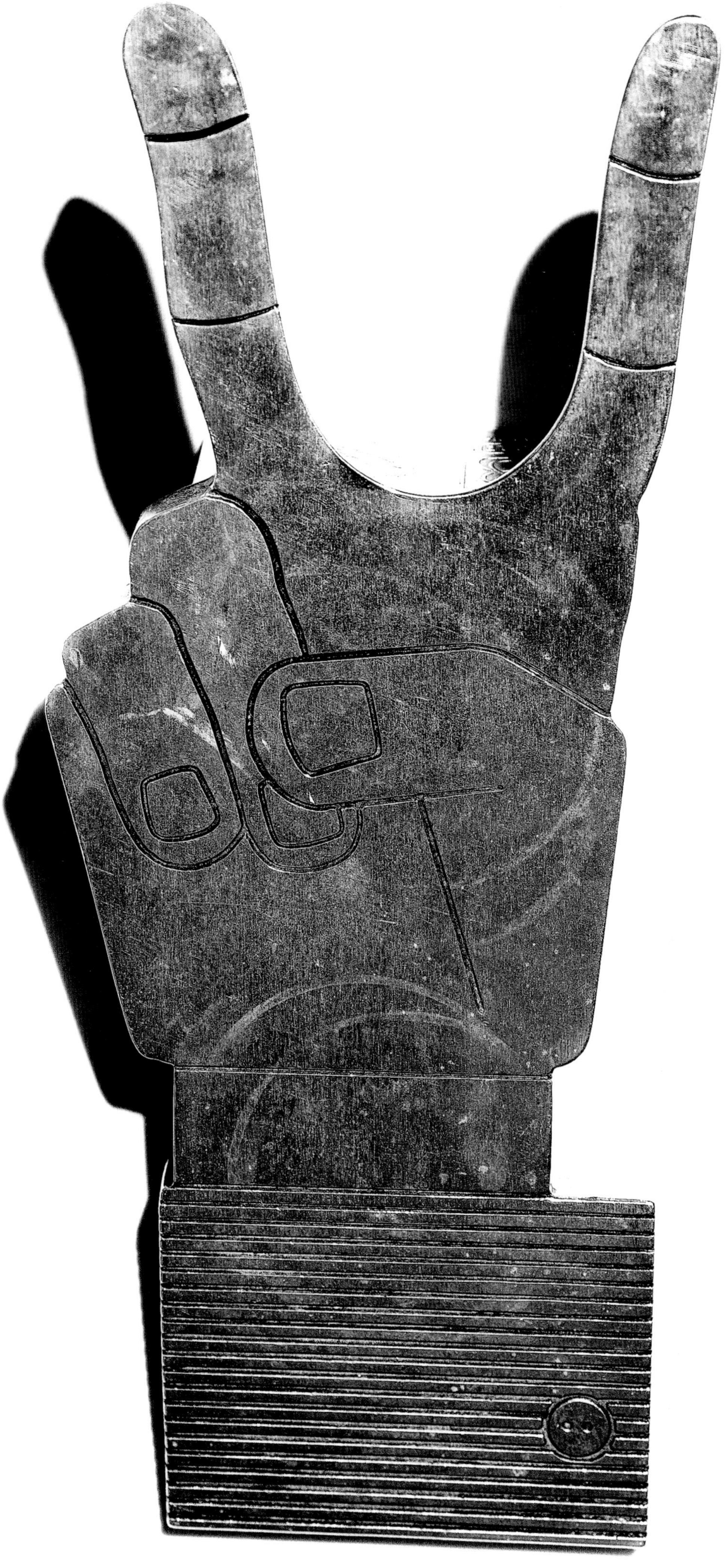

AL JACKSON JR.'S BOOT BUTLER

# Acknowledgments

Thom Gilbert acknowledges:
Lisa Allen (Director), Tim Sampson (Communications Director), and Levon Williams (Curator of Collections/Registrar) from the Stax Museum of American Soul Music, Memphis, Tennessee
Ben Harper
Christine Kane
Wayne Jackson (author of the three-volume autobiography *In My Wildest Dreams: A Collection of Rock and Roll Tales—Take 1, Take 2, Take 3*)
Amy Jackson (editor of *In My Wildest Dreams*)
Jeffrey Banks
John Doyle, Executive Director @ the Rock 'n' Soul Museum, Memphis, Tennessee
Chuck Porter
Joe Chambers, Founder and CEO @ the Musicians Hall of Fame & Museum, Nashville, Tennessee
My agent, Michael Ginsberg
Marco Jellinek, Publisher @ Officina Libraria
Wikipedia
E. J. Devokaitis, Curator/Archivist, and Richard Brent @ "The Big House," Allman Brothers Band Museum, Macon, Georgia
Stephanie Goldman
Eddie Braddock
My good friends at Hasselblad USA
Boo Mitchell @ Royal Studios, Tennessee
Rick Hall @ FAME Studios, Georgia
Al Bell
Larry Moss
Light in the Attic Records
Larry Nix
Scot LaMar
Francis Galluccio
Spooner Oldham
Lannie DeWalt
Tina France
Steve White @ Four Seasons Auction Gallery, Alpharetta, Georgia

All the musicians from Memphis and other places I was able to brush a bit of history with.

Finally, my dog Ellie who missed me the most while on the road.

# Credits

Portion of the proceeds from this book will go to the Stax Music Academy.

**Stax Music Academy** promotes the overall philanthropic work of the Soulsville Foundation through music education, community partnerships, and high-profile performance opportunities.

Further donations to the Stax Music Academy can be given at http://www.soulsvillefoundation.org/donate/

Thom Gilbert is represented by Michael Ginsburg (mg@michaelginsburg.com).

# Photo credits

Portrait, location, and still-life photography by Thom Gilbert. Thom and Officina Libraria wish to express their appreciation to the following individuals and institutions who provided items and, in the case of Getty Images, stock images as follows:

Pages 8, 9, 31, 36, 42–43, 150, 182, 225, 255: Stax Museum, Memphis, Tennessee
Pages 10, 11, 14 (top, bottom), 69 (top): Getty Images
Page 12: "Arizona Soul Man" artwork, John Good
Page 15: Sam Moore Collection
Pages 16, 17, 230, 231: Four Seasons Auction Gallery, Alpharetta, Georgia
Pages 16, 17, 242: Chuck Porter Collection
Page 18: Charles Lloyd
Page 38: Larry Dodson Collection
Page 56: Larry Moss Collection
Page 58 (groups): Don Nix and Estelle Axton Collection
Pages 58 (tape), 99, 214: Chips Moman Archives
Pages 59, 151, 220, 221: Johnny Rawls Collection
Pages 60, 61: Eddie Braddock Collection
Pages 71, 224, 240: Musicians Hall of Fame & Museum, Nashville, Tennessee
Page 81: Overton Wright
Page 103: Johnny Keys
Page 114: Jimmy Johnson
Page 176: Richard Williams
Pages 194, 195: The Big House, Allman Brothers Band Museum, Macon, Georgia;
Page 195: Scot LaMar Collection
Pages 146, 218, 219: Rock 'n' Soul Museum, Memphis, Tennessee

MIX
Paper from responsible sources
FSC www.fsc.org
FSC® C017635

Printed in Italy by Petruzzi Stampa,
Città di Castello (Perugia), in August 2014
*ex Officina Libraria Jellinek et Gallerani*